S0-CFP-897

208424
Leach Library
Londonderry, NH 03053

DISCARD

Further Praise for

Artie Shaw, King of the Clarinet

"I've .... ures, with
the .... se settle
for .... voiding
bot .... sides of
thi .... *hronicle*

"C .... *o News*

"M .... *ahoman*

"E .... ags-to-
rich .... r faults
wit

.... *Booklist*

"Tc .... t-hand
rese .... .chable
pros .... a man
botl .... iet and
crea .... *z Lives*

Leach Library
276 Mammoth Road
Londonderry, NH 03053
Adult Services 432-1132
Children's Services 432-1127

"Breezily written yet painstakingly detailed . . . estimably candid."
—Christopher Loudon, *Jazz Times*

"Tom Nolan has done a remarkable job of capturing Shaw on paper, in all his glory and self-inflicted misery. . . . This is a rich and rewarding portrait." —Leonard Maltin, *Leonard Maltin's Movie Crazy*

"Riveting. . . . Tom Nolan recovers the genius, the legend, the ego and blocked emotions of an enigmatic American icon."
—Kevin Starr, University of Southern California

"At last, the lively, continually imaginative life of the most creative clarinetist in jazz history." —Nat Hentoff, author of
At the Jazz Band Ball: Sixty Years at the Jazz Scene

A *January Magazine* "Best Book of 2010"

ALSO BY TOM NOLAN

Ross Macdonald: A Biography

EDITED BY TOM NOLAN

Strangers in Town: Three Newly Discovered Mysteries by Ross Macdonald

The Couple Next Door by Margaret Millar

The Archer Files by Ross Macdonald

LEACH LIBRARY
276 Mammoth Road
Londonderry, NH 03053

ARTIE SHAW, KING OF

=== *the* ===

CLARINET

His Life and Times

TOM NOLAN

W. W. NORTON & COMPANY
New York • London

781.65
SHA

Frontispiece: The charismatic maestro of "deluxe swing," 1940.
Michael Ochs Archives / Getty Images

Copyright © 2010 by Tom Nolan
Originally published under the title
Three Chords for Beauty's Sake: The Life of Artie Shaw

All rights reserved
Printed in the United States of America
First published as a Norton paperback 2011

For information about permission to reproduce selections from this book,
write to Permissions, W. W. Norton & Company, Inc.,
500 Fifth Avenue, New York, NY 10110

For information about special discounts for bulk purchases, please contact
W. W. Norton Special Sales at specialsales@wwnorton.com or 800-233-4830

Manufacturing by Courier Westford
Book design by Dana Sloan
Production manager: Anna Oler

The Library of Congress has catalogued the hardcover edition as follows:

Nolan, Tom.
Three chords for beauty's sake : the life of Artie Shaw / Tom Nolan.
p. cm.
Includes bibliographical references and index.
ISBN 978-0-393-06201-4 (hardcover)
1. Shaw, Artie, 1910–2004. 2. Jazz musicians—United
States—Biography. I. Title.
ML419.S52N65 2010
788.6'2165092—dc22
[B]
2010006301

ISBN 978-0-393-34010-5 pbk.

W. W. Norton & Company, Inc.
500 Fifth Avenue, New York, N.Y. 10110
www.wwnorton.com

W. W. Norton & Company Ltd.
Castle House, 75/76 Wells Street, London W1T 3QT

1 2 3 4 5 6 7 8 9 0

For Mary

Contents

Contents

Contents

= Preface =

IN THE exuberant decade between 1935 and 1945, when America's indigenous art form—jazz—was also the nation's popular music, no musical performer was more famous, controversial, admired, and reviled than Artie Shaw: the brilliant, handsome, outspoken, and unpredictable clarinetist and bandleader whose hit recordings ("Begin the Beguine," "Frenesi," "Star Dust," "Summit Ridge Drive") sold millions, whose marriages to several beautiful women (including movie stars Lana Turner and Ava Gardner) made headlines, who risked alienating his public by calling a large chunk of them "morons," and whose frequent abdications from the kingdom of swing earned him a reputation as jazz's Hamlet.

With no formal training, Artie Shaw became a virtuoso musician almost without peer: a clarinet player influenced as much by trumpeters, violinists, pianists, and even painters as by fellow reedmen. His lyrical solos seemed to evoke visual images: a bird in flight, a tree moved by wind, a sailboat in the moonlight. On a ballad, his harmonically adventurous playing explored every gorgeous nook and cranny of a melody; on a rousing swing tune, his euphoric horn soared high and joyous enough to raise the roof.

He grew up as a player in the 1920s jazz age of Bix Beiderbecke and Louis Armstrong; reigned in the 1930s and '40s swing era alongside Benny Goodman, Duke Ellington, and Tommy Dorsey; navigated past the '40s bebop revolution of Charlie Parker and Dizzy Gillespie (who both admired his playing) to make beautiful and remarkable chamber jazz in the early 1950s—then, at the peak of his powers, retired from performing, prompting admirers ever since to ask, *Why?*

The answers were as simple and complex, as open and hidden, as the man who provoked the question. Artie Shaw was a study in contradictions: an artist who made a fortune as a supposed entertainer; a musician who would just as soon have become a teacher or writer and who identified with prizefighters; a Jew who said he wanted to be a Gentile and felt most inspired in the company of African-Americans; a shy fellow who depended on crowds for his living; a loner who married eight times and had dozens more affairs; a man who adored children but had little to do with his own two sons; a household name with a lifetime supply of semi-aliases (Arthur Arshawsky, Art Shaw, Sid Shawfellow, Mr. Cinderella, Arthur J. Shaw, Arthur Sanders, Artichaut, Artixo, James Braddock, Albie Snow, and sometimes just A Shaw); a misanthrope who was at heart a romantic; an alleged agnostic who combed books of science and wisdom for answers to cosmic riddles; a constant complainer who wouldn't tolerate criticism.

Some found him cold and cynical, "with ice water in his veins"; others knew him as a generous mentor. As a player, a bandleader, an arranger, and a musical editor, he had impeccable taste; but his own behavior—with women, with friends, with colleagues (but not with employees)—was often appalling. "He was like a prism," thought Tony Pastor Jr., son of one of his oldest pals, "depending on how the light hit him, you know? He could be arrogant, he could show pathos, he might be tearful, he could be laughing—but under it all was this complex man."

So complex did this man seem even to himself that he subtitled his well-regarded memoir "An Outline of Identity"—and conceded that that identity, at age forty-two, had yet to be resolved. In the meantime, Artie Shaw was such an iconic figure he moved into the realm of fiction, earning mentions in works penned by luminaries from P. G. Wodehouse to Thomas Pynchon, Jack Kerouac to Philip Roth.

Such literary lights were the stars Shaw preferred to cultivate. This terrific musician who backed Bessie Smith, sat in with Count Basie, hired Billie Holiday, and inspired Ray Charles savored most of all his acquaintanceship with authors, including Sinclair Lewis, Ernest Hemingway, William Saroyan, Budd Schulberg, Ralph Ellison, and Terry Southern. When he abandoned music for long periods during his thirty-year career, it was in order to write. After giving up the clarinet, he labored for decades on a mammoth autobiographical novel.

Many jazz legends led lives cut short by alcohol or drug abuse or misadventure. The abstemious Shaw voluntarily ended his own jazz career at age forty-four—and lived another half-century in the wake of his formidable achievements.

The best of those achievements deserve to be appreciated forever. Yet Artie Shaw left no formal archive of correspondence and decreed that his possessions be sold to fund scholarships. How might one attempt to write a biography of a celebrity who made sure his papers would be scattered to the winds? Early in life, Shaw heeded the advice of a lawyer who warned, "Every time you write a letter, four people are reading over your shoulder," and he often treated the facts like a set of chord changes to be improvised on.

I have written this biography with care, respect, and affection—and by drawing on dozens of printed and broadcast sources, including the subject's own memoir, several conversations with Artie Shaw from 1990 to 2004, and interviews with a hundred other individuals willing to share memories and insights regarding one of the greatest popular artists of the twentieth century. Artie Shaw was a man who thrilled millions with his music, but whose own most consistent pleasure seemed to come from sitting alone with a book.

ARTIE SHAW, KING OF *the* CLARINET

CHAPTER ONE

Avenue C

ONCE UPON a time, on the twenty-third of May, in the year 1910, a son was born to Harold and Sarah Arshawsky of 255 East Seventh Street, on the Lower East Side of New York City.

The circumcising rabbi proclaimed the boy Avraham Ben-Yitzhak Arshawsky. His mother called him Arthur. Near the end of his life, in the early years of a future century, Arthur recalled his earliest memory: "I don't know how old I was," he said at ninety-two, "but I was in a crib—I had to be a kid—and I looked up. . . . I saw a head up on the ceiling—shadows, lights from the outside—and it was like a devil. I didn't know what a devil was, all I knew was it was this *frightening* thing; and I screamed, as a kid. And my father came and picked me up and—comforted me."

Harold was a stocky man, born in Russia, in the Black Sea port of Odessa, in 1880. At eight, he came with his family to America. As a young man, he went west and ran a saloon. By the early years of the twentieth century, he was living in New York, where he met and married Sarah Straus, a young woman born in Austria and raised in Sambor, near the shifting Polish-Austrian border. Sarah was fifteen when she came with her family to America in 1899, speaking German and some Polish; she was twenty-four when she married twenty-eight-year-old Harry Arshawsky on January 24, 1909.

Sarah had seamstress experience, and Harold worked with her as a tailor, both of them living at 723 East Sixth Street. When Arthur was born, the Arshawskys moved to East Seventh.

Harold aspired to be much more. He had spent childhood years in Odessa: a city of artists and merchants and adventurers, where Isaac Babel (born fourteen years after Harry) would write of bandits and Cossacks, and where gifted children became famous fiddlers. Harry Arshawsky, dressed in a three-piece suit, faded into the multitude on the Lower East Side, but at a picnic in the open air, wearing a homespun shirt, he looked like a figure from Turgenev or Chekhov. The spirit of Odessa smoldered in his eyes.

By 1915, Harold was a portrait photographer with a studio at 42 Avenue C, home to him and his wife and child. Harry often used his son as a subject. Five-year-old Arthur was a beautiful boy, with a guileless gaze and a tentative smile. For some portraits, he wore a European sailor's suit made for him by his mother, with knee-high stockings and white button-shoes. Resting his arm on a carved-wood chair, his hair cut pageboy style, Arthur looked like the favored son of a Russian czar.

But Arshawsky's photo studio failed. By 1916, Harry was once more doing tailor work.

The Arshawskys still lived at 42 Avenue C, in a building with a dozen other residents, including Harry's brother Joseph (Yussel), a house painter who had just arrived from Russia, and other Russians, Austrians, Hungarians, and Germans. In nearby buildings were families from Ireland and Italy. Many in the neighborhood were Jewish. Harold and Sarah were not devout, but they took their boy to a synagogue once or twice, where Arthur heard the Kol Nidre.

In the city, the common music was ragtime, and rhythmic songs with "ragtime" in their titles. In 1917, as Arthur turned seven, New York was gripped by another music craze when a New Orleans group called the Original Dixieland Jazz (or Jass) Band played at Reisenweber's on Fifty-eighth. The Jazz Band's sounds caused a sensation. Their 78-rpm records ("Livery Stable Blues," "Clarinet Marmalade Blues," "Tiger Rag") spread those sounds through the land and around the world.

Maybe Arthur heard Jazz Band records in his neighborhood, a district where gaslight was being replaced by electric lamps, and the streets were full of interesting sounds and sights.

"There's somethin' to be said for the days when people walked around, and the air was clean," Art said. "But the air was full of horse-shit too. People were riding in carriages; streetcars, trolley cars pulled by great big horses. So there was horseshit all over the street! And guys with white uniforms, cleaning it up."

The nearby river was the kids' swimming hole. Here every child was equal. But there were common hazards too: The "Spanish influenza" swept New York like the black plague. Thousands died in days. Arthur himself became ill: "Sick unto death, as they say." Doctors came and diagnosed him with flu; they said he wouldn't survive. *No*, said Harry. "He gave me a dose of castor oil," Art remembered in 2003, "that I *still* haven't gotten over. But whatever I had, went away. I shit it out, and I was okay. He was great," Arthur said of Harry. "He saved my life."

Harry had gone into partnership with another fellow, Israel Lamb, in a dressmaking business at 148 West Twenty-third Street, where Sarah pitched in. "My mother was a plodder," her son said. "And she supported him. At one point, they were fairly well to do. And then he became a sport, you know: big guy, coat with a mink lining?"

But the good times ended. In 1918, Arshawsky and Lamb declared themselves bankrupt. Sarah complained of the bad situation Harry had brought about; Harold answered in anger. And Arthur was afraid of his father.

HAROLD AND SARAH decided the family would relocate to New Haven, Connecticut, where the couple had friends. The Arshawskys moved into 215½ York Street, and Arthur enrolled at Dwight Street School. On his first day there, when he stood to say his name, other students laughed. In New Haven, "Arshawsky" was a funny sound.

Other things were different too.

"There was a little girl, I liked her," he would remember the rest of his life, "so I walked along with her, and I took her books; and I was holding her books, she just—let me. So we came to a street called Goffe Street ... crossed the street. And she was gonna turn off at the next block, and I had to take a leak. So I said, 'Would you hold this a second?' So she held the books. I went to the curb and—unbuttoned my fly and started taking a leak. Well, *crash!* The books went to the ground. She *ran.* I said, 'What's the matter with her?' On the Lower East Side, that's what you *did:* you pissed into the curb. No one thought anything about it. New Haven, you couldn't *do* that.

"And I suddenly realized—I didn't know the word 'gauche,' but I knew that was *not* the thing to do. And she wouldn't *talk* to me anymore. Word got around: 'This guy stops and *pees* right in the *street.*' Seemed absolutely *normal* to me. My *back* was to her . . ."

Playing in the schoolyard during recess, Arthur found an anthill: he interrupted a baseball game with his shouts for all to come see what he'd "discovered." *Hey, fellas—look what I found!* Older kids mocked him with a chant that grew and grew: "Columbus Arshawsky, *Columbus Arshawsky*, COLUMBUS—ARSHAWSKY!"

The ringleader of playground bullies cornered Arthur after school and warned him not to recite the Lord's Prayer with the rest of them in class: "Go on home and say your lousy kike prayers, and keep your dirty sheeny nose out of other people's prayers, you hear what I'm telling you?"

He ran home, chased by boys throwing taunts and stones.

IN NEW HAVEN, Harry Arshawsky made another attempt to break free from the clothing trade. He bought a Pilot automobile and, working with a friend, took the car apart and rebuilt it with what would be called a rumble seat. "Nobody'd ever seen one before," said an older Arthur, proud in memory. But the rebuilt auto was too unusual, and the Pilot was not a popular make. Harry couldn't sell his creation.

"He was a frustrated artist," Arthur later realized. "He wanted to do things, and he couldn't get support. My father couldn't stick to one thing and do it superbly. He couldn't take the guff that went with it. He got disillusioned—lost his 'dream' of being somebody—and ended up: nowhere." Harold had to be a "vassal" for his wife. Arthur's judgment was harsh: "I didn't think he knew his ass from his elbow—and he *didn't*."

This was the gruff figure Arthur, at eight and nine, began to avoid—the man Arthur blamed for the family's poverty and his own despised name. When Arthur was outside playing with friends and saw Harry coming, he would hide until the old man passed, lest his father, with his "impossible" Yiddish-English, shame him by speaking.

The shy boy withdrew. He found escape when Harry's brother Joseph showed up with a barrel of books salvaged from a worksite. Arthur dug into the trove and came up with treasures—for instance, *An Encyclopedia of Wit and Humor*, filled with riddles:

Q.: What's the difference between a bachelor and a married man?

A.: One kisses his missus, and the other misses his kisses.

Wow! That would have the kids at school in stitches.

There were other finds, among them Robert Louis Stevenson's *Kidnapped*: a thrilling story of a youth in quest of an inheritance. One detail in the novel leaped out at Arthur: the grand manor where the young hero, David Balfour, claimed his birthright was the House of Shaws—*Shaw*—a name contained in Arthur's own last name. Maybe Arthur had that hero concealed within: a daring young Shaw who would seek and find his own fortune.

For now, Arthur walked into solo adventures. "As a boy," he would say, "everything I ever did turned out wrong." One Sunday he strolled out Orange Street to a formation known as East Rock and started to climb it: "I got halfway up and couldn't go one way or another, and they finally called out the fire department to rescue me." Another time, he explored an old well at "the Castle" on York Street, fell in, and again had to be helped by firemen. The worst happened at a swimming hole: seized with cramps, he went underwater and was fished out to be revived by respirator.

He was small and had no siblings to guide him. And he won no love at school when, now an avid reader, he raised his hand with right answers.

Not everyone disliked him. He made friends with a doctor's son named Rand, who invited him to his house: a huge place with a stable in back. Rand had a shelf of microscopes which, if Arthur was careful, he could look through. Rand had a nice sister. It was quite a contrast to the Arshawskys' cramped existence. "Mom," Arthur asked his mother when he got home, "why can't we live in a *doctor's* house?"

Arthur hated his family's acceptance of their lot in life. He cringed at his father's Yiddish accent ("I *gotta* do better than that," he thought), but he hated the stinky-rich kids of New Haven. "I had dreams as a kid," he would say, "of being a strong man, a wrestler. Charles Atlas—remember that? We were little people. . . . It's a difficult thing to be, a young kid. 'Specially being the only one."

Arthur acted out resentments in furtive ways. He took some of his mother's dressmaker pins onto a balcony on top of the family's quarters. "Had a little parapet outside the front window, with a thing you could hide behind," he said. "I'd learned something: you'd take a pin, and bend it; and get a little rubber-band—take the pin, and shoot. So I'd wait until someone came by, and I'd shoot the pin—and duck. Some poor prick: 'What's goin' on, raining *pins*?' That was, for me, very funny. I'd peek down—watch—see—look *around*—Never got caught. I was really a fuckin' idiot. Jesus, at that age, I was nuts."

He got hold of a BB gun. "I went out in the back yard; and there were buildings across and over the fence. And there was a window open. And I held the gun up to the window, and shot. It just rattled around. The next thing I heard, all this commotion: it was in a class-room! This BB hit the ceiling, and bounced around.

"Next day, detectives came, took the gun away."

He hadn't been aiming to hurt anyone, Arthur insisted: "Kids are trying to *discover* what's going *on* in the world. They're not aware of consequences." One consequence was that Harold became disgusted with his troublemaking son. "My father had no *use* for any of that."

Harold was so fed up that even when Arthur did something worth praising, the father squelched him—as when Art made use of the thin-cardboard boxes that held his parents' dressmaking pins. The boy cut up some of these cartons to make model airplanes—biplanes, with fuselages and double wings, and straight pins for struts. He fashioned cardboard wheels and a folded-cardboard tail, even a spinning cardboard propeller. Arthur made half a dozen of these craft: a whole fleet. He was playing with them on the floor when Harold came out of the workroom and saw them. On purpose, he *stepped* on the planes, crushing each. "Oh he was a son of a bitch," Art said.

Sarah had a plan. The Arshawskys got a piano, and Sarah arranged for lessons for Arthur from a woman nearby. A bored, complaining Arthur spent afternoons after school "churning" through Czerny's beginner's book when he would rather be outside climbing trees. The lessons ended when he turned ten; his "graduation" came with playing Robert Schumann's "Träumerei" for a friend of his mother's, who gave him a quarter. Later, in the Boy Scouts, Arthur learned to play the ukulele. Music was a way to fit in and stand out.

CHAPTER TWO

Dreamy Melody

THE ARSHAWSKYS moved four times in four years within New Haven. In 1922, Harry was proprietor of the DeMode Dress Shop, at 841 Howard. In 1923, it was "Harry Arshawsky, cloaks and suits," at 913 Grand. Harry was the man up front; Sarah made the clothes. Arthur attended Orange Street School and sold *New Haven Registers* on the city green.

But then the family relocated to 899½ Grand: a cheap railroad flat in a rundown neighborhood. Arthur joined a gang of kids who shoplifted items from dime stores; he was the best of these artful dodgers, until a do-gooder fingered him to store detectives. At home, Art received blows from Harry: "Open hand, but smacked me—on my head. I couldn't believe what he was doing."

Again the family moved, to 340 Orange. Arthur, thirteen, enrolled in New Haven High School, where he did well in English, History, and Algebra; fair in Science; poor in Latin. He was marked "average" in personality and "below-average" in dependability and leadership; in boxes for "integrity" and "conduct," Arthur's teacher entered question marks.

UNHAPPY AT HOME, out of place at school, Arthur played hooky. He found refuge at Poli's Palace Theatre, New Haven's vaudeville house.

Arthur ducked around to a side exit; when a patron left, Arshawsky slipped inside. The Palace had its pick of the best New York acts: comics with ethnic brogues, dancers and jugglers—and a music act that changed Arthur's life.

A small orchestra, wearing blue-and-white-striped blazers, performed onstage for a group of chorus girls. A saxophonist knelt on one knee to play the popular tune "Dreamy Melody." Arthur was bedazzled by the gleaming saxophone, bewitched by the chorus girls. *I could do that,* he said. *That's* what I'll do.

He needed a saxophone. There was a secondhand one for sale in the window of Wrozina's Music Shop, for forty dollars. His mother wasn't hard to convince. A scheme was hatched: Arthur would take a summer errand-boy job at Eli Gorn's delicatessen and earn four dollars a week. At the end of ten weeks, Arthur owned a C-melody sax.

A Wrozina's employee showed him some fingerings, but the man angered Art by saying he should study scales first: "You gotta walk before you can run." Arthur was damned if he would. "I wanted to run," he would say later. "Guess I was in a hurry."

ART ANNOYED his father plenty with the squawks and screeches of his saxophone. The boy practiced until his teeth ached and his mouth bled. At last he had enough skill to play at a little-theater amateur contest. In a knickers suit (sewn by Sarah) and yellow polka-dot bow tie, Arthur Arshawsky performed "Charley, My Boy." The prize was five dollars. Arthur won.

He took the money home in triumph. Arthur and his mother were thrilled, but his father was scornful: "Five dollars—for playing the *blosser?*" "Blosser" was Yiddish for something blown into, like a kazoo.

"I remember him kinda makin' fun of me," Art said. "It wasn't a manly thing to do, to go up there and blow a horn in front of a lotta people." Another father would have patted his boy on the back; Arthur's dad instilled cruel doubt. "As he got older, he got very nasty, very disappointed in life," Art saw. "He was a sick man, a failure. And he didn't respond well to failure."

At least he didn't threaten them anymore. In years past, Arthur lay awake in fear, listening to his parents argue. "I used to *cringe* under the [covers]," Art said. "Thought he was gonna come and kill her, and *me!* And I would think to her, 'Why don't you shut *up* . . . Stop *naggin'* him, you're gonna—He'll *murder* you . . .' Aaaah—what a way to live."

Harry chose a less violent method to rid himself of wife and child: he left home.

In late 1924 or early 1925, Harold Arshawsky quit New Haven for Los Angeles, where his brother Joseph had already moved. The plan was for Harold to settle in L.A. and send for Sarah and Arthur, but, according to his son, Harold never followed through. "He had to be a selfish bastard," Art said as an old man, "just got up and left. No more money, no more nothin'." Young Arthur was chagrined to think maybe it was his constant practicing (and the money he had made) that prompted Harold to flee.

"So, my mother raised me," Art said, "and that was not the best on earth, but I didn't know it as a kid. I'd say to her, 'Don't worry, Mom, I'll always take care o' you.' I *meant* it."

ARTHUR KEPT practicing, imitating records bought and played on the Victrola: Rudy Wiedoeft, "Saxophobia"; Edgar Benson Orchestra, "I Never Miss the Sunshine," with saxophone solo by Frankie Trumbauer.

He and a banjo-playing kid from school toured the local amateur-show circuit. Next Art joined three other boys in the Peter Pan Novelty Orchestra; they dressed in matching Peter Pan outfits Sarah made, and worked parties, showers, and weddings, earning two bucks apiece. Then Arthur became leader of a six-piece high school band playing for school dances and after basketball games. He switched from C-melody to alto sax, buying the horn from a guy next door. Arshawsky was making twenty-five bucks a month.

He needed now to learn from real musicians, the best of whom worked at the Cinderella Ballroom at Orange and Court. Art focused on one sax player: dark-haired, stocky Tony Pestritto, from nearby Middletown, twenty years old.

"Every night that I took my seat on the bandstand," Pestritto wrote seventeen years later, when both he and Arshawsky had become famous under different names, "a kid in short pants would plunk himself as close to me as the management would allow, and his eyes and ears would follow every move and sound I made. . . . He would tell me about his ambitions and wondered if he'd ever be a musician. . . . I saw this kid had the right spirit."

In the summer of 1925, Art was tapped by a drummer named Dave Yudkin to audition for Johnny Cavallaro's band at the Cinderella Ballroom. Art was hired. At fifteen years old, he turned pro—not as the foreign-sounding Arthur Arshawsky but as the forward-looking "Art Shaw."

"As 'Arthur Arshawsky,' I would never have got to first base," he said. "In those days, you had to be a Gentile in America, to work. I know it was embarrassing to be a Jew. But I *wasn't*, and I could see no point in going around admitting to being something that I didn't *work* at, that I didn't *believe* in. I don't know if that's rationalization or what it is, but— if somebody said, 'What is a Jew?' I couldn't have answered. I didn't have their religion; I didn't belong to any Zionist movements; anything that had to do with being Jewish, I had nothing to do with. To this *day*, that's true."

So "Arshawsky" became "Shaw." It meant more though than just ridding himself of a handicap. "That's a big deal, you know, when you change your name," Shaw said. "It's like assuming a new identity."

Arthur Arshawsky was shy and wary; Art Shaw was brash and confident. Arshawsky held back, afraid of rejection; Shaw rushed in, knowing he was better than most. "I was nobody from nowhere," Shaw said, "and I had to elbow people aside to get anywhere." Of the assured manner others said they saw in him: "They mistook desperation for self-confidence."

There was so much to learn.

"The nuances of playing . . . very few people understand," Art said. "There's about twenty-eight ways to play a quarter-note. . . . You can go *dit—dot—dooh*; you can go *aaah*. A million ways. Most people know,

'You play the *note*.' That's—got nothin' to *do* with anything. You *shade* that note, depending on what it's comin' *out* of, and where it's *going*. It's a relationship of one note to another that a musician is interested in. If he's *good*."

Sarah, still sewing, was grateful for the money Arthur brought home. Financially, he had more than taken the place of his father. But Sarah expected her son to continue his schoolwork. Art had a different idea.

He found out that if he got four F's in a row, the school had to expel him.

Arthur Arshawsky left New Haven High, without a diploma, at age fifteen and two-thirds. Art Shaw was now free to do as he pleased—to chart a course to his very own House of Shaws.

CAVALLARO'S ORCHESTRA played the summer at Bantam Lake, a resort near New Haven. The men in the band shared a single cabin. One of the seven had a special interest in ragging Shaw, this eager kid who was always practicing—when he didn't have his nose in a book. One Sunday, with Cavallaro away, this troublemaker gave Art his first liquor: shots of rye, with beer chasers. "In Prohibition," Shaw said, "booze was an Emancipation Proclamation. If you didn't drink, you're—" A baby, a sissy. "I wasn't drinking 'cause I *wanted* to, I was drinking 'cause I didn't want to be an outcast. . . . If you were a player of an instrument, that's what you hadda do."

Art passed out. No one woke him. When he came to, still wearing the one-piece red bathing suit that was his daytime Bantam Lake attire, everyone was gone. It was nine-thirty at night. He threw on a pair of trousers and ran to the dance hall. The silent movie was still playing; he could hear the band accompanying it. Art took his seat onstage. When the lights came up, there was Shaw, in the midst of half-a-dozen tux-edoed band members, wearing the red-shirted bathing suit. A roar of laughter burst through the hall. Cavallaro went berserk. He chased Art off the bandstand, and the next day he fired him, despite Art's efforts to explain.

Later the leader claimed he had just been trying to scare some sense into the kid. But Art took him at his word, and he was outraged. Fine. He would make it on his own. Shaw fell in with some teenaged musicians who had a job lined up in Lexington, Kentucky. In two old jalopies, they started south. Art rode perched on the rolled-up canvas top of one of the convertible roadsters. When the driver swerved accidentally into a ditch, Art was thrown forward; his right thumb went through the windshield. "Thought the thumb was gonna come off," he said decades later, wiggling it. "It's still there."

They reached Lexington and the Joyland Casino: a beat-up dance hall. A week later, the place shut down. The other youngsters made arrangements to get home. Art wasn't about to get in touch with his mother, though, who thought he was still at Bantam Lake.

He slept in the park. In the daytime, he went to the library. He pawned his horns for food money; when that ran out, he washed dishes for meals. Art was looking seedy by the time a band came to Lexington to play one night at the Hotel Lafayette. Shaw talked its leader into letting him sit in with a borrowed horn. The leader gave Art a job and loaned him the money to get his instruments out of hock.

With this band, he traveled to Tennessee. Art wrote his mother now, describing his odyssey as a grand tour. He started smoking cigarettes, the start of a half-century habit. In Florida, he repaid the money he had borrowed and caught a bus to New Haven.

Art acted like a success, and his mother let him, despite the fact that he came home without a cent. No matter: before long, John Cavallaro called with an offer for Art to rejoin his orchestra for a winter-season engagement in Miami. The sixteen-year-old condescended to accept, even though Cavallaro insisted Art "double" on clarinet, an instrument Shaw had not learned yet.

Clarinet called for a whole different embouchure: the way you held your mouth and applied lip pressure, how you tensed your face and throat. The fingering was different from the saxophone's. And the horn was finicky: get one thing wrong and you produced an awful squeal.

Shaw hadn't made much progress on clarinet by the time the band reached Miami. But the more he played, the better he got. By the end of three months, he wasn't bad.

THE LITTLE Miami casino-ballroom was packed with patrons the night 1926 became 1927. Shaw was the obvious star of the band. Also in Cavallaro's crew was substitute drummer Charley "Chuck" Cantor, a Cleveland man who'd come south for the winter. Cantor was bowled over by Shaw's ability. On the next day he had Shaw show off his stuff to two other Cleveland players. Trumpeters Lee Repp and Willis Kelley agreed: Shaw was the best sax man they had ever heard. They all urged Art to come to Cleveland and work in Charley's brother Joe's orchestra.

Shaw was flattered but cautious. He jammed a few more nights with the Cleveland musicians, but when the season ended, he went back to New Haven. There the Publix Presentation outfit was starting live stage shows at the Olympia movie theater, with a pit band of New York musicians and a New York conductor, Alex Hyde. Auditions were held for local men. Shaw was hired as lead alto.

Now he learned how to read a score not *as* he played each bar but three or four measures ahead, how and when to produce different tones on the horn, how to vary a vibrato, how "dynamics" worked. He had to consider about seven different aspects of every note, by second nature. Art could barely sleep for digesting all this.

And he could hardly wake up. His mother had a hell of a time rousing him for work. "Get down!" Sarah would shout in broken English. "Get down off the bed!" Sometimes she would burn paper in a frying pan and wave the smoke under his nose, crying, "Fire! Fire!" What worked best was throwing cold water in his face.

Working thirteen hours a day, Art was making $125 a week. He bought a red car, a little Studebaker Erskine. One night he drove out to Savin Park to hear Barney Rapp's orchestra. Friends introduced Art to a cute girl in a red dress. "We drove out into the woods," he said. "It was a summer night. I took the back seat out of the car and we lay down on it, and that is how I officially lost my virginity. It was very fumbly and embarrassing. She just hiked up her dress and I pulled down my pants and we went at it like two little animals. . . . I just thought, 'Well, it's over. Thank Christ I did it. . . . Now I can get on about my business and my life.' I drove her home and never saw her again."

AS SOON as he became aware of a new music technique, he mastered it. One day, the New York trombone player complimented him on a brief solo: "That was damn good, Art. Sounded like a real pro." No tribute he would ever receive would mean more to Artie Shaw. Still, the better he got, the more he saw the distance between where he was and where he wanted to be. Up on a mountain were Frank Trumbauer and Bix Beiderbecke, idols to dance-band players all over the country.

Bix and "Tram" in early 1927 did a 78-rpm recording called "Singin' the Blues" that was so good that musicians carried it in their instrument cases and learned its solos by heart. Trumbauer was an inspiration on the sax, with plenty of technique but without being a show-off; he had his own "voice," and you knew it when you heard it. The cornetist Beiderbecke was something else: gorgeous tone, and so expressive—the sweetest sound you ever heard and your saddest memory, all at once. Trumbauer and Beiderbecke were stars in the Jean Goldkette Orchestra, based at Detroit's Greystone Ballroom. The fourteen-piece Goldkette band was on tour and scheduled to play in Bridgeport, twenty-five miles from New Haven. Shaw wanted to be there.

Later in life, Art called the trip a "hegira": a religious pilgrimage. He was not disappointed. And he wasn't alone. Tuxedoed musicians from all over the territory crowded up to the bandstand. When Bix played a four-bar break, they let out a roar. What took you by surprise, Art said, was his *power*. "When you heard him in a room—that horn literally shook! You could almost feel the bell vibrating. He got a sound totally unlike anything anybody ever heard." It wasn't so much what he played, Art thought, but the *sound* of it. "When he blew into that band, it came to *life*; you could not *believe* what he did. Trumbauer did similar things, with a saxophone."

And there was also Steve Brown, the standup bass man, playing with terrific force; he would do cross-rhythms with drummer Chauncey Morehouse, darting in and out of the beat. The band's arrangements were out of this world, the best of them by a fellow named Bill Challis, who wrote for sections the way Bix played his horn. "It was the first really great white big band," Shaw said. "Unbelievable. It swung like mad. I stood in front of that band open-mouthed."

Back at the Olympia in New Haven, Art continued to shine. Alex Hyde said he wanted to take Art with him back to New York. But for now, the work was a grind: four live stage shows a day, plus rehearsals, plus outside gigs. Things got worse when Hyde's crew was given a new duty: playing accompaniment for the silent pictures screened between the stage shows. Art was working from eleven in the morning until midnight; he couldn't even leave the building.

It was the perfect time for Chuck Cantor and Willis Kelley to show up and repeat their offer, contract in hand: a year's employment with Chuck's brother Joe's band at the Far East Restaurant in Cleveland, Ohio, at a hundred dollars a week. Art had no qualms giving notice at the Olympia. When his two weeks were up, he got in his Erskine and started for Cleveland. His mother would join him there once he got settled. She said she needed to go—to "take care" of him.

CHAPTER THREE

I'm Sitting on Top of the World

JOE CANTOR had a good little band: alto, tenor; trumpet and trombone; drums, piano, banjo—and the leader, Joe, who just "led."

Using pointers picked up in Lexington, Art had already written a few section arrangements for John Cavallaro. He had had his ears opened by the Goldkette band's scores, and at the Olympia he had watched carefully as one of the New York men wrote out some passages. With the Cantor band, Shaw started learning to arrange in earnest. "Wabash Blues," an Isham Jones hit, was his first full-fledged effort. Soon he was turning out arrangements for other Cleveland outfits too.

"He was a bug for staying up late and listening to concert records," Chuck Cantor said. "Such stuff as [Holst's] 'The Planets' by the London Symphony and the works of Beethoven. He'd listen to the record, then pick up his clarinet and interpret the tune in his own way."

"It wasn't long," Lee Repp said, "before the boys in the band nicknamed him 'Little Beethoven.' He could sit down with a pencil and paper and dash off neat arrangements just like you'd write a letter."

"When we played the Far East, Art was always getting new ideas for arrangements and wanting to try them out," Chuck Cantor said. "So during the intermission, when we were supposed to be resting, three or four of us would carry our instruments out to the alley in back of the place and jam for him."

Late at night Art went to see "colored" bands and players who came to Cleveland—including, in the summer of 1927, the Fletcher Henderson Orchestra, which played Oster's Ballroom at East Forty-sixth and Euclid. After being wowed in Bridgeport by the Goldkette band, Shaw was not much impressed by this New York ensemble. "Fletcher had *no* band," as far as Art was concerned. "You went to hear the band so you could hear Coleman Hawkins."

That Henderson star was the first important soloist on tenor saxophone, which he played in a rhythmical "slap-tongue" fashion. But Hawkins's approach changed once he went with other bandsmen to an after-hours club in Toledo to hear the eighteen-year-old pianist Art Tatum, who startled these New Yorkers with his advanced harmonic conception and technique. "Coleman Hawkins was so taken by Tatum's playing," cornetist Rex Stewart wrote, "that he immediately started creating another style for himself, based on what he'd heard Tatum play."

Tatum moved to Cleveland soon and became a fixture at Val's in the Alley, a little club off Cedar Avenue near East Eighty-seventh, where many musicians, black and white, including Art Shaw, made early-morning visits to hear him.

"JAZZ" HAD already grown a lot since 1917. Small groups, white and black, proliferated across the country, spreading a rhythm gospel of collective improvisation, while dance-band orchestras blended elements of "hot music" into a sweeter ensemble sound.

Then there was Paul Whiteman, a larger-than-life figure (he weighed three hundred pounds) billed as "the king of jazz." Whiteman offered something for everyone's taste, from Tchaikovsky overtures to hot-jazz solos, from kick-in-the-pants slapstick to a man who squeezed tunes from an automobile pump. When Jean Goldkette's orchestra broke up in the fall of 1927, Whiteman hired the best of the bunch: arranger Bill Challis, bassist Steve Brown, Frank Trumbauer, and Bix Beiderbecke.

"BIX COMING TO CLEVELAND WITH PAUL WHITEMAN" read the headline on the entertainment page of the *Cleveland Press* in December, heralding the arrival of Whiteman and his twenty-four-man orchestra at the Allen Theatre. "Bix Biederbeck [*sic*] and the Dorsey boys will be with Paul Whiteman," wrote Billie Thomas. "Bix and the Dorseys are creators of ultra-modern dance music." The young Dorsey brothers (Jimmy on reeds, Tommy on brass) had come out of Pennsylvania and a band called the Scranton Sirens. It was Jimmy who had played the eight-bar clarinet solo on "Singin' the Blues."

The Allen was "crowded to the doors" on opening day: fifteen thousand people, Art among them, attended Whiteman's four shows. There was plenty of hokum in Whiteman's act, as well as a lot of music. And there was Bix.

The cornet player, sporting a dark moustache and seeming to glow with pride, was featured on a song called "Changes." With a mute jammed in his cornet, he stood and ripped sixteen bars of hot fingering before the band swallowed him up; he was gone before he started.

The show ended with a rousing performance of the *1812 Overture*, complete with cannon shots. When the curtain came down, Shaw made his way backstage, eager to glimpse or even maybe talk with Bix, Tram, Whiteman, or whoever was around. Shaw was irritated by some of Whiteman's presentation—the "showmanship"—but he admired the professionalism and the musicianship, and how each element served the whole. And he admired the *success*.

ART HAD GONE as far as he could with Joe Cantor by 1928. But right at the end of his stay, the Cantor band went to Richmond, Indiana, to make four sides for the Gennett label. Shaw, his first time in a recording studio, paid close attention.

There the Gennett people played them a record some other kids had made not long before: an instrumental by the group's piano player, Hoagland Carmichael. It was a jazzy line that shifted in and out of the beat; it was obvious "Hoagy" had written a tune taking off from Bix's style. Carmichael called his number "Star Dust."

Back in Cleveland, Shaw played a while with Merle Jacobs's orchestra at the Pirates' Hole; he took a paycut from what he had been getting, for the chance to play more jazz.

And he explored other diversions available to a good-looking young musician.

"The first time I remember having sex that was intensely satisfying," he told authors Karl and Anne Taylor Fleming, "was in Cleveland when I was about nineteen. There was this woman of about twenty, a kept woman whose boyfriend was out of town, and she picked me up at this place we were playing. She got a couple of other girls. A couple of other guys and myself went to this hotel where they had a suite, and we went into an all-night bout of drinking and sex. There was great sexual release, but it was all impersonal. I mean, I was being used, and she was being used. There wasn't any exchange of feelings between two human beings."

Shaw left Merle Jacobs for the better-paying dance band of Austin Wylie, a fixture at the New Piccadilly and Golden Pheasant restaurants. Wylie's was probably the top ensemble in Cleveland; it already had a good jazzman in nineteen-year-old trombonist Jack Jenney. Shaw was hired not only to play but to write arrangements, for which Wylie had constant need. In addition to his restaurant work, he made regular broadcasts from radio station WTAM. Art would also rehearse the band.

In June of 1929, Wylie's orchestra took a summer engagement at Wille's Lake Shore Gardens, on the outskirts of Cleveland. Here Art made the acquaintance of someone who would become as close a friend as he'd ever have.

He couldn't help but notice this fellow his own age, hanging around the bandstand. Claude Thornhill was "a funny-looking gent, with that potato nose and round German face," and reddish hair that stuck up like straw. Thornhill was a pianist, in Cleveland with a traveling orchestra. Who wrote those fine arrangements? he asked. Shaw admitted *he* had.

Very *good*, said Thornhill. Art bloomed under flattery. To test Claude's musicianship, though, Art asked him to play something. The pianist ran through some pieces of his own. Not only was he an outstanding keyboard man but an excellent composer.

Shaw drove Thornhill to Thornhill's hotel, then sat in the parked car and talked with him until six in the morning. Art, lonely all his life but especially in Cleveland, told Claude all sorts of personal things: that he was Jewish, for instance, and how alien this made him feel. Thornhill, not Jewish, seemed to understand. "Although I had only known him for one night," Shaw wrote, "I felt far closer to him than to anyone."

Neither man wanted their new friendship to end. But Claude was leaving town. Art hit on a solution: he would get Austin Wylie to hire Claude as arranger and second pianist. It worked. Thornhill joined Wylie's roster as the band was about to start another resident engagement at the Golden Pheasant Restaurant.

Shaw had another idea: he would use the occasion to move out of the place he shared with his mother and into a room with Thornhill at the Winton Hotel, next door to the Golden Pheasant. He would be free at last of Sarah Arshawsky's supervision.

ART WAS EARNING a grown man's wages; he wanted to be on his own. But whenever he suggested that Sarah get her own place (let alone go back to New Haven), she threw a fit: she was his *mother*; she had to take *care* of him. Christ, *he* was the one taking care of *her*. He had plenty of money: Wylie was paying him $175 a week. What was the point of working so hard if you couldn't live your own life? But his mother wouldn't hear of it. "She was like a *leech*," he would say. "She wouldn't let *go*."

Art was adamant. It edged Sarah past some brink. She went from pleading to threatening: picking up a butcher knife, she came at him, he said, knife raised. "Oh yeah! And I took the knife away, and I *pushed* her, and she fell down. And I was filled with *guilt*. 'Jesus, Mom, you know—

I didn't mean—' Blah blah blah. She'd have killed me," he said—or thought so, or said he thought so.

Years later, a woman he knew suggested that Sarah—forty-five years old in 1929—had been going through menopause at the time. Made sense to Art: "I never thought about that. That's what it was. She was goin' crazy; she was really goin' a little nuts." That image was burned in his unconscious for life: "'Crazy' was a woman with black hair, coming at me with a butcher knife."

Jesus, Mom—I didn't mean to—

But he was still determined to leave.

"When you get downstairs," she said as he was on his way out their upstairs flat for good, "you'll find my body on the sidewalk."

Art said good-bye, left, closed the door. Walked downstairs—took his time, maybe—and went outside.

Checked the sidewalk. No body.

CHAPTER FOUR

Why Was I Born?

T HE HOTEL WINTON suite Art shared with Claude was small, but
there was room for a Victrola. "We'd play records and—do whatever
young musicians do," Shaw said. "I remember we were both great fans
of Helen Morgan. Remember the record, 'Why Was I Born?' Oscar
Hammerstein wrote the lyric, Jerry Kern wrote the song." It was a great
ballad written in 1929 by an already legendary duo, for the most distinctive white female singer of the time.

"They had people like Helen Morgan who could sing an octave and
a sixth—almost two-octave range. And nowadays," at the dawn of the
twenty-first century, "all you gotta do is an octave and a note or two: a
ninth, or a tenth; a tenth is a stretch, for most singers." In 1929, when
singers sang for real, Art and Claude listened over and over to the musical emoting of Helen Morgan.

Other times, Claude and Art practiced basic aspects of craft.
"Those were the days when we were *learning*, what we had to do,"
Shaw said. "Claude and I would take afternoons off and go down
in the Chinese restaurant, and he'd sit at the piano, or I'd sit at the
piano—and hit random notes. And you had to call out the note:
'G'—'B sharp'—'F'—'F sharp'—'E flat'—'D.' We could call 'em.
And we rarely *missed*. A note goes three octaves down on the key-

board, it loses a lot of the timbre it had, up *there*. But we—trained our ears."

Claude had perfect pitch. Art had more: he heard quarter tones and eighth tones most people couldn't.

Art practiced and practiced. "As many hours as it took," he said. "I could play until my chops got ragged." Claude, too, was a demon at his keyboard. "He practiced things like 'Danse Negre' for hours," Art said, and Bach's "Inventions," to keep his fingers nimble. "He had a great musical ear but not much time—in a jazz sense." But Claude was great at creating musical moods, his own tone poems.

Claude and Art sought out other sounds on 78s. Most of what they heard was bad. But one disc, from Chicago, impressed them: the McKenzie-Condon Band's "You're Nobody's Sweetheart Now." Bud Freeman, Jimmy McPartland, Frank Teschemacher—the so-called Austin High Gang: white Chicago youngsters, mostly, barely out of their teens—little sons-of-Bix's, with (unbeknownst to Art) the sounds of black players from Chicago's South Side clubs also ringing in their ears.

Claude admired Art. "He called me Shawfellow," Art recalled. "Sid Shawfellow." It was a same-syllable play on Art Arshawsky (a name Claude was one of few to know), and an alternative to Art's own alternate identity. "Then *one* day he came up with Emerald Shawfellow. I thought, 'What the fuck is the *emerald* for?' Took me a long time; I finally found out: Emerald was my birthstone. So I became 'Emerald Shawfellow.'" Art was charmed. He would adopt this habit of tagging his *own* favorite people with private nicknames.

But Art could be an annoying roommate. Stumbling home past midnight, he would fall into a slumber deep as a coma. When Claude tried to wake him for their luncheon-set, often as not Art was immovable.

Shawfellow came up with an ingenious solution: a string tied to his little toe that Claude was to yank to wake him up. The first time they tried it, a still-asleep Shaw leapt from his bed and started choking Thornhill. Claude broke free and went to work, saying Art could get *himself* up from now on.

. . .

FORAGING THROUGH a pile of 78s in a Cleveland warehouse, Art found some "race records" made for the Negro market by a cornet player named Louis Armstrong—"Louis Armstrong and his Hot Five"—who played in a crackling style that moved to an inner beat. These records changed Art's life. "I couldn't believe my ears," he would say. "No one had done that on a trumpet, before him. No one knows how he *got* to that. I *didn't* understand that, and I *still* don't." With Armstrong's "West End Blues," Shaw said, "I began to see vistas in music, in popular or in jazz playing, that I had not even *imagined* or *conceived* of."

Listening to Armstrong, he hadn't forgotten Bix. "They were the best there was, and they did things no one had done before in terms of emotion, technical ability and the element of surprise." Armstrong brought "swing" to the fore: that rhythmic feel that marked the difference between what was jazz and what wasn't. The rhythms and patterns that poured from his horn showed the way to the future—for jazz, and for Art.

But Thornhill didn't care for Armstrong. He thought Art was just trying to cop hot licks. "I couldn't make him understand," Shaw said. "It wasn't the *notes*, I wasn't stealing *riffs*—just an *approach*. He *composed* a solo."

ART FOUND SOMEONE besides Claude to focus on: Betty, a beautiful blonde from Conneaut, Ohio, a greengrocer's daughter he had first met two years before while traveling with a band. Now here she was in Cleveland, eighteen years old, lovelier than ever, with cornflower-blue eyes and hair the color of wheat. For some reason, this gorgeous girl seemed to be in love with him. It was understood that she and Art would marry. Betty was the "nice" girl with whom he could live the dream life of popular songs—in their love nest, under their own blue heaven . . .

Soon Claude had a girl too: Polly, whom he had met in Lexington, Kentucky, when he had worked there a while back.

As full as Art's life was, he still had restless hours; with his screwy schedule, he was prone to insomnia. One night he saw a contest announced in the newspaper in connection with national airplane races to be held soon in Cleveland; the idea was to come up with the name of a song celebrating flying—just a title, not a real song—and an "essay" of 150 words. Right away Art had a title—"Song of the Skies"—and then he had the essay. "Just for the hell of it," he submitted his entry. A few days later, he won. The prize was an all-expenses-paid eleven-day *airplane* trip to Hollywood, a fantasy journey the benevolent Austin Wylie was happy to let Art take.

Shaw winged from Cleveland to the West Coast, arriving in Los Angeles on September 6. His name and those of the eight other regional winners were printed that morning in the *Los Angeles Times* ("Arthur Shaw, Cleveland"). Waiting at the airport were several civic officials and publicity people.

And Art's father.

Almost fifty, Harold looked as if he had shrunk. Art had mixed feelings at seeing him. "Jesus, that was weird," he would say. "It was very strange. . . . 'Who needs you? Where were you when I needed you?', and alla that; at the same time, it was my *father*, so—" People were ready to take Shaw to his hotel. Harry said he would call later.

Art stayed at the two-year-old Hollywood Roosevelt Hotel on Hollywood Boulevard, a four-hundred-room, twelve-story place financed by movie people. Four months ago, the motion-picture folk held their first "Merit Awards," or "Academy Awards," in the Roosevelt's Blossom Room. The Roosevelt was across the street from Sid Grauman's Chinese Theatre, a fantastic new movie palace.

There was an orchestra booked in the Roosevelt's Blossom Room: Irving Aaronson and his Commanders, a well-known outfit from the East. After dinner, Shaw took a table on the indoor balcony so he could see them. Aaronson's was an "entertaining band," though, doing novelty songs and funny routines—nothing to write home about. But the Blossom Room patrons made Shaw's jaw drop: the greatest bunch of movie stars you could imagine. Joan Crawford. Richard Barthelmess. William Powell. Art couldn't believe it. Look—yes—Charlie Chaplin!

Shaw went down to the lobby when the orchestra broke. Some band members wandered through. Art got a shock: one of Aaronson's men was someone he knew, Charlie Trotta, from the Olympia in New Haven. Art got another jolt when Trotta told him who *else* was in Aaronson's band: Tony Pestritto, whose saxophone case Art used to carry from the Cinderella Ballroom. The Aaronson band had been in a Broadway musical, *Paris*, with songs by Cole Porter; the band would tour soon with Irene Bordoni's road-show production of the play. Pestritto and Trotta had an idea: since the boss wanted to hire more men next year, why didn't Art join Aaronson's band?

HARRY ARSHAWSKY had things to tell Art too, when father and son met the next day for lunch. He was working as a tailor in a costume shop, all alone (but for his brother) and seeming miserable and lost. Art felt sorry for his dad, though he didn't mind telling him how much he was making in Cleveland: $175 a week. "He couldn't believe his *ears*. With the *blosser!*" Harold was impressed, maybe even proud. Art offered his father some cash, but the older man refused it. He asked Art for a favor: try to talk Sarah into coming to live with him in Los Angeles. His son said he would see what he could do.

Quite a trip this had turned into. There was more to come.

On September 11, Shaw went with the other contest winners to the Metro-Goldwyn-Mayer studios in Culver City, where they posed against a soundstage wall for a photograph with the platinum-blonde picture-star Bessie Love. Handsome Art Shaw—dressed in shirt, tie, stylish sweater, tan plus-fours, and brown-and-white Oxfords—stood with arms crossed to show off his chic Art Deco wristwatch; he was a confident focal point in this otherwise stodgy-looking bunch of Babbitts and bromides. Art looked as if he belonged, with that pretty blonde movie star, not outside but *inside* the MGM soundstage.

Give him time.

CHAPTER FIVE

The Girl Friend

I RVING AARONSON came to Cleveland with Irene Bordoni's show. The leader made Art a firm offer to join the Commanders, who were booked to be back at the Hollywood Roosevelt come spring; from there, Aaronson's band would go to Chicago, then New York.

It made sense for Shaw to join them: Aaronson had a national reputation; Wylie was just a big fish in a little pond. Times were changing: the stock market had blown a gasket. Maybe people would soon stop going to Chinese restaurants. But Art hesitated. He didn't like Aaronson's band. And he would have to leave Betty and Claude. But Claude urged him to go, and Betty vowed that if he didn't take this chance she would no longer be his girl.

Shaw wired Aaronson he was on his way.

In L.A., Art was a member of a "world-famous" orchestra, playing in a mecca for beautiful people. Just twenty, handsome as a motion-picture leading man, Shaw caught the eye of one of the young actresses who flocked to the Blossom Room. In theory, Art shared a Hollywood room with Tony Pestritto; in fact, he was all but living with his pretty new flame. He felt some guilt at the thought of Betty, but he shoved it to the back of his mind.

For the first time, Art could relax. And yet—he was embarrassed about the band he had joined, a "showmanship" outfit full of guys who sang, told jokes, and did specialties. Shaw was ashamed of these shenanigans but at the same time felt inadequate: *he* couldn't do anything like that. Still, he felt fated to break through to some golden realm where wishes were met and dreams fulfilled.

HE MET AGAIN with his father, unemployed now. Harold was disappointed but not surprised to learn Sarah refused to join him. Shaw felt sorry for his dad, but he also felt distance. There was nothing he could do for him. They went their separate ways.

All this time, Shaw had kept up his constant reading. Chummy MacGregor, Aaronson's pianist-arranger, steered him to *The "Genius"* by Theodore Dreiser. Shaw fell hard under the spell of that 1915 novel of an American artist wrestling with questions of craft and commerce, sex and spirituality—a book in its way as thrilling as *Kidnapped*:

> *He would go. He would save up his money until he had one hundred and fifty or two hundred dollars and then try his luck in the East. He would leave Ruby and Angela, the latter only temporarily, the former for good very likely, though he only vaguely confessed this to himself. He would make some money and then he would come back and marry his dream. . . . Then he would bring her back with him to New York—he, Eugene Witla, already famous in the East. Already the lure of the big eastern city was in his mind, its palaces, its wealth, its fame. . . . He would go to it now, shortly. What would he be there? How great? How soon?*

Aaronson's Commanders were booked for the summer into Chicago's Casa Granada, from where they made nightly "remote-control" broadcasts over the Columbia Broadcasting System via radio station WBBM. After his Aaronson duty, Shaw went all over the city's South Side in search of jazz.

A lot of "the Austin High gang" had moved to New York or elsewhere, but there were still lots of hot white players for Art to jam with.

Playing alto, he sat in with one bunch at a gin-fueled marathon-dance contest: drummer Gene Krupa, trombonist Floyd O'Brien, pianist Joe Sullivan, clarinetist Frank Teschemacher. Chicago men played four even beats to the bar, giving the music a relaxed feel; they did popular songs ("Liza," "Louise") instead of New Orleans pieces.

These kids had grown up listening to great black players. Teschemacher's inspiration was Louisiana-born Jimmie Noone, who'd spent much of his life and career in Chicago. (Another local clarinet player, nineteen-year-old Benny Goodman, had also built his style from Noone's; Goodman had gone to New York.) Noone, whose theme song was "Sweet Lorraine," held forth at the Apex Club, where Shaw liked what he heard: "He was a good player, yeah; he knew what he was doing."

Then there was Earl Hines, the black pianist who had collaborated with Louis Armstrong on such sky-shaking Chicago platters as "West End Blues." Armstrong had long since made it east; but Hines was leading an orchestra at the Grand Terrace Ballroom. Shaw sat in one night with Hines's band and found himself next to the well-known white trumpeter Muggsy Spanier. He listened closely to anyone who did anything he hadn't yet done.

His wide-open ears led him one day to a record shop in Chicago's Loop where customers previewed discs in listening booths before buying them. "I heard some music coming from a nearby booth . . . ," Shaw told radio interviewer Ted Hallock. "Some *strange* chord-structures and—passages that sounded different from anything I'd ever heard: There was no drumbeat, there was no pulse, no steady beat or any of that; and it—threw me.

"So I went out and asked the clerk, 'What was that?' And he said, 'It's Stravinsky, it's called *The Firebird*; it's a ballet piece.' . . . So I then asked if they had anything else like that; and he gave me *Afternoon of a Faun*— *L'après-midi d'un faune*—by Debussy. . . . The music was *delicious,* to my ears; I just *loved* it. So I bought those two records, and then I bought *Sacre du Printemps—The Rites of Spring*—and I brought those home, and the guys in the band thought I was *nuts*: 'What *is* that? What kinda *crap* are you listening to?' And I would *play* it—and listen and listen and listen. Changed my ear, changed my entire approach to music. Even the jazz that I played was affected by it. . . . Because it got to the point where beyond Louis, there wasn't much to hear."

If these modern works were news to Art and his Aaronson bandmates, they weren't to Chicago players such as Bud Freeman and Jess Stacy: Bix Beiderbecke five years ago had taught his midwestern buddies all about Ravel and Debussy, Holst and Schoenberg, Eastwood Lane and Edward MacDowell. Compared to those who already knew what was what, Art was playing catch-up.

But it was ever thus, for a kid who felt he had to discover the world all on his own.

ART HAD BEEN in Chicago with Aaronson's band for about two months when a Chicago plainclothes detective came into the Casa Granada one night asking for Shaw. Gangsters of all sorts were plentiful in the music world Art lived in, but police were a less frequent sight. Art was nervous; what was this all about? The cop told him: his father Harold was very sick, in County General Hospital in Los Angeles. The L.A. police, at the request of Harry's brother Joseph, asked Chicago authorities to contact his son.

Art didn't know what to do. He called the L.A. hospital but couldn't reach his uncle and his father was unconscious. Art thought about flying to L.A., but that was expensive and he would have to find a substitute to take his place with Aaronson. Instead, Shaw returned to his hotel and went to sleep.

His pals Tony and Charlie woke him at noon the next day with a telegram from Art's uncle: Harold had died. Art succumbed to a fit of hysterical laughter, which appalled and offended Pestritto and Trotta. Later Shaw apologized, and his friends forgave him. But, as Art would write, "I couldn't make myself *feel* anything. . . . It was all mixed up and confused. . . . [T]here was a sense of something *lacking* in me, a feeling of guilt at not feeling more. . . . [M]y mind began to feel like one of those Chinese boxes-within-boxes-within-boxes. . . . I eventually came to understand that there was no use condemning myself. . . . [H]e was probably far better off dead."

WHEN ART WENT with the Aaronson band to New York City in the fall of 1930, he was returning home in a sense—to the city where he was born and lived during his first eight years, and where his mother now lived, having moved back once her son joined Aaronson's touring outfit.

The orchestra opened at the Beacon Theatre on Broadway in early October, playing between showings of the new John Barrymore movie, *Moby Dick*. Art was soon learning his adult way around his childhood town. Trumpeter Max Kaminsky, visiting from Chicago, met Shaw at a party in the apartment of pretty female pianist Gladys Mosier, drinking bootleg whiskey and listening to jazz records.

A young woman more important to Art was in town this month: his girl Betty, from Ohio. In a fortuitous-seeming turn of events, she had come to New York at the same time as Art, to be maid of honor at the wedding of one of her best friends: the daughter of the deputy police commissioner of Mount Vernon, New York. Betty was staying at the Hotel Marseilles. She probably went to see Art play with the Aaronson band the night of Tuesday, October 14. Betty and Art were together later, early Wednesday morning, after he got off work—together in his red roadster when, at Broadway and Ninety-first Street, about seventeen blocks from the Beacon Theatre, Shaw's car struck and killed a sixty-year-old yacht-chef named George Woods, who stepped off the curb and into the path of Art's car, which sped from the scene. Witnesses gave its license-plate number to police, who found Art and Betty in the car two hours later on Columbus Avenue. Police said Shaw told them he had thought what he had hit was a traffic stanchion.

It was hard for Art to imagine a more calamitous event, as he was poised on the brink of a plausible New York success, and reunited with the girl he said he loved and hoped to marry—all on the heels of the sudden death of his father. Was some cosmic force punishing him for achieving too much, too soon? Was he thwarting himself through some inscrutable impulse of anger or dread or guilt, emanating from deep within a mental box within a box within a box? Was this the price extracted for running before you learned to walk? Or was this plain bad luck?

Art was cleared of criminal charges, but the dead man's family filed a civil suit for eighty thousand dollars in damages—a fee in wild excess of anything Art might hope to pay. In fact, since Shaw was under twenty-one, his mother was sued too. The two of them moved in together, into a tiny apartment on the Grand Concourse, while legal fees ate up their savings in the weeks and months to come. Sarah took in sewing to earn what she could, and got loans from friends and relatives. Art had to stay in New York and see these legal matters through. Once Aaronson's band left town, he was forbidden by union restrictions from taking music jobs until he had lived in the city three to six months and could claim his local 802 card. And Betty was out of his life, it seemed, for good, their relationship another victim of the fatal accident.

Desperate and depressed, Shaw stared into the abyss of a bleak-seeming future. He slunk around the city at night on his own, riding the subway for hours and falling asleep until the car reached the end of the line, then making the return trip. He discovered Greenwich Village and haunted its seedy bars and clip joints, where his mournful air and candid manner earned him pity and a few free drinks. He couldn't explain himself to his mother, and for the most part he shunned her company. The future hung over his head like a dark cloud.

But his survival instincts were stronger than he knew: he pulled himself together enough to find his way, with instruments, to Harlem, where Max Kaminsky said the real jazz was played; maybe he could sit in somewhere.

"I came around a corner," he would say much later, "134th and Lexington. And here was this little place: the Patagonia Club, or Pod's and Jerry's. I'm always comin' around a *corner*—and there it is! To me, I thought it was just pure luck; well—you *make* your luck too: you're *there*. I must have been *lookin'* for that corner, you know."

The spot Shaw found was a basement club down two flights of stairs, marked by an outside canopy. He stood on the sidewalk and listened, fascinated, to the sound of a pianist playing some sort of ragtime, it sounded like, but with a very driving beat. "I thought, 'Oooh, what the *hell* is *that*?' The guy was playing his ass off, you know; really great piano." After a while the music stopped, and a big black fellow, about forty-three, came outside, wearing a derby hat and smoking a cigar. "I said, 'Who's that cat in there playin'? That's great shit!' He says, 'You lookin' at him.' I said, 'You're *kiddin'* me! Are you the guy?' He said, 'Yeah.' I said, 'Can I sit in?' He says, 'That's your horn?' He talked: 'haaawn.' He says, 'Sure.'"

Shaw went downstairs and inside. "I was the only white guy in the place, and I felt very self-conscious about it; but after a while, it was all right." The club's piano was a beat-up wreck: an old scarred upright with chipped keys, and the whole front part missing so the hammers were exposed. That didn't bother this fellow; he made it sound great. He knew what he was doing.

The two men, both seated, made music just for themselves, and whoever else was around. "He had a peculiar way of playing," Shaw said, "not like anything I'd ever heard. Riffs that were so strange: changing keys in the middle, and coming back. He was very interesting." Willie "the Lion" Smith was the man's name, and it was clear he was born to play the piano. "He'd sit very straight," Art said, "and his fingers would do these *things*. He'd make these hawking noises—'*hok, hok, hok*'—off beat; I figured that's why they called him 'the Lion.' *Haw-haw-haw*, like a little roar. He was quite a guy, absolutely natural. He had this ability."

The Lion's music drew from many traditions: ragtime, Victorian parlor piano, German classical. He said practicing Bach strengthened his left hand. Strains and patterns of American impressionists such as Mac-Dowell could be heard in his compositions; yet he was as powerful a stride man as his buddy James P. Johnson. Willie borrowed from what he liked, but his playing was all his own. "First time I heard him play," Art said, "it really floored me, but I got with it pretty soon. I found it very exhilarating, very exciting. . . . I listened hard to what he did, and I tried to do the equivalent of that with my alto and clarinet. . . . [W]hen we came down, he had been playing stuff I knew was over my head . . . 'cause he'd been doing things I had not heard before, and I was trying to stretch out to meet that. . . . I learned a lot. . . . He was very nice to me, and he liked what I played; he said . . . 'Where did you learn to play like that, kid? You blow purty good.' . . . He asked me, 'Who do you listen to?' . . . I said, 'Pops Whiteman, Armstrong, and Bix.'"

Art returned often to Pod's and Jerry's to play with the Lion, and the Lion let him. "We got to know each other pretty well," Shaw said. " . . . He was a very sweet guy. . . . He had this kind of nice, almost arrogant way about him. It wasn't arrogant; he just knew who he was, he knew what he was about." That was something for Art to aim at: to become as sure of himself as the Lion was. To do your best—and to do it your own way.

Other white guys came to Pod's and Jerry's, one or two at a time, including Max Kaminsky, guitar player Eddie Condon, and the Chicago saxophonist Bud Freeman, whose first records Art remembered from Cleveland. Other black performers worked at the club on a casual basis, including a fifteen-year-old girl named Billie Holiday, who, the Lion said, drank and messed around too much, but she could sing like nobody's business.

The Lion, married but childless, had many musical cubs, black and white. None did he favor more than young Shaw, whom he called "Artie my boy" and escorted to several other clubs. "Willie was my open-sesame," Shaw said. "He took me all over Harlem. . . . You'd go from the Savoy [Ballroom] . . . to Connie's, to Smalls Paradise . . . the Shim-Sham place, Dicky Well's—all right in a little cluster. . . . It was a little world of its own. . . . I even went up and sat in the Cotton Club with Duke [Ellington]; I got to know Johnny Hodges."

Art, it turned out, excelled at the blues: a form developed by black Americans with chords and notes akin to tones from the Eastern European Pale of Settlement where Jews and Turks and Greeks and Palestinians played for and borrowed music from one another. No less a blues master than New Orleans clarinetist and soprano saxophonist Sidney

Bechet said one Harlem night of Shaw to Smith: "He is a good blues-man."

So welcome was Art made to feel in Harlem, he almost thought it his real home. On some deep musical and personal level, he yearned to be black. And in the strange cosmological scheme of things, Art's mentor in this welcoming world—his newfound adoptive father, as it were—thought himself a Jew. William Henry Joseph Bonaparte Bertholoff was the Lion's real name. His father had been part Jewish, and the Lion followed that faith. He was a Harlem cantor. He spoke some Yiddish and had business cards printed in Yiddish: a Harlem incongruity, for sure. Arthur Arshawsky was amazed; but he kept his own secrets, even with—especially with—this mentor. "He didn't know that I was Jewish," Art said. "I didn't tell him that."

CHAPTER SIX

Just One More Chance

I N HIS DARKEST hours of 1930, as his legal travails dragged on (coming to a resolution at last, but only after he had declared bankruptcy like his father before him), Art was not as alone as he pictured it later. There were friends to share these days and nights that tried his soul.

Claude and Polly Thornhill, now married, had moved to New York from Ohio around the time Art had. Art took Claude to Pod's and Jerry's to listen to and learn from Willie the Lion Smith, and Claude loved it. Then there was Roland Bernard "Bunny" Berigan, a blue-eyed trumpet player from Wisconsin, whom, as Artie later told it, he had first met in Cleveland when Berigan came through with the sweetish band of Hal Kemp. Or maybe Art met him elsewhere, through Thornhill; Claude too was on Kemp's band for a time. In any case, Art knew Bunny in New York, and knew what a fine trumpet man he was—with some of Bix's melancholy and a lot of Armstrong's raw passion. "Every time he blew into that horn," as the saying went, "fire came out."

Art and Bunny sat in at little Manhattan clubs, and they roomed together for a while in a rundown, dollar-a-night hotel near Broadway that catered to jazz musicians. Together they shared what little money, food, bootleg booze, or marijuana there was.

Geoff Miller, a Los Angeles magazine editor who came to know

Shaw late in life, shared this story Art told him of his Manhattan scuffling days: "He was sweating out his musician's card, and rooming with Bunny Berigan; and they had one joint between them, and just enough money to buy a bowl of soup—I mean, this is how poor they were in New York. And they walked along Broadway and went to some restaurant near Times Square, and sat in the upper portion of it, looking down on where the swells were. And they had their soup, half-stoned, and Artie says he remembers this incredibly gorgeous red-headed girl coming in from a Broadway show, and—*dancing* on the table! And it was Ginger Rogers."

The previously unknown Rogers was Broadway's latest sensation, star of the new George Gershwin musical *Girl Crazy* in which she introduced the ballad "Embraceable You"; in the same show, newcomer Ethel Merman became an overnight rage belting out the instant hit "I Got Rhythm." The pit band for *Girl Crazy* at the Alvin Theatre was cornetist Red Nichols's outfit, stocked with several young white jazzmen who had gotten to New York a year before Shaw and Berigan: Benny Goodman, Gene Krupa, Jack Teagarden, the Dorsey brothers, and Glenn Miller.

Art wouldn't mind having that pit-band gig. And—his sensations and pleasure centers stimulated by weed and hunger and the fierce anxieties of his young life—as Geoff Miller heard it from him all those years later, "He just wanted that dancing girl, Ginger Rogers, more than anything else in the world!" *Some day*, Art vowed . . .

FOR A WHILE Art roomed in a beat-up apartment behind the Winter Garden Theater with bassist Artie Bernstein and violin player Harry Bluestone and a trombonist named Larry, who mixed homemade gin in the bathtub.

Then one day there was Bix.

"He'd come up for sessions," Shaw said. "That was when he was on his way *out*. . . . I moved in with him, for a while. Bix was broke, and— It was hot, summer day; he was stayin' at the 44th Street Hotel. And so

I—found myself sharing a room with him. And boy, it was rough, 'cause he—wouldn't bathe. . . . Bix was—drunk all the time. He was a heavy drinker. Anyway, I moved out of there pretty soon; I only stayed there about two weeks. I couldn't *handle* it, although I *loved* his *playing*. But by that time, he was out of it. He'd show up at jam sessions, and you could hear him *trying*, to make somethin' happen. He couldn't, you know. That great *blot* that he had, that *sound*, was gone."

In the spring of 1931, Art at last got his local union card. He had begun hanging out at Plunkett's, a speakeasy on West Fifty-third Street that served as an informal hiring hall for jazz players and leaders. Shaw was there one day when Tommy Dorsey was rounding up men for a pick-up band to play a Princeton party. Berigan and guitarist Dick McDonough praised Art. "Think you can cut [play better than] my brother?" the gruff and mischievous Dorsey asked, with Jimmy standing right there. Art said, "I don't *think* I can, I *know* I can." Tommy hired him.

Also in the band that night of May 8 were Berigan, Bix Beiderbecke, tenor man Eddie Miller, and guitarist Carl Kress. "Tommy and Jimmy took turns standing out in front of the band that night," Shaw recalled. "When it was Tommy's turn, I played lead alto, 'cause that's what I did. Jimmy couldn't play lead alto. . . . Tommy had me get up and play a chorus, but I played about twelve choruses. Bix put his thumb and index finger around his nose and then touched his ear lobe indicating how much he liked what I'd played."

"He was telling me about that, one time," said Larry Rose, Shaw's personal assistant the last several years of his life, "and he said, 'You know, that time I met Tommy Dorsey, and they invited me to go play a gig with them—that was the turning-point. After that, there was no lookin' back.'"

IN JULY, Art was hired to play clarinet and alto in a Red Nichols outfit at the Park Central Hotel. He had been with the Nichols band a month when, on the morning of Friday, August 7, he heard the bad news. "I remember being in Jimmy Plunkett's saloon," he said. "And Frank

Henry, a trombone player with the Whiteman band—About eleven in the morning, getting ready to go to rehearsal, and Frank walked in. And there was nobody there, just the two of us; and he said: 'Bix just died.' And man, that was a—sad moment, for me. 'Cause I'd grown *up* with him, on him, you know."

Bix gone, at twenty-eight—and with him, that uncanny beauty.

"Playing the *sound* that you get," Shaw said, trying a lifetime later to articulate what it was that made Bix and others so special. "Most people don't seem to understand that that's what it's about. It isn't how many notes, or how *good* your playing is—nothin' to *do* with that. The *sound* of the *horn*—what you *do* with the instrument."

AND THE INSTRUMENT was subject to change.

Shaw's alto sound—a Trumbauer approach—didn't "make it" in New York, Art learned: it wasn't crisp enough to register well through a microphone. Nichols's tenor-sax man Babe Russin gave him the word when the band made some records in August. Art needed a new mouthpiece and reed, a whole new tone. Once he had that, he was ready. He soon became known as one of the best saxophonists in town.

In August, Art was hired as a member of the CBS radio orchestra. Shaw would now be working every day in company with the best players in New York: Manny Klein; Bunny Berigan; Tommy Dorsey and another trombonist, Jerry Colonna; Jimmy Dorsey (often playing second alto to Art's lead); violinist Joe Venuti; guitarist Eddie Lang. All the best white jazzmen were in the network radio orchestras; it was the only way they could make a living.

Art was on the Fred Rich band, which worked from noon to ten at night. The music they had to play was often terrible; the shows, ridiculous; the sponsors, meddlesome nitwits. But it was a living, and there were occasional glimmers of better things to come.

On September 2, 1931, a month after the death of Bix, a series debuted on CBS that would change American popular music. It starred the singer Bing Crosby.

Art had first seen and heard Bing in Cleveland when Crosby was part of Paul Whiteman's Rhythm Boys trio. He had met Crosby a year ago in Hollywood, when Bing came by the Blossom Room to sing with the Aaronson band a few times. Now Art was in the orchestra for Crosby's CBS broadcasts, along with Tommy Dorsey, Joe Venuti, and (right by Bing's side, feeding him rhythm) Eddie Lang. Crosby—who had already recorded with the best white jazzmen, including Bix, and caroused and sung with black performers such as Louis Armstrong and Duke Ellington—was an immediate coast-to-coast hit with his relaxed jazz-derived "crooning."

"Bing was an enormous influence," Shaw told Crosby biographer Gary Giddins. "You couldn't avoid him. He had a good beat. He was a jazz singer, he knew what jazz was, and could sing a lyric, say the words, and make you hear the notes. Bing could swing."

Crosby perhaps was on Shaw's mind when he stood in Central Park one evening with an unnamed friend—maybe Claude Thornhill—and gazed at the thousands of windows in the buildings of the Manhattan skyline. His friend asked him what he was thinking about, and without hesitation Art, now with the glimpse of a brighter future ahead—said, "See all those windows up there with all those lights going on in them? Well, back of every one of those there's somebody. And one of these days everyone of those people up there behind every one of those windows—is going to know my name."

IN A WAY, his progress had been extraordinary. At the age of twenty-one (twenty-two, in May), Art Shaw was the first-call alto studio-man in New York City, with an apartment on West Fifty-seventh Street crammed with books and records, and take-home pay of two to three hundred dollars a week. The problem was, he didn't like what he was doing. With the Depression having brought most things to a standstill, the radio shows were the only paying game in town, and the radio shows were pretty awful. "They used the best musicians in New York," Shaw said, "for some of the worst music."

So Shaw (with the guidance and encouragement of another mentor, Guy d'Isere, a well-read CBS classical clarinetist, his intellectual Willie the Lion Smith) kept studying—learning all he could, trying to improve himself, thinking maybe he was in the wrong line of work. Maybe he should try to be a journalist, or a novelist. At Columbia University extension, he enrolled in some writing courses.

In this confused state of being, Art encountered Jane Carns, a doctor's daughter from Ashtabula, Ohio, whom he had first met when he'd played at Bantam Lake with Joe Cantor. Now she was all grown up, or near as like: a beautiful girl of seventeen. Maybe Jane reminded Art of the Betty he'd lost. Though Jane was under the age of legal consent, she and Art eloped. But the two were approaching life from different angles of experience; the marriage, Art said, wasn't consummated. Jane's mother came and took her away. Her father had the marriage annulled.

Another hope for a happy life dashed. Shaw's self-prescribed cure: more work.

In the middle of 1932, Shaw took to the road, in a reprise of the odyssey that had gotten him to New York. Due to "economic pressure" CBS cut staff and reduced pay for those who stayed. Shaw could make more money in a hotel band.

Art got an offer from Roger Wolfe Kahn at three hundred dollars a week. He took a boat down to Florida and then a train, joining up with Kahn in New Orleans, where he played lead alto and solo clarinet alongside top-notch players such as Chicago pianist Joe Sullivan, trumpeter Charlie Teagarden, and ex-Goldkette drummer Chauncey Morehouse. After three months in New Orleans, the ensemble headed north; Shaw himself drove Kahn's Lincoln up to New York, where the orchestra was booked in the Pennsylvania Hotel. Shaw was featured on records Kahn made and was also seen playing with the group in a Vitaphone movie short.

It was a good band, but business at the Pennsylvania was poor. Rather than break up the orchestra, Kahn got it hired as the pit band for a musical with songs by the Gershwin brothers. But *Pardon My English* closed in a month, and Shaw went back to radio work—which he now loathed all the more. Not that he wasn't grateful for a living, in a year when there were "breadlines stretching four-abreast from the soup kitchen at the World Theater all the way to Sixth Avenue," as trumpeter Pee Wee Erwin wrote.

More and more, Art took refuge in books, and his mind returned to the notion of being a writer. If only he could make a living at *that*. There were lots of writers in Greenwich Village, where Art took to hanging out. Edna St. Vincent Millay, whose poetry Art loved, was the Village's patron saint. Someone said Theodore Dreiser was still in New York, living at the Empire Hotel. One day Art went over there, marched up to the front desk, and asked them to ring Mr. Dreiser's room. He said into the phone, with the confidence of a fellow making two or three hundred dollars a week, "My name is Art Shaw. I'd like to meet you, Mr. Dreiser."

"And I met him! It must have been pretty vacuous to *him*. But he was kinda pleased: There was a young guy, there, obviously *intent*. And I told him, you know—how much his books *meant* to me. Here was this guy—who was *God*. He'd written *Sister Carrie*, he had written *An American Tragedy*. I'd never written a *line*, I had no *idea*. Wanted to rub up against *greatness*."

Decades later, Shaw would fashion some rules for how to become a genius: "One: Find yourself a genius. Two: Follow him around. Three: Do what he does." The author of *The "Genius"* was a genius, for sure, but Art could hardly follow him around. What might Art do, though, that Dreiser had done? What could he write that might evoke the same feelings and response as, say, *An American Tragedy*? What did Art know?

Well—there was Bix Beiderbecke: a tragic figure if Art ever met one, and a genius too. Bix had done things no one else did, and there was no accounting for it, no explanation in his background. What else was genius but that?

If Art could write a book about Bix—a tragedy about a musical genius who couldn't make a place for himself, who the world and the times passed by—yes, people might want to *read* that.

CHAPTER SEVEN

A Deserted Farm

Hanging out on West Tenth and West Eleventh, Art encountered other Greenwich Village characters: Joe Gould, Maxwell Bodenheim, John Coffee.

"John Coffee was like—an untutored poet," Art said. "He'd been at Matewan, for the criminally insane, you know? They sent him there; he didn't fit the pattern. And he would come up with things like—He'd be drunk, he'd have a hangover; used to sleep on a pool table, in the—Village. And he would say, 'I feel like a leaf, dropped from the tree of myself.' He'd *speak* like that. A rough, tough guy. I got to know him pretty well. Big influence in my life. Turned me on to Veblen—and Joseph Wood Krutch—and writers like that, that I'd never heard of." Also anarchist authors: Kropotkin, Bakunin.

Coffee had gotten into real estate to help artists move to Bucks County, Pennsylvania, where they could live and work cheap, about seventy miles away from the city. It was an appealing notion to Art, and plausible once he met a sweet and kind dental nurse named Marge Allen, who moved in with him, Village-style. Coffee told them of a place for sale, a farm owned by *New Masses* poet and activist Isidore Schneider: twenty-seven acres, with an old house and barn, near Erwinna, Pennsylvania, for three thousand dollars. Art and Marge pooled their money and bought the farm in both their names.

"We had no [running] water," Art said. "A well; you pumped water into the kitchen—a pump, you know?" No electricity. There was a wood-stove for cooking and a fireplace for heat. The privy was an outhouse. Winter came. It snowed. "Froze my *balls* off at night," Art said. "Went to bed with a *hat* on—a nightcap. It was *cold*, Jesus Christ! Unbelievable."

But Art loved the countryside, next to the Delaware River. They lived well enough on fifteen dollars a week. That sum came from a system concocted by Coffee: Shaw cut firewood from trees and plantings, which he and Coffee trucked to New York and sold in the Village. Art kept bread and milk and steak on the table, and continued to support his mother in New York, while he tried to get his novel going. When friends like Claude and Polly Thornhill visited to suggest that Art go back to music (Claude was sure he could get Shaw onto Ray Noble's band), Art said *no, no, no.*

For information and inspiration, Shaw turned to books John Coffee gave him. "*Theory of the Leisure Class*—[Thorstein] Veblen. That was a helluva book. Opened up my eyes. Joseph Wood Krutch: *The Modern Temper*. That was a big thing." Yet these books were vexing: they made Art aware of how *un*-aware he was.

Krutch made a reference to the speed of light which sent Art to the encyclopedia for a definition. He found one but could make no sense of it. "You know, it was very, very, very clear—but gibberish, to me." He thought he didn't know enough to write. He would have to go back to school.

Whether or not this discouraging train of thought was to blame, Shaw had a mishap hacking firewood: he nearly chopped off his left forefinger. "And I swear," he said, "the very first thought I had was, 'I'll never have to play the clarinet again.'" But "Marge was a nurse; she sewed it back on, and it took."

Just as well. With his writing hopes dashed, he would have to make a decent wage again. In the early weeks of 1934, Art Shaw was back in Manhattan, horn in hand, once more in search of a gig.

. . .

THIS TIME he would arrange things differently: just do a *couple* of radio shows a week—enough to buy groceries and pay his (and his mother's) New York rent. The rest of the time, he would read and study.

Shaw lined up assignments on record and transcription dates with the orchestras of Richard Himber, Adrian Rollini, and Ben Selvin. The latter's crew was featured on *The Taystee Breadwinners*, a transcribed program where Art again worked with the top session players in town: the Dorseys, trumpeters Manny Klein and Sterling Bose—and a certain reedman in whose path he had been following, one way or another, all his young life.

BENNY GOODMAN was born in the same month as Artie Shaw—on May 30, to Shaw's May 23—but a year earlier, in 1909. He had been at least one step ahead of Art ever since. Like Art's father, Benny's was a Polish-Russian Jewish immigrant, who worked as a tailor. Unlike Harold Arshawsky, David Goodman, who settled in Chicago, acted in loving ways toward his family, which included twelve children (Benny was the ninth). And where Harold Arshawsky mocked Art's playing the "blosser," David Goodman was responsible for Benny's music making: first getting him enrolled in a settlement-house band and later paying for lessons with a classically trained clarinetist (who also taught the black players Jimmie Noone and Buster Bailey). Benny was encouraged to make a career of music; he, like Art, made his first five dollars as a kid in an amateur contest. Goodman joined the musicians' union at the age of thirteen; and by sixteen, he was a member of Ben Pollack's band, which traveled all the way to Los Angeles.

Goodman's jazz credentials were impressive: By age twenty-one, he had worked or recorded with Bix Beiderbecke, the Dorsey brothers, Jack Teagarden, Dave Tough, Bud Freeman, Hoagy Carmichael, Wingy Manone, Venuti and Lang, Red Nichols, Jimmy McPartland, and Miff Mole. He moved his family to New York after his father's death at the age of fifty-four, and there he established himself as a top session player.

By age twenty-five, Goodman had also recorded with Bessie Smith, Ethel Waters, a teenaged Billie Holiday, Frankie Newton, Chu Berry, Bunny Berigan, Red Norvo, the Boswell Sisters, the Mills Brothers, Bing Crosby, Muggsy Spanier, and many others. He made his first record date as a leader in 1928, and in 1933 he put together his own first orchestra to audition for a radio program to be sponsored by Lucky Strike cigarettes.

The latter event occasioned the first known time Goodman's path crossed Shaw's. Art had been hearing about Benny for years. While he said an adamant no to Claude Thornhill's offer to help get him onto Ray Noble's band, Shaw did consent to come into New York from Bucks County during 1933 to join the ranks of Goodman's short-lived audition ensemble, which also included the Dorsey brothers, Bunny Berigan, and Artie Bernstein. Here was a band that might be fun to play with. But at the crucial audition, the sponsor fell asleep. The orchestra dispersed. By 1934, Goodman was back to freelance record and radio work—where he and Shaw now often found themselves sitting side by side in various commercial reed sections.

Shaw, in later years, prompted by a mixture of brutal honesty, envy, mischievousness, and even maybe perverse affection, would tell a number of "anecdotes" designed to show Goodman's stupidity (and Shaw's cleverness), Benny's limitations (and Artie's wider vistas).

Here is Shaw's recollection of one incident he said took place in 1934, when Art and Benny doubled on alto and clarinet in such session orchestras as Richard Himber's, Ben Selvin's, Adrian Rollini's, and Johnny Green's: "I used to play lead alto; Benny played second alto—he had a *lousy* saxophone sound; terrible. And—we were playin' a program together one time. There was a part written in an arrangement, piece was 'Lover'—*dum*-da, dum da *dum*-da, dum da *dum*—lead alto, playing a sort of, obbligato, against the brass. It was in my part; I was playin' lead. And it was a nice-sounding thing; radio music was so awful, mostly, that it was always kind of marvelous to have something that you could play with a *little*, sense of music. So we played it, went through part of a rehearsal; and at one point, Benny said, 'Hey Pops, lemme—lemme play that.' I said, 'Sure. Take it.' I didn't care; we were all getting union scale. So I handed him the part, and we went into it again. And the leader, I forget who it was, said, 'Who's playin' that?' And I—leaned back. Benny said, '*I* am.' 'Give it back to Artie.'

"Benny always remembered that; *bothered* him a lot. . . . He didn't *blame* me; he just—knew he didn't make it. That was *galling*. But he had a lousy sound, on an alto; just didn't *sound* good. And I was a very good alto player."

Shaw would recall another radio show he and Goodman worked together, with Richard Himber conducting, in which Benny was nervous in Art's presence, Art thought: "And Benny squeaked, on the air: clarinet. I had that sort of effect on him; we used to call it 'Indian sign.' . . . He never quite got over that. . . . All the years I knew him—I was one of the few guys he kinda respected. [Louis] Armstrong was another."

Another Goodman encounter Shaw would recall took place late in their careers, he would say, around 1949: "One day we're having lunch, at the Oak Room, in New York. I had wanted to enlist his support on something I was trying to do; had to do with agencies who were running the business. I thought the big bands should have their own agent; run their own agency, and *hire* the agent to do it, and have a share at—you know, a communal kind of owning of this thing; corporate, cooperative agency, in which we would share, in terms of profit. . . . Tommy [Dorsey] was willing; everybody I knew. Guy *Lombardo* was willing! Benny said no; I said, 'Why not?' He said, 'Ahh, I got my own lawyers.' I said, 'Benny, for Chrissake, we're not talking about that.' . . . 'Yeah, but—'

"All he wanted to talk about was the clarinet. . . . He said, 'I heard that Mozart you played—' . . . I went in one day to WOR [radio], they had a house quartet, we ran down the piece and played it. No rehearsal, none of that. . . . He said, 'Not bad.' I said, 'It wasn't *meant* to be, Benny.' And he looked at me, kind of, you know—He was *not* the *brightest* guy you ever knew. 'Yuhhh'—

"Then he started asking about Reginald Kell, about Simeon Bellison, about this guy and that guy, and—I had reservations about a lot of 'em.

He said, 'Who do you like?' I said, 'Dan Bonade!' Dan Bonade was a *helluva* clarinet; he worked in the CBS Symphony Orchestra . . . and *I* had the pleasure of sitting next to him; he was a *helluva* sonofabitchin' clarinet. He later became head of clarinet for *Juilliard*. Anyway—long story.

   "So at a certain point I said, 'Benny, Jesus Christ, you know—you're too hung up on the goddam *clar-*inet.' So he looked up and said, 'That's what we *play*, isn't it?' I said, 'No, I'm trying to play *music*.' And a funny little thing occurred: he looked at me like it was the first time that he ever considered the idea that the clarinet was an instrument—a *means* by which you did something. He *heard* it—but then he went right back to talking about clarinet. To the end of his life, that was all he knew about."

   Art's most elaborate putdowns of Benny would come after decades of counting mixed blessings and eating sour grapes. But in 1934, Art and Ben were both talented and ambitious players, each yet to make his mark. They would joust as professionals for decades, and their clashes would benefit popular culture as much as the "battles" of Hemingway and Fitzgerald shaped American writing, or the duels of Picasso and Matisse informed European painting, or the contrasting styles of Coleman Hawkins and Lester Young created two schools of jazz tenor-saxophone playing. Youthful music fans would soon feel impelled to choose sides between Artie Shaw and Benny Goodman, but America was lucky to have them both. In order for their rewarding game to commence, though, one of them needed to put the ball in play.

SOME OTHER SIDEMEN in 1934 were about to take matters into their own hands, prompted by the success of the Casa Loma Orchestra, a brassy white ensemble that played with "machine-like" precision and was popular with college kids.

   Tommy and Jimmy Dorsey, who had made records under their own names and done enough college gigs to pick up a campus following too, thought they might give the Casa Lomans a run for their money. They signed with the Rockwell-O'Keefe talent agency (who handled

Bing Crosby) and, with thirty-year-old session trombonist Glenn Miller writing arrangements, began rehearsing an eleven-man band in the spring of 1934.

Benny Goodman's brother Harry urged *him* to form a band to audition for a spot at the Music Hall, a club being built at Fifty-second and Broadway by promoter Billy Rose. Goodman once more began assembling an orchestra made up of men he had worked with, including Claude Thornhill. The Dorseys also tried out for that Music Hall job, but Rose hired Goodman's band; Benny's outfit opened the club in June. The Dorseys' orchestra then went on the road, in hopes of building a momentum that would lead to a good New York booking; Tommy and Jimmy's boy singer, thanks to Rockwell-O'Keefe, was Bing Crosby's younger brother Bob.

Art kept his nose to his chosen grindstone. He had enrolled in a tutoring school to get the equivalent of the high school diploma he'd never received, hoping to attend college. To make a living, he kept doing radio: playing in the orchestra for Ed Wynn's *Texaco Fire Chief Hour*, working for conductor-composer Johnny Green on a show with singer Ruth Etting; and playing in ensembles led by conductors such as André Kostelanetz, Victor Young, Howard Barlow, and Sigmund Romberg.

More satisfying on a musical level were some record dates Art took part in, thanks to the wealthy young promoter-producer John Hammond. Passionate in his love of jazz and devoted to using music to promote racial integration, Hammond had already taken an intense interest in Benny Goodman's career. (Goodman would eventually marry Hammond's sister.) Shaw too had come to Hammond's notice, and in August, John hired Art to play clarinet on a record session with an eight-man "mixed" combo led by the one-armed white New Orleans trumpet player Wingy Manone. Bud Freeman was also on that date, which alternated "colored" keyboard men: newcomer Teddy Wilson, and the veteran Jelly Roll Morton.

Hammond used Shaw again a month later for a Red Norvo septet date featuring Wilson along with the young white tenor-saxophonist Charlie Barnet and Jack Jenney, whom Shaw knew from Cleveland.

Shaw and the others did another Norvo record date in October, about which Hammond said, "Shaw and Teddy Wilson were again superb."

But it was at a non-Hammond session on November 20 of 1934 that Art showed just how exciting a player he could be. Leader of this twelve-man date was Art's old idol Frank Trumbauer. Bunny Berigan played lead trumpet. Also on the date was trombonist Glenn Miller. The pianist was Roy Bargy, a Whiteman vet; Artie Bernstein was on bass, and the drummer was Johnny Williams (whose son John would distinguish himself later in the century as a movie-soundtrack composer). "Frankie Trumbauer and His Orchestra" cut three sides this day before wrapping things up with "Troubled": an intense, insidious, relentless number that all but tore the roof off the Victor studio.

"Troubled" was an intricate line, graceful but jittery, done in a spare and clever arrangement (maybe by Miller). Trumbauer and Berigan were heard in brief solos; then Shaw came in on alto sax for a subtle, forceful eight bars. Frankie took a half-chorus C-melody solo full of his loping, lyrical rumination. Then Art returned—on clarinet, with sixteen bars of reined-in ecstasy, gleeful as an imp dancing on a grave. The ensemble played a brief passage before Berigan took off on a fiery solo as Williams kicked things along with an urgent *whomp* on each fourth beat. The whole ensemble returned for the final ride-out, with Shaw's euphoric clarinet soaring above like the wrath and love of God. Tension and release, drama and catharsis—an unforgettable experience in under three minutes. Shaw might choose to labor forever in the radio mills, or read books and keep studying until insight overtook him—but somewhere in his heart or head or gut, young Art must have known he was born to make music like this.

═ CHAPTER EIGHT ═

Broadway Rhythm

CHANGE was in the air.

Benny Goodman, with his new orchestra, got a job as one of a trio of bandleaders on a three-hour Saturday-night NBC-radio music program, *Let's Dance,* to start in December. Claude Thornhill left Goodman's crew before the show debuted, but Benny hired Bunny Berigan and the Chicago drummer Gene Krupa. Doing Goodman's arrangements would be Fletcher Henderson, the best black writer for hot band this side of Duke Ellington.

The whole New York scene seemed revitalized. With Prohibition repealed and liquor once more legal, speakeasies turned into joints with entertainment: small combos, "intimate" singers, raucous comedy. Clubs sprang up along Fifty-second Street.

One was the Onyx, where money for a liquor license was raised with funds from radio and session men including Art Shaw. The Onyx was a musicians' clubhouse, where session cats sat in after their day jobs. Art was glad for the chance to play with men like guitarist Dick McDonough; he said, "Dick was okay. I liked him. He was a nice guy. We used to play together a lot. I remember 'The Devil and the Deep Blue Sea'—he would play that. The middle of the bridge of that—it's a strange chord structure. So he played the chords, and

I would—play ad lib above him. These were strange days, 'cause we were learning a craft that never existed before. We were making it up."

Art took music as seriously as anything in life, and it bothered him when others didn't. "I 'member listening to Jimmy [Dorsey] one time, play—and I got so impatient," he said, recalling one night at another club, the Famous Door. "Well in those days you didn't have your horn, you had your *mouthpiece* with you, and you'd *borrow* a horn. So, Jimmy was playing, and—I said, 'Ah, this is *shit*.'"

"Artie . . . was a fantastic lead alto," said trumpeter Manny Klein, who was with him that night. "[H]e kept shaking his head. Finally . . . he got on the stand—and he played! You never heard such sax playing in your life. He was a demon! But that was Artie Shaw, a meshuggener if there ever was one."

"And I was not *known*, and I got up and—blew him out of the room, as you'd say now," as Artie told it near the end of his life. "Jimmy never got *over* that. 'Where's that *comin'* from?' Come from anywhere, man. We're *all* listening to the same *records*."

The Dorsey brothers were back from their band tour in the spring of 1935. On May 15, they opened at the Glen Island Casino. During the May 30 matinee, their temperaments clashed. The aggressive Tommy beat off a brisk tempo for "I'll Never Say 'Never Again' Again." The low-key Jimmy complained, "Hey Mac, that's a little fast, isn't it?" "You want to take over?" Tommy asked. "It's yours. Take it"—and stomped off the stand, and out of the Dorsey Brothers Orchestra. Jimmy became sole leader; Tommy found a second band to helm. Both brothers would win success in the music-mad years to come.

BUT WHAT CONCERN was it to Art Shaw if the Dorseys, Goodman, and whoever else traveled from town to town, as Art had done three years ago with Roger Wolfe Kahn? Endless travel got you nowhere. Shaw had his own life to lead.

Art and Marge were having problems, though. Her religious parents were giving her a hard time about living in sin. "She hadda choose," Art said, "between staying with me, unmarried, the way we were—or her *family*: her father, and mother, and all that shit. So she—was too *scared* of that. She was gonna *leave*. And I wasn't *ready* for her to leave. And so—" And so they wed, giving them new problems. "That was a real marriage," Art insisted. "She was an okay woman. She had one big problem: she was also a spoiled Catholic, and we didn't want children. And the only answer to that would be: birth control. And that was a sin. So we lived with that—her problems, with that. And her parents; she allowed them to dictate her life." Marge knew better, Art said. "But she couldn't deal with the emotion." They were together three years. "And the last year was hopeless." Before they married, things were fine. "Marriage is a great—great, destroyer." Or so it was proving, in his experience.

As for his studies—there too Art was thwarted. A cynical prep-school teacher mocked Shaw's desire to pursue education while already earning a decent living. A more sympathetic academic was dismayed by Art's plan to teach, and convinced him he would hate the life. And an instructor in a required course failed Shaw for his unorthodox answer to an essay question.

"You weren't graded by what you knew or how well you thought," a disgusted Art saw, "you were graded by the books you were told to read. I remember flunking a class, a history course, American history. 'Name three causes of the American Civil War.' So I named three. One of 'em, seemed to me, was that the North couldn't compete with Southern slave labor; so obviously they wanted to put slavery away. Had nothin' to do with being humane; the humane was window dressing. Well, that was no good. The guy said, 'We didn't ask you to read Marx.' I didn't realize it, but I was giving him a Marxian interpretation; I hadn't read Marx, at the time. So, you know—I got mad as hell; I walked out of school. 'Ah well fuck it, I gotta do it on my own.'"

His life-motto.

Art was back to square one.

. . .

LIFE AS a sideman wasn't without fringe benefits, though. Art befriended interesting people, including the popular sports-columnist Jimmy Cannon, who did Art a neat favor the night of September 24, 1935: he smuggled Shaw, a boxing fan, into a ringside seat to see Joe Louis, "the Brown Bomber," battle former champion Max Baer in a heavyweight bout at Yankee Stadium.

Clutching a pencil and a yellow notepad, Shaw was disguised as a reporter; he sat just a few feet away from the boxers. People were expecting a terrific struggle, but the whole thing was over early, when Louis knocked down Baer in the first seconds of the fourth round. "I was in awe of Joe Louis," Shaw said. "Very, very powerful man. I was sittin' right *there*, watching this fight. And all of a sudden Baer is lyin' on the floor, bein' counted out. I didn't *see* anything. And I thought to myself, 'Well—if I didn't see it—*he* didn't see it.' Not a glimpse, and he's watchin'! Baer was a very cute fighter.

"So we all left, afterwards—a lotta reporters, and I was along with Jimmy, went to Joe Louis's apartment. He was married to a woman named Marva. And—I think it was in Harlem—we all went to the apartment, where he was eating a *huge mound* of vanilla ice cream. He loved vanilla ice cream; and when you're in training, you can't *do* that.

"I'm standing with Jack Blackburn, his trainer. And it made me inquisitive: 'What the hell is it, with Joe? What *is* that, that he does?' And Blackburn said, 'He's a *counter*-puncher.' I said, 'What're you talkin' about?' 'Joe got great eyes. When a fighter's gonna hit you—he *does* somethin'. And if you got good eyes, you do it first.' He's counterin' somethin' that never happened yet.

"Blackburn says: 'Joe, get up.' Joe got up; whatever Blackburn said, he trusted him. So standin' in the corner is a phonograph—wind-up, on a cabinet. Record on it: a 78. And Blackburn turned it on. He said, 'Joe, read the title.' The light—wasn't very good. So—Joe read the title. *Wuuuhh*, I'm tryna read it. Then he said, 'Read the—smaller print.' Joe read the small print. And then: 'Find the little print.' 'Not licensed for radio broadcast'—Joe read it. He went back and ate his ice cream. I said,

'That's pretty—crazy.' He said, 'Yeah.' He said, 'Well that's what he got. Joe got that. When he lose that, he's through.'"

Art had good eyes too. But it took him a while to see the counter-punching possibilities right under his own nose.

OUT IN Los Angeles, late in August, Benny Goodman scored a triumph when college-age fans of his *Let's Dance* broadcasts turned out in thousands to cheer his band at the Palomar Ballroom through an engagement that went down in history as the birth of the swing era.

Most folks back east didn't get the news until November, when Goodman's crew began an incredible six-month stay at the Congress Hotel in Chicago, and the band's half-hour weekly remote broadcasts were picked up in New York by the NBC network.

Shaw said he was visiting the farm in Bucks County when he heard Goodman's orchestra on the radio from the Congress. "I *knew* he always wanted to have a band of his own," he said, "and I had all but given up on the music business, I was totally disgusted with it. And—he got on that Camel program, he and some guy like Xavier Cugat—and some sort of American band, terrible; they were the three. Well none of us could have known that was gonna result in this success that he had when he got to the West Coast. Which in a way, established the *popularity* of that kind of music. Casa Loma band was there *ahead* of time; they were doing the same thing, but not very good. Benny at least had good men, and he *played* a helluva good *clar*-inet. Anyway—

"I'm up on a farm—had a radio hooked to a car battery, didn't even have electricity . . ."

Presenting Benny Goodman and his music! Benny Goodman, ladies and gentlemen, the man with the torrid clarinet, and the even more torrid band, who purvey these sorts of rhythms—all danceable—in the Joseph Urban Room at the Congress Hotel, on Michigan Avenue in downtown Chicago—

"I wrote him a letter! At the Congress Hotel. I wrote him and said, 'Jesus Christ, Benny, I heard your band, it's a *bitch*!' You know: 'Great; isn't that marvelous.' He used to say to me later, 'I'm gonna blackmail you.' I said, 'What *with?*' He says, 'That letter.' I said, 'Well I *meant* it. Why would you blackmail me? Go ahead and publish it.' But he had this attitude that, you know, there's a *rivalry. I* didn't want to get into any rivalry; I played clarinet, he played clarinet."

But Art couldn't help but admire what Benny had done: seen his chance, taken his shot, hit it big. If Goodman's run held—and there was every indication it would—he had cracked open a gate through which many might follow.

And Art Shaw—twenty-five years old, half out of a marriage he no longer believed in, not yet able to take another swing at writing, no happier in his day work than he had ever been—saw possibilities. Because if Benny Goodman could do this—Benny, who probably never read a book in his whole *life*; Benny, the *second*-best alto player in New York City (and just maybe, in Art's opinion, the second-best *clarinetist*)—why then, so could Art Shaw.

══ CHAPTER NINE ══

There's Something in the Air

NEW YORK and the country exploded with music. Many types of swing were for sale. Art Shaw was rushing from gig to gig.

In early 1936 he worked record dates with the singing Boswell Sisters, and with his friend Bunny Berigan. In April, Shaw took part in a Berigan session that produced the first version of what would become a swing-era classic. Pianist Joe Bushkin, then nineteen, later told pianist and radio host Marian McPartland how a friend of his bought the sheet music of a new Vernon Duke and Ira Gershwin song from the lobby of the theater where it was being featured in the *Ziegfeld Follies*: "He brought it down to the Famous Door, where I was playing with Berigan and Eddie Condon and a whole buncha cats; we outnumbered the audience, many nights. And Eddie Condon set up the chord-changes. . . . They're all four-part harmony, 'cause he played a four-string guitar. . . . And then we went into a studio and just recorded it just that way." Berigan cut the number on April 13 with a seven-man group including Bushkin on piano, the black drummer Cozy Cole, and Art Shaw playing soulful clarinet obbligato behind Bunny's vocal of Ira Gershwin's topical lyrics to "I Can't Get Started (with You)."

. . .

AS THE SWING craze grew, musicians of all sorts were attempting to become bandleaders. Bill Challis, the arranger who had written for Gold-kette and Whiteman, was showcasing a radio ensemble; in February and March he recorded a couple-of-dozen numbers for broadcast syndication. "We went up sometimes after midnight, and did a date for about three, four hours," Challis told Chip Deffaa. "Jesus, I had the best people in the whole business. I had Charlie Margulis, Manny Klein, Wilber Schwick-tenberg [Will Bradley], Jack Jenney . . . Artie Shaw. And I had all those fiddle players, you know," among them Harry Bluestone. "I remember one time, the guys gave me a hard time about something. And Artie comes up; he goes over in front of the cello and he bangs for the tempo! . . . I should have done something like that, but I wasn't that type of guy."

Whether or not he wanted a band of his own, Shaw was already acting as if he had one.

"Just for some relaxation on the side," Art would say, he started holding weekly rehearsals with some of the best string players in New York. "Every Thursday evening at the apartment of a friend of mine," he'd write, "I would take part in a sort of string jam session—only we played chiefly Brahms and Mozart quintets. In addition to this I had occasionally sat in with [black violinist] Stuff Smith at the Onyx Club. So the idea of playing with strings was by this time quite familiar to me." And he'd been listening to and loving strings-laden classical and Paul White-man records for a decade. Debussy and boogie-woogie pianist Pinetop Smith were other composers tackled by Shaw and his pals. Art also wrote pieces of his own: "I wrote a jazz quintet in movements, which bore such names as 'Blues,' 'Stomp,' and so on, instead of the more customary 'Allegro,' 'Andante,' etc." Shaw was onto something fresh with this combination of reed and strings. Like Challis, he was creating a showcase with which to present himself should a proper occasion arise.

IT WAS BILLED as "New York's First Swing Music Concert": a needy-musicians benefit arranged by the Onyx Club's Joe Helbock, to be held

at the Imperial Theatre on Sunday evening, May 24, 1936. The roster would include the cream of the crop from Fifty-second Street and
beyond: Tommy Dorsey and his Clambake Seven (including Bud Freeman, Max Kaminsky, and drummer Dave Tough); Red Norvo's Swing-
tette, with his singer-wife Mildred Bailey and pianist Teddy Wilson;
Stuff Smith and the Onyx Club Band; Bunny Berigan and his swing
band (with Condon and Bushkin); the Casa Loma Orchestra; the new
Bob Crosby band; Chicago pianist Meade Lux Lewis; Wingy Manone;
Willie the Lion Smith; Joe Venuti (with Jerry Colonna); a combo from
the Whiteman orchestra that included Frank Trumbauer and the Teagarden brothers; the guitar duo of Carl Kress and Dick McDonough—
and even Louis Armstrong. "A stillion bucks worth of talent, Jack," as
Wingy Manone put it.

And Helbock invited Art Shaw to join this fabulous roster and play
whatever he chose. Here was a golden opportunity for Art to show what
he could do in front of everyone who mattered in the New York swing
world. He had damned well better play something worth hearing.

The sold-out concert took place the night after Shaw's twenty-sixth
birthday. Art almost got bumped from the bill at the last minute, but
then was told he could go on as scheduled.

Glen Gray's Casa Loma Orchestra started the show. Next came a
swing harmonica octet. Then Wingy Manone's combo, then Stuff Smith's
ensemble—then Art Shaw's string ensemble.

Eight men strode onstage: Art, a rhythm section, and four string
players from his Thursday-night rehearsal group. With the audience still
abuzz over Stuff Smith, Shaw and company launched into Art's original
piece, "Interlude in B-flat." "I was terrified," he would tell jazz historian
Richard Sudhalter, "but when we went into the 'jazz' section, I realized
that people were actually starting to applaud!"

Sudhalter described the "Interlude" as "an essay in contrasts," finding
its opening string passage "strongly reminiscent of Ravel's 1905 'Introduction and Allegro.'" Others heard the same fragment as a paraphrase
of Tommy Dorsey's theme song, "I'm Gettin' Sentimental Over You."
"Shaw enters with a brief, and highly romantic, cadenza," Sudhalter

wrote, "then launches into a technically intricate theme based on the chord structure of the old standard 'Shine.' The introduction turns out to have been a phrase fragment belonging to an expansive middle section, now played with considerable tenderness by clarinet and strings. A return to the 'Shine' section sees things home."

Down Beat's man-on-the-scene captured in telegraphic fashion the moment's excitement: "Artie Shaw and his string swing ensemble . . . stole the show for novelty. . . . He has what is probably the only new creation in modern music within the past five years. . . . Arrangements were by Shaw, I believe, and were distinctly outstanding. . . . Intro on first selection, which was probably original, had four bar string (no rhythm) playing sustained harmonics a la Debussy and Ravel . . . then with a fanfare of rhythm, Shaw came in for some dynamic clarinet work that will probably keep Goodman awake for several nights to come . . . absolutely masterful on technique and tone. . . . Rates with Goodman any day . . . after each chorus strings would pick up modulations in subdued style and then rhythm would whip back into high style swingin' with Shaw playing variations on the theme. . . . Applause tore down house and necessitated many a bow . . . Four Star stuff."

The next day, Shaw's telephone began to ring.

CHAPTER TEN

No Regrets

T HE MOST PERSISTENT caller was Tommy Rockwell, of the Rockwell-O'Keefe agency, who wanted Shaw to expand his Imperial Theatre group into a big band to play hotel engagements and "one-nighters" around the country.

Shaw told Rockwell he wasn't sure he wanted to do that. What the agent described would take Art away from his life's goals—though he couldn't quite say what those were, exactly, beyond more reading and study. Rockwell asked, How much money would Shaw need to pursue those goals? Twenty-five thousand dollars was the colossal figure Art gave, at a time when a good teacher made thirteen hundred a year. Well, Rockwell said, why not lead a band a while? If it took off, Art was sure to make enough to leave music for whatever else he wanted to do. That made sense. Shaw could always quit.

Rockwell had his own agenda: his agency wanted a bandleader to compete with the Music Corporation of America's headliner Benny Goodman, "the king of swing." Artie Shaw as a rival for Benny Goodman was Rockwell's big idea from the start.

EVEN BEFORE the agent got to him, Art had made a deal with the Brunswick label. Eighteen days after the Imperial concert, Shaw was in Brunswick's studio with a pick-up group recording four tunes, one of them "Japanese Sandman"—the 1920 song that had also been Paul Whiteman's first recorded number.

That done, Shaw began finding and hiring musicians for a working orchestra with a lineup of two violins, a viola, a cello, two trumpets, a trombone, a tenor sax, Shaw, and four rhythm: a band flexible enough for ballrooms, theater stages, and hotel cafés. The leader needed help with arrangements; there was no way he could write them all himself. Shaw hired Joe Lippman, a pianist-arranger who had worked with Berigan. Lippman recommended a twenty-year-old "hot fiddle" from Boston, Generoso Graziano, whom Shaw could coach to do orchestrations. Art told him to change his name. "Jerry Gray" would be a crucial part of Shaw's endeavors.

Another key man came when Shaw ran into Tony Pestritto—now "Tony Pastor"—in the lobby of the New Yorker Hotel. Pastor had been on the road with Vincent Lopez; but now, with his wife pregnant, he was scuffling for a gig. Shaw hired his twenty-nine-year-old pal on the spot.

As trumpet soloist, he got Lee Castaldo, a handsome twenty-one-year-old kid from New York. As his necessary girl singer—hotels and ballrooms demanded one—he chose singer-actress Peg La Centra, whom he had worked with in radio.

Rockwell-O'Keefe advanced him seed money. Artie was also still doing radio and record dates to pick up cash, and sitting in at joints around town. He went to the Famous Door to play with Berigan's outfit that included Bushkin, Condon, Bud Freeman and Dave Tough. Back in February, Art and this Famous Door bunch had backed the great blues singer Bessie Smith for her first and last Fifty-second Street appearance: "She had a voice like a trumpet," Art marveled. "No mikes." Now, this summer, some of these same cronies—Berigan, Shaw, Bushkin, Dick McDonough, and bassist Pete Peterson—got called for a record session with the twenty-one-year-old Billie Holiday at the Brunswick studio on Friday, July 10.

Billie had been singing on Teddy Wilson platters with pick-up groups for a year. Now Brunswick wanted her to do discs under her own name for their budget Vocalion label. This Friday session would yield the first-ever sides by "Billie Holiday and her Orchestra." Bernie Hanighen, a Harvard-educated sometime-songwriter (and Billie's current boyfriend), produced the session, though John Hammond was also in attendance. English jazz journalist Leonard Feather also fell by. It was sweltering in the studio. Drummer Cozy Cole sat behind his kit in his undershirt, his skin glistening with sweat. The scent of marijuana was in the air; Billie indulged, as did Hanighen.

"Did I Remember?" from a Jean Harlow picture was the first tune. The two horns played obbligato behind the singer's lead. Artie took a nice middle-register half-chorus, followed by sixteen bars of Berigan.

Dick McDonough's eight-bar introduction set up Billie's saucy reading of "No Regrets," a lover's-parting shot that (thanks to the song pluggers who got paid to make things happen) was recorded by several folks this season, among them Shaw on his own first Brunswick session. "Most people would sing, 'No re-*grets*,'" said Shaw, going upward with the note as written. "She went: 'No! Re! Grets!' *Pow, pow, pow*—right on the beat!" He laughed, excited sixty-five years later by the memory of Holiday's art. "*My! Time!* You know? She had a way of making a song *hers*. She'd *inhabit* the song. She would take it *over*—and re-*do* it. That's a *quality*. I don't think you *learn* that. You *polish* it. But she *had* that."

"Summertime" was third, a song fresh from George Gershwin's short-running Broadway opera *Porgy and Bess*. In the future, most singers would do "Summertime" as a semi-aria; in the summer of 1936, Holiday and company made it a swinging blues. Berigan began with a growling lower-register intro, so down and dirty he sounded like a trombone; Shaw's clarinet wailed in sympathetic counterpoint. Billie worked her sorcery. Art's sixteen-bar solo, with Bunny's commentary, was graceful and emotional.

The fourth song didn't go well; Hanighen threw it out. Why not do a blues? Hammond suggested. Billie made up lyrics on the spot; Shaw and Berigan filled the spaces between her words. The whole thing clocked in at just two and a half minutes. It was Holiday's first songwriting credit, "Billie's Blues"—a number she would do the rest of her life.

IN THE AUTUMN of 1936, Art Shaw's major energies were focused on his orchestra, scheduled to open in the Silver Grill of the Hotel Lexington on Forty-eighth Street on the twenty-first of August, with a remote wire hooked to the CBS radio network. The day before, Shaw said he was told he'd need a theme to play at the start and stop of the broadcasts. Most orchestras used a Tin Pan Alley number. Benny Goodman's was "Let's Dance."

With no time to find a proper tune, Art composed his own. "I just wrote the notes and quickly orchestrated it for the band," he told *Jazz Journal International* in 1987. Shaw's dark and bluesy theme was simple but striking—unsettling, even. Song sleuths would claim to trace its main device to a variety of sources, from King Oliver's "Call of the Freaks" to Igor Stravinsky's *Firebird*. Tony Pastor took credit for naming the piece: when he first heard Art play it at four o'clock one morning, he said he thought he was having a nightmare.

"It sounded kind of nightmarish," Artie later allowed, with Shaw's clarinet swooping like a bird of prey while the band moaned and swayed like zombies. "Nightmare" was a wail from the lower depths of Dostoevsky, or the pulp-*noir* hangover-square of Cornell Woolrich. With its twisting gyre of doom and angst, "Nightmare" was a surrealistic blues: an up-to-the-minute item that stirred ethnic memory.

When eleven-year-old future jazz journalist Nat Hentoff heard this piece coming from a record-store speaker on Boston's main street, he yelled out loud with pleasure. "It *reached* me, *viscerally*, the way no other music had until then except for cantorial music: the improvising *hazan* in the synagogue." (Hentoff wrote, "The *hazan* sounded at times as if he was arguing with God, and the depth of his witnessing to the human condition later connected me with black blues.") "I rushed into the record store: 'What's *that*?' It was Artie Shaw's 'Nightmare.' And that started me in jazz. I found out years later, 'Nightmare' was based on a *nigun*: a melody that these cantors sang."

Then there was the classical violinist who had his musical horizon expanded when he was booked on the same radio program as Shaw and happened to hear the clarinetist's mesmeric intro. "Artie and his boys began playing their theme song, 'Nightmare,'" journalist Mel Adams wrote at the time. "Another artist appearing on the program walked to the wings and confessed to a bystander: 'I've always hated swing, but now I find it has definition and clarity.' And he picked up his violin and, unannounced, accompanied the swing band in its strange tempo. The unheralded accompanist was Efram Zimbalist!"

Efram Zimbalist Senior: one of the greatest fiddle players in the world, born of Jewish parentage in 1890 in the Russian city of Rostov on Don—about four hundred miles from Odessa, birthplace of the father of Arthur Arshawsky.

CHAPTER ELEVEN

It Ain't Right

T HE BAND LOOKED sharp on opening night, in dark double-breasted suits with white pocket-handkerchiefs. Peg La Centra wore a high-necked, long-sleeved dress. Musicians and other colleagues—singer-songwriter Johnny Mercer, guitarists Carl Kress and Dick McDonough—jammed into the Silver Grill for the public debut of Art Shaw's "sweet swing" orchestra. But after opening night, despite its weekend broadcasts, newcomer Shaw's band couldn't fill the room. One of the Silver Grill's few enthusiastic patrons was a sweet-faced fourteen-year-old girl visiting from Los Angeles, who came up to Art and introduced herself as Judy Garland: "I'm a singer with Metro [Goldwyn Mayer]," she said. "I just had to tell you how great your music is."

The "sweet swing" outfit's next commitment was six weeks at the French Casino, a theater-restaurant at Seventh and Fiftieth, where the orchestra played between performances of an imported floorshow. "When we went through the stage entrance to do our playing," trumpeter Zeke Zarchy said, "we had to go through the girls' dressing room. All the girls were from England, and none of them would cover their boobs; they were, like, oblivious of us. So we had that special treat!"

Artie had hired the twenty-one-year-old Zarchy right out of Benny Goodman's orchestra. "After a few months with Benny Goodman's band," Zarchy said, "I got tired of *listening* to Benny; it was kind of—dull, you know? Artie offered me a raise in salary. And I liked the *band*, I liked that *style*; I really enjoyed playing with it."

Zeke was with Art on October 30 when Shaw's orchestra made four new Brunswick sides: an instrumental of "Skeleton in the Closet," from a soon-to-be-released Bing Crosby picture; two numbers with Peg La Centra ("There's Something in the Air," "There's Frost on the Moon"); and "Take Another Guess," with a Tony Pastor vocal.

"Artie was very *loyal* to Tony," Zarchy said. "That was quite noticeable. Made him our *vocalist, and* our soloist with the tenor saxophone. He was a stylist, in a way, and did a good job." Artie himself was a pleasure to hear, Zeke said. "I had tremendous respect for his talent; I think I preferred listening to him a lot more than Benny. He was more of a musical player; Benny just showed off a lot of technique most of the time. And Artie didn't rely much on his technique, which was also of a very high degree; but he had a nicer *sound*, a more musical sound. And made more music when he played."

When Shaw had to replace his trombone player, he got seventeen-year-old Moe Zudecoff to leave Eddy Duchin's society band. "I gave up a great job for him," the trombonist said. "I was making $187.50 a week—to go with Artie for $70 a week. But that's because I was grateful to him."

Shaw was responsible for Zudecoff, a New Haven native, coming to Manhattan in the first place. On the recommendation of Dave Hudkins (Yudkin), Art brought Moe to audition for Tommy Dorsey as part of a player swap that fell through. "He loaned me money to stay in New York," Moe said. "Which he promptly accepted when I had it to give back to him." Shaw made calls to Fifty-second Street figures, recommending the new man for allowable one-night gigs while he waited out his union card. "He established a situation where I *could* be a New York musician; I was tutored in the beginning by Artie Shaw, how to fit into the music scene." And when Shaw needed the trombonist, in November of 1936, Zudecoff was happy to serve. Artie had another piece of practical advice: change your name. Moe Zudecoff became Buddy Morrow.

Art had filled this first band not with veteran players (whom he couldn't afford) but with men eager to play and learn, Morrow said: "Guys who wanted to be under his tutelage." And Shaw was a great teacher: "Artie would take an ordinary sax section, and by the time he was through with them, they were in the top echelon." The leader had just as firm a hand with arrangers. Buddy said, "Artie had impeccable taste. He knew how to separate the wheat from the chaff, you know? He knew how to eliminate the superfluous—to just look at an arrangement and take it apart, and see whether it was suited for him or not."

Morrow's first record date with Shaw was November 30, when the orchestra cut four more numbers at Brunswick. Each member was paid a flat twenty dollars for three hours' work. Given the way sides were done straight to wax, the pressure was always on to make a perfect take: "The only editing was, 'This cut was better than the other cut.'" One way or another, though, Buddy said, "Artie always came out with great product. Always."

AFTER THE FRENCH Casino gig, which also failed to draw many customers, the Shaw band did a brief tour of nearby colleges before opening in December for nine days at New York's Paramount Theatre, the premier Manhattan venue for popular-music orchestras, where the band rose up to audience view on a giant stage-elevator.

"I remember standing on the stage of the Paramount elevator, when we were gonna come up" the first time, Shaw said many years later, "and I heard the first quivering of it, and I thought: 'Oh my God—lemme outa here.' I'd have given anything, to get the hell *away* from there. And I hadda get up there and—say what I hadda say. Scary. You're not *trained* for that. Nothing in life *prepares* you for that kind of thing."

"I was never so nervous in my life as on the first performance," Art wrote in a music paper a month after the fact, "but in a few days I had all the confidence I needed."

Shaw had hired Chicago drummer George Wettling during the French Casino engagement. For the Paramount, he needed a substitute guitarist and turned to Eddie Condon, who hustled to keep the breakneck tempo of "Streamline," a Shaw original written to show off his own technique. "I wanted to play a showpiece with that group," Art told Richard Sudhalter, ". . . Just me, the strings and the rhythm. I wanted to show people that I could play the clarinet; and I'll tell you . . . it worked, worked like crazy." On "Streamline," Art played almost faster than the ear could hear or the brain comprehend. The idea was to demonstrate that Shaw could execute as well as Goodman, but in his own style. "Goodman came along, and he invented the instrument," Shaw said. "It was very hard, to go around him. You had to go *through* him. I had to do a lotta work, to get to be my own man, in *playing*."

Shaw failed to fill the Paramount too. Playing that big a venue early in the band's career was a mistake, he saw. One person who did buy a ticket to see Shaw was a jazz-happy teenager named George Avakian, a student at the Horace Mann School for Boys; in a few years, Avakian would be a pioneer in the jazz-reissue movement and then a significant record producer in his own right. Shaw's outfit was good, Avakian said: "That was a wonderful band, because it had such a variety of sound. And the Dixieland instrumentation of trumpet, trombone, clarinet was very effective. And for ballads and so forth, the strings put a good floor on it; so you didn't miss, say, a sax section, or anything like that."

But Shaw needed a decent booking in a venue where he and his band could shine. The Adolphus hotel in Dallas, Texas, sounded ideal; but in person, in January, it was a catastrophe.

"We played a noon session, and an evening session," Zeke Zarchy said. "It was not a large room, and they were on our ass *all* the time, because the room was full of mirrors; can you imagine that, putting an orchestra in there? We never really were able to play naturally; we were always holding it down, you know—so people could either talk, or *eat*. The luncheon session, of course we had to play everything way down in the volume. And—I don't think we were well known enough to draw large crowds for the evening, which was probably the reason we were only there for four weeks."

To make matters more humiliating, across the street from the Adolphus was the Baker Hotel, where Tommy Dorsey was riding high. With Bunny Berigan on trumpet and a couple of hit records ("Marie," "Song of India") breaking wide open, Dorsey was on the brink of a fantastic year.

Artie took what solace he could from the local beauties. "He was always on the loose," Zarchy said, "looking for a pretty, well-made ankle; and made several attempts at a few nice-looking girls in Dallas. I don't know how well he *scored*, but I know that one in particular—Constance Moore [later a movie actress, but at the time a band vocalist]—preferred Lee Castaldo over Artie."

More important things were going awry.

Back when he had hired Zeke, Art told the trumpeter the band was all but signed to perform with Bing Crosby on NBC's weekly *Kraft Music Hall*. But when the show went on the air, the band with Bing was Jimmy Dorsey's. (Shaw would later blame Crosby's mixed signals on an unwillingness to say no, a wish to get along: "To be a *good guy*: hail-fellow well-met. . . . Bing needed to be *liked* by people. . . . 'Swhy he died on a golf course.")

Zeke had no beef with Art. But when Crosby didn't come through, and other hotels canceled bookings in the wake of the Adolphus flop, Shaw's trumpeter gave notice: "I told Artie, 'Like the guy said to the horse when the horse farted, I can't live on promises.'"

Meanwhile, Benny Goodman went from triumph to triumph. "Artie talked a lot about Benny!" Zarchy said. "They had a kind of a rivalry, because they were both the top freelance clarinet soloists or alto players, you know, in the days of radio, before they got their bands. I knew all about both of them; we all did." It was a "friendly" rivalry Shaw often stoked, despite later protestations to the contrary. "Benny had made a *mistake* on one radio show—missed a note or somethin'," Zarchy said, "and Artie asked me to *remind* Benny of it. Which I did *not*."

THE PARAMOUNT THEATRE in New York's Times Square, site of Shaw's nerve-wracking stage debut, had been booking big bands as an added attraction to the week's feature film for a year. Benny Goodman's Paramount debut occurred the first week of March in 1937. At six in the morning on Goodman's opening day, there were already three thousand people—mostly high school kids—waiting in line outside. An astounding twenty-one thousand teens bought tickets this day. When the stage platform rose on its elevator lift and brought Goodman's band into view playing "Let's Dance," the kids' roar was enormous.

A few youngsters were given money (some said by the Paramount's publicist; others, by Goodman's PR men) to dance in the aisles. Once these ringers were out of their seats and doing the Lindy Hop, the Suzie-Q, and the shag, others joined in. ("Monkey see, monkey do," a sardonic Shaw said.) The stunt made a splash in the papers, further proof of the unprecedented popularity of big-band jazz. Swing was king—and Benny Goodman was the king of swing.

The lesson wasn't lost on Shaw, laboring with his band through a mediocre engagement at Frank Dailey's Meadowbrook Ballroom in New Jersey. To succeed, Shaw needed the public clamoring for *his* music; but what the public wanted was Goodman's brash ensemble, not Artie's subtle sounds. The public wanted *loud*.

Art decided to give it to them. After nearly a year's struggle and expense to build up this "swing-strings" band, he announced he would fold the ensemble—and start fresh, with a louder, Goodman-style orchestra.

To his advisers, it seemed a crazy idea, an almost criminal move. But Art could see that his great little band was going nowhere; people just didn't want to hear it. Better to join the parade than march down some side street all on your own. If you're at least in the mainstream, then you have a chance to work your way to the front.

Shaw told Buddy Morrow, "I'm gonna get the loudest God-damn swing band you ever heard—and *then* we'll see."

Morrow had lunch with Shaw in New York, where he had already rejoined Eddie Duchin; he was available if needed, he told Shaw. "We talked about it, and he said, 'I can't afford you,' which was true; I had to make money, in the height of the Depression." Shaw advised Morrow to stay with a hot-music band like Goodman's or Dorsey's rather than go with Whiteman or a radio band; Morrow needed to keep growing as a jazz player. "Always good advice, always sincere," Buddy said of Art's counsel. "Never for a price. Except he's a tough guy with a buck."

As for Shaw, he would make do with the best men he could get for seventy dollars a week. And Art had developed some new rules on how to handle them.

"One of his mottoes," Buddy said, "was: 'Never write anything they can't play drunk.'"

CHAPTER TWELVE

I Got Rhythm

SHAW HAD TO arrange financial backing, sort things out with Brunswick, hire new men (keeping Tony Pastor and Jerry Gray), get arrangements, rehearse—same as before, but with double urgency. "I was a wild man, a crazy man," he wrote. "I cajoled when I couldn't browbeat. I browbeat when I couldn't cajole. All I knew was that I had started something and I wasn't going to quit it until I'd either licked it or it had licked me."

The woman Shaw was still married to no longer saw a place for herself in his life. Marge encouraged Art to pursue his dream; she didn't think he would be happy until he achieved success. But it was nothing she wanted any part of. The fellow she married had been an earnest, private guy, living out in the country and trying to write a novel. In the past couple of years, Art Shaw had become another person: a Fifty-second Street figure, a young man on the rise. This wasn't what she had bargained for. Marge didn't want to be married to someone famous; she wanted just plain Art. She stayed away from his gigs and didn't tell anyone she was the wife of that new bandleader. But for Art, there was no turning back; nor should there be, Marge thought. They agreed to divorce, on the grounds of adultery: in New York at that time, it was the only way. Marge kept the farm.

· · ·

IN THE WEEKS before his new band's debut, Shaw maintained a public profile doing radio guest spots and sitting in at clubs (including Clark Monroe's Uptown House, where one night he backed Billie Holiday). In mid-March, he took part in another well-publicized event that would become legendary in the annals of Manhattan swing.

It was a jam session, but different from the sort at the Onyx or Uptown. This one, at the Brunswick building on Sunday, March 14, was almost a concert. It was also a photo session for *Life* magazine, a publicity event for two new record labels, a gala gathering of the United Hot Clubs of America, and a showcase for the new-to-New-York Count Basie band brought to the Big Apple from Kansas City by the smart and tireless John Hammond.

At three in the afternoon, Brunswick's biggest room was filled with five hundred sharply dressed New Yorkers, both black and white. A seven-man unit from the Basie band began playing in the Kansas City manner, its soloists including Lester Young, a Trumbauer-influenced tenor saxophonist whose elliptical style was a league apart from the blustery Coleman Hawkins's ("He could *allude* to notes you never heard," Shaw said of Young). Benny Goodman, rushing over between performances at the Paramount, followed Basie's bunch in a trio with Joey Bushkin and drummer-bandleader Chick Webb.

The black, hunchbacked Webb, a powerhouse percussion man, later backed up his band's eighteen-year-old singer Ella Fitzgerald, who did three songs along with trumpeter Rex Stewart, and Duke Ellington on piano. Next Webb and Ellington formed a trio with a slick-looking Art Shaw, dapper in a dark-blue double-breasted pinstripe suit.

For more than ten minutes, they played theme and variations on that jam-session Gershwin staple, "I Got Rhythm." Starting off subdued, the trio built in intensity, with Ellington comping chords and cocking his head to hear the men behind him. Webb, beating time with wire brushes on a snare drum, stared at Shaw as the clarinetist unfurled chorus after rhythmic, inventive chorus. Shaw was grinning around his clarinet's mouthpiece as he brought the number to an emphatic close. The producer of CBS radio's *Saturday Night Swing Club* hurried across in hopes of getting the three men to agree to re-create their performance on his network program. This jam-session "I Got Rhythm" became an instant jazz legend, thanks to journalists present who wrote of it in American and European publications. It would be included in a WPA account of the New York music scene; thirty years later, Duke Ellington's son Mercer would recount it with wonder in his memoirs.

A photo was taken in the set's after-flush of a gleeful Webb, a happy Duke, a beaming Shaw—and a chortling Benny Goodman. Yes, Benny was smiling, but Artie's grin seemed about three times as wide.

FATE SMILED in a different way on Claude Thornhill, now writing radio-orchestra arrangements at CBS. A female "colored" singer from Philadelphia named Marietta Williams entered his life, introduced by pianist Gladys Mosier. Claude renamed her "Maxine Sullivan," got her a record date, and wrote the session's arrangements in a "chamber jazz" manner perfect for this singer's gentle swing. *The New Yorker* ran a piece on Sullivan, and patrons flocked to the Onyx Club to hear her. Maxine and Claude made more records, including Thornhill's swing version of the Scottish folk tune "Loch Lomond," which became one of the biggest hit records of the year. Benny Goodman covered it with Martha Tilton, and he had a hit with it too.

SHAW NEEDED a hit of his own.

"Art Shaw and His New Music" was the tag for his revamped outfit, whose first record session took place in the Brunswick studio on May 13. This rethought ensemble was built around Art's clarinet, and the leader rose to the concept with playing even more precise and accomplished.

Also emphasized were the vocals of Tony Pastor, whose singing style, thanks to Shaw's prodding, was more spontaneous now, more like Louis Armstrong's. "Artie would wear two hats," Tony Pastor Jr. said. "He was your best friend in the world, but when it came to the musicianship—if he *knew* you could do better, he would absolutely cut you off at the knees, you know, and say, 'Come on, do it *right*.' I think that in a lotta ways, Artie helped my dad to become a very very excellent lyric reader."

Other men in the new band included drummer Cliff Leeman, saxophonist Les Robinson, and a trumpet player from North Carolina named John Best, who was reluctant to join at first because he was in the midst of his six-month waiting period for his union card; but Art assured him he would square things with the New York local's president so Best wouldn't lose the waiting time he had already put in.

Key to the new band's identity, Art figured, would be its use of the best songs by the best songwriters. Composers such as Jerome Kern, George Gershwin, Irving Berlin, Cole Porter, and Richard Rodgers had by now written dozens of popular songs that might be termed "standards"—tunes that had risen above the run-of-the-mill to become secular American classics. The trick was to arrange and perform such material in the best and most appealing way. Quality and beauty would be Art Shaw's "gimmicks."

But at Shaw's second new Brunswick session on August 4, a more basic Americana was featured.

RCA Victor this spring had cut an all-star record with Bunny Berigan, Tommy Dorsey, the black pianist Fats Waller, and Dick McDonough: a series of loose-limbed improvisations titled "The Blues." Shaw and his men did their own easy-jointed "Blues," to be spread over two sides of a Brunswick 78. Cliff Leeman lay down its shag beat. The first solo, two forceful choruses, was by trumpeter Best. Tony Pastor's tenor played the next pair of stanzas; then brass riffed with rhythm until Shaw showed up. Pianist Les Burness ended "part A" with a wistful twelve bars. "Part B" began with two choruses of George Arus trombone. Then Shaw took leader's prerogative of three choruses and earned it, with a solo both simple and intricate, earthy yet elegant. The whole six minutes was (in the parlance of the day) "in the pocket," "in the crease," "in the groove."

Another side, "The Chant," was a take-off on Benny Goodman's nine-minute killer-diller "Sing Sing Sing." Shaw's three-minute "Chant" was nearly identical in feel to Goodman's flag waver, with Leeman doing a creditable imitation of Gene Krupa's tom-toms; Shaw's solo was briefer than Goodman's but more soulful, showing Art could take on Benny and maybe best him in yet another regard.

"THE CHANT" turned one of the band's early one-nighters on the road into an unforgettable occasion. The gig was in Carbondale, Pennsylvania, John Best told Sheila Tracy: "[T]he people that hired the band had heard [Art's] strings and that was the band they thought they were getting. The hall wasn't too big, and we came on with this loud band—we played just about top volume all the time—and [the ballroom manager] complained, and he made Artie mad. Artie said to pull out some stock arrangements, Guy Lombardo's 'Boo-Hoo' and so on; but that didn't help." The ballroom manager continued to bug and heckle Shaw all through the dance. "[A]nd now Artie was really mad," Best went on, "so then he said, 'What's the loudest thing we have in the book?'" It was "The Chant." "We got that out, and then this guy got mad and started screaming while Artie was playing it." The stage was only about three feet off the floor where the irate manager stood. Shaw leaned down, aimed his clarinet in the man's ear—and played his most piercing note. "[T]he guy got furious," Best said, "and he jumped up on the stand and started swinging; and we went out of there with a police escort!"

CHAPTER THIRTEEN

If It's the Last Thing I Do

ART HAD LIED to John Best: his New York union card had been pulled as soon as he had gone on the road with Shaw. When Best learned of this in August, he got mad and quit. Shaw had to find a new lead trumpet almost overnight. Living across from Art on West Forty-ninth was Max Kaminsky, fresh from Tommy Dorsey's trumpet section. Maxie was at liberty, though it looked as if Benny Goodman, with whom he had been subbing at the Pennsylvania, was getting ready to offer him third-trumpet chair.

Not if Art got to him first.

Shaw sent his band manager over to Maxie's on a Sunday afternoon, his day off from Goodman's band, to roust him out of bed. Could Max help Art by playing a gig that night in Bridgeport, Connecticut? A bushed Kaminsky said no; but half an hour later, Shaw's man came back—then back again. Max gave in, went downstairs, and got on the band bus.

Afterward, Art drove Max back to New York in the old Rolls-Royce he'd acquired. "He talked and I listened," Kaminsky wrote, "while Artie turned on the old charm, with his marvelous laugh and his wonderful way of making you feel he was a real friend. . . . [B]efore I knew it I was in Artie's band."

Best had been getting seventy-five dollars a week from Shaw, but Art told Max all his men were getting forty-five. He offered Kaminsky sixty-five. Max took it.

Art had another record date coming up, and again there was a last-minute panic. But he was able to call for a favor on one of his ex-dates: Bea Wain, whom he had gone out with a few times a year ago ("Wasn't a big romance or anything," she said), until she found out he was married. Wain still considered Art a good friend.

"I was singing on the [CBS radio show *Your*] *Hit Parade*," she said, "and he came backstage to the rehearsal and said he had a problem: he was recording the next day, and his girl singer was sick; could I help? I had a reputation for being a good singer, and dependable. This was a fast step-in, and I had to hurry up and learn this song. He gave me the tune, 'If It's the Last Thing I Do'—a pretty ballad—and I worked on it at home, and I came to the studio, and I did the take."

Then Wain stayed to hear Shaw do a number with a very different singer.

Vocalists were a trial for Art. "I didn't like singers in the records," he said, "because—one little singer on the mike, and you got eighteen men back there blowing their hearts out: where are they? It's easy for a singer to reach an audience, 'cause he's singing a buncha sentimental *sop*. . . . So lyrics were a thing that the *audience* liked. And the band didn't play a lyric." Yet Shaw had to have a vocalist. "It was an absolute necessity," he said. "The contract would read: 'Thirteen, or fourteen, men—*and* a singer.' So I would hire a singer—and hopefully, one that was not too bad."

Peg La Centra, after a stint with Benny Goodman, came on Shaw's new band and cut four sides in July and August—then was gone by September. Dolores O'Neill traveled with Shaw a couple of months and made one platter ("A Strange Loneliness") before she too departed. By the winter of 1937, Art's singer was Cliff Leeman's wife, Nita Bradley, who recorded with him "One Song," "Goodnight Angel," and "There's a New Moon over the Old Mill."

All these women's sides earned praise ("goose-pimply" was a favored adjective of swing journalists to describe the frisson induced by such "thrushes"), and some of their numbers became "jukebox hits." But none of them was what Shaw wanted, and none gave the band the big push it needed.

So Art pursued more unorthodox effects.

Leo Watson—small, strong, dark-skinned—was a Fifty-second Street fixture, singing in a mostly wordless scat that crooned and burbled, stuttered and caressed. With or without words, Leo sounded like a horn player—one with a full heart, a fevered brain, and a sense of humor as quick as mercury.

This was Art Shaw's surprise guest vocalist on September 18.

The first of the three sides Watson cut was a brand-new Cole Porter song, "I've a Strange New Rhythm in My Heart." "What he did to it was just terrific," Bea Wain said. "It was—unusual. It was not a *pretty* vocal; it was a scat-sing, with syllables."

A strange new rhythm, indeed. Shaw's solo had a gritty edge. Watson burst into the ear again, full of vim. Shaw returned, sounding like a kid on a Sunday afternoon rolling a hoop down an empty Fifty-second Street.

The second number was "Shoot the Likker to Me, John Boy," in tribute to a Harlem bartender. Leo scatted a wordless ululation emulating whiskey rolling around the mouth and down the throat; Art's solo extended the trope with a flurry of notes like the blossoming rush of liquor hitting the brain.

Watson's third side, the up-tempo "Freewheeling," had Shaw sounding as smooth and rhythmic as a stone skipping on water. Art was as good as the people he played with. Watson brought out dazzling facets in his work. There was no substitute for the creative jolt Art got from a true original.

BUT IT WAS Benny Goodman still in the forefront of swing consciousness in early 1938. Newspapers, magazines, and radio air-waves buzzed with his latest triumph: Benny and his orchestra played Carnegie Hall!

The king of swing had captured the high-culture castle. It was a press agent's dream; in fact, a press agent dreamed it up.

Art Shaw, meanwhile, struggled to make his payroll. Sometimes he couldn't, and the men took half-salaries, with Art's promise that they would get the rest later. Road life was hard. The constant pressure was getting to Art. He had migraine headaches, which he fought off with aspirin, then with Emperin-codeine. Music papers liked the band, but it wasn't catching on. Shaw quit one booking agency for another, then switched back; he stayed awake nights trying to figure out how to make things work. He needed help.

His lawyer Andrew Weinberger put him in touch with Si Shribman, a Boston-based operator who, with his brother Charlie, owned a string of ballrooms all over New England. "When he hit Boston," Si's nephew Joe Shribman told Max Jones, "Shaw wasn't doing anything. He'd spent all his dough and was rooming with trumpeter Max Kaminsky. Si booked him for the State."

Boston's Roseland State Ballroom was the Shribmans' main base; Si agreed to feature the Shaw band there two nights a week and keep it busy in other venues from Maine to New Jersey. In addition, Shaw said, "He gave us one thousand dollars a week and was supposed to make up any shortfalls if expenses went over, in exchange for ten per cent of the gross."

Shribman had another idea: to put a network-radio wire into the Boston ballroom. It took some doing, since New York had most of the airtime locked up; but Shribman persisted, and the result was a coast-to-coast CBS hookup. "It meant two broadcasts a week," Joe Shribman said, "and though the band was playing at first to a half-empty hall, it was being heard by millions of people."

The Roseland State was around the corner from Levaggi's Restaurant, where Chick Webb's band was in residence. Webb sometimes sat in with the Shaw orchestra. His beat and the precision with which he played were incredible. Shaw held close the memory of something Chick Webb told him this spring: "He listened to a rehearsal of my band one day; he said: 'Some day I'm gonna be walkin' down the street one way, you gonna be comin' down the street the other way—and you're gonna say, 'Hello, best colored band in the world,' and I'm gonna say, 'Hello, best white band in the world.' That was Chick's—compliment to me."

Shaw wanted his band to pulse with the same energy as Webb's.

Back in 1937, Art frequented a Harlem club where clarinetist Mezz Mezzrow led an integrated combo that included Max Kaminsky and the veteran black drummer Zutty Singleton, who had worked with Louis Armstrong in Chicago. Now, in Boston in 1938, he put Singleton on the band's payroll—not to be a regular band member, but to sit in at times and coach the band: to instill the jazz spirit in some of the younger men.

Shaw wasn't the only white jazzman chasing the spirit with the help of black musicians. Benny Goodman never swung harder nor played prettier than when he had pianist Teddy Wilson and vibraphonist Lionel Hampton in concert with him. Goodman's trio (with Wilson) and quartet (with Hamp) were specialty units, traveling with but playing separately from his orchestra; no black musician was a member of a white big band. But Goodman's integrated combos opened the door.

There was a budding demand from critics and fans for black female singers to be featured with white bands. Claude Thornhill's records with Maxine Sullivan were a catalyst. June Richmond cut a few sides with Jimmy Dorsey. Now swing-world insiders learned that the best "sepia thrush" of all, Billie Holiday, was about to quit her gig with Count Basie's orchestra. Art's friend John Hammond knew of Billie's decision; so did Si Shribman, who had booked Basie in New England.

Whoever had the idea first, Art Shaw grabbed it: "I got in the car one night after work," he said, "I think it was one in the morning. Maxie Kaminsky was with me, he . . . knew Billie too, and we both got in the car, drove down to New York, down to Harlem, asked around, found out where Billie was living with her mother in some little flat, and went up and got her." Holiday recalled her mom fixing fried chicken for an early-morning breakfast, before she and the men took off in Artie's car.

If Benny Goodman (who had recorded with Holiday, and for a time dated her) had thought about hiring Billie, he'd been outflanked. But no leader had a greater appreciation for this singer's gifts than Artie Shaw. "I gave her a record of Debussy's L'après-midi d'un faune," he said. "She could sing the whole thing, the top line: 'Da, da-da-da da da-da dee—' She could do the whole thing. Didn't have the range for it—but she had a very good ear."

Billie Holiday made her first appearance with the Art Shaw Orchestra in spectacular fashion: in Madison Square Garden at the Harvest Moon Ball, a citywide dance contest drawing twenty thousand spectators. Then, on March 15, Holiday and Shaw were in Boston for the band's opening at the Roseland State, where they would play each Tuesday and Saturday night for the next three months.

Holiday had made an earlier Boston splash with Basie at the Ritz-Carlton, singing numbers like "Swing, Brother, Swing," "I Can't Get Started," and "When My Dreamboat Comes Home." "[T]hose college students from up at Harvard and those places were crazy about her," the Count said. Her college fans must have been among those who jammed the Roseland State now, where business was at "capacity" and the Shaw band drew "record gates." Metronome referred to this revitalized crew as "the new Shaw-Holiday combo" but said Shaw was still "stealing the show with his clarinet work."

The two made a striking couple: he dark and handsome in the double-breasted suits he favored, two months shy of his twenty-eighth birthday; she, almost twenty-three, vibrant in a floral dress with bare shoulders and slight décolleté. On its radio broadcasts, at six-thirty in the evening on Saturdays and at midnight on Tuesdays, the band tried different things, including an ever-lengthening version of Shaw's "The Blues," with Artie and Billie swapping verse after ad-lib verse.

Among those crowding the Roseland State were members of the Chick Webb band, including tenor-sax player and arranger Teddy McRae. "One night [Art] asked if I could do some instrumentals for him," McRae said. "I told him, half as a joke, that I'd have a big hit for him when I got back next weekend." McRae was commuting by train between Boston and Manhattan; when he wrote his piece for Shaw's band, he tried to re-create the sensation of that experience: "In those days, everything closed down tight in Boston on Sunday and, when they'd finished on Saturday night, all the musicians would rush for the 1:05 train to New York. The saxes in 'Back Bay Shuffle' play the sounds we used to hear of the wheels coming around the bend as we dashed for the train in Back Bay Station." Shaw liked the piece; it swung with the black feel he wanted.

Chick Webb, on the other hand, seemed to be aiming for a commercial white (or "ofay") sound as he reshaped his band to showcase singer Ella Fitzgerald. Inspired by Maxine Sullivan's "Loch Lomond," Ella came up with a jumping version of the children's song "A-Tisket, A-Tasket" to record with Webb. If a Scottish folk song had been a "nickel-grabber" at the jukeboxes, why not a nursery rhyme?

"Back Bay Shuffle" or "A-Tisket A-Tasket"—Shaw and Webb weren't far apart in their musical ambitions. What each craved in the spring of 1938 was a great big hit.

THOSE NETWORK remotes were proving a mixed blessing for Art. Yes, they spread Shaw's music to farther corners, but they drew the attention of the music-business song pluggers. Shaw's coast-to-coast radio broadcasts made him a valuable resource: a performer with the sort of network feed these men got paid to have songs heard on.

While Shaw and swing-journal critics and kids from Harvard might be delighted for Billie Holiday to sing "Travelin' All Alone" (written in 1929) and "I Must Have That Man" (1928) and seventeen choruses of the nameless, timeless, uncopyrighted blues for half an hour on the CBS network, song pluggers were livid. One was not supposed to—not *allowed* to—squander golden opportunities. One was supposed to perform "Love Is the Thing" or "Dancing with a Debutante" or "I'll Be Seeing You" or "Jeepers Creepers" or "I've Got a Pocketful of Dreams"—or whatever other new tunes of the month one was beseeched to perform by these men with cash in their pockets and gifts in their cars and glints in their eyes. And perform it *right*: words *and* music, maestro, please.

Because a proper plug contained the lyric. Why would people buy a song if they didn't know the words? And the words had to be sung right—not by some jazzbo who slurred syllables and screwed with the beat and changed the notes around.

The song pluggers started a whispering campaign against Billie Holiday with the aim of getting Shaw to replace her; Billie was too demanding and temperamental, the grumblers said, and not suited for singing with a band of Shaw's "type" (in other words, a white band). The "complaints" grew loud enough to prompt a stinging piece in *Down Beat* by George Frazier. Art was outraged. But Si Shribman thought the song pluggers had a point—and Shribman had to be listened to. After all, he was backing Art with his own money, not to mention the fact that he had a virtual lock on all the New England ballrooms.

"Art Shaw will keep vocalist Billie Halliday [sic]," *Variety* reported on May 4. "Talk of her exit not so, he says. Just wants another girl with band so he'll have alternates." Shaw brought back Cliff Leeman's wife, Nita Bradley.

There was another change in the trumpet section. Max Kaminsky, long at odds with Shaw and now entangled with a married woman, had begun to show up late for shows. Max would have to go.

Out of the blue came a solution: John Best, of all people, wrote Shaw a letter.

After quitting Art in the fall of 1937, the trumpeter had gone home to North Carolina and played local college gigs for eight months. He remembered Shaw said John hadn't heard enough early Louis Armstrong. "I went to a record store and found a whole stack of old records that had been on juke-boxes and were worn—but there was a big stack of Louis Armstrong. They were ten cents apiece. I didn't have much money, but I bought as many as I could and went back home and started to listen to them. . . . 'Wild Man Blues,' and all those old things. . . . I finally realized what they were talking about." That's when he wrote Art. Shaw responded by telephone: Did Best want to rejoin?

Best didn't have to sleep on it. Without waiting a day, he drove all the way from North Carolina to New York, where he left his car with his brother and took a train to Boston. Exhausted, he made his way with trumpet and baggage to the Roseland State. "The band was on the stand at the time; and when I spoke to Artie, he immediately asked, 'Have you got your horn?' I told him yes, but that I was really too tired to play. He said, 'Come on, you're gonna have to play anyway.' So I got on the stand, and the band began to ad lib some blues—he did a lot of that—and I played two or three choruses."

If he had been expecting a hero's welcome, Best was disappointed. "Artie came to my room and said, 'John, I want you to play the jazz in the band until I find a trumpet player I really like.'"

CHAPTER FOURTEEN

Green Key Jump

IN 1938, THE MOST popular dance orchestra in America was Tommy Dorsey's, an all-purpose ensemble that played sweet, hot, swinging, *or* mellow. Dorsey's crew was headlining Dartmouth's Green Key prom in May, and filling out the bill was Art Shaw's rambunctious mob of Boston-based newcomers. Shaw admired Dorsey and had gained much from knowing him; they even collaborated on a tune, "Green Key Jump," to be played at the dance. But underdog Art, on fire with ambition, had not come to Dartmouth to show professional courtesy. Shaw's band blew Dorsey's off the stage.

"Billie Holiday was singing with us, and we cut [Dorsey's] great band, which was the number-one band. . . . We cut them a brand new one," Cliff Leeman said, "that's how *that* goes." The trade papers, the audience members, and the musicians agreed: Shaw's "savages" had triumphed. Tommy Dorsey stalked off the stage in fury; he was not a man who liked to lose.

From Dartmouth, Shaw and company went to Nutting's-on-Charles, a Shribman ballroom in Waltham, Massachusetts, for a match-up with the Red Norvo orchestra. This was billed as a "battle of music," and *Metronome* called it "the greatest attraction of the month," with Norvo's featured vocalist being his wife Mildred Bailey. "Billie Holliday [*sic*] and

Mildred Bailey waged a war within a war," *Metronome* reported, "with Nita Bradley . . . doing her bit between rounds." According to the *Met*, "Shaw, who had previously nicked T. Dorsey at Dartmouth, also edged Norvo."

The all-day, open-air "Carnival of Swing" at New York's Randall's Island on Sunday, May 29, was no cutting contest; it featured twenty-six name bands and swing combos in performance for the approval of twenty-five thousand spectators. The event, a benefit for the New York musicians' hospital fund, was staged by radio host Martin Block, whose *Make-Believe Ballroom* program was a key showcase for swing artists.

Vincent Lopez called the crowd to attention with "The Star-Spangled Banner." Then the show began: a parade of headliners and newcomers, black and white, including Chick Webb (with Ella Fitzgerald), Charlie Barnet, Duke Ellington, Larry Clinton, Count Basie, Kay Kyser, Slim and Slam, Bobby Hackett, Stuff Smith, and the Andrews Sisters. The Hickory House's dynamo of a teenaged percussionist, Buddy Rich, broke a few drumsticks to the delight of the audience.

Police put in a good day's work trying to keep thousands of exuberant adolescents in their stadium seats and off the infield grass, where they tried to dance the shag and the Lindy Hop. Bands arrived throughout the afternoon by bus, train, and plane. It was said that Benny Goodman, booked in Atlantic City, might come—but at the last minute, it was announced he wouldn't. "The mob howled its disappointment," *Variety* said.

But there were cheers each time Block gave an update on the progress of the bus bearing the Art Shaw band from Boston. By the time Shaw's vehicle pulled into the stadium, the jitterbugs were in a near frenzy. When the orchestra took the stage and cut loose, the kids seated on the infield stood on their metal folding chairs and danced in place. "Nightmare" never sounded so sweet.

THE BAND SEEMED to get better every week. At the heart of its esprit de corps was Shaw's relationship with Tony Pastor, which went back fifteen years to when Arthur Arshawsky met Antonio Pestritto in New Haven, Connecticut. "Dad and he saw a mirror in each other," Tony Pastor Jr. said. "The two of them were like strange soul mates. I think Artie was very much like my dad, who was a terribly sensitive man: when he was happy, he would cry; when he was sad, he would cry. I think Artie and Dad *shared* that, but Artie never *showed* that; but my father always *saw* that in Artie. I think that's what he and Artie really shared artistically, was the pathos—the melodic pathos for the structure of the tune, and pathos for the emotion you could put into it."

The bond Tony and Arthur shared extended through the orchestra. "These guys in the band," Tony Jr. said, "they were like *family*." Tony's nephew Joseph Tauro was often present at informal gatherings of Shaw band members at Tony's summer place in Soundview, Connecticut: "I was a seven- or eight-year-old kid; all I used to do was just listen, and gape at them with my mouth open. They'd have jam sessions in the back yard. They were a very happy crew; that's the way it seemed."

There was someone else nephew Joseph would remember: a young black lady named Billie, who used to spend quite a bit of time at the Pastors' house in Hartford. "She and Tony were very close friends," said Joe, who in later years learned a lot more about Billie Holiday. "Tony was a big factor in her life. She depended on him to sort of *be* there for her, when she was doing her engagements with the Shaw band. 'Cause you can imagine how tough it must have been, being on the road anyway in the '30s: the highways that they had were all dirt roads; and then on top of that, not to be able to even go in and get something to eat at a greasy spoon because you were black. He had many fights, Tony did about that, protecting her."

"If you've got one of those Italian boys like Tony in your corner," Billie Holiday would write, "they'll go to hell for you and die for you."

"She was very nice," Joe Tauro would say of the young Billie he met at his uncle's house in 1938. "But one thing I remember about her: She used to tell me, 'Joseph, you better be good—or I'm gonna put a stamp on your forehead and mail you away.' Now, that—I was only seven or eight, but I remember bein' scared shitless. Gonna put a stamp on my forehead and mail me away!"

It worked though: Joseph Tauro *was* good—and grew up to become chief justice of Boston's First District Federal Court.

IN PRIVATE or on stage, Billie made an impression. One customer who saw her perform in the summer of 1938 was a nineteen-year-old swing fan from Pennsylvania named Jack Klugman, who said of Holiday seventy years later, "She was sen-*sational!*" Klugman would earn fame in the 1950s as a stage, film, and television actor; but as Art Shaw's and Billie Holiday's stars were on their ascents in 1938, he was a mere swing-happy kid. Benny Goodman was the first artist whose music "sent" Klugman: "I liked that group; I liked Wilson, I liked Krupa; I loved that band. Artie Shaw came along later. Oh, God, they were wonderful days—wonderful days! I liked Benny, I *think*, better, but—Aw, I *loved* Artie Shaw's band. He was—he was great; *he was an innovator.*" The teenaged Klugman saw Shaw's band at the Ocean Pier in Wildwood, New Jersey, when Artie's great innovation that season was (as the music papers called her) his "sepia songstress," his "colored canary," his "bronze bombshell." Billie Holiday thrilled the crowds who thronged to see Artie Shaw in 1938. "*God*, she was wonderful," said Klugman. "But she would get up and sing—not like the other singers—she didn't just sing that one song and go back; she would sing maybe two or *three* songs, and the people would go crazy."

"It wasn't like a Hollywood movie or something," a revisionist Artie Shaw would insist, decades later, maybe not wanting to acknowledge how much Holiday had meant to the crowds back then, or to the band, or to him. "It wasn't like she got up there and sang, and the people went crazy, or something."

But it was.

CHAPTER FIFTEEN

Begin the Beguine

S HAW HAD LET his Brunswick contract expire six months before and
hadn't signed with any label until he was sure his new orchestra was
ready to record. Now, with the band's reputation on the rise, Art okayed
a contract with RCA Victor.

With the new deal came a new name for the leader. A Victor executive thought "Art Shaw," said fast, sounded like a sneeze and might lead
to unwanted gags: "*Art-Shaw.*" "*Gesundheit.*" Henceforth, it was decreed,
this RCA artist would be billed "Artie Shaw." Sneeze or no, it helped
mark Shaw's split with his "sweet swing" past, and it put him on a first-
name basis with "Benny" and "Tommy" and "Ozzie" and "Charlie" and
all the other hit-seeking bandleaders.

The number Artie Shaw thought he held as his ace when his orchestra gathered for its first session at Victor's New York studio on the
afternoon of Sunday, July 24, 1938, was his very own up-to-date arrangement of Rudolf Friml's vintage "Indian Love Call."

The Prague-born Friml's operettas had been 1920s Broadway hits.
A 1936 movie of his *Rose Marie*, with Jeanette MacDonald and Nelson
Eddy, had yielded a million-selling record of "Indian Love Call." Artie's
swing-style send-up of that song was as different from Nelson's and
Jeanette's reverent call-and-response as "Stompin' at the Savoy" from a

Strauss waltz. It featured Tony Pastor's semi-scat vocal in tandem with a hepster chorus of bandsmen chanting droll comments—a device more or less invented by black leader-arranger Don Redman and brought to the fore by Tommy Dorsey the previous year with "Marie." Shaw's band had been doing this swingopated "Love Call" at gigs, and it was a crowd pleaser.

But before recording "Love Call," Art had a warmup number to wax: an all-but-forgotten song from the unsuccessful 1935 Cole Porter show *Jubilee*. This one didn't sound so good though to the wise men at RCA, especially (Art wrote) the label's recording manager, who thought Shaw's doing the tune would be "a complete waste of time."

NO ONE but Xavier Cugat had recorded "Begin the Beguine" before— or even knew quite what it was. One critic who reviewed *Jubilee* called the number a waltz, while *The New Yorker*'s Robert Benchley groused, "Why throw in just another rumba?" The tune was of mixed parentage. In 1925, Porter saw a performance by a Martinique troupe whose native dance was the beguine; "begin the beguine," he jotted in a notebook. Ten years later, he viewed a different native dance in New Guinea and notated its melody, then joined notes to title for a number for *Jubilee*. "Begin the Beguine," at 108 measures, was thought to be "the longest popular song ever written."

Once *Jubilee* closed, its music went into limbo. There would be nearly as many anecdotes about how "Begin the Beguine" ended up in Shaw's band book as there were men in his orchestra.

Here's one, put forth in a Time-Life Records account of the swing era: "By 1938 Artie Shaw was playing for a dance at Syracuse University, he recalls, when some of the fans asked him if he could play 'Begin the Beguine.' Artie had never heard of it but found it was a jam session favorite with some of his sidemen."

Another version: "It all started in a hotel room in Boston," alto-sax player Hank Freeman told Burt Korall. "Artie and Jerry Gray got to talking about this Cole Porter tune that never made it: 'Begin the Beguine.'

Chuck Peterson said something about gimmicking it up, rhythmically. Artie and Jerry figured out a pulsating introduction which, in its way, was innovative."

Max Kaminsky, who left Shaw's band months before its first Victor session, would try to take credit: "One day at a rehearsal, when I started to noodle around with the song, Artie told his arranger to copy it that way."

Cliff Leeman said, "Jerry Gray scored the original 'Begin the Beguine'"—but added, "Artie used to give him a chart to go by, and how to style it; and then Jerry Gray would arrange."

Shaw shrugged off such stories with show-biz resignation, telling Vladimir Simosko, "Everyone wants to get in on the act."

"We rehearsed it one afternoon," guitarist Al Avola told Time-Life, "and it wasn't even part way through when Artie stopped us. It was arranged in a beguine rhythm—*bhum bhum, bhum pah bhum*—and Artie wouldn't stand for that. He was always figuring how a song would play at the Waldorf and that wasn't the sort of stuff he thought they wanted. So he said, 'Let's do it in four-four time,' so we changed the time but kept Jerry Gray's chords."

Blip! went the brass.

Ba-dooby-doo, bop!—bop! said the reeds.

Blip! blip!

Ba-dooby-doo, bop! Baa!

In four bars the band grabbed the listener by the ears; then Art's silken-smooth clarinet entered with the beguiling melody. The band kept going, maintaining a suave platform from which Shaw uttered perfect little phrases. Tony Pastor came in on tenor, graceful as an otter, polished as an old boot—*Bump! ba dodda-dodda*—

The orchestra built it up, came down in volume, then rose up again, as Shaw led it out with his soon-to-be-patented upward glissando. The song seemed over almost as soon as it started, yet you felt you had dreamed a whole love affair in its spell. "Begin the Beguine" was slick, romantic, and swinging. As soon as it was done, you wanted to hear it again.

With "Beguine" captured, the band turned to "Indian Love Call."

Shaw began in exotic mode: his lone clarinet over Leeman's tom-toms. Then the ensemble came in, as a bunch of the men chorused "*cheep-cheep!*" in playful commentary. Shaw's arrangement was full of surprises: Dixieland-sounding passages; that trick of having the band *stop* for a few seconds, before jumping in full throttle; then a burst of Sousa-like fireworks to set up Pastor's scat-soaked vocal, which was nothing like Nelson Eddy but more like Louis Armstrong splitting a riff with Leo Watson.

By eight-thirty in the evening, Art and the band had cut six sides, each good enough to blast the orchestra out of the workaday music world and into the swing empyrean. But everyone from Shaw to Pastor to RCA's music director was certain "Indian Love Call" was the hit.

When it came to predicting hits, though, the only certainty was that no one—especially the "experts"—knew anything at all.

THEN THE BAND was on the move, and the road trip stretched out through August. Some engagements would take the band down South, where the locals' possible reactions to Shaw's "colored canary" caused both leader and singer anxiety. Holiday thought Art was trying to build as large a national audience as possible before trying an extended Manhattan gig. But once committed to something, she wrote, he wouldn't back down: "He's . . . amazing and a good cat deep down. He's not one to go back on his word."

She saw Shaw turn words into deeds when they got to Lexington, Kentucky: "[W]e couldn't find a place that would rent me a room. Finally Artie got sore and picked out the biggest hotel in town. . . . He got eight cats out of the band and they escorted me to the registration desk. . . . I think the man at the desk figured it couldn't be true what he thought he saw . . . so they gave me a nice room and no back talk."

She wrote too of an onstage incident in what seems to have been Clarkesville, Tennessee: "When I came on, the sheriff walked up to the raised bandstand; Artie's back was to the dance floor, so he pulled Artie's pants leg and said, 'Hey you!' Artie turned around. 'Don't touch me,' he hollered over the music. But the sheriff . . . pulled Artie's leg again. 'Hey you,' he said. Artie turned around. 'You want to get kicked?' he asked him. Still the old cracker sheriff didn't give up. . . . 'Hey you,' he said. Then he turned to me and, so loud everybody could hear, he said, 'What's Blackie going to sing?' Artie looked like it was the end of the world—and the tour. I guess he thought I was going to break down and have a collapse or something. But I was laughing like hell."

But other scenes and taunts, in and out of the South, were harder to laugh off, and the constant battle for food, lodging, and bathroom rights wore on everyone's nerves.

Alto player Les Robinson said, "Especially in the South, they didn't like the idea of a black girl sitting on the bandstand. They didn't care if she sang, as long as after she finished she returned to her place, as they would say." Mostly, Robinson, thought, "[Billie] just sort of took it in her stride. . . . It was the same old thing everywhere we went—hotels, restaurants. And the guys stood behind her. Artie did too."

The band kept on, doing one-nighters in Pennsylvania, Ohio, New Jersey, Massachusetts, and New York. All the hard travel, bad food, missed sleep, and (for some) overindulgence caught up with several band members in September. Holiday had to see a doctor. Les Robinson caught pneumonia and checked into a New York hospital. One trombonist was replaced. Even Artie, who had a strong constitution, proved susceptible.

On the night of September 16, the Shaw band was in New York City in pitched swing battle with the Tommy Dorsey Orchestra for a charity event at the 105th Regiment Armory, before an audience sprinkled with music-biz colleagues including Glenn Miller, Ozzie Nelson, and Count Basie. Suffering from the flu, Art had to be helped offstage and into a doctor's care—but not before giving Dorsey's crew another solid drubbing, according to Metronome's George Simon: "Holding back nothing, Artie and his men shelled out as few white bands have ever shelled before. Their rhythmic attack was devastating; their pace scorching; their effect upon the assembled jitterbugs downright murderous."

Nine days later, Artie was back in RCA Victor's Studio 2 for the second of his Bluebird recording sessions.

But Billie wasn't with him.

SHAW LATER BLAMED Holiday, saying she had re-signed with Brunswick without telling him. Billie blamed RCA for putting out Art's records on their budget-priced thirty-five-cent Bluebird label—thus competing with her budget-priced Vocalions, which made Brunswick cry foul.

Whatever the case, Victor yanked "Any Old Time"—the side she'd made with Shaw on July 24—and stopped Shaw from recording again with Holiday: another annoyance for Art, who now had to hire a second female singer to make the band's quota of girl-vocal platters.

He called on a white Washington, D.C., vocalist brought to his attention in 1937 by Goodman's trumpet player Ziggy Elman. Benny had walked out on this singer in a D.C. club, but Art thought she had potential. In the summer of 1938, Helen Forrest was ready to make good on that promise.

Forrest learned some phrasings from Holiday, but her approach was her own: precise and polished, with banked emotions and her own subdued swing. She was well suited to good show tunes.

But the pair of movie songs Forrest was given to do at her first session with Shaw was a far cry from the deluxe material Art vowed he would specialize in. "I Have Eyes" and "You're a Sweet Little Headache" were on a par with the most jejune items from Shaw's Brunswick days. Art was appalled at being induced by RCA to commit this material to disc. Half a century later, he would say, only half-jokingly, "That was the beginning of the end: the day I let them talk me into recording 'You're a Sweet Little Headache.'"

Shaw's orchestra made four other sides on September 27, all instrumentals, each first rate: a moody "Nightmare"; another Shaw original, "Non-Stop Flight"; Cole Porter's "What Is This Thing Called Love?"; and Jerome Kern's "Yesterdays." The five-hour session produced four top-notch tracks—plus two banal examples of someone else's idea of a possible hit.

Art would soon start quoting an anonymous poem about a musician who summed up his pragmatic modus vivendi as "Three chords for beauty's sake, and one to pay the rent." On September 27, Shaw played four chords for beauty and two to pay the rent. It was a ratio Art Shaw guessed he could live with, so long as it didn't tilt any farther.

CHAPTER SIXTEEN

Non-Stop Flight

BUT WHAT IF HE wouldn't get to play the music he wanted? Already he was being told what he ought to record, and he'd lost the right to make discs with his first-choice singer. Not only that: Billie told him her days with the band itself were numbered. She thought she could make a living on Fifty-second Street, and she wasn't crazy about life with a big band—*any* band. She would give Art a few more months, she said, and then leave.

With Billie soon to depart, and more inevitable *schlock* in his RCA Victor future, maybe the race was already lost. Maybe Art should do what he had done with the swing-strings orchestra: pack it in, give it up, start from scratch.

"And [when] we left town, [Artie] was thinking of dissolving the band," Cliff Leeman said. "But he had a commitment in a hotel in St. Louis." The gig was three weeks at the Chase Hotel, and the promoter made it clear Shaw had to have a white female vocalist. Fair enough; Shaw hired Helen Forrest for ballads, and Billie could sing her blues and swing.

Opening on September 30, the band drew a thousand customers, breaking a house record; it topped that the next night, with fourteen hundred.

On a Monday off from the hotel gig, the Shaw band went to Chicago to play the annual "Negro Christmas Basket Fund" benefit sponsored by the *Defender* newspaper. Some five thousand people, nearly all black, filled the Savoy Ballroom to see a show billed as "Billie Holiday, with Artie Shaw and his Orchestra." Joe Shribman said, "It was very funny, because they opened up and Artie really laid it on, 'cause he'd found out they didn't really know who he was. The band was tight; it was a great band. The reception was wild. When Billie came out, she tore the joint down."

BUT IT WAS back at the Chase that Art's life changed forever. As with other pivotal events in his history, there are different stories about what happened.

In one, he had just started playing that Cole Porter number they had recorded in July when the crowd all of a sudden gave a roar. Shaw peered out to see what was going on, because often a couple drew a big reaction with some ambitious jitterbugging. When he realized the crowd was cheering the tune, Art guessed they had a hit.

But Cliff Leeman, also on the scene, told a different tale: "[I]n the middle of the engagement, after a week or two in St. Louis, [Art] got a call one day from RCA Victor—this is only two months later—from Leonard Joy, who was a big man there, saying to come back [to New York]. [Shaw] was already gonna dissolve the band, now. But 'Begin the Beguine' . . . is a sensation, it is sweeping the nation. Well, as a bunch of kids, you don't know how thrilled we were."

"Begin the Beguine" had been the B-side of "Indian Love Call," but disc jockeys and jukebox patrons flipped the record over and fell in love with "Beguine." Maybe they liked that the clarinet came in sooner.

Nobody knew why "Beguine" took off, not even the man who made it, although he took a few guesses in later years.

"What is 'Begin the Beguine'?" Shaw asked in 1990, when his 1938 record in one form or another was *still* being bought. "It's the first time that anybody played a real *melody* down with a jazz *beat*. That's what that *was*. After the fact; I couldn't have known a-*head* of time. Still holds *up*; that goes *on* and *on* and *on*. You'd think that's the only thing I ever *did*."

To someone else, Shaw said the record's appeal was that it combined swing rhythm with a Latin beat. But on another occasion, Art admitted, "I don't know why that tune caught on; I have no idea. . . . I tried to play the song the way I thought it would sound good. When you do something that does go off on its own and it's a standout thing—you don't *mean* it to *do* that; you just play a particular song, and you happen to hit a way of doing it that for some unknown reason the public buys, en masse. . . . Trouble with that is, they want you to keep doing the same *thing*. If you had done the same thing to start with, you'd not have played *that*. So—it's a cockeyed business. When you're dealing with the public—it's cockeyed."

Artie Shaw's record of "Beguine" made Cole Porter's all-but-unknown four-year-old song "really big-time stuff," in Porter's phrase. Biographer William McBrien would write in 1998, "Porter was pleased with Shaw's version and invited him to a party, where Cole greeted him: 'Happy to meet my collaborator.' 'Does that involve royalties?' asked Shaw. 'I'm afraid not,' countered Cole."

Overnight, "Begin the Beguine" made Artie Shaw a household name. But another tune might just as well have done the trick. The band and its leader were more than ready, and "Back Bay Shuffle" or "Yesterdays" could as easily have lit their fuse.

Shaw might well have been grateful it was "Beguine," though, and not "Indian Love Call" that became his signature hit. While he would grow weary over the decades of having to play Porter's melody again and again and again, how much more annoyed might he have been at having to hear two or three generations of sidemen chirping "*cheep cheep!*" the rest of his musical life?

CHAPTER SEVENTEEN

Indian Love Call

EVEN BEFORE going to St. Louis, Artie Shaw and his orchestra had been booked "for the season" (October through January) into the Blue Room of the renovated Hotel Lincoln. Shaw got a tremendous "build-up" via half-hour remotes from the Lincoln over the NBC network. These broadcasts began just as Bluebird's new single of "Nightmare" (backed with "Non-Stop Flight") hit record stores, and Artie's theme song became an integral part of his on-the-air identity. Riding the wave of the already huge "Beguine," Shaw's band was a Blue Room sensation.

Bea Wain and her new husband, radio announcer André Baruch, were among those dancing to the music of Artie Shaw at the Hotel Lincoln in the autumn of 1938. "We followed him around pretty good," she said, "from one engagement to another." So did many other swing enthusiasts—including Benny Goodman. "Benny took me to hear Artie Shaw at the Lincoln Hotel," said singer Helen Ward. "Benny admired Artie. He said he was damn good. He never made any bones about that. He thought Artie was a great clarinetist."

Goodman downplayed the rivalry promoted by the music press and by Art's agents (who now billed him "king of the clarinet," in contrast to Benny's *Down Beat*-bestowed title "king of swing"). But how could Goodman not be envious of "Begin the Beguine," which was turning into the biggest record of 1938? Within a month, Goodman also began featuring Porter's tune in performance. But it was Shaw's "Beguine" that was the anthem of the hour, and his orchestra the band of the day.

Artie was especially popular at colleges, where kids liked both his swinging sides and his romantic numbers. His popularity extended to black campuses, said writer Albert Murray, who was a student from 1935 to 1939 at Alabama's Tuskegee Institute. "Jazz was the big thing on radio, with special programs and so forth, and Artie Shaw was among those very popular at Tuskegee—as was Benny Goodman. You see? And many people thought that he was very very *very* good competition for Benny Goodman. And in many ways, this guy Artie—well he wasn't gonna be outdone so far as *effort* was concerned, by Benny Goodman! He was a *challenge*, to how much of the instrument you really had to *know*! His actual mastery of his horn, and his invention—outside musical devices, and so forth—that was a challenge, to all. And of course, the Negroes liked him because—he's a friend of Billie Holiday's, and—he liked to hang *out*, in that part of *town*."

With Shaw at the Lincoln, new business partners appeared. "That's when they came in with all the contracts and so forth," Leeman said. "He hadn't been there more than a month," Joe Shribman said, "when he got one of the biggest plums in the business: the Old Gold radio show. And they came looking for Shaw!"

Old Gold cigarettes had sponsored Paul Whiteman a decade ago. Now they were putting together a show with Robert ("Why throw in just another rumba?") Benchley, who in addition to being a *New Yorker* writer was also starring in a popular series of MGM movie short-subjects. *Melody and Madness* was to be the title of Old Gold's half-hour CBS Sunday-night radio series. Benchley would provide the madness and Shaw the melodies, starting November 20.

But neither the sponsor nor the network wanted controversy. Shaw's singers on the series would be Helen Forrest and baritone Richard Todd. Billie Holiday would not be part of the show.

"A lot of people including [Art's] manager, booking agents and producers put a lot of pressure on him not to use [Billie]," Forrest wrote, "and he used her less and less as time went on. He had it in his mind to do right by her, but his skull was caving in from the pressure."

Shaw said there were other factors involved. "She quit because some guys got hold of her and promised her the sun, the moon, and the stars," he said. "And by that time she was becoming well known. My band just got over, and—pow! We were stars; and so she was a *star*, right away. And people got their hooks into her, and they wanted her to do a single."

Art acknowledged, though, it was the Lincoln situation that led Billie to fire herself, as she put it. "The woman who ran the hotel [Maria Kramer] . . . she said, 'Artie, could you talk to Billie and ask her—See if you could get Billie to go on with Helen, and use the freight elevator to go up?' See there was no 'mixing' [of races]. People come in the elevator and see a 'colored woman'—they wouldn't *stay* in the hotel. I said, 'I don't think she's gonna *like* it, but I'll try.'

"So I said to her, 'Billie, you know, this—has nothin' to do with *me*, has to do with the way the *world* is.' She heard me. She said, 'Yeah—I don't think I'm gonna like this.' I said, 'Wadya wanna do? I'll buy you gowns, whatever you need.' She said, 'No, I got these people—' So she went out on her own. That was the end."

Billie didn't blame Artie, as time went by. She would write, "There aren't many people who fought harder than Artie against the vicious people in the music business or the crummy side of second-class citizenship which eats at the guts of so many musicians. He didn't win. But he didn't lose either." By the end of the year, Holiday would be the debut headliner at a new club in Greenwich Village, Café Society, where races would "mix" onstage and off. During her multimonth stay at this popular nitery, Billie came into her own as a solo performer—especially after a patron asked her to feature a provocative "protest" song he had written, "Strange Fruit."

VICTOR WANTED more sides from the pistol-hot Artie Shaw; the record men cut the gap between his studio sessions from two months to one. Art complained that there was barely enough time to rehearse new material.

At a Victor session on December 19, Shaw recorded four Helen Forrest vocals, an up-tempo instrumental of the old Isham Jones song "It Had To Be You" and a moody "Jungle Drums," featuring the band's newest member, tenor man Georgie Auld, whose up-to-the-minute style (influenced by black saxophonist Ben Webster) would complement Tony Pastor's riffs. Also coming onto the band was pianist Bob Kitsis. When drummer Cliff Leeman had to leave for medical reasons, Shaw first used George Wettling as a substitute, then hired Buddy Rich from Bunny Berigan's band (where Auld had also been working). "Buddy provided a spark we never had before," Shaw said. This fine-tuning had the desired effect: the band was being praised as the best all-round swing outfit in white America—better even than Goodman's, which some felt had been weakened by the departure of Gene Krupa and others.

Art's newly refined orchestra had become the real star of *Melody and Madness*, which had turned into "a classic stand for Artie Shaw," radio historian John Dunning wrote. "The band burst into 1939 with a free and happy sound. . . . [I]t captured its moment as vividly as a photograph."

As 1938 closed, Shaw devotees had a unique opportunity to compare their new idol with Benny Goodman—not as a bandleader, but as a clarinet virtuoso on a legendary concert stage. Paul Whiteman had been presenting jazz-influenced compositions in concert venues since 1924, when he commissioned and debuted George Gershwin's "Rhapsody in Blue" at Aeolian Hall. On Christmas night of 1938, Whiteman sponsored another "experiment in modern American music" at Carnegie Hall. Artie Shaw was invited as a featured soloist. Whiteman would showcase Shaw in the same auditorium where Goodman that year had made his most prestigious splash.

Art concocted a twelve-and-a-half-minute opus with the working title "A Mess of Blues." Irving Szathmary, one of Whiteman's arrangers, wrote out band parts from Art's sketch. When it came time for Art's solo passages, well, Shaw would improvise.

The event began Christmas night, at eight-thirty. Shaw's turn came forty minutes into a two-hour bill emceed by musicologist Deems Taylor and featuring works by (among others) Duke Ellington, Morton

Gould, Richard Rodgers, and the late George Gershwin (who had died in 1937, shockingly at the age of thirty nine). As at the Imperial Theatre swing concert, Artie walked into a comfortable occasion filled with friends and colleagues: Whiteman's sixty-piece ensemble included Jack and Charlie Teagarden and George Wettling, who until a few days ago had been Shaw's own drummer.

The piece, in Szathmary's arrangement, began with a vampy wah-wah strain over which Art quickly ascended the scale into a free-form meditative glide. Shaw ornamented a traditional twelve-bar line with his own warm musings, until a quick change in tempo introduced W. C. Handy's "St. Louis Blues." Shaw went to swing town on the melody.

Another tempo change, to slow-drag march-time, had Shaw's lines twining vine-like around the orchestra's framework; his clarinet sounded tender, reflective—and Jewish. *Variety's* Abel Green wrote, "His blends of the immortal 'St. Louis Blues' were but incidental to the original minor Semitic strains blended with the major Magyar mood of the 'Blues.'" George Wettling lay down the tom-tom beat Shaw now preferred for extended improvisation. With a nod from Art, the orchestra returned for a half-chorus—but dropped out again for Shaw's prolonged cadenza, which led to a final soaring upward slide ending on a nearly out-of-sight high note, an altissimo C above high-C, cleanly hit and held. The Carnegie Hall applause lasted a full minute—but like an apparition, Shaw was already gone. "He's not here!" Deems Taylor cried. "He's gone broadcasting!"

Shaw had rushed offstage and into a car waiting to whisk him to CBS for his weekly Sunday-night series.

To move without misstep between concert stage and radio studio, recording booth and nightclub bandbox, was the mark of a consummate pro. But somewhere a doubt gnawed. Could this be the curse of a much-desired gift? Would the dream, once made real, consume its recipient? "Did you ever feel," Artie Shaw asked late in life, "that once you finally got what you wanted, it wasn't at all what you thought it would be?"

CHAPTER EIGHTEEN

King for a Day

H IS RATE FOR THEATER dates climbed to $6,500 a week (and by year's end it would jump to $10,000). College proms and one-night stands paid $3,500. *Melody and Madness* gave him $2,500 each Sunday. The contract he would renegotiate soon with Victor would bring $50,000 a year. It kept adding up and up—in a time when the average family could be fed, housed, and clothed on a hundred dollars a month.

But Shaw needed to do *more*, be *better*: make his band the heavyweight outfit it had to be to beat Goodman's as undisputed champion.

His new drummer helped. Bernard "Buddy" Rich was a powerhouse. The twenty-one-year-old Rich lit a blaze beneath the Shaw orchestra, then tossed in two handfuls of firecrackers. Rich had been on the band a couple months when it won the *Down Beat* readers' poll in early 1939, beating Goodman's outfit by a mere thirty-eight votes. "In Person: Artie Shaw and his Orchestra: 1939 New King of Swing" read the banner beneath the marquee of the Strand Theatre on Broadway in February.

Recognition was sweet for Shaw's musicians. To the self-conscious Art, it was bittersweet: "I felt as if I were going around in a fish bowl with people staring and pointing at me and telling other people, who in turn stared and pointed and ogled and giggled and whispered to each other. I began to develop a near-paranoid kind of behavior. Only unlike a paranoiac, my behavior was based on the fact that people actually *were* following me around."

But there was a plus: he had become one of the charmed and chosen people, his company sought, his opinions valued.

His first use of his fame outside the swing arena came in mid-January, when he was in the forefront of a group flying to Washington to protest proposed congressional cuts to President Roosevelt's funding for the Federal Arts Project. "I went there," Shaw said with a rueful chuckle, "with, of all people, [actor] John Garfield—[nicknamed] Julie Garfield—and [actress] Frances Farmer. Three-person delegation, from the Theater Arts Committee, to talk to people in Washington, about continuing the WPA program for *theater*! Well, we got shunted from one to another. The congressmen said things like, 'You people can go on all you want, but—' I said, 'Who do you think we *are*? We're the ones who *put* you here; we're the constituency. Not like, we're coming here *asking* you for something; no, we're giving you the idea of what we think should be *done*. If we're mistaken, all right; but we don't *think* we are.'" The trio persevered all the way to the White House, where they received a more courteous hearing—from Franklin D. Roosevelt himself.

"I was the talker," Shaw said, with another chuckle. "You can see why. Julie didn't talk very much, and Frances was full of fervor but she didn't have much to say. So I laid out the dilemma. And Roosevelt listened very *carefully*; he was quite a man. He listened, hard. We didn't have very *long* with him; he had a full plate! We wanted to have a new committee started, instead of WPA whose function was over; start something else to support, governmentally, theater. It seemed like a reasonable thing: Most countries *do* have a state-run theater; America didn't. Well, Roosevelt agreed with us; but he said, 'It's a lost cause; you haven't got a constituency. There aren't enough people like you to constitute votes for the senators and the congressmen; you're not gonna get it. I can't use up my influence—that's for bigger issues—to go in there and say to 'em, you need more *theater*. Congress won't buy it.' So he said, 'I sympathize,

I understand—but you can't win.' But he was at least civil about it; he gave us a very clear answer. Roosevelt was courteous, and to the point; and he *heard* you. He heard what you were saying, he knew you weren't wrong; but he knew there was no way to get it done. Well—'lost cause.' He made us *see* that. It was very smart."

ON THREE DAYS in January, the Shaw orchestra cut sixteen sides for Bluebird, including such soon-to-be-favorites as "Rosalie" (a Pastor vocal), "The Man I Love," "The Donkey Serenade," a sizzling, Rich-propelled "Carioca," and "Bill," an old Helen Morgan favorite, sung by Helen Forrest.

Art gave Helen complete freedom on her numbers. On the romantic standards Shaw preferred, such as "Deep Purple," she showed style and class. Such was the case with Jerome Kern's "All the Things You Are," written for the 1939 Broadway musical *Very Warm for May*. "It followed a kind of complicated line melodically and wasn't easy to sing," Forrest said. *Very Warm for May* soon closed, but records of "All the Things You Are" by Shaw and others turned that song into a jukebox hit and then a popular classic. With its haunting melody and intriguing chord changes, it became a favorite of jazz musicians for the next half-century. "Kern credits our recording with bringing it to life," Forrest wrote, "and making it the standard it became."

Helen Forrest would become many listeners' favorite big-band vocalist. She was an attractive woman, but her relationship with Shaw was strictly professional. A different singer had Art's personal attention in 1939.

LEE WILEY, born in Port Gibson, Oklahoma, showed up in New York at the turn of the 1930s with stories of being a Cherokee princess. Her vocals simmered over a low, erotic flame. She made the poetry of Richard Rodgers and Larry Hart sound like the murmurs of her secret heart, and she wrote her own down-home bedroom-blues.

Wiley romanced good mentors. Conductor-composer Victor Young was her supporter; and Bunny Berigan neglected his wife for "that snake eyes," as Mrs. Berigan called her.

Lee's husky style was entwined with her sultry look. She wore slit skirts and had the gaze of a Circe. She was a blonde-haired vamp in a Harris Tweed coat, a torch singer who became a jazz thrush with one shrug of her beautiful shoulders. "The one I wish I could have recorded was Lee Wiley," Artie Shaw said with regret. "She was a good singer. Great sense of—what worked. I remember she'd go, '. . . And what is there, *to* do?' One note higher. Marvelous note! She had that kind of ear."

Art came under Lee's spell in late 1938. "We went together for quite a while," Shaw said. "She was a—beautiful young *woman*. When I was playin' at the Lincoln Hotel; used to see her almost every night, after work. We'd go to the hotel where she lived. The Astor—the old Astor Hotel. In bed, she would say things like, 'You are lying next to the greatest ass in New York.'" Art laughed. "She was a funny woman! And very hip. Smart broad. Yeah. We used to have fun."

Art relished private fun in a hectic year. His new refuge was Sherman Billingsley's Stork Club on East Fifty-third, haven for movers and shakers: captains of industry, columnists, authors, Broadway headliners, movie stars. Here everyone was famous; nobody gawked. Shaw enjoyed being among people *he* wanted to meet, especially writers and editors. Sometimes he sat near *The New Yorker*'s Harold Ross, and while he couldn't get much shoptalk from that magazine captain ("You'd ask him, 'Who's the better writer: Wolcott Gibbs, or Alexander Woolcott?' and he'd kind of shrug, and smile"), Shaw got a kick just out of being in his presence.

The Stork Club gave Shaw respite from the raucous world of swing, where Art's poll-victory over Goodman hadn't stopped the rivalry but stoked it. He described going backstage to Benny's dressing room at the Paramount to pay his respects after the *Down Beat* contest. As Art told it, Benny greeted him with, "So you're the new King of Swing, eh?"

"Well—"

"Thirty-eight votes, huh?"

"*Abee gesunt*," Shaw said he said in Yiddish: *As long as you've got your health.*

FROM THE LINCOLN, the Shaw band moved in February to the Strand Theatre, where the patrons were young and noisy and began pouring in at nine in the morning. Artie played to full houses through six or seven sets.

"Every time we went into the ['Nightmare'] theme," Georgie Auld said, "thirty, forty kids would jump up on the stage. Security would have to come up and put them out. One show we did, as the pit was going down, this little broad jumped on top of the pit, grabbed hold of Artie, and started to dry-hump him! He's holding his clarinet above his head; he don't want to break his reed."

It was such frenzied kids as these whom promoters did their damnedest, in early 1939, to lure into competing Newark, New Jersey, theaters for a money-making contest between Benny Goodman and Artie Shaw. The "Battle of the Killer-Dillers" is how *Variety* billed the hectic week in which Goodman and his orchestra would play six shows a day at Newark's Shubert while Shaw and his band worked fifteen hours at the nearby Paramount.

Jersey jitterbugs cut school and came out in force, especially for Artie, whose opening-day morning show was sold out before the theater opened. Once inside, the crowd was so noisy that Shaw's band had to start early—at which point seventy-five kids swarmed onstage to express themselves. Police were called to quell what the Newark paper termed a minor riot.

Hooky-playing swing kids thronged to see Benny too. "At the Shubert," *Time* wrote, "a girl swooned clean away." Back at the Paramount, one lad leapt from a balcony onto the stage and broke his leg; Shaw claimed to quip, "John Wilkes Booth, I presume?"

Pandemonium continued through the week, with Art drawing one hundred percent attendance, spilling into standing room. "If Goodman is beaten at the [box office] by Shaw's figures," wrote *Variety*'s Bernie Woods, "he'll have one consolation—that of having given a better show than Shaw. . . . Shaw's shortcoming is in his coldness onstage. . . . Goodman, on the other hand, has a stage presence that gets to the kids he's playing for."

"Rivalry was bitter throughout," *Metronome* said. Goodman called Woods to thank him for noting Shaw's venue was "on a main drag" while Benny's was "hidden on a side street"—hence accounting for Goodman's slightly lower attendance. Shaw would still bristle sixty years later that Goodman was thought the better showman: "When Benny played a 'hot lick' he thought was swell, he'd raise his leg a little bit or something—hop around on one leg—and people would think that was so *great*. Ridiculous!"

BENNY GOODMAN'S biggest record of 1938 was "Bei Mir Bist du Schoen," an Andrews Sisters smash hit adapted from a Yiddish-theater song. Benny's version had a Ziggy Elman trumpet interlude in the form of a *fraylich*, a Jewish wedding dance. Elman (a cantor's son) then crafted his own Yiddish-style number, "Frailach in Swing"; with Johnny Mercer's lyrics, it became "And the Angels Sing." Goodman recorded that too and had another big hit.

Benny's swing *fraylichs* came as Adolf Hitler was overrunning Europe and persecuting Jews. Goodman now added to his stage show a medley of folk numbers from the Diaspora. Artie Shaw then chose to end *his* set in the same manner. Maybe it was an expression of competitive pride: "I can do that, *better*." It gave Arthur Arshawsky the perfect opportunity to express the sound he found with ease at the back of his throat: the Eastern European *krecht*, a cry of joy and pain not unlike the growl and groan of American blues. Shaw retrieved "The Chant" from his 1937 book and revamped it to bring out its unexpected resemblance to "Khosn Kale, Mazeltov," a Jewish wedding piece.

Shaw and his orchestra performed this "Chant"—"a number guaranteed not only to send you," his radio announcer promised, "but to bring

you back"—on the Old Gold show on March 12. Spurred by Buddy
Rich's tom-toms, Art took off on a klezmer ride of a solo into which
were woven bits from "Bei Mir Bist du Schoen" and "Yossel, Yossel,"
"Patsh Tants," and "Ukrainian Kamarinska." Bernard Rich urged Arthur
Arshawsky on with shouts of "oi-oi!" The New York studio audience
stirred in recognition of the tunes; at the end of Shaw's two-chorus solo,
the crowd burst into fervid applause. It was an astonishing moment on
network radio; it might be seen as the dropping of a mask—or was it
the donning of one? Art Shaw assumed the guise of a klezmer player to
release the *krecht* in his blood and bones—but only once. Now you see
me, now you don't.

CHAPTER NINETEEN

One Foot in the Groove

For SHAW, the pace was killing. It seemed he never stopped: going sometimes from *Melody and Madness* on Sunday night right into the Victor studio for a four-and-a-half-hour session ending at four in the morning, then getting ready to hit the road for another week. In the spring, Art began to get sick. He canceled the odd one-nighter, or let the band play without him for part of a dance. He said he needed a vacation; his doctors agreed. He dropped out of a week at the Cleveland Palace; it was reported he had pneumonia.

There was one April gig, though, that Art was determined to make: a six-week run at the Palomar, the Los Angeles ballroom where Benny Goodman had flung open the gates to the swing era. Goodman himself was soon due into Hollywood's Cocoanut Grove. No way would Art miss a chance to beat Benny to town with a splashy debut on the site of the ex-king's first triumph. A new sulfa drug was administered; Shaw, against doctor's orders, claimed he was fit to work.

Artie and his orchestra drew 8,753 patrons on April 19, a Palomar opening-night record. But the doctors were right: it *was* too soon. Shaw fainted onstage. The next day he checked into Cedars of Lebanon hospital with a fever of 105 degrees and a strep-throat infection that became the often fatal blood disease agranulocytosis, brought on by misjudged dosages of that sulfa drug. In a semi-stupor, Art was transported to Good Samaritan Hospital for the administering of another drug flown in from the Mayo Clinic. Being prepped for treatment, he said, he heard a nurse murmur "something about one chance in a hundred." The chance took. By April 27, he was out of the woods.

The sudden collapse, the long-odds recovery—the whole sequence took on an aura of outsized drama consistent with the image of "Artie Shaw," a larger-than-life figure like a character from a book or a movie. Long live the king! And it was perfect timing to coincide with his latest Victor platter: "One Foot in the Groove."

IN YEARS to come, Shaw would say the first thing he saw after his life-saving hospital treatment was the smiling face of sixteen-year-old Judy Garland: that wonderful girl who had introduced herself to him at the Hotel Lexington in 1936. Judy had just finished shooting a big MGM musical, *The Wizard of Oz*, and already begun another, *Babes in Arms*, with young Mickey Rooney. (Some of *Babe's* vocal arrangements were being written by Claude Thornhill, newly lured to Hollywood.)

Art had many other visitors, including a chortling Robert Benchley, photographed delivering a punch line that had a propped-in-bed, back-from-the-dead Artie roaring with laughter. Also photographed in Art's room was his mother, Sarah, straight-faced and gray-haired, in L.A. on a visit. Then Shaw was shown in bed reading John Steinbeck's *In Dubious Battle*, a novel about Communist labor organizers. Freethinker Art found plenty of fuel for outrage in the thick of success; it was still a stinky-rich-kid's world. Once or twice, Shaw tried to get Benchley to join him in a discussion of Marxian economics, but the Harvard-educated writer begged off: "I can't even keep my checkbook balanced."

The band carried on without Shaw at the Palomar, and there was no slacking off at the box office. Onstage, Pastor led the band; Jerry Gray took charge during Old Gold broadcasts (now being done from Hollywood). Art was happy to let them. He had had a lot to think about: How long did he want to continue this insane life? "The one-night stands, the long brutal jumps from town to town in rainstorms and blizzards, the bottles of aspirin I had consumed to keep me going and blowing," he would write soon in a piece for the *Saturday Evening Post*. "What for? To die at twenty-eight?"

As if to underscore his point, news came from Baltimore of the death of Chick Webb, felled by a liver ailment and spinal tuberculosis at thirty-seven.

This whole carousel ride began, Shaw recalled, when an agent said Art could quit once he had made enough to write his novel. And how much money had that been three years ago? Twenty-five thousand dollars: about what he and the band earned in one month at a movie house. No, Shaw decided, he had had it. When Gray and Pastor told him how well the band was coping without him, he said, "You can keep it." He was serious; let *them* have the orchestra.

But the timing wasn't right, come to think of it. Shaw had at least two big commitments to fulfill: that lucrative RCA Victor contract and a deal to play the Hotel Pennsylvania in New York. But Shaw made up his mind he *would* call it quits in the not-distant future, once he had worked off the contracts and put that "reasonable" sum aside.

What might be a proper amount, then, in lieu of that now laughable twenty-five thousand? How about a million? That was it: Artie Shaw would quit the music business once he had a million dollars.

OUT OF the hospital, Art began to explore Hollywood in the company of Judy Garland. On a Sunday afternoon in June, Judy and Artie went to actress Dorothy Lamour's house for a garden cocktail party attended by actors, directors, and producers: Cary Grant, Randolph Scott, John Ford, Sam Goldwyn. The stolid Charlie Barnet was there, dapper as a redwood tree in a sport coat and tie; it was clear the hostess was sweet on him. Late in the evening, Lamour, a former band vocalist, sang "Moonlight and Shadows," a tune Artie had recorded with Peg La Centra a long sixteen months ago.

Garland said she had a great idea: Why didn't Artie hire Judy to sing with his band? Art had to be straight with her. "I respected her, I thought she had great talent," he said. "But she couldn't sing with my band. She was a *belter*, you know, and I didn't want it. I needed a café singer—different thing. But she had good chops, good ears." It was crazy, anyhow. Judy was now a hot studio property. MGM would never allow her to go off with a band—just as they weren't about to let Lamour and Barnet get married.

Judy just wanted an excuse to be with Art, whom she told a newspaper writer she had a "violent" crush on. Artie claimed he saw Judy as a kid sister. He liked her a lot though.

And he liked her new house: a four-bedroom place she and her mother had built on Stone Canyon Road, up above Sunset, in Bel Air, beyond Beverly Hills and halfway to the ocean. It was rural enough that they needed to put up a fence in the backyard to keep out deer. Artie, who had loved the countryside since he was a kid, was charmed.

"You could live out where there were trees, and birds, and butterflies—and still go to work at night?" he would recall realizing. "Couldn't do that in New York, which was a metropolitan experience. . . . Whereas Hollywood was a country place; still is. . . . You know, it's a different way of life. I liked that, about Hollywood: that you could live comfortably in a nice house—and go to work at night, and come home, same night. There's a new idea." Shaw soon bought a house of his own on Summit Ridge Drive, up in Benedict Canyon (where his neighbor was the noted conductor Leopold Stokowski). Artie looked forward to enjoying the pleasures of staying home.

But he was soon back leading the band at the Palomar, and on June 18, they played for twenty-six thousand people at a daytime jitterbug dance contest at the L.A. Coliseum. The same month, he and the band went into Victor's Hollywood studio to record the first sides for that two-year, $100,000 contract. In June, they cut sixteen numbers, including "Out of Nowhere" (a Johnny Green ballad), a couple of pop tunes with Helen Forrest ("Comes Love" and Art's own "Moonray"), and a killer-diller by Teddy McRae, "Traffic Jam," which would be the band's featured number in *Dancing Co-Ed*, an MGM movie they were about to make for $50,000.

The movie assignment made Art nervous. "I never had mike-fright in radio," he told the *Boston Globe*, "but I had it pretty badly in Hollywood." He masked his fear with a condescending bravado that turned the cast and crew against him.

"Artie was despised on the set because of his arrogance," wrote Lana Turner, the eighteen-year-old "hot chick" costarring in the picture. "He never missed a chance to complain that it was beneath him to appear in a Hollywood movie. The crew plotted to drop an arc light on his head."

Shaw was playing "himself" but didn't like the dialogue he was given. He tried buying his way out of the picture, but too much footage had been shot. "I'm pretty awful as an actor, but I know it," Artie told columnist Hedda Hopper. "I know a little about music, nothing about acting."

He knew what he liked about Hollywood, though: beautiful young women, many of whom hovered around Art like hummingbirds at a feeder. A production still showed Shaw, in gleaming black tux, surrounded by Lana Turner, Ann Rutherford, and June Preisser: a swing-band sultan in a high school harem. Here was his youthful Poli Palace vision come true. "All these great chicks—comin' *at* you," he said. "I was like a kid in a candy store."

THE MOST BEAUTIFUL creature he met in Hollywood, Art said, was twenty-two-year-old Betty Grable: a sometime singer, sometime dancer, sometime movie actress married to Jackie Coogan, who as a child in the 1920s had been one of the most famous screen stars in the world. In 1939, Coogan was suing his mother and stepfather for the millions of dollars he had earned as a kid. Art liked Jackie—and he really liked Betty: "She had the most gorgeous body I'd ever seen, though not much going on upstairs. A total, complete Hollywood creature."

The three of them—Jackie, Betty, Artie—did the town and were photographed together in clubs, Art with a grim grin. "You know, we're sitting there at the table," he would say, "she's rubbing her knee against me. I knew what she wanted. And then there was that body—"

Shaw called a halt to such outings, he said: "'Jackie, come on, I can't do this.' He said, 'Wadya mean?' I said, 'Your wife *likes* me, Jackie.' He said, 'Oh, she likes everybody.' I said, 'Not like *that*.'"

Then Betty telephoned: "She'd call me up, want to come over. I said, 'Not as long as you're married to Jackie.' Because he was a friend of mine."

Grable was fed up with her husband's boorish behavior. According to Coogan's biographer Diana Serra Cary, Betty came home one night to find Jackie had sold their wedding presents for "ready cash." On another evening, as a drunken "joke," he urinated on his sleeping wife. On July 17th, Grable split from Coogan.

"She called and said, 'I've left Jackie,'" Shaw said. "And so I said, 'Well come on over.'" The king of the clarinet and the budding blonde bombshell began an affair.

A DIFFERENT RIVALRY continued in July in northern California, where Shaw and Goodman "did battle" at the San Francisco Golden Gate Exposition, though this time a difference in venues precluded any "winner" from being declared. Goodman's band spent the month playing free open-air concerts on Treasure Island, twenty-five thousand spectators per show. Shaw's orchestra was booked in the Golden Gate Theatre, where they broke the house's opening-day box-office record.

Betty Grable worked San Francisco too, teaming with Jack Haley for two weeks of vaudeville singing and dancing. Broadway's Buddy DeSylva offered her a feature part in a new Cole Porter musical that would open in New Haven and Boston before going on to New York. Betty took the job. It was a nice coincidence: Artie would head east soon for bookings in Boston and New York. They would have lots of time together.

In August, the Shaw band took to the road for a string of one-nighters: Salt Lake City, Kansas City, Grand Rapids, Milwaukee, Detroit.

"I'll tell you," Buddy Rich said to Joe Smith, "it was so romantic then. . . . It was a love thing that permeated places in those days."

For sure, Rich got lots of cheers from fans. But there was little love coming Buddy's way from colleagues. The gargoyle-handsome drummer was "cocky, rashly outspoken and brutally sarcastic," Metronome's Bob Bach said. "You almost had to stand in line to be able to get a sock at him." His loud mouth was bad, but his pranks were worse—as when he stuck the stage piano's keys together with chewing gum before Bob Kitsis's solos. "Oh, he was a little prick, is what he was," Shaw said of Rich with a chortle, years later.

But there were other matters on Art's mind.

The jazz-driven swing that Goodman had pioneered and Shaw refashioned was a bit less popular now, just as Art himself was tiring of its more predictable patterns. New sounds were in the air: the loping Kansas City beat of the Count Basie orchestra, the inventive voicings of Duke Ellington's band, the sophisticated arrangements of the John Kirby Sextet (whose theme song, "Pastel Blue," was co-credited to Shaw). Meanwhile, the mainstream audience was responding to the sweeter, "whiter" sounds mocked by jazz fans as "Mickey Mouse" music: the vocal-heavy ballads of Tommy Dorsey, the cornball trickeration of Kay Kyser, and, especially, the bland musical malted milkshakes and moonlight cocktails of trombonist-arranger Glenn Miller and his popular new orchestra.

Music-biz people urged Artie (and Benny) to follow Glenn's trend of pasteurized swing, but the pablum Miller purveyed was the last thing Art would dish out. Shaw was ready for change, but his own sort. To Clarissa Start, of the St. Louis Post-Dispatch, Art said, "I've gone as far as I can with this band playing our present style. What I'd like to do is organize an American symphonic band to play American music in the swing idiom or jazz idiom or whatever you want to call it. . . . I'd use my present band as a nucleus, of course, and augment it with string instruments, woodwinds, that sort of thing."

Artie Shaw was tired of having the loudest goddam swing band in the world.

CHAPTER TWENTY

Nightmare

S HAW HADN'T been back to Boston since before "Beguine." The town's swing fans were galvanized by the band's extended engagement at the Summer Terrace of the Ritz-Carlton. On August 23, the Terrace manager told Art he was committed to perform a free concert the following afternoon on the Boston Common.

A huge crowd showed up: maybe twenty thousand people. Artie and the band played; shag-happy jitterbugs shrieked and screamed. When the show was over, as *The New Yorker's* Robert Lewis Taylor would write much later, Shaw got into a limousine with the mayor of Boston. "But the crowd, despite forty policemen in attendance, declined to open a way. Chanting, it took to rocking the car, which finally turned turtle, with a crash of glass. When Shaw had regained a measure of composure and mobility, he fought a retreating action on foot, fending off grasping hands all the way back to the Ritz. His lapels were ripped off, his jacket was split down the middle, his face was badly scratched, his hair was askew, his tie had been squeezed to a string, and his trousers were limp bags." Someone in the mob yanked out a hank of his hair. Shaw was ready to quit, million dollars or no. It took the hotel manager three hours to talk Artie into going to work that night.

. . .

SHAW WAS ALREADY nostalgic for "the early days" when the band was struggling but blessed with a special camaraderie. There had always been an extra closeness between Art and Tony Pastor. Now Tony, in the autumn of 1939, said it was time to go out on his own; thanks to Art, he had enough of a name to form his own band. Shaw understood and Tony promised to stay until Arthur found a replacement. But his close pal's imminent departure was another disappointment. Meanwhile the pace continued. On August 27, Shaw and his men took a plane from Boston to New York for a noon-to-four Victor session, then flew back the same day so as not to miss a single night of their Ritz-Carlton gig.

The orchestra was booked Labor Day evening for the Crystal Beach Ballroom in Ontario, Canada, near Buffalo, New York. Art, driving alone, got there an hour before the scheduled nine o'clock show, but the band was delayed by a slow train and then by customs and immigration. They went onstage an hour late. The show's Buffalo promoter claimed he had to refund money to patrons upset over the tardy start, and he was withholding four hundred dollars of the band's two-thousand-dollar fee. A wrangle ensued, and Art pulled the band offstage.

Twenty-five hundred attendees reacted in anger. Ballroom employee Fred Truckenbrodt described how "they went wild! . . . Then Artie Shaw wouldn't come down because of the riot, and he remained marooned upstairs. It was a disaster." Enraged patrons broke hundreds of windows. "On top of all this, it was Labor Day, the biggest day of the year for cash; and the upstairs office had all the money . . . in the safe, over half a million dollars. My father [working part-time security] was ordered to stand at the top of the stairs with a machine-gun. . . . But people were not interested in coming upstairs. They were rioting because Artie Shaw had given them a dirty deal." Canadian Provincial police arrived to restore order.

Shaw and the band went on to play without mishap at the Toronto Exposition and in Montreal, but as Art, after an all-night drive from Quebec, entered the States on September 8, he was hailed by a fellow who asked for an autograph. Shaw took the paper. It was a summons: he was being sued by the Buffalo promoter for ten thousand dollars.

A *Cleveland Press* team encountered an exhausted Artie Shaw later that day backstage at the RKO Palace, drinking black coffee and running a band rehearsal while dressed in a bathrobe and bedroom slippers. He stood still for the *Press* photographer's flash-camera, looking dazed (the *Press* reporter seemed happy to note Shaw was "shorter and heavier than he appears in pictures"), then sequestered himself in a telephone booth to call Betty Grable, who was in Cleveland too.

Years later, Shaw said, "We met one time in Cleveland, she came in at the train station. I *grabbed* her, and we went straight to the hotel. And I remember her saying to me," plaintively, "'All we ever do is *this*.' I said, 'Well, what's better?' But—later I saw, she was right."

, Quizzed by the *Cleveland Press* on his relationship with the "estranged wife of Jackie Coogan," Shaw said, "No, we're not engaged yet. Just friends." The reporter got a quote from Grable, too: "We met on the coast. We have lots of fun together. He likes my dancing and I like his music. It's not at all serious. Really."

SHAW WAS BACK in New York in late September for a week's run at the Strand. The jitterbug squads had gotten worse. Near the end of one night, an exhibitionistic male dancer flung his female partner around in the air; her shoe heels came within a hair's breadth of knocking the clarinet from Art's mouth. A furious Shaw strode offstage and into the wings, where he found Michel Mok, a *New York Post* feature columnist, who asked, "Want to talk?" Sprawling on a dressing-room sofa, loosening his thick-silk blue-and-white tie, bourbon-and-water in hand, Art began to let off steam.

"I don't like the damned music business," he said. "The music business stinks—and you can quote me! . . . In a month and a half they haven't given me a minute to work out something worth-while with my band. . . . They won't give you a chance to breathe. . . .

"And I don't like the crowds. I'm not interested in giving people what they want—I'm interested in making music. Autograph hunters? To hell with them! . . . Nothing doing! I'm too busy with my job. . . . My friends, my advisers tell me that I'm a damned fool. 'Look here, Artie,' they say, 'you can't do that! Those people *made* you!' Want to know my answer? I tell them, 'If I was made by a bunch of morons, that's just too bad.'"

Mok's piece, titled "A Band Leader THINKS," caused a sensation when it was printed on September 26. The word "morons" provoked outrage and in particular irked Shaw's radio sponsor. "Modern as a Jitterbug" was one of the phrases Old Gold was using to pitch its 1939 "Double-Mellow" cigarettes to "fashionable" young consumers. "Modern as a Moron" didn't sound quite so good.

Shaw's efforts to clarify his remarks prolonged the controversy. Regarding jitterbugs, he told *Metronome*, "I meant the ones who continually yank at your coat and who keep shouting at the band all night long so that you can't concentrate. . . . There's only one in a hundred in any group of dancers; and if they're the ones who are sore at me, I don't care. They should be told off, both for music's sake and for the other ninety-nine dancers who know how to act." Of his interview with Mok: "Everything I said, I feel. Frankly, I'm unhappy in the music business. Maybe I don't even belong in it. I like the music part—love it and live it, in fact—but for me the business part plain stinks!"

Old Gold and CBS got so much angry mail from listeners that the sponsor, the network, and Shaw all agreed he should leave *Melody and Madness* mid-season. In public, Artie claimed it a blessing. "The show was built all wrong for me," he told *Metronome*. "Besides, it was on a weak network, thus killing its rating. . . . When I asked for a one-week vacation because I was so tired, and they wouldn't give it to me unless I quit the show entirely, I quit the show entirely." Old Gold's ad agency put it this way: "He asked us for a week's rest, so we gave him seven."

ON SUNDAY, October 8, Art arrived in L.A. by rail, getting off the same Union Pacific Streamliner as Betty Grable. Photographers wanted the two to pose together, but they refused, despite the urging of Betty's mother, also present: "Why don't you? You've got nothing to be ashamed of."

Grable was in town for the court hearing on her divorce from Jackie

Coogan. An interlocutory decree was granted on grounds of extreme cruelty, with the divorce to become final in a year. Reporters asked Grable if she would now marry Shaw; Betty echoed Artie: "We are just friends." Grable and Shaw were photographed together the next day, though, enjoying themselves at the Brown Derby: Betty pointing to the camera and looking with glee at Artie, who grinned straight at the lens like the cat who stole the canary.

After Grable got her decree, as Shaw told it much later, Art got a visit at his L.A. digs from a distraught Jackie Coogan, who showed up drunk—and armed.

"He comes in with a gun in his hand," Shaw said. "I told him, 'Come on, Jackie—she didn't leave you because o' me; I was just an excuse. She'd have left you anyway, you know that.'

"He says, 'Give me one good reason why I shouldn't shoot you.'

"I said, 'Oh, I'll give you a couple. One, I don't *want* you to. Two, *you* don't want to. Think of all that would entail.' He thought about it—said, 'Yeah,' and put the gun down.

"And we stayed friends, for the rest of his life."

"Well—" Art thought about it. "Friend-*ly*."

BETTY GRABLE told Sidney Skolsky, "I can't marry for a year, until the divorce becomes final. I *will* say that I like Artie very much, and if we feel the same way a year from now I'll marry him." She and Shaw took the same Twentieth Century train to Manhattan, arriving October 16.

Art's next engagement was a three-month stand in the Hotel Pennsylvania, where Benny Goodman had held forth for seven solid months in 1936 and 1937. Art's press agents got busy. In the days before Shaw's opening on October 19 at the new Café Rouge, two major pieces on Shaw were printed in *Down Beat* and *Esquire*. They were sympathetic explications of his personality and actions, both of which made reference to his eventual retirement—with *Esquire* quoting Artie guessing it would happen in three years, while *Down Beat*'s Dave Dexter Jr. stated without doubt, "That time isn't far off."

New Yorkers turned out in force for Art's opening night. Shaw went out of his way to be nice to dancers and autograph seekers. The jitter-bugs kept coming, week after week; the band was a solid hit. But at the height of this triumph, Art endured a misery of doubt.

"It's funny," he told an interviewer from the *Clarinet* magazine, years later. "I didn't think I'd done anything worthwhile. . . . I had a very screwed-up opinion of myself. In short, if I did it, it couldn't really be much good. I felt I was kidding people, that they were being taken in by me. Even at the peak of my success part of me kept saying, 'Oh well, that's okay but I don't really value any of it.'" It would take five years and a world war before Art Shaw would begin to realize such feelings had tenterhooks in a forlorn childhood spent with a father who held Art's music in contempt.

Even as Art felt like an imposter, he was being encouraged by others to see himself as extraordinary. "Big star—everybody bows and scrapes," he said. "And the trouble is: people really *do* look at you and—bow and scrape. So, what are you gonna say? I went through that wringer."

One afternoon, out driving with one of his managers, Art glimpsed a new Packard in a showroom window: a neat red roadster, not unlike his first car—the one in which he had driven away from his dreary childhood.

"Stop!" Shaw commanded. "*That's* what I want! Buy me that—right now!"

But that makes no sense, the manager said, take your time, shop around. "So I fired him on the spot," Shaw said, with a little laugh part embarrassed and part still proud. "Sure. Couldn't have my judgment—my authority questioned."

He bought the car.

WHAT WAS the fun of having money and clout, if you couldn't use them?

But new problems cropped up every day. In November, *Variety* reported that Eli Oberstein, former artists-and-repertoire chief at RCA

Victor, was suing Art for $30,000, for professional advice he said he gave Shaw between April 1937 and May 1938; and for ten percent of Shaw's earnings from May to December 1938. (Shaw's lawyers claimed Oberstein's deal with Art was illegal and "made under duress.")

And there were orchestra problems, Art felt. "The band's morale is still high, thank God, though there are a couple of guys who feel they're too important," he told *Metronome*. "That'll have to change. No prima donnas in this band!"

Buddy Rich had begun "going off on his own" in his playing, "doing things that were good for him but not for the band." Shaw didn't fire Rich outright: "With me, it was a little different: I'd talk to the guy. I called Buddy in and said, 'Who are you playing for: you, or the band?' He said, 'Well, I guess—me.' I says, 'Buddy, you know, you're not gonna *like* it here, if you stay long.' I never fired him. He said, 'Wadya *mean*?' I said, 'Well I'm gonna be on your *ass*; I'll be *ridin'* you, Buddy. You're not gonna be *happy*.' He says, 'Well *Tommy* [Dorsey] wants me.' I said, 'Go.' So he went; that was it."

Shaw got drummer Ralph Hawkins to give two weeks' notice to Harry James; Hawkins joined Art's band mid-November.

Café Rouge crowds were still capacity. But Artie was often feeling rotten. Some nights he sat out the first several numbers. He had headaches, stomachaches. He kept saying he needed a vacation, but his managers told him that wasn't possible: he and the band were booked into 1940.

ART FULFILLED another obligation on November 15, performing at the sixth annual "Night of Stars" show in Madison Square Garden on behalf of the United Palestine Appeal. It was a gala event with a hundred headliners, from jazz players to theater people to movie actors to sports stars. There was also the greatest classical fiddler in the world.

When he heard Jascha Heifetz play, Shaw said, he couldn't believe his ears: "I thought, *holy Jesus!* You know—there are a lotta violin players, but he could do things that nobody was doing—nobody could *do*. But he'd—*hear* things, and he'd *shade* things in his playing, in a way that you said, 'This guy is *thinking*. He's not just playing *notes*. He's *feeling* somethin' happen.' Those are the—subtleties that make the difference. But the *audience* doesn't know that; they don't hear that. The only guy who can really appreciate a fine musician—is another fine musician."

Heifetz and his pianist performed Bach's "Air on a G String," and it was the most remarkable thing Art ever heard. The fiddler got a countermelody going, using two fingers of his left hand, that created an extraordinary effect of eerie beauty. Art couldn't help but go back to Heifetz's dressing room afterward. "Jascha," he presumed, "that was really—magnificent."

"Oh really?" Heifetz asked. "I thought it was—a little bit off."

No false modesty; Heifetz was serious. Art looked at him: a rather bleak-looking figure, standing in his terrycloth robe, frozen smile in place, sweating a little.

Art had an epiphany.

"I realized that Heifetz was aiming at a hundred," he told Gary Giddins years later, "and he probably hits ninety-four regularly. So that night he only hit a ninety-three, and it bothered him. There's not much difference, but he can hear it. And it's the same with the clarinet. If you really play honestly, if you're cursed with that, and you take even one day off, then you can't hit ninety-four."

Art couldn't stand to play less than his best; that's one reason why he stayed away from the bandstand until he felt ready. But if he kept aiming for a hundred, sooner or later the pressure would kill him.

"So that's why I quit," he concluded.

Then he added (just to make things clearer or more obscure), "Of all the reasons I've ever given for quitting—that one's closest to the truth."

HE NEVER SAID what the final provocation was, but it came in the Café Rouge room of the Hotel Pennsylvania around eleven at night on Tuesday, November 14. Was it someone jabbing his leg with a pin? Asking him to sign an autograph on a wet napkin? Maybe someone taunting: "You know, we *made* you!"

"At the stage I was then in," he'd write, "any little thing would have been sufficient; and so, because of a slight unpleasantness with some idiot on the floor in front of the band . . . I suddenly decided I'd had it. Instead of kicking him in the teeth, I walked off the bandstand."

"When we finished the set," Helen Forrest wrote, "Tony got a message that Artie wanted to see us in his room upstairs in the hotel. We all went up and crowded in and there was Artie, bags partly packed, clothes strewn around the room, propped up in bed. He said, 'I'm leaving the band.' Tony asked, 'Are you sick?' And Artie said, 'No, just sick of the business. And I'm finished with it forever.' We just stood and stared at him. We couldn't believe it. Someone said, 'You've got a million dollars' worth of bookings.' Artie said, 'I don't give a damn about that.' Someone said, 'They could sue.' Artie said, 'Let 'em sue. If I don't have a band, what're they going to sue me for?'"

He called his lawyer, Andrew Weinberger, who rushed over from Long Island. Also quick to arrive was agent Tommy Rockwell. They discussed, argued, pleaded. Rockwell promised Shaw that if he would just keep working another two years, he'd never have to worry about money the rest of his life. Art said, "If I stay two more years, I won't be *able* to worry anymore."

Talking continued for days; each night the band played without Artie. Patrons were given no explanation. The idea formed of the band becoming a cooperative unit, with Shaw donating existing arrangements. Who wanted to be leader, Art asked: Tony? Georgie? He even asked Helen; why not? Ella took over Chick Webb's orchestra, didn't she?

Tony said he would lead the co-op band, but others had different ideas.

According to Pastor's nephew Joe Tauro, "When Shaw broke up, Si Shribman, the band booker, made a date to come to see Tony Pastor at his summer cottage in Hartford; my aunt Dorothy [Tony's wife] told me this story. Si Shribman wanted to hire Tony to play tenor sax for the

Glenn Miller band. They were waiting for Tony to get dressed and come downstairs; and my aunt Dorothy said to Si Shribman, 'Mr. Shribman, if Tony Pastor can do it for Glenn Miller, he can do it for himself. You let him have his *own* band.' When Tony came downstairs, Shribman said, 'You know your wife thinks that *you* oughta have a band.' And that's exactly how it happened."

Georgie Auld was voted new head of the co-op orchestra.

Benny Goodman was happy to hire Helen Forrest—as long as she accepted a cut in pay from Artie's $175 a week to Benny's $85. "I took it," she wrote. "I wanted to work."

Some of the men in the band resented Art's decision; others were proud of him for doing what he thought he needed to do. "It was like the end of the world," Les Robinson said. "I damn near cried." Art got in touch with his mother, to make sure she had enough cash. He told Tommy Rockwell he intended to "go away and meditate"—probably in Mexico, but maybe in the South Sea Islands. On Tuesday, November 21, he was ready to leave—in the Packard roadster he had bought on impulse.

He of all people knew what he was abandoning. "It was a bitch of a band," he would say. "It breathed together, thought together, played together. It was as close to black music as a white band can get. I never played better. . . . At that time I became an artist." As *Billboard* had written a couple of months earlier, "The crew is billed as the band of the year, but in sober truth they rate with the great pop aggregations of all time."

"There we were," Georgie Auld said. "Artie got into his red Packard and drove off. And suddenly I was a band leader."

CHAPTER TWENTY-ONE

Over the Rainbow

ARTIE SHAW'S abdication from the kingdom of swing was front-page news, prompting a range of reactions from stunned to outraged to admiring.

His exit stirred mixed feelings in Shaw too. Yes, he had warned people he'd quit the business once he had a million dollars. But he also said all he really wanted was a vacation. And while it was one thing to walk out on a string of one-nighters and a bunch of hotel gigs, it was quite another to tell a major record company to go take a hike.

Shaw knew all along, in the back and front of his mind, that sooner or later he would have to return. But when he did, it would be on his terms: with the sort of outfit he had been talking about for a while.

There it was, hidden in plain sight on the front page of *Variety*, in the midst of the storm of controversy over Shaw's vanishing act: a precise summary of his future plans. "Artie Shaw, Jivist, Will Do Comeback as String Dance Band" was the headline of a story saying that Shaw in time would head "a string dance combo, backed by a hot clarinet (meaning himself) . . . a complete switch for one of the country's topflight out-of-this world swingologists." It was "no secret," the piece went on, "Shaw isn't serious about retiring professionally despite his walkout."

Even the *New York Times* reported, "Mr. Shaw, it was said, would organize a new band on his return from Mexico several months hence."

But talk of Shaw's comeback got less notice than reports of his dramatic departure, which convinced even the people closest to Art. "It was a big surprise," said Joseph Tauro. "And everybody thought it was for *real*, and for *good*."

For now, Shaw was free and on his own. But even in self-imposed exile in a foreign country, he couldn't escape the klieg light of publicity.

IT HAPPENED on a beach called Pie de la Cuesta, in the sleepy fishing village of Acapulco, Mexico.

The surf there was extraordinary. Shaw was on the beach one day when he witnessed a teenaged girl being knocked down and pulled out to sea by a wave. He plunged in after her and was pulling her back by her wrist when a much larger wave rose up and crashed down on them both, flinging them up on the beach. The girl was all right, but Art's right leg was throbbing with pain. He was taken to Mexico City for treatment.

Shaw's kneecap, banged on the rocky shore, was fractured in four places; he had torn several ligaments. The mishap put him back in the headlines—"Artie Shaw Saves Girl from Death"—and soured him on his south-of-the-border trip.

"I could have bought, *did* buy, a beautiful piece of land in Mexico, for five thousand dollars," he said. "Two rocks thrown up against one another: great site for a house. Had plans drawn up; still have 'em. But I [hurt] my leg, rescuing a girl—got discouraged, wanted my money back. The fella I'd bought it from—one of the major developers of Acapulco—gave it back; said, 'You're foolish.' Later, that became the site of the United States Hotel. But I figured, what's the point of having a house down there if I'm never going to go back? And I never *did* go back."

But he did return to music.

Shaw was an adept improviser, in life as in jazz; deft entrances and exits were his specialties. His leaving the scene had all but stopped the show, prompting the *New York Times* to editorialize, "Any commentary that might occur to us would be lost in our sense of admiration at the Shakespearean sweep of Mr. Shaw's exodus. . . ."

But the exodus was brief. In the middle of January, 1940, his knee in a cast, Shaw flew to L.A. to ease back into a career he had never quite intended to abandon for good.

JUST IN THIS short time, much had happened.

Claude Thornhill had returned to New York and become a bandleader.

Bunny Berigan, induced in 1938 to form an orchestra in the wake of his success as a soloist with Goodman's and Dorsey's outfits, had gone bankrupt, folded his band, and rejoined Tommy's.

"He didn't have the quality that it took," Shaw said of Berigan. "Certain people don't. Bunny could play the *hell* out of a trumpet; couldn't lead a band. Jack Teagarden couldn't lead a band; tried. Tommy Dorsey *could*. Jimmy Dorsey *couldn't*." (Though he did anyway.) "It's a quality of—sort of, self-assertiveness. Plus, the ability to be able to—*get* something out of the men, that they didn't know they *had*."

Tommy Dorsey hired a new boy singer, twenty-four-year-old Frank Sinatra, from the Harry James band. (Sinatra's audition piece for Dorsey was "Begin the Beguine.")

Georgie Auld carried on as leader of the Shaw co-op unit.

Tony Pastor and his band cut their first singles for Bluebird.

Glenn Miller's ensemble continued to sell lots and lots of records.

But the outfit of most interest to Shaw, as always, was Benny Goodman's, which had won both the *Down Beat* and *Metronome* readers' polls for 1939. Benny was suffering with sciatica. He canceled several weeks' work and decamped to Hot Springs, Arkansas, vowing he would open at Hollywood's Cocoanut Grove in March.

UP ON Summit Ridge Drive, his knee on the mend, Artie Shaw was lonesome.

He wanted to see Judy Garland again, but Judy's mother wasn't keen on her seventeen-year-old daughter palling around anymore with this notorious and maybe unstable twenty-nine-year-old character. Judy found a solution. She asked young actor Jackie Cooper if he would pretend to be dating her: pick her up in his car, take her where she could meet Artie, then later bring her home. Cooper did this for a while, until he started dating another girl. After that, one of Judy's sisters pretended Judy was at *her* house.

Art and Judy took long drives in the jasmine- and sage- and orange blossom–scented air. Judy found Artie handsome, brilliant, funny, appreciative. For Art, Judy was enchanting, talented, and smart enough to *talk* to. She lapped it up and said to her sister, "If only he'd ask me to marry him."

Art talked about Judy to Phil Silvers, a New York comic brought out to L.A. by MGM. Phil was friends with Judy too; he was also close to Betty Grable (as was his and Art's New York songwriter-pal Sammy Cahn).

Grable, continuing on Broadway in *Du Barry Was a Lady*, kept a warm place in her heart for Shaw, who still fed Betty's torch with romantic letters from the West Coast, which Grable read aloud to Cahn in her dressing room at the Forty-sixth Street Theatre.

Up on Summit Ridge Drive, Shaw talked about Grable too, Silvers wrote:

> [Artie] complained that he was sick of being separated from Betty. "What does she really want? The gold pants? The tinsel? Or me? I make enough to take care of her."
>
> "Did you ever tell her that?" I asked.
>
> He thought a minute. "No."
>
> I suggested he write a letter telling her exactly where he stood.
>
> And he did.

A few days later, though, on Monday, February 12, Phil suggested that Art drive with him over to Metro, where Silvers was under contract. The two men walked onto the set of *Two Girls on Broadway*, a production costarring Lana Turner, who had just turned nineteen. Lana veered straight for Art, Phil wrote, "like a bee making for the honey." This wasn't the testy girl Shaw had worked with last year but a beguiling creature in a green-satin gown so tight it looked painted on. Art asked her to dinner. She suggested lunch sometime.

Shaw went home but was restless. He found a phone number for another actress from *Dancing Co-Ed*, and called to ask her out. Her mother answered—and warned Shaw to stay away from her daughter.

Art's thoughts returned to Lana. Boy, was she hot!

Lana had just gotten off the phone with Greg Bautzer, the Hollywood lawyer alleged to be her fiancé; she and Greg were to have gone out that night, but Bautzer had called to cancel. A moment later, her phone rang again: Artie Shaw. Lana, furious with Bautzer, said she would go to dinner with Art.

Shaw asked Phil Silvers to accompany them "because she might bring me down." ("He was always afraid of rejection on some level," his later friend Jan Curran said, "especially with intimacy.") The three drove to Victor Hugo's, a Beverly Hills supper-club Lana chose. The band, Silvers said, was Guy Lombardo's Royal Canadians: the same Mickey Mouse orchestra that got its start in Cleveland across the street from Austin Wylie. "Lombardo's musicians," Silvers wrote, "in awe of Artie, tootled as if their fingers were stuck on fly paper."

Shaw began unreeling to Turner a line Silvers had heard before: how he was sick and tired of these phony Hollywood females; what he wanted was a girl who could be happy with him alone. That night, Silvers wrote, Turner returned Shaw's serves, saying, "That's exactly what *I* want: a man who has the brains to be satisfied with me only." To the teenaged Turner, upset with a cavalier fiancé, the picture Shaw painted was the one she had to have. "Artie built me a romantic dream," she would write, "with a white picket fence around it. His eloquence stirred me, and the evening took on a romantic glow as we parked in a spot overlooking the ocean."

Holding hands with Lana, Artie spoke of his hopes and dreams:

"about the concert orchestra he was planning . . . about how he wanted to write music and someday write books. . . . What he wanted now were the basic things—a good, solid marriage, a home, and children." *Me, too,* Lana said.

"It was a dare," Artie said later. "We played chicken, you know: 'You wouldn't.' 'Yes I would.' 'Naw, you would not, you're just talkin'.' . . . Didn't know what the hell we were doing; I had no idea. I had that whole myth—American myth—'Somebody to come home to.' We had heard all that stuff about the wife and kids—'somebody to—'Aw, it was all—very stupid."

A strange thing was happening, with or without Art's awareness: Four years earlier, Shaw had sat in New York's Onyx Club with Claude Thornhill and watched Charlie Barnet turn an instant infatuation with a pretty vocalist into a spur-of-the-moment marriage proposal, which was accepted and instantly acted on. Artie and Claude accompanied Charlie and the girl that night by train to Montauk, New York, where couples could wed without waiting for a license; Shaw was Barnet's best man. (The marriage was never consummated and soon annulled.) Here in Hollywood, Shaw seemed to be reenacting that event—with himself in Barnet's role, and Silvers playing Claude.

"I married these women," Art said of his wives near the end of his life, "each time thinking this was the *one.* I was *serious* about it." Lana was as desirable a woman as any man might come home to. "I thought, *you* know, 'Why *not?* What's wrong with it. We'll make it work.' We had that sense of—my analyst, my first analyst, used to call it 'omnipotence.'"

Julia Jean Mildred Frances Turner had a sense of preordained omnipotence to match Arthur Jacob Arshawsky's: "It was destined to happen like this." Lana too wanted to live happily ever after—and to get even with Gregson Bautzer.

By now it was Tuesday. Art and Lana drove to the Burbank airport and at one in the morning chartered a plane to Las Vegas. Silvers didn't want to fly; he returned Art's car to Summit Ridge Drive.

In Vegas, the wedding party (pilot included) procured a marriage license and took a cab to a justice of the peace, who at four in the morning joined Art Shaw and Lana Turner in legal matrimony, with pilot and taxi driver as witnesses and Artie's blue-sapphire-and-platinum pinkie ring as Lana's wedding band. "There I was," Art recalled feeling years later, "a little guy from the Lower East Side, with this ravishing creature."

Turner sent her mother a telegram saying she just got married.

By the time Artie and Lana flew back to Burbank and pulled up in a cab to Summit Ridge Drive, the street was full of reporters and photographers. Shaw erupted. Lana said, "I had never heard cursing like that before. . . . [I]t was worse than he'd ever been on the set." Art dragged his bride inside his house and slammed and locked the door. The press pounded to be let in. A window broke.

Shaw and Turner were under siege. MGM sent people to sweet-talk the press into leaving, with promises of a visit soon. At midnight, Art and Lana sneaked over to Art's movie producer friend Edgar Selwyn's house. There, in the flower-filled guestroom, in the early hours of Valentine's Day, the newlyweds made love.

After breakfast, the couple went to Summit Ridge Drive to meet the press. Lana, in the same navy-blue dress she had worn to dinner Monday, hadn't had much sleep, but fatigue gave her a heightened allure as she half-gazed through slumbrous lids. Artie—back straight, jaw firm, mouth set—was Dreiser's *Genius* in a tweed sports jacket.

Judy Garland read the news in the morning paper. Her sobs brought her mother on the run. Judy spilled the secret of her friendship with Art. An irate parent reached Shaw by phone and read him the riot act. "I never *touched* your daughter!" Shaw insisted. But still he broke her heart.

AND WHAT of the woman who had left Jackie Coogan to be with Artie Shaw? Why, Art was asked years later, didn't he marry Betty Grable?

His face assumed a look of irritated candor. "She wasn't a *lady*. I was very much into the idea of wanting—that a woman should be a *lady*; I learned that later in analysis. Betty was rather—*coarse*. Lana was much closer to my idea of what a lady should be." To live in a castle, even one with a picket fence, a wife should have a regal air. The earthy Betty Grable, who swore like Tommy Dorsey and practically felt you up under the table, did not fill that bill. The divine Lana Turner, with her air of poise and entitlement, did—or at least *seemed* to.

"Does that," Artie Shaw asked his interrogator, "answer your *question?*"

CHAPTER TWENTY-TWO

Summit Ridge Drive

AFRICAN-AMERICAN orchestrator–composer William Grant Still was a talent of the first order; he had "done it all," from vaudeville to Broadway to the movie studios to the Hollywood Bowl. Bill Still had written arrangements for W. C. Handy and for Paul Whiteman. His own long-form pieces had been played on the concert stage. He was the first man of color in America to lead a symphony in public performance of his own work.

But Art knew Bill Still from working with him in New York radio, six years ago. This was the man Shaw asked to orchestrate half-a-dozen numbers for his "comeback" session at Victor on Sunday evening, March 3, 1940.

The thirty-two-piece orchestra included some of the best studio musicians now on the West Coast, among them some recent New York transplants who knew Shaw well: trumpeters Manny Klein and Charlie Margulis and violinist Harry Bluestone. Altogether there were six brass, four saxes, a bass clarinet, a flute, an oboe, a French horn, fourteen string-players, four rhythm, plus Shaw's clarinet. Artie wanted to create something beautiful that would also be a hit.

"Oh I believe strongly in success," he would say. "Success enables you to do what you'd like to do. But you don't want to keep doing the same thing over and over again. . . . That's why I kept quitting. The audience would get to where they liked what I did to the point where they wouldn't let me keep growing. And you know, it's very uncomfortable to have a suit that's too tight. . . . So I added strings—which *no one* had ever thought of doing . . . strings and French horns."

Shaw was fit and rested, tanned from Mexico, his white teeth flashing in a wide grin; he looked dashing, in shirt and tie, as he prepared to lead this orchestra in music he hoped would rock the popular-music world on its ear.

The first number cut was "Frenesi": a tune Shaw heard played so often by an Acapulco-restaurant mariachi band that he had memorized it. His and Still's rendering with full orchestra was a revelation. A three-bar intro of strings above tom-toms set the tone for something new under the dance-band sun. Art's clarinet sang the melody for sixteen bars above a magic carpet of cellos, violins, and violas. The French and other horns took the eight-bar bridge, then Art returned with an enchanting eight-bar variation. There was joy in Shaw's playing—a percolating pleasure, an impeccable grace. Strings and woodwinds mingled in sophisticated interplay. At a mere three minutes and three seconds "Frenesi" was done: an enticing mix of Latin, swing, and concert elements that left you refreshed yet wanting more.

"Adios Marquita Linda," another tune from Mexico, began with violins. Not until ninety seconds into this three-and-a-half-minute number did Art's clarinet ornament the theme. His playing had tang, like lemon icing on a cake. Classical instruments ended the piece with a dark-toned coda. No doubt about it: this would be the A-side of Shaw's next 78. "We thought it was gonna be big," Art said. "You just never know."

The day's first song with a singer was "Gloomy Sunday," a mordant Hungarian number that had kicked around Tin Pan Alley for years. It was a morbid item, a suicide note. Not everyone had the vocal and emotional chops for it, but Shaw, with his ear and eye for talent, had found the right singer. Pauline Byrne was lead voice with Six Hits and a Miss, an innovative vocal group on Bob Hope's *Pepsodent* radio program (broadcasts of which Art had attended with Judy Garland). Art plucked Pauline to be solo vocalist on his Victor session.

"Gloomy Sunday" had a superb Still arrangement. Art's sinuous clarinet conjured the hypnotic melody like a snake rising from a basket. Byrne's voice evoked Eros and Thanatos as she promised her departed lover that the black coach of sorrow would bring her soon, through death, to his side. Klein's muted trumpet played obbligato counterpoint to the singer's sacrilegious kaddish. As the singer left the spotlight, the band kicked into wailing mode, giving out with a demonic cakewalk, a suicide shag, a gavotte to the scaffold. Then the unholy wedding march paused, the clarinet reared back—and the cobra struck!

WITH SIX dynamite sides done, and his wife having finished work in her latest MGM movie, Shaw took Turner to New York the last week of March for another installment of their "honeymoon."

"Look, baby," a wire-service reporter heard Art tell Lana in their twenty-first-floor suite at Manhattan's Sherry-Netherland, "I'll be damned if you're going to have the usual Hollywood tour of New York: from the Stork Club to El Morocco to 21 to Monte Carlo and back again. By the time I get through with you, you'll have seen something!"

"Yes, dear," Lana said.

Highlights of Shaw's planned itinerary included Staten Island, the aquarium, the Statue of Liberty, and Grant's Tomb. But first Art took his bride to view his childhood haunts on Avenue C in the Lower East Side. "Do her good to see how the other half lives under the stinking conditions we call civilization," the former Arthur Arshawsky said. Art introduced Lana to "two of his aged feminine relatives" (probably a favorite aunt and cousin), but he kept his mother out of sight. As Turner remembered it, Shaw was furious after she went alone to visit Sarah.

Dr. Colter Rule, a physician and psychiatrist who would later become friends with Shaw, said Art's relationship with his mother was always strained: "I think he was ashamed of her and resented having to take care of her in many ways. He was ashamed of himself, and his background; I don't think that's too unusual. You know you like to think—like all my classmates and schoolmates—'I am to the manner born, and am entitled to this honored position.' And if you have to absolutely question your origins—right? Poor Artie's father left, and his mother was a seamstress, and this was it. It's not much of a foundation for status, is it? He didn't *have* any. But he *did* have fight, and he did have a good head, and he did have musical talent—and he *built* somethin' out of it. So, it's a remarkable story."

But not one Art was eager to share with his brand-new wife.

LANA WAS obviously closer to her mother than Art was to his. But there were days, once the Shaws returned to Summit Ridge Drive, when even she wanted to put distance between herself and her surviving parent. "Her mother used to come busting in all the time at very odd or inconvenient moments," Art said. "And Lana didn't want it anymore than I did. And I said, 'I'll fix it; you wanna let me fix it?' She said, 'Sure.' I said, 'The next time your mother comes, I'll have Herbie'—my cook-valet-housekeeper guy—'he'll let me know she's at the door.' So he did. And I stripped buck-naked—and went to the door, and opened the door. I said, 'Oh, Mildred, I didn't know—' She *shrieked*, and left. And after that, she called, before she came.

"Lana thought that was very funny; she giggled. How to get rid of a pest, huh."

"DELUXE SWING" is what the record company tagged Shaw's innovative new music. The public was quick to pick "Frenesi" over "Adios Marquita Linda" (maybe because the clarinet entered sooner) and make it the hit of the summer, then of the year, then of an era. Like "Begin the Beguine," "Frenesi" sold and sold and sold. Shaw's career was back on track, in high gear—and on *his* terms.

Lana (despite her avowal that she didn't care about making movies) started a new MGM picture with Lew Ayres. Shaw quashed rumors he might costar in a film with his wife but said he was glad for her to stay in front of the cameras: "He doesn't want Lana Turner to give up her career, but thinks she'd be happier working," Hedda Hopper wrote. "Then, if anything should happen she'd never be able to blame him for interfering with her screen work."

SHAW SEALED a deal to appear, with orchestra, on radio's weekly *George Burns and Gracie Allen Show*, starting July 1. Shaw now had to assemble a working band with which to rehearse, broadcast four times a month, and maybe tour with. He had a cheeky idea: Why not ask Tony Pastor if Art could take over *his* new outfit? Shaw's old pal's ensemble had been together six months, long enough to work well as a unit.

Tony and his men were in Southern California to play the Casa Manana, near MGM. "It was one of the first contacts that they'd had, after Tony left Artie's band," Joe Tauro said. "Artie came in and asked Tony if Tony would mind him talking to the musicians. Tony, gracious as he was, said, 'Sure, go ahead.' So they all went out on the terrace, and Artie made the pitch. And the guys in the band took a vote—and they said, 'No, we're gonna stay with Tony.' Which was, you know, a very very nice thing. I remember Tony tellin' that story with great satisfaction; very proud of that."

Shaw didn't miss a beat. He would find the nucleus of his new band in an even more promising outfit.

Benny Goodman, playing on Southern California's Catalina Island, was still having such bad back trouble that he left mid-engagement for an operation at the Mayo Clinic. Artie Shaw, Kay Kyser, and other leaders took turns fronting Goodman's outfit for the rest of his booking. "[Benny] says, 'I don't know when I'm coming back; it may be in the fall or something like that,'" tenor-saxophonist Jerry Jerome told Monk Rowe. "This was summertime; and he said, 'I'll call you.' But meanwhile, all six of us joined Artie Shaw; the day after we left Catalina, he was waiting for us: [trombonist] Vernon Brown, myself, [drummer] Nick Fatool, [altoist and Shaw veteran] Les Robinson."

Leaders had been pillaging one another's ranks for years; it was standard swing-era practice. This move by Shaw wasn't even a raid, as such: Goodman had in effect disbanded. Artie also acquired Johnny Guarnieri, an excellent young pianist Goodman hadn't liked much. And from Bob Crosby, Shaw got Billy Butterfield, a terrific first trumpet-player of the period who could really swing a band.

To sing, Artie hired Anita Boyer, a clear-toned vocalist who had worked for Tommy Dorsey. To do arrangements, he took on Lennie Hayton, for whom Art had worked in New York radio and whose writing experience went back to Whiteman; William Grant Still, that other Whiteman alum, would also do charts.

AS HIS MUSIC world coalesced, though, his home life was coming apart.

The friction had begun as soon as Lana moved into Summit Ridge Drive, which was short of closet space (at least by a starlet's standards). Mrs. Shaw needed a whole bedroom to store her clothes—and another bedroom just for her *shoes*. While Art couldn't tell his wife to get rid of her wardrobe, he did insist she not be done up like an MGM actress when she was at home. No makeup in the house, he decreed; and he insisted she was always to wear just a simple skirt, blouse, and loafers. And there were other rules. "By the third day of our marriage," Lana said, "I knew I was in trouble."

For Art, it took longer. But it dawned on him with a thud: Lana was no Judy. Lana didn't love books. Lana was of humble background, a girl who had had some tough years before being "discovered" by a movie-biz hot shot. Of course she would put her career first; it meant everything to her.

"Lana used to thrust out her bosom like a pouter pigeon," Art said, "when some guy was around; they would stand at attention. That was what she *had*; that was her *merchandise*. I would note it—though I didn't really care about it. We were only really married, in the sense of being together, three or four months. Didn't even last that long."

But what vexed him most was how *stupid* he thought she was; or rather, how stupid *he* had been for marrying someone like her: a girl who thought her work was on an equal plane with his—which, by his lights, it most certainly was *not*.

And when she wouldn't cater to his wants and needs—when she came in late and went to bed early, to get up in time to go back to the studio—he lost face in front of his friends. Why shouldn't the wife serve the husband? Did she think the husband served the wife? Damned if he would be her vassal, like his father had been Sarah's.

Art caused humiliating scenes, Lana said: demanding she make dinner after her day at work, then in disgust throwing what she served on the carpet and saying, "Clean up that mess."

"He told me," Jan Curran said, "he came home one day, and there Lana was with her hair needing to be done; and he said to her, her hair looked terrible. And she said, 'Well did you marry me for my *looks*?' And he said, '*Yes*.' Well—cut her to the quick: there wasn't anything *about* her he liked, 'cept to *look* at her. That's a *mean* thing to *say* to someone."

It made Art mad when life didn't give him what he wanted, *right now*. Thwarted by a door, he would bust it down. If he forgot his keys, he broke a window. Miffed by a marriage that didn't work, he fell back on patterns learned from a mother who complained and manipulated and a father who stepped on dreams.

"We lived in the little cottage of my fantasy," Turner wrote, "but without two loving people inside it."

"I saw marriage as a long cat-fight," Shaw admitted late in life, "because that's how I grew up."

LANA LEFT HIM on Saturday, June 29.

On Monday, July 1, Art needed a favor: He and his band were making their debut on the Burns and Allen show. Art's handlers, mindful he had had to quit the Old Gold program in the wake of his moronic-jitterbugs remark, didn't want Shaw to lose another series through controversy. Would Lana come pose with Art after the broadcast, to show she and he were still a happy couple?

Lana was there Monday night in the NBC radio studio at Sunset and Vine when the Burns and Allen show went off the air. Artie and Lana stood side by side in front of photographers and reporters. Red-headed Lana was dressed in all black. She put her arm around Art and smiled, but when someone asked, "Won't you please kiss him?" she balked: "Kiss him! I've just *left* him."

It was "one of the wildest-eyed interviews ever held in Hollywood," claimed United Press correspondent Fred Othman, with Turner spilling the beans of their estrangement even as she squeezed Shaw's hand.

All they had ever done was fight, she said. That wasn't true, he parried. Back and forth they went—she saying she had her own apartment, he claiming they lived together—until Lana said, "Goodbye," and left. United Press quoted Artie's last word: "*Whew.*"

Married for Valentine's Day, she had declared independence in time for the Fourth of July. She and Art let attorney Greg Bautzer handle everything, the three of them coming to easy terms (no alimony) over a restaurant lunch.

But Lana and Artie stayed friends, closer than most people knew.

Yet they stood up to each other.

When movers came to take Lana's belongings from Summit Ridge Drive, Art kept the piano her mother gave them as a wedding gift because, he said, he played it and she didn't. Turner was livid: "I'll *never* forgive him for that!"

She wouldn't have to. Unbeknownst to him, Turner stole Artie Shaw's best clarinet.

CHAPTER TWENTY-THREE

In the Mood

WHILE IN CHICAGO for an urgent meeting with American Federation of Musicians president James C. Petrillo to make sure a threatened labor strike against radio networks wouldn't interfere with Shaw's Burns and Allen broadcasts (it didn't), Art went to the Hotel Sherman's Panther Room to hear the Glenn Miller orchestra, now the most popular band in the country. Miller fans were lined up outside the hotel and halfway down the block, but that didn't affect Shaw's candor: "Artie managed to get down to tell Miller how bad his band was," *Down Beat*'s Ted Toll wrote, "and to complain about . . . everything else about the room that most of us in this jerkwater town seem to enjoy."

Decades later, Shaw was happy to expand on his dislike of the Miller style: "Glenn doesn't even count, as far as I'm concerned. What did he ever do, musically? He was Lawrence Welk, with a jazz accent. Miller never had much of a band; it was a drilled buncha guys doing the same things, they never made a mistake. You never heard a clinker, 'cause they played within strictly defined, safe limits. And for me, unless you made a mistake once in a while, I knew you weren't trying.

"What Glenn did was *safe*; you felt *comfortable*. That's not what it's about; it's supposed to be *exciting*. Ellington had that. Lunceford had it.

Uh, what's his name—Fletcher Henderson, *didn't*. Count Basie had it. . . . With Glenn, it was like: 'Once you hit a good groove, *stay* with that.' That's got nothin' to do with jazz. I wasn't sure where I was gonna go— but I knew it wasn't gonna be the same *thing*."

Where Art went next with his own new band, in the autumn of 1940, was someplace he had vowed he would never return to: a movie studio. "But finally a friend of mine came along with that 'Second Chorus' script," he said. "I took that picture on the proviso that I would be able to rewrite any language they put in my mouth; I'm playing 'Artie Shaw' again, in a fictional situation. So, you know, I was working with people I *knew*: Frank Cavett wrote the script, Hank Potter was the director; Johnny Mercer and I were scoring the film. We were supposed to have Julie [John] Garfield, and it was gonna be a serious story about a young trumpet player. Anyway—Boris Morros, the producer, didn't get along with Jack Warner, and Jack Warner rescinded his deal to lend us Julie Garfield. So we didn't have a star!

"So uh—our friend, Boris Morros, comes over to the Chateau Marmont where we were working—says, 'I got a *staah*.' We says, 'Who you got?' 'Fred Astaire.' I said, 'Wait a-minute! This is a serious story about a trumpet player!' 'So you'll change the story.' Well, at that point—That's the last movie I ever did, the last movie I ever *would* do."

Shaw was pleased, though, with the song composed for the picture. "I wrote a tune called 'Would You Like to Be the Love of My Life?' with Johnny Mercer, for Fred Astaire to sing to Paulette Goddard. Is he a good singer? No. But he was a good Fred Astaire singer; he did that superbly well. He didn't pretend to be Louis Armstrong or Bing Crosby or any of that; he was 'Fred Astaire'—and when you say that, you're giving it a brand name, a title.

"So anyway, that tune, 'Would You Like to Be the Love of My Life?'—it's a good song." Shaw attributed half of its appeal to the man who wrote the lyric. "Johnny knew what he was doing, Mercer. Kind of a prick as a guy, but he wrote good lyrics. He didn't like me because Judy Garland threw him out of her house when he made a critical or disparaging remark about me. And she would not have it! 'Cause she was—she was nuts about me. And he *hated* that. I said, 'Jesus Christ, Johnny—I can't help that! What do you *want* from me?'

"I think he had a little faggotry in him, somewhere. He sat in my house one night, and I was talkin' to Bart [Herbert] Marshall and his wife; and I'm here, and Johnny's over there, in a corner. And I turned, and he was drunk; you know: 'in vino,' et cetera. He said, 'You handsome bastard.' That's a funny thing to *say*. I said, 'I'm what I *am*; I can't change. You want me to break my nose?'

"Ah, well. But he had talent; Johnny was a—helluva lyricist."

MOVIE WORK was by nature boring—lots of waiting around—but Art's men didn't mind. "How could it not be fun looking at Paulette Goddard?" Jerry Jerome asked. "Short skirts; my goodness, it was great." The movie though was just a diversion. Shaw's main work was the new orchestra, with which he hoped to depart from the going clichés; and a six-man "band within the band," intended for "tasty" swing.

Art had the makings of an excellent small group in Billy Butterfield, Johnny Guarnieri, bassist Jud DeNaut, guitarist Al Hendrickson, drummer Nick Fatool, and of course Shaw himself. He thought of a gimmick to make the outfit stand out even more: Guarnieri would play not a standard piano but a baroque-period harpsichord.

The first time Guarnieri heard of this, he later told jazz pianist–radio host Marian McPartland, was on September 2, 1940: "I said, 'Artie, I don't know what a harpsichord *is*.' I said, 'I know my father makes violins and—I *suppose* it's an old-fashioned kind of a piana.' And he said, 'Yes it is.' He says, 'I have one up [at] the house; let's go up there tonight—and we'll rehearse, and we'll make some records tomorrow.'"

At rehearsal, Shaw played his own catchy composition, "Summit Ridge Drive." The men worked out a head arrangement (nothing written down), then practiced another Shaw original and two pop tunes, all "with Butterfield's muted trumpet voiced a minor third below Shaw's clarinet," wrote Shaw expert Vladimir Simosko, "and drummer Nick Fatool usually using brushes."

The recording session began the next morning at eight. Artie's other original piece, "Special Delivery Stomp," was done first: a speedy item that announced itself with four descending harpsichord tones, then took off at a fast clip, allowing Shaw and Guarnieri half- or quarter-chorus solos.

"Summit Ridge Drive" cruised at a danceable pace, giving DeNaut a walk with Guarnieri before Butterfield's muted gutbucket solo. Shaw tossed his musical mane and frisked around the corral. A fugue-like groove riff took the tune home.

The lazy-shuffle "Keepin' Myself for You," stated by Artie, then Butterfield, then Hendrickson over a kicking rhythm trio, was a winning old show tune that swung like a hammock. "Cross Your Heart," another Broadway oldie, turned into a harpsichord boogie-woogie halfway through, before coming to an abrupt stop at two and a half minutes.

Four sides in four hours; the men were done by noon. That was the start of Artie Shaw and his Gramercy 5: a winning sextet named for a New York City telephone exchange but thriving in the L.A. sunshine. The group wouldn't record many sides, but everything it did had crisp appeal and was note perfect, with an irresistible pace and swing. The Gramercy 5 was bluesy but classy, gutsy yet sophisticated. It was a fine vehicle for jazz, and it had instant jukebox appeal. "Everything was made for the jukebox then," Butterfield said, "which was three minutes at most. . . . [I]f you had a number on the jukes, that was very good publicity for the band." Jud DeNaut said, "The group was about as much fun as anything I can think of."

SHAW TOOK the fun on the road in September for an extended location engagement in the Rose Room of San Francisco's Palace Hotel. This Northern California gig would be the first time Shaw had played in public since abandoning the bandstand ten months ago. This time around, Artie was aloof, not giving patrons the first chance to make him feel bad. "[T]he way he used to treat the public was something to see," Billy Butterfield told Alan Littlejohn, "I mean downright rude, and very contemptuous. Still, they loved it, and he got away with it, so who's wrong?

"He had this big band with strings, maybe [twenty-two] guys, and we were playing at this fine old hotel. . . . We had just got two new band uniforms each, neither of which were tuxedos. So this elderly lady who owned the hotel says to Artie, 'I trust the band will be wearing tuxedos when they appear.' Artie replied to the effect that the band were not waiters but businessmen and would be wearing business suits. She didn't like this at all; and there they were, arguing for hours. This was one time Artie did not get his own way, because in the end we wore the tuxes! Mind you, his way of getting even with her was not to show up himself until about twelve-thirty. . . . [H]e used to disappear with Paulette Goddard, and then trombonist Jack Jenney used to front the band; and Johnny Guarnieri would play the clarinet solos on piano!"

Herb Caen, at the start of a decades-long run as the columnist bard of the Bay Area, in October 1940 wove a glimpse of Shaw into the newspaper prose-piece "What Is San Francisco?": "It's the Saturday tea *dansant* at the Palace—where the most beautiful girls in the world gather under one roof not to be admired, but to admire Artie Shaw, who only looks the other way."

Caen offered Shaw entrée to his concert pianist sister Estelle's convivial gatherings of such luminaries as union-activist Harry Bridges, physicist J. Robert Oppenheimer, conductor Pierre Monteux, and artist Dong Kingman. Estelle was a gifted hostess, her brother said—"one of those remarkable cooks who could keep four pots and five conversations going at the same time"—and Artie felt comfortable at her informal salons where, Caen wrote, "the mix was heady, the dialogue crisp, the politics left." Another salon guest would become a friend of Artie's: thirty-two-year-old author William Saroyan—like Shaw, a darkly handsome, self-made man of immigrant parentage. Saroyan's play *The Time of Your Life* won the Pulitzer Prize that year, an honor the indifferent author refused to accept. An artist after Artie Shaw's heart. Saroyan began coming to the Palace's Rose Room for Shaw's last set. Afterward, according to the author's dual biographers Barry Gifford and Lawrence Lee, "the two men often . . . wound up their evenings at Sally Stanford's, where both were fond of the society madam's Chinese cook and his way with a scrambled egg."

Shaw had a good time in San Francisco, where he began a rest-of-his-lifetime appreciation of the visual arts. At a group show, he bought a work by female artist Gene Kloss: "I think I paid three or four hundred bucks for it," he would say sixty-four years later. "Gene Kloss is in Taos, now; last time I saw her, she offered me ten thousand for it; she wants it back. Well—" Art also viewed an important Monet exhibit: "Some remarkable paintings. Cézanne is supposed to have said about Monet, 'Nothing but an eye, but what an eye.' I guess he didn't feel Monet had much of a philosophical understanding of what he was doing." Didn't matter to Art, who was knocked out by the old Frenchman. Shaw was certain his clarinet playing was influenced by the paintings he looked at.

"You're influenced by *everything*," he insisted. "Sight and sound are not that far apart. They all deal with sensibility. Sensibility is, finally, your ability to *sense*. These are all mysterious things, though, you know; I don't think anyone's ever examined this particular mental transmutation that takes place. When I say I was influenced by a Van Gogh *tree*—this green *flame*, that he said was a cypress tree—I don't mean deliberately influenced in what I'm trying to play, or write—but it's *there*. I've been transformed, to a degree, by Van Gogh's tree; I've been transformed, by Monet's water lily. *Why*? I've no *idea* why."

But he could guess. "People ask me who are my influences. I say, 'Well a Monet water lily was as much of an influence on me as some other musician.' 'Well wadya *mean*?' I'd say, 'Well what's the sign, the characteristic, of a Monet water lily?' 'I don't know what you're talkin' about.' 'Well if you don't know what I'm *talking* about, I'm not gonna *talk* about it anymore. It's a *metaphor*.' Excellence, is what we're talkin' about." In any case: "I loved painting. And painting's a lot like jazz, too. The great ones: same thing."

THE BAND was a hit at the Palace from opening night, when an overflow mob jammed the Rose Room to catch the return of Artie Shaw.

He and his twenty-two men were the band of the hour, being on radio weekly with Burns and Allen, on local and network remotes from the Rose Room, and with "Frenesi" all the while in nationwide play.

Artie and the men also flew to Hollywood in September to record new platters: two Anita Boyer vocals (including "If It's You," a Shaw tune); "Temptation," a swinging Latin number from a 1933 Crosby movie; and "Chantez Les Bas" ("Swing 'em Low"), a first-recording of a W. C. Handy blues piece arranged by Bill Still. What with record sessions and radio work, Art was making two L.A. plane trips a week. He also had a nonbusiness reason for going to Hollywood: brunette actress Frances Neal.

Shaw was at the Halloween-night opening of the new Hollywood Palladium, a gala event with Tommy Dorsey's orchestra that drew sixty-five hundred patrons: an unbroken sea of dancers filling the ballroom's eleven-thousand-square-foot floor. Dorsey this week had the number-one record in the country, "I'll Never Smile Again" (with Joe Bushkin on celesta)—a *vocal* record, with Frank Sinatra.

In fact, skinny Frank approached Art this Halloween with an offer he hoped Shaw couldn't refuse: How would he like to hire a new singer for his band? Sinatra was chafing under the iron hand of the domineering Dorsey, and annoyed with the obnoxious behavior of Dorsey's drummer, Buddy Rich, whose recent beating by a pair of thugs Sinatra was suspected of having arranged.

"But I don't use boy singers," Artie begged off.

"What about Tony Pastor?" Sinatra countered.

"You call that a *singer*?" Art joked. "I like Tony, he makes me laugh."

No, let Tommy keep this handful of trouble, *and* his sensitive vocal stylings. Tommy liked *stars*, and a big-circus atmosphere, with something to please every customer. Artie Shaw, on the other hand, just wanted to make *music*.

A LOT had happened to Hoagland Carmichael's "Star Dust" since the eighteen-year-old Shaw heard its first peppy, raggedy-time record version at the Gennett Studios in Richmond, Indiana, in 1928.

Earl Hines in Chicago used to let Carmichael play his tune some-times with Hines's orchestra. Don Redman picked it up and gave it to Jean Goldkette, who gave it to arranger-composer Victor Young, who slowed the instrumental down to ballad tempo for his boss Isham Jones, who in 1930—at last—made a hit of it. Lyrics were added by Tin Pan Alley writer Mitchell Parrish, and in 1931 both Bing Crosby and Louis Armstrong did vocal versions of it.

Five years later, Benny Goodman and Tommy Dorsey each recorded "Star Dust" for RCA Victor, Goodman's in a Fletcher Henderson arrange-ment and Dorsey's with a vocal by Edythe Wright; the label issued these as two sides of the same 78, and the platter became Victor's biggest-selling disc of 1936.

By 1940, Artie Shaw had been playing "Star Dust" live for at least four years. The idea of Shaw making a record of "Star Dust" came from RCA Victor's Harry Myerson; the exec suggested Shaw and Dorsey duplicate the label's 1936 stunt of a two-sided "Star Dust." Fine, Art said; he had Lennie Hayton, his right-hand arranger, score the piece. Shaw's band cut "Star Dust" during the night of October 7, 1940.

Hayton's arrangement, from Art's sketch, gave the first solo to Billy Butterfield, who began the record with a bravura trumpet burst of full-toned melody as romantic as anything in the swing era. Shaw's sixteen-bar solo, though, was the one that pierced the heart: Art's improvisation had the symmetry of an inspired composition, and it dazzled other players for years. "His chorus on 'Star Dust' was almost like a bebop chorus," bop vibraphonist Terry Gibbs thought. "If you listen to that chorus, he was playing double-time figures with great feeling. I never heard anybody play a better chorus on 'Star Dust' than Artie Shaw." In 1982, Buddy DeFranco would tell Whitney Balliett, "It's the greatest clarinet solo of all time."

But the record wasn't over. Flowing without pause from Art's final phrase was Jack Jenney's eight-bar ad lib, his trombone so in keep-ing with Shaw's rumination that it seemed to continue the clarinet's thought. The full orchestra took the song home in an unwinding Hay-ton coda where the strings traced a drifting burst of shimmering star-dust in air.

Artie knew what he had as soon as he had it. He said, "Certain things, I thought, 'Well that's pretty damn good, leave it alone; don't mess with it.' 'Star Dust,' which is a record that will live—Ah, it's *there*; I don't know why it was good. I know we made a take—and I said to the band, 'Let's go home; this is it, it ain't gonna get any better.' You know— it was one take! I couldn't have made 'Star Dust' as it was without Billy Butterfield, Jack Jenney, and my own particular ability—which came to a peak, in that thing. Whatever I've ever done in my life came to a culmination, at that point."

A few weeks later, Shaw said, he asked to hear what Tommy Dorsey had done for the record's other side. Myerson claimed Dorsey reneged on the project after hearing what Shaw recorded; "I'm not gettin' on the back of that!" he's supposed to have said, in tribute to Art's achieve- ment (or maybe Jack Jenney's).

Tommy cut his own "Star Dust," a vocal showcase for Frank Sinatra and the Pied Pipers, a few weeks later, for separate release. It sold well enough. But Shaw's disc went through the roof.

Artie Shaw's "Star Dust" was one of his all-time biggest records— and the most popular recording ever of Hoagy Carmichael's most pop- ular tune. Before Shaw, "Star Dust" was a well-known song; after Shaw, it was a standard, a classic, an American evergreen. It was a side for the ages, a record that pleased forever: the sort of thing it seemed second nature for Art to produce in a year that brought so many successes—and still had great things to yield.

CHAPTER TWENTY-FOUR

Concerto for Clarinet

"CONCERTO for Clarinet" was just meant to fill a spot in a movie, Shaw insisted, but this bravura piece would become Art's best-known composition.

The title was misleading: this was no concerto in the classical sense, but a showboating piece in the tradition of "Streamline" and that Whiteman-concert "Blues." After a fanfare from the band, Art began a slow, out-of-tempo blues soliloquy against seductive strings. Faster than you could say Meade-Lux-Lewis, Johnny Guarnieri jumped in with some boogie-woogie, setting up Art's chorus of fast improvisation. Les Robinson's alto was heard, then Butterfield's trumpet; then Art's musings found blue notes within Semitic scales. When Fatool's tom-toms started, the clarinet soared. Shaw glided and glissaded through a full-minute spiral of a cadenza as full of breathtaking vistas as Jack's ascent of the beanstalk. Up and up he went—from concert double-F through high B-flat—to land (à la Shaw's showpiece with Whiteman at Carnegie Hall) on a hard-to-believe-your-ears altissimo high-C, held for a full five seconds.

With a three-note tag from the orchestra, this "Concerto" was done: nine and a quarter minutes unlike anything ever heard before.

RCA Victor put it out on a two-sided twelve-inch 78, and it found favor. Mills Music published its music in 1942, with Art's improvisations included. Precocious students (and professionals) wrestled with Shaw's quicksilver phrases. Shaw's non-concerto persisted into future decades as a performance piece from New York's Alice Tully Hall to London's Royal Festival Hall to Queensland, Australia's City Hall—done by aggregations from the Cleveland Orchestra to the Boston Pops to the U.S. Marine Band. A British disc version would be played behind the Iron Curtain by Hungarian Radio. Over a dozen virtuosi, jazz and classical, would record the work in the next fifty years.

But no one performed "Concerto for Clarinet" to such thrilling effect as the man who devised it to show off his own extraordinary abilities. Shaw wrote, "A well-known clarinet player came into my dressing-room after a show I'd just played in a theatre (we did five or six shows a day in those days, seven days a week, sometimes for *months* on end); I used to play my 'Concerto for Clarinet' at the end of every one, and he said, 'Artie, do you end every show with that piece?' I said, 'Yes. Why?' He said, 'You mean you always end on that top C?' I said, 'Of course. That's how the piece ends.' 'I know,' he said. 'But aren't you ever afraid you'll miss?' I said, 'Put your hand on the table.' He did, and I said, 'Raise your index finger.' He did. I said, 'Were you afraid you'd miss?' 'Well, no,' he said, and then, 'You mean, it's like that?' 'If it isn't,' I said, 'don't mess with it.'"

SHAW AND his band began a six-week stay at the Hollywood Palladium on December 12. By then, RCA had lots of great Shaw in the can; *Second Chorus* would soon be released, and the Artie Shaw orchestra sounded better than ever (as demonstrated each week on the Burns and Allen show).

As for Art's private life—

Down Beat informed readers, "The Frances Neal-Artie Shaw twosome hit a snag and his friends will tell you Artie still worships Lana Turner (and Betty Grable's friends will tell you she still thinks Artie's just about tops)."

In the autumn of 1940, Lana Turner moved in with her mother—to a house just down the hill from Artie's. Tenor man Jerry Jerome said, "I recall at Christmas, Lana Turner had us [band members] select a present for Artie. We all chipped in and got him a pool table."

Lana gave him a different gift.

"Christmas, I was playing at the Palladium," Shaw said. "Came home—alone—Christmas Eve, and she popped up from behind the couch; and there were Christmas trees, and—she had decorated the whole bloody place. She wanted to come back."

Art was touched. Lana spent the night. "I *almost* went back with her then," he said. "But—I kept thinking about that hundred pair of shoes that she hadda have. Had to have a whole *room*—just to shelve her shoes. Why a hundred? 'Cause that was her—her little—girlish dream, of glory."

There would be no roomful of shoes at Summit Ridge Drive, and no second-chorus remarriage.

But that didn't mean they couldn't *see* each other once in a while.

WAR AND RUMORS of war had plagued Europe for the last several years, but America stayed neutral. Germany's bombing of England in 1940, though, made things more urgent. U.S. males between twenty-one and thirty-six were required to register for military call-up; the fulfillment of this obligation by Artie Shaw and many other celebrities was well publicized. By February 1941, some big-band ranks were being depleted by players caught in the early draft. Art wasn't worried: he had a deferment as sole support of his surviving parent. Shaw went about his life with zest. He was seen dancing with Betty Grable at Ciro's, and holding hands with Alice Faye in another club.

Art met new girls too, including a teenaged brunette dancer named Yvonne De Carlo, part of the floor show at the Florentine Gardens on Hollywood Boulevard. Yvonne was drawn to Artie, she would write,

There was a masculine intensity about him that was almost overpowering, and he was remarkably bright and articulate. . . . What I did—which probably endeared me to him more than anything else—was listen.

*. . . He freely discussed the other women in his life and philosophized
about his requisites for a wife. The girl had to be neat and attractive, have a
sense of humor, and above all be intelligent. Actually, his standards were so
high he could never find a girl to meet the requirements. . . .*

. . . "I'd really like to be a singer," I said.

*His train of thought was derailed. "Don't you realize you can't just be
a singer. It takes study, my girl! . . . Tell me this—how do you expect to get
anywhere working in a dump like the Florentine Gardens? . . . Look," he
said, "you're not just in a rut, you're in a hole. In a rut you can at least move
in one direction. I advise you to quit—right now."*

*Quit the Florentine? Me? . . . "Look, kid," he said. "I know you can't
afford to be out of work, so I'll make a deal with you. Quit your job, start
studying singing, get yourself a movie agent—and I'll pay your salary for
a month." He must have read my mind, because he added, "No strings
attached, I promise."*

*I don't know why I let him talk me into it, but I did. . . . I lost no time
in getting an actor's agent. . . . Artie Shaw kept his word about the month's
salary, but now Artie was off somewhere with his band and was no longer a
factor in my life.*

But De Carlo was launched on the path to becoming a movie star.

WHERE SHAW went with his band was New York City, where the Burns
and Allen show relocated for the end of its 1941 season. Most of Art's
men went with him, and the band had an extended stay at the Strand, a
gig said to pay ten thousand a week.

Artie stayed in a suite at the literary-minded Algonquin Hotel. There
he entertained *New York World-Telegram* writer William Brennan with
an advance copy of his recording of "I Cover the Waterfront," made in
Hollywood in January; the two men admired its "symphonic" structure
and soothing strings. "My music is still solid," Art said, "but it doesn't
kick you in the face anymore."

That music generated big royalties: twenty thousand dollars so far just for "Frenesi." Art could afford to relax. He complained to Brennan that he hadn't had time to read any of the books piling up in his Algonquin suite. When Burns and Allen went off the air in March, Shaw disbanded his orchestra. But he continued his studies. In Hollywood, he had received instruction in counterpoint from composer David Diamond; in New York he studied orchestration and arranging with German conductor Hans Byrns.

At Barney Josephson's Café Society, Art became acquainted with Hazel Scott, a twenty-year-old Trinidad-born pianist causing a sensation with her swing versions of Bach, Chopin, and Rachmaninoff. Also performing at Café Society was singer Lena (Helena) Horne, a twenty-three-year-old "colored thrush" who had made records with Charlie Barnet and toured with his orchestra (though not when he had gone down South). Horne sang with a supper-club poise far removed from the earthy swing of Billie Holiday. Shaw thought she had potential—and God knows, she was gorgeous.

Again Art became a habitué of Sherman Billingsley's Stork Club. Shaw was of special note there as one of the most eligible bachelors in the room: "a combination," feature writer Inez Robb wrote, "of dream prince and glamour boy."

BENNY GOODMAN'S latest band opened at New York's Paramount in April. *Down Beat*'s George Frazier thought Goodman's new outfit sounded too much like his old ones, but duller: "it's a great big disappointment." The same magazine's Dave Dexter differed, saying, "Goodman no longer is fighting to be a success, but *experimenting*"—citing fresh arrangements by Eddie Sauter. But Goodman didn't play Sauter's scores much, and according to trumpeter Jimmy Maxwell, "Benny used to edit [them] brutally—just brutally." This arranger would have more luck impressing Artie Shaw.

Artie and Benny ran into each other at the Hotel Lincoln, the night of Harry James's Rose Room opening. Benny seemed cheerful; he owned a chunk of his former sideman's band, and it looked as though James would make a success of it. Tony Pastor was also on hand to wish

James well. Tony had done all right with his own band in the past year and a half, playing an easy-to-like style one wit dubbed "pastor-ized swing." Musicians respected Tony's talent ("Benny Goodman once confided to me," Bill Gottlieb would write in 1941, "that he thought Pastor the greatest of white tenor saxophonists"), but what drew the public were Pastor's stage presence and his vocals. He had a hit singing Cole Porter's "Let's Do It."

Another old friend, Claude Thornhill, was holding forth at Long Island's Glen Island Casino, still trying to make a go of an orchestra that critics liked but the public hadn't discovered. Thornhill's latest gambit was a souped-up repertoire of classic strains by Brahms, Grieg, and the like. The best of the batch was a piece that Emerald Shawfellow maybe once played on the piano for Claude Thornhill back in Cleveland: Robert Schumann's "Träumerei."

CHAPTER TWENTY-FIVE

This Time the Dream's on Me

W HEN ARTIE SHAW returned to the recording studio in June 1941, it was with seven black jazz musicians, thirteen white strings players, a female harpist, and singer Lena Horne. The concept was intriguing: to juxtapose the sonic textures and rhythmic feel of pure-jazz men with those of classically trained players. The stellar jazzmen included trumpeter Henry "Red" Allen, trombonist Jay C. Higginbotham, and alto-saxophonist Benny Carter.

On the 1930 standard "(I'm) Confessin' (That I Love You)," Carter and Higginbotham alternated solos with Shaw over the weaving of strings and horns. "Beyond the Blue Horizon" had sixteen bars of Higginbotham; Shaw sketched graceful aerial maneuvers against the string players' cloudless sky. The other two sides were Tin Pan Alley vocal tunes: "Love Me a Little" had a beguiling feel, and Lena Horne's restrained delivery was effective. On "Don't Take Your Love from Me," Horne gave the lyric a sophisticated touch. Each side was a superior piece of popular music; Art's experiment could be judged a success.

Lena Horne thought the date might lead to bigger things.

"Lena was the type of person who . . . wanted to be a big star," Shaw said six decades later, recalling the aftermath of that June afternoon. "She wanted to marry *me*. . . . I was a very big name, at that time. And we were—we were—in bed, you know. It was good, sexually, but—that's not enough to get *married*. I said, 'Lena, you know, this is the *wrong thing*, we're not gonna *do* it.' She—couldn't handle that. That's Lena's problem. I couldn't begin to figure out what she had in mind."

Shaw put distance between himself and Horne. Soon the columnists had Art linked with society-girl Barbara Bannister, the Smithfield hams heiress and screen-hopeful said to be "Shaw's current inspiration." But Bannister too vanished from Shaw's New York orbit.

THE DISCS SHAW made at the end of 1940 were coming out at a steady clip now: four platters in May alone. *Down Beat*'s Dave Dexter marveled at the high quality of Artie's sides: the sublime "Marinella," the bluesy "Chantez Les Bas," the winning "Alone Together," the beautiful "Moonglow." When Art's two-sided version of William Still's "Blues" was released in June, Dexter deemed it "a really sensational biscuit . . . a 'must' record on any count."

Shaw was now Victor's best-selling artist. Art had realized one of his long-standing ambitions: to make a commercial and artistic success playing the best American popular songs. As summer turned to autumn, Art pursued a more audacious goal.

AS SOON as word leaked out that Artie Shaw was forming a new band, players from Benny Goodman's orchestra began showing up in Art's company at Nola Studios, the rehearsal hall on Broadway and Fifty-first. Alto-man Les Robinson played out his two-week notice with Goodman and joined Shaw's roster. Johnny Guarnieri, who had quit Benny in May, signed on with Artie and brought drummer Dave Tough, who'd left Goodman's band at the same time. Georgie Auld slipped out of Benny's ranks—to once more fill Art's tenor-sax chair. Mike Bryan, Goodman's rhythm guitarist in the spring, by the fall was in Shaw's crew.

Big-band musicians switched allegiances often, but lots of Benny's players seemed more than eager to work for Art. For one thing, Shaw paid better. For another, many found his music more challenging and interesting. Last but not least, Shaw treated his men with a courtesy that on the whole eluded Goodman. As drummer Nick Fatool put it, "Artie's a little more of a gentleman, I would say."

Ray Conniff and Jack Jenney both broke up their own bands to join Shaw's. Jenney's wife, Bonnie Lake, became Art's singer. Lee (Castaldo) Castle jumped into Shaw's trumpet section, as did Max Kaminsky. Bassist Ed McKinney left Tony Pastor for Art. It was turning into a formidable ensemble: thirty-two men, including strings players; quite a sight when spread out and seated at music stands in one of the larger rooms at Nola's, where Shaw held practice sessions beginning on August 15. "Watching him . . . is a revelation," Dave Dexter wrote. "Shaw gets discipline without ever asking for it; without flashing a 'death ray' at the sidemen"—this in reference to Goodman's notorious stare of disapproval.

Art started rehearsing the strings at ten in the morning, then stayed until six at night polishing nuances ("Smack it!") with the saxes and brass. He hadn't worked so hard since 1938, but this would be his first barnstorming tour in two years.

The one-nighters began in August. Boston's finicky George Frazier wrote: "[Shaw] has assembled a group of stars and has succeeded in making them play irreproachably. The brand of jazz they produce is always substantial and at times . . . thrilling." For Frazier, the essential man was drummer Dave Tough, who weighed a mere hundred pounds but pushed the orchestra like a Mack truck in second gear. The antithesis of a Buddy Rich, Tough avoided flashy moves and rarely took a solo; but he brought out the best in an orchestra and from each of its players.

Shaw's real star was the African-American trumpeter, vocalist, and showman Oran Thaddeus "Hot Lips" Page. Born in Texas, Page had performed with blues-singers Bessie Smith and Ma Rainey before going to Kansas City and becoming a member of Count Basie's Reno Club orchestra, the band John Hammond brought east in 1936. "Lips" went to New York then too but opted for a solo career. Shaw was giving

Page the showcase he had deserved for years and getting an ace performer who electrified everyone from mindless dancers to stuffy jazz buffs. "Lips" Page was front and center during the band's first recording session in New York City on September 2.

"Blues in the Night" was a brand-new Harold Arlen and Johnny Mercer movie song. To arrange it, Shaw turned to an old colleague with matchless experience writing for a colossus band with a brilliant brass soloist: Bill Challis, who had done scores for Goldkette and Whiteman when Bix was in ascendance. Page played nothing like Bix, and Challis had moved on in style, but Bill knew his business, and the dynamics were right. Shaw's "Blues in the Night" began with eight bars of Page's growling, plunger-muted trumpet, then quick-vamped into Lips's affecting rough-and-ready vocal: Art's clarinet skirled in between Lips's voice and a strings-and-reeds interlude, then Page's open horn blasted through the final eighteen bars to bring this 78 full circle.

Artie recorded another Arlen-Mercer number, "This Time the Dream's on Me," with a distracted vocal by Bonnie Lake, whose thin tone and tentative manner created an almost avant-garde effect. This "Dream," with its unusual chord changes and cooled-out manner, would hold special appeal for the most adventurous jazz musicians of the time.

More to the point of Shaw's own daring theories was "Nocturne," a 1928 composition by Thomas Griselle. Jerry Sears, whom Art knew from Roger Wolfe Kahn's band, brought him an arrangement of this jazz-tinged tone poem which seemed just the sort of "native American music" Shaw wanted to play with his "concert-jazz" orchestra. "Nocturne" had solo parts for trumpet, saxophone, and clarinet but no improvisation. Griselle's piece was not for dancing or soloing but for listening.

"Nocturne" too was recorded on September 2, in a six-hour session that also preserved versions of Hoagy Carmichael's "Rockin' Chair," Vincent Youmans's "Through the Years," and the 1933 semi-standard "If I Love Again." Once more, with style and an innovative conception, Artie Shaw had achieved his ideal of three (or three-and-a-half) chords for beauty and one to pay the rent. How long might he maintain this golden mean?

ARTIE SHAW and his "symphonic swing" orchestra broke box-office records everywhere they went: Clear Lake, Iowa; Oklahoma City; St. Louis; Omaha. Artie canceled a scheduled thirty-two-city foray into the Deep South, though, when bookers told him Lips Page's presence would necessitate a special arrangement. The only way this black musician could be on a southern stage with a white band, they said, was if he stayed fifteen feet away from the rest of the men. Artie said to hell with it. The band wouldn't go to the South; they would make up the lost dates by adding new ones in the North.

While in Chicago, Art met twenty-five-year-old composer-arranger Paul Jordan, who played Shaw some of his original pieces including "Evensong" and "Suite No. 8," half-jazz and half-classical compositions of great sophistication. Artie hired him on the spot to move to New York and compose for the band. The first number Jordan created for Shaw's outfit, the trade paper said, had the working title "Dance of the Drunken Spirochete."

Was there nothing this crackerjack outfit of Shaw's couldn't play? By the time the band reached Philadelphia in mid-November, it was as loose as a goose and as tight as a drum.

Then without warning came the sort of magical live set Shaw had experienced once or twice before with his 1938 band. This 1941 orchestra's unforgettable night took place in the Midwest. Ray Coniff remembered, "I think it was in Kansas. . . . The places we used to play sometimes—they were Quonset-huts, these metal barracks-type things. . . . The temperature in the day in the sun must have been up to one fifteen or one twenty. . . . And you can imagine this metal barracks at eight p.m. when we were going to start; it was like a furnace in there. It was absolutely stifling—and the place was packed. The temperature was so high that all the brass instruments were sharp because of the change in the size of the metal; we couldn't get tuned to the piano. Artie didn't

even come up on the stand; he was down in the dressing-room somewhere in the basement."

Shaw thought Conniff's "Just Foolin' Around" was the number the
band was into when the magic struck. As Conniff recalled,

> *"Hot Lips Page was the first to play a solo. I don't know what happened,
> but something he played just suddenly inspired the whole band. . . . It was
> an electrifying thing: The band started to swing like I've never heard a band
> swing before or since. The people all stopped dancing and got as close to the
> stand as they could. As each guy played, he just played way over his head.
> I remember when I played it was like I wasn't moving the [trombone] slide
> myself; everything went automatically by itself.*
>
> *"Artie . . . grabbed his clarinet and came up on the stand and joined in.
> When we got to the end of the arrangement—he gave the signal with one
> finger up, and we all went back to the top again; we didn't even stop. We just
> went back to the top of the whole arrangement and played it down through
> again; we all played solos again. That was one of the most memorable experi-
> ences I've ever had in my entire life in the music-business."*

"Hot Lips Page was playing," Art said in awe, over sixty years later,
"and the band caught fire. The god-damn thing—Suddenly, there was
a *thing* in the *air*: this band was blowing up a *storm*. The *tempo*, and the
time—everything just *came* together. We all *stared* at each other: *What's
happening?*

"Many many years later—only recently—Ray said, 'You remember that night?' I said, 'I know exactly the night you're talking about.
Low ceiling—' He said, 'That's right. Hot Lips was playing—' And the
band—went crazy. Everyone! Everybody—staring at each other. . . .
That's somethin' you never *get* over," Shaw said at ninety-three.

THE BAND WORKED its way back east. In New York, in mid-November,
Art had a nightclub supper with a vacationing Lana Turner (whose
divorce from him became final that September). "I liked Lana," Shaw

told Vladimir Simosko. "She wasn't a malicious person." Art joked to a passing newsman that he and the former Mrs. Shaw were about to remarry. Lana went along with the gag, but when called later to confirm the rumor, she squelched it.

Besides, Shaw was said to be competing with Al Jolson, of all people, for the attentions of B-movie actress Peggy Moran.

At the same time, Art made further forays into the world of letters.

"I had a friend named Paul Peters," Shaw said, "he was drama editor for *Life* magazine; and Ivan von Auw was a literary agent, who [later] represented Salinger and a few others. Paul and Ivan *lived* together. I at that time was so naïve, I didn't know what homosexuals were; they didn't *seem* to be. But—so it was. They had an apartment on—East Tenth. They moved to—Port-au-Prince? I guess they're dead by now.

"Anyway, they came to *see* me at a theater I played, the Paramount or the Strand; and after the show they came backstage, and Paul said, 'Who *is* that guy up on the stage? It's not *you*, is it?' I said, 'No, it's not the me *you* know; that's Artie Shaw. I *play* him; I play him pretty skillfully.' They couldn't get over the—enormous difference. 'Cause when I was with *them*, I was pretty intense; we would *talk* about things."

What Art most liked to talk about was writing. Peters and von Auw knew lots of authors, several of whom Shaw met at their apartment. Dawn Powell was one; another was Nancy Wilson Ross, a novelist and journalist a year younger than Art. Nancy and Art were attracted to one another. "I know she liked me," he would say. "But she didn't have that—theatrical quality of beauty, that for me was the hallmark." Maybe too he was shy of Ross's intelligence and ability. Decades later, Art told another woman writer, "I never married an intellectual, because I was scared to; I went the other way: broads you could make it with." Art dealt with Nancy by playing matchmaker. "I introduced Nancy Wilson Ross to Stanley Young," he said, "who was the Young of [the publishing house of] Farrar Straus and Young. They got married [in 1942] and lived, as they say, happily ever after."

Art was free once more to pursue his craft and calling.

"I've been looking around at the world," he told columnist Earl

Wilson, "and it seems to me the only thing for a guy to do is find a job and do it. I'm past thinking about security. What's the sense of piling up money and saying 'I'm secure'? Your hands, your ability, are your security." As for "running away from it all," as he had seemed to do when he fled to Mexico: "Somebody said, I forget who, 'Every time you escape you have to take yourself along.' That's about it."

Art didn't *want* to escape now. Shaw *liked* his work now. But that part of the world that was merrily going to hell was about to pull him along.

CHAPTER TWENTY-SIX

Someone's Rocking My Dreamboat

ARTIE SHAW and his orchestra were playing a theater date in Providence, Rhode Island, on the Sunday afternoon of December 7, 1941.

"I went back in the wings," Shaw told radio interviewer Terry Gross, ". . . and the stage-hand's radio was on; and we were hearing a hysterical announcer talking about the Japs having bombed Pearl Harbor. . . . I got a note from the manager: 'Please announce that all military personnel are to report to their bases immediately.' This was right near Newport, where there was a naval base, air-force base, all that. So I went out onstage and did that—and about three-quarters of the house got empty. I hadn't realized . . . World War II was out there, but it seemed somehow distant."

Shaw (like Benny Goodman) had made appearances on behalf of Russian War Relief. In response to a government appeal for citizens to conserve wool, Artie had had his band's winter suits made single-breasted and without vests. Otherwise, his engagement with world affairs had been nil.

Even after Pearl Harbor and a U.S. declaration of war on Japan and Germany, Artie, and many of his colleagues, felt fighting was best left to the experts. There were indications that U.S. officials shared this view, and that big-band leaders would be kept out of war for the sake of domestic morale. Anyway, Shaw had that 3-A deferment as sole provider for his mother, and in the weeks after December 7, Art and his orchestra kept to their schedule.

On December 8, they opened at Loew's State in New York City, where crowd response (affected perhaps by current events) was extraordinary. Patrons loved everything Art played, including such demanding fare as Paul Jordan's four-and-a-half-minute "Evensong."

Art was leading as innovative a band as any he had ever had. And it was popular, placing fourth (behind Miller's, Dorsey's, and sweetish Kay Kyser's) in *Billboard*'s survey of college favorites. Artie himself was voted third-favorite soloist (behind Goodman and Harry James) in that year's *Down Beat* poll. Many of Shaw's 1941 records were praised as among the best of the year, not only by *Down Beat* and *Metronome* but also by the *New York Times*. And Art had done it all on his own terms.

There would always be some who preferred Artie's 1938 band to this 1941 outfit. But there were enough who wanted what Art had to offer now to make it feasible for him to keep playing what he liked. "It's not a question of making a lot of money," he said, "but of supporting the best orchestra I can get." He was shelling out nearly three thousand a week in salaries, while taking in maybe five thousand—with much of the surplus reinvested in new arrangements to keep him ahead of the curve, in front of the parade.

BUT WHAT HAPPENED in January 1942 changed all that.

"[W]e were doing a record date at Victor," Max Kaminsky wrote, "when Artie's manager handed him his letter of greetings from Uncle Sam. The band was immediately given its notice."

Shaw's draft classification had been changed to 1-A. At once he began exploring alternative-service possibilities. After a two-week stay in New York's Roosevelt Hospital, recuperating from the flu, Shaw left Manhattan and arrived in L.A. by train on January 31.

There he right away ran into William Saroyan, who was in Hollywood on MGM business and tooling around in a sky-blue Cadillac convertible. Also in L.A. were composer David Diamond and a gaggle of other old and new Shaw cronies from both coasts, including playwright Clifford Odets.

Lee Wiley was in town too. Close to Valentine's Day, Shaw had dinner with her and Rosheen Marcus, a friend of Lee's from back east. Picking them up beforehand, Artie made the acquaintance of Rosheen's beautiful, blonde, sixteen-year-old daughter Carol, who would write,

One night Mother and Lee told me they were going to go out to dinner with Artie Shaw. When I heard the name, I nearly fainted. In those days bandleaders were such big heroes, you have no idea.

He came to pick them up and he said, "Oh, who are you?"

"I'm her daughter."

"What are you doing in California?"

"I am going to be a good actress, or a star."

"Have you ever acted?"

"Yes, I just finished a play before I came out here: [a Princeton University production of] Jim Dandy by William Saroyan."

"He's my best friend. Did you know he's out here now?"

"William Saroyan?"

"Yes."

"Not dead?"

"Not dead. Definitely not dead."

He told me what a terrific person Bill was and how he'd be very interested in meeting me. Artie himself began calling me to have dinner, but for so early in the evening that I fully expected the next time we'd have dinner would be at three in the afternoon. I'd always ask him, "Who's your real date tonight?" I knew he just considered me a child.

About a week later, I was out with some people at the Players Club, a Hollywood restaurant. Artie came over to our table and said, "I'm with Bill over there in the corner. I just told him all about you; why don't you come over and say hello?"

The teenager and the thirty-three-year-old playwright began keeping company. Soon they would marry.

WHILE IN L.A., Shaw sat in (as did Harry James and Buddy Rich) with black bands in the clubs on Central Avenue in Watts. And he went to a tiny boîte called The Little Troc, where he caught the act of the migratory Lena Horne, who would write of that club, "We quickly became that year's 'in' place for the Hollywood crowd. I did not see any of them socially, of course, but I remember John Barrymore coming in several times. And Marlene Dietrich, and Artie Shaw, whom I had known in New York, and Artie's immediate ex, Lana Turner, who was going around with Steve Crane at the time."

Art's own new companion was Elizabeth "Betty" Kern, the twenty-three-year-old daughter of the great Jerome Kern, whose "All the Things You Are" Shaw made a hit and a standard, and who this year would win the Academy Award for his and Oscar Hammerstein's "The Last Time I Saw Paris." Betty was a cool-looking blonde. Like Nancy Wilson Ross, she lacked Shaw's preferred "hallmark of great beauty," but he thought she was still good looking, and her musical bloodline was an incredible plus.

Once again Art was in the marrying mood. He was almost thirty-two, which seemed old as hell. How long could he go on wasting his time with swoony teenagers and empty-headed actresses? He had his life to live and, what with the world going to blazes, maybe he had better start living it.

IT WAS a surprise to most when Jerome Kern told Hollywood reporters on March 3 that Artie Shaw had married the composer's daughter in Yuma, Arizona. This was no elopement, Kern said; the couple had been accompanied by Betty's mother: "They have our blessings and best wishes."

Again Shaw had startled the public and press with a "whirlwind courtship." His other dates were surprised too. When Hedda Hopper saw Art at a Russian War Relief benefit in New York, where he and Betty relocated to Shaw's studio apartment facing Central Park West, the columnist asked if Lana Turner had congratulated him. "She called me on the phone three times without mentioning the fact of my marriage," Art said, "and finally I introduced Betty over the telephone to her. You know, Lana's a sweet kid, but I wonder if she wouldn't have been happier if she had been allowed to sit at that soda fountain, marry one of her school friends and have a brace of kiddies."

IN APRIL, Shaw's plans changed again. Sole support of his mother or not, he was going to have to serve his country.

What he proposed, with the help of the William Morris Agency (which had ties to the USO), was novel: he would travel to Army camps and organize servicemen's bands, rehearsing each orchestra for two weeks and supplying it with free arrangements. "This isn't a fancy-pants job I've got," he assured *Down Beat*. The idea was to organize an entertainment center in each camp, with acting and producing groups to back visiting performers.

But it wasn't to be. "Shaw had cleared his proposed USO camp job with everybody but his draft board," *Down Beat* wrote. "They got very huffy about the whole thing." On the morning of April 28, Betty Kern Shaw drove her husband in a Lincoln convertible to the New York recruitment center, where he enlisted in the United States Navy.

He began active duty two months later, but not as an officer. The bandleader didn't feel entitled to a commission. "I went in as an apprentice-seaman," he would tell Terry Gross, "as low as you could get. . . . I thought the Navy would have enough rationality to put me into the job I could do best for *them*—and then give me whatever rate or rank I needed. . . . I didn't realize that the military service doesn't *operate* rationally."

Art took his basic training on Staten Island: "They looked at one stripe, or no stripe, and they gave me a swab: 'Swab the deck, sailor.' Well that's kinda stupid. I was building shelves, under a stairway, to put mops and buckets on. . . . Six or eight weeks of mine-sweeper duty, off Staten Island, this that and the other."

Things got worse when Art was promoted to chief petty officer, sent to the Newport naval base, and told to lead and perform with the band there. This fourteen-man ensemble was dreadful. Twelve of them couldn't play worth a damn, so Shaw told the other two to follow the poor ones' lead; let them *all* play bad. Soon he was getting compliments on how *good* the band now sounded. He couldn't take it.

He began to get migraines, so severe he couldn't see straight. And he had trouble with the base commander, a man he couldn't abide. "I had a breakdown; they put me in the hospital." After five days, he bribed someone to look the other way while he went AWOL to Washington to see Undersecretary of the Navy James Forrestal, a former investment banker he'd met (probably at the Stork Club) who'd told Art to look him up if he had any trouble.

Art, in civilian clothes, talked his way into Forrestal's office and told him why he was there and what he wanted: If he had to run a Navy band, he wanted it to be a *good* band. And he wanted it to play out where the action was—wherever the men were fighting.

Forrestal said okay. *Just like that,* he made a call to a man in Washington who gave Art a slip of paper that told one and all that Chief Petty Officer Arthur Shaw had one month and carte blanche to find enough 1-A men (in any service branch) to enlist in the Navy and make up a proper orchestra. Now Shaw was in business! War or no war, Artie Shaw would have a new band this year.

CHAPTER TWENTY-SEVEN

I Ask the Stars

S HAW WOULD boast he had used psychology to persuade men to join his service band. He would stare at a fellow and say, "They'll get you in this war anyhow, and they'll put you to doing something else. When it's over, you won't be able to play. *Your lip will be gone.*"

But in truth, Artie didn't need to do much persuading. Most players were as eager to serve in Art's naval orchestra as they were to be in his civilian outfits.

John Best spurned offers from Glenn Miller and Benny Goodman to go with Artie. Max Kaminsky, who had already gotten his draft notice, switched over to Art's Navy branch. Tenor-saxophonist Sam Donohue had been leading his own orchestra before the draft board broke it up; he too joined the Navy to sign on with Art's ensemble. Claude Thornhill had been doing well with his outfit at the Glen Island Casino. But Claude said he wanted to serve as a member of Artie Shaw's naval band. "He *begged* me," Shaw said, and Art said okay, although he had already signed up a piano player. Claude could write arrangements.

For his drummer, Shaw picked Dave Tough. There was no doubt of Dave's ability. But the alcoholic, epileptic Tough didn't seem seaworthy; he now weighed just ninety-two pounds. Tough though was admitted with a medical waiver (as was Max Kaminsky).

Shaw's lineup was complete by December: twenty men, including himself, an accordionist (to substitute for a pianist in remote areas), and two arrangers. Navy Band 501—Shaw's "Rangers"—was stationed for a few weeks at Pier 92 on West Fifty-second Street. Betty Kern, staying in the Whitby Hotel, was pregnant. The Shaws broke this news (where better?) in the house bulletin of the Stork Club.

ART WANTED to go where the action was, out in the Pacific, but the Rangers' first posting, though tropical, was not in the hardship zone. From January to April 1943, Navy Band 501 played three afternoons a week at the Breakers, an enlisted-men's club at the edge of Waikiki Beach. Shaw lived at the Halekulani Hotel; Thornhill stayed with a friend in Honolulu; the rest of the men were in barracks on the site of an old pineapple plantation. In the evenings, the orchestra served up sounds at the Pearl Harbor officers' club. On days off from the Breakers, they gave concerts at service camps on nearby islands and on ships docked at Pearl.

It was an extended shakedown gig, a chance for the Rangers to learn the ropes. But the younger men (several of whom struck up romances in Honolulu) had trouble adjusting to even this easeful duty. They clashed with Shaw, whose high standards of bandstand decorum were raised to another level as a chief petty officer in charge of enlisted men.

And Art was soon at cross-purposes with his second-oldest friend. Artie went out of his way to showcase Claude, turning the orchestra over to him mid-set. But CPO Shaw had to insist on Navy discipline, and Thornhill was lackadaisical. "I was the leader of the band," Shaw said, "and he was used to being his *own* leader; wanted to be. Just didn't work: he wouldn't show *up*, he'd be *late*; he knew I was covering for him. I finally said, 'Look, I can't do this anymore. You have to show up at muster—every morning, you know; it's the Navy.'"

Playing piano at an officers' party one night, in a combo with Kaminsky and Tough, Thornhill caught the ear of Admiral Chester Nimitz. The pianist told the admiral that he would like to lead a Navy band of his own, and Nimitz arranged for it.

. . .

AT LAST, the Waikiki gig was over. After a month at sea, Shaw's Rangers debarked the battleship SS *North Carolina* at Nouméa, capital of New Caledonia, a French colony whose residents had taken it over in the name of resistance figure General Charles de Gaulle. Several thousand troops were on the island, which was Admiral William Halsey's headquarters. The band was based there for weeks. Drinking water was rationed (as were showers), and tainted Navy chow often caused food poisoning. Disease-carrying mosquitoes attacked at night.

Each morning, Shaw and the others gathered at the pier to be ferried out for concerts on one or more of the harbored ships or to perform on neighboring islands. The Rangers often played in jungle clearings. Once, wearing heavy-weather ponchos, they played at night in a pouring rain for GIs who were so excited by their presence that they didn't want them to leave.

Then there was the time Shaw and his men performed an evening show aboard the aircraft-carrier *Saratoga*, a performance that no one who saw it ever forgot.

"Since it was night," Kaminsky wrote,

> the men were gathered on the lower deck, and our entrance alone sent them off into an uproar. We set up the bandstand on the huge aircraft elevator and began playing our theme song, "Nightmare," as we descended slowly into the midst of the wildly cheering men. It was like being back in the Paramount Theatre again. . . . As I sat there looking out at these thousands and thousands of sailors and feeling the waves of homesickness flow out of them at the sound of the familiar songs, I began to fill up so much that when I stood up to take my solo on the "St. Louis Blues," I blew like a madman. On hearing me let loose, Dave [Tough] started to swing the beat, and when I picked up my plunger and started to growl, those three thousand men went stark, raving crazy.

It was Shaw's responsibility to cadge rides, arrange for "concerts," and secure food and tents for his men. "We hitch-hiked everywhere," he told a *Metronome* writer. "Sometimes on a large ship, then a smaller one, and sometimes by airplane. We traveled any way we could."

"I was the lowest of the low," he would tell a *New Yorker* writer twenty years later. "The brass considered our mission silly, and I heard a lot of 'You're not in Hollywood now.' . . . But there were things that made it all worthwhile. . . . Sometimes those forlorn, homesick birds would throw their hats in the air and cheer for five minutes. It made a lump come into my throat, I can tell you."

In time the Rangers left Nouméa and went north by plane to a new base on Espiritu Santo; from there they made jaunts through the New Hebrides and the Solomons, as they got closer to the front.

In July they arrived at Guadalcanal, where the ground battle was almost over but nightly Japanese bombing runs continued. Artie Shaw was the first American "act" to reach the battle-torn island. The troops housed Shaw's Rangers in tents so full of bullet holes they looked like Swiss cheese. Art and his men stayed for several weeks, spending almost as much time in foxholes as in their bunks. "Sometimes we'd be set up to play and have to run for the foxholes," Artie told Vladimir Simosko. "One night bombs landed close by the foxhole I was in, one on each side, bracketing it. We were deafened, and my hearing never came back in my left ear." (Shaw feared he might not be able to play again as a civilian, but he would find ways of adapting—holding his good ear toward the piano, for instance—that would allow him to cope.)

On Guadalcanal, the band heard "Begin the Beguine" and other Shaw records played over Radio Tokyo's *Zero Hour* program. In English, a Tokyo announcer reported that Shaw and his band this minute were playing at the St. Francis Hotel in San Francisco. "The idea was to make American boys homesick," Shaw told *Metronome*. "Out there on a tiny island, thousands of miles from the mainland, the boys and I got quite a kick from that spiel."

Also on Guadalcanal, Shaw learned by shortwave that Betty had given birth in Los Angeles to their baby: a seven-pound, one-ounce boy.

. . .

THROUGHOUT THESE extreme events, Shaw was still Shaw: high-strung, dogmatic—and a close man with a buck. Kaminsky told this anecdote: "We were on this battleship out there in and around the islands, and I wanted a cold drink, like a Coke; so I asked Artie to let me have a half-dollar. Now you know, you got to get the scene: there's a war going on, and they're blasting. Well, Shaw gives me a half-buck—then calmly reaches into his pocket, takes out a notebook, and marks it down."

In a civilian band, if Artie irked a guy or vice versa, it was two weeks' notice and the guy was gone. Here there was no way out. Cliques solidified; resentments grew. One group of players, including trumpeter Conrad Gozzo (a former Thornhill band member who came to the Rangers out of Goodman's orchestra), signed a pact that whoever could get Shaw near the side of a moving ship would push him overboard.

On and near Guadalcanal, the temperature was often a humid 110 degrees. Jungle rot disintegrated everything from boots to books. Instruments fell apart; saxes separated at the metal seams, leather pads fell off.

The men were coming apart too. Dave Tough and Max Kaminsky got dengue fever; Kaminsky had screaming nightmares. All around, people were wounded and killed.

The breaking point for Shaw came one night on Guadalcanal: he found himself setting out on a sudden hike. "I just took off walking," he said. "I was headed into the jungle. This officer in a jeep, he *saw* me; he knew what was goin' on. He drove right over, pulled up along-side. He says, 'Where you headed, sailor?' I said, 'I dunno.' He just said, 'Get in.' And I started to cry."

Displaying symptoms of battle fatigue, or "shell shock," Shaw got driven to a hospital and put to bed. *The New Yorker*'s Robert Lewis Taylor, in a 1962 Shaw profile, wrote,

A few days later, Dr. Mark Gerstle, the psychiatrist who was treating him, said briskly, "We're going to ask you to play a concert for the entire fleet tomorrow. Can you do it?"

"I can't blow a note," said Shaw. "I couldn't get out of this bed if my life depended on it."

"All right," the Doctor told him, "you're a goldbricking son of a bitch."

Shaw leaped up, drew on his trousers, and cried, "I'll show you, and, by God, you're no friend of mine!" The next day, he played perhaps the best concert of his naval career, before twenty thousand men, who practically went berserk with pleasure. "Oh, boy, how we hit it, how we hit it!" Shaw recalls with satisfaction.

The biggest men in the fighting Navy were aware of how Shaw and his men were hitting it, day in day out. "After we got down to the South Pacific, in the combat area . . . Admiral Halsey and other people came down, such as Admiral Nimitz, and led me to believe I did a good job down there," Shaw told a congressional committee in 1953. A candid picture was taken of Admirals Halsey and Fitch with Shaw, in the excited flush of a 1943 concert triumph: all three aglow with pride and mutual respect, like chiefs who have just won the big battle. But there's a hollow aspect to Art's grinning visage, as if his skull is a year-old jack-o'-lantern.

In August, the Rangers were pulled away from the front and sent back down the chain of islands they had visited before. Shaw and his band were assigned a one-month tour of New Zealand. They played at bases and hospitals and at servicemen's concerts and dances in Auckland and Wellington. The Rangers provoked reactions like those Shaw stirred at the Strand in 1938. "While Kiwi dads frowned on what they called 'that jungle music,'" a retrospective 1999 *Wellington Dominion* piece read, "Shaw's clarinet would have the local lasses jiving and jitterbugging as if their lives depended on it. And there was swooning aplenty when Shaw would call for the prettiest woman there to join him on the dance floor."

In September they went to Vella Lavella and other Solomon Islands, then to Australia and the cities of Melbourne, Brisbane, and Sydney. In Rockhampton, Shaw's Rangers had an overflow crowd jitterbugging in the streets. Max Kaminsky remembered playing in a huge stadium for an audience of fifty thousand.

Wherever he was, Shaw drew the attention of beautiful women. "[H]e was a natural target," Kaminsky wrote, "for the bored Navy wives, who all trained their guns on him at every dance we played." Asked, in his early nineties, if he had cheated on any of his wives, Shaw said, "Only one": Betty Kern. "Yeah, 'cause I was in the war. She was back here [in California]—and in the war, in Australia, and New Zealand, you *had* to. You were always out with a broad, they were always *after* you. And you're six thousand miles away, or whatever. Sure. The first time was awkward," he admitted. "I didn't—*do* it," he said, meaning the sexual act. "I'm a one-person person, or I *was*."

Shaw and his Rangers, having traveled maybe a hundred thousand miles, at last were out of gas: deemed unfit, at least for now, to further serve. From Brisbane, the whole band was sent back to the States for medical inspection, rest, and rehabilitation. In the past six months, they had survived seventeen bombing and strafing runs. Their luck held through a final voyage: Artie and his Rangers, without escort, made it all the way to San Francisco, often through sub-infested waters, on a lone Liberty Merchant ship. A news photographer snapped a picture of Shaw disembarking on November 11 in San Francisco: Art got down on his knees and kissed the dock.

CHAPTER TWENTY-EIGHT

Dearly Beloved

THE NAVY PUT Shaw in Oak Knoll Hospital in the Bay Area, where it was confirmed he had lost hearing in his left ear. He still had incapacitating migraines, he was twenty pounds under normal weight, and his teeth were bad. But his illness was more than physical: Art was morose, withdrawn, depressed. He was moved to a Section 8 ward for psychiatric observation.

"[There] a guy would ask me the God-damnedest questions you ever heard," Shaw told a pair of writers years later, "and I would look at him in utter astonishment. 'Do you hear voices?' I said, 'Yeah, I do.' 'Whose?' 'Mine, yours, kids out there in the yard hollering at each other. I hear all those voices. What do you expect. You mean like Joan of Arc?' He said, 'You hear Joan of Arc?'"

Given a month's leave, Art went south to Los Angeles. His Hollywood house was rented out now, and he couldn't make its occupants leave; there were wartime restrictions. Betty and their four-month-old baby, Steven Kern Shaw, were staying with her parents in Beverly Hills, which is where Art stayed too.

Steven was a cute, plump, sleepy-eyed blonde kid; Art adored him but didn't know how to relate to the infant. He tried whistling to see if the tyke would react, and he did—but only to "Pony Boy"; anything else—nothing. "For him there's just one tune in the books," Art said. At least it wasn't "Begin the Beguine."

A team from *Metronome* came to the Kern house to see Artie, who had been named that magazine's "Musician of the Year." Shaw spoke and posed on cue, but he was restless and self-conscious. "I couldn't do anything," he said, sixty years later. "I came back from the Navy burnt-out. I've seen pictures of me at that point; I look like a hollowed-out nothing. And I was."

The Navy gave Shaw, Tough, and Kaminsky medical discharges; Art was released from service in February 1944. Tenor-sax man Sam Donohue took over what was left of the Rangers and led them on a tour of Europe. Artie wouldn't say what his plans were, except he and Betty were house-hunting.

They found a Tudor-style home on Bedford Drive in Beverly Hills, not far from the Kerns' home on Whittier Drive. Jerome Kern, who doted on his daughter, took charge of remodeling the Shaws' house. Nothing was too good for Betty—or for little Steven, the new apple of his grandfather's eye.

Kern's feelings toward his famous son-in-law were ambivalent. The composer valued Shaw's musicianship ("a virtuoso, if I ever heard one," he wrote in praise of Art's 1938 recording of "Yesterdays"), but Art's "wide-ranging and probing fascination with all sorts of nickel knowledge sometimes confounded" him, according to Gerold Bordman.

Shaw's attitude toward Kern was also mixed. He had admired the composer since the 1920s and recorded nearly a dozen of his tunes, but he had also been criticized by the master. Guitarist Steve Jordan wrote, "Artie told me that Kern had a habit of writing letters to bandleaders, whether he knew them or not, after he heard them play one of his songs on the radio. He'd compliment them or—when he didn't like the arrangement—tell them that his song shouldn't be played that way. Shaw said he was most familiar with such Kern criticism long before he married Kern's daughter."

It seemed Kern cared more for his grandson than he did for Art, who may even have been jealous of Steven. But the composer spared no expense furnishing the Shaws' house with antique Chippendale and Sheraton furniture. "It was all too much," Art said.

Shaw did what he often did in uncomfortable circumstances: he took off. "I rented a car and drove around California for a while," he would testify nine years later. "I was sort of at loose ends. I didn't know quite what I was going to do with myself. I was pretty beat up at that time."

When he returned "home" to Beverly Hills, he went to his room. Just lying in bed, he was making enough in royalties to live in comfort. He had no reason at all to get up each day. But he could see that wasn't healthy.

Someone told him of a psychoanalyst in Beverly Hills, May Romm, who was easy to talk to. Art went to see her and had no trouble speaking for a whole hour about some of the things on his mind: the insanity of the world, his confusion about his place in it. When he was done, Romm said she thought he would benefit from analysis: he was articulate and could say what was bothering him. Shaw began a rigorous schedule of Freudian-analytic sessions, five mornings a week. He had a lot to sort out.

One of the things confronting him was the ambiguous state of his marriage. He didn't feel he belonged in it; it no longer seemed real to him. He had to understand why he had gotten married in the first place, and whether he ought to remain so.

For better or worse, answers came.

AFTER A COUPLE of months' therapy, Shaw started easing his way back into the public eye. On June 10, at NBC's Sunset and Vine studio, Artie Shaw recorded a number for the Armed Forces Radio Service program *Command Performance*, his first clarinet work since the Navy: a staid rendition, with studio orchestra, of "Long Ago and Far Away."

Also in June, Shaw sat down for an intense talk with Barry Ulanov, the bright young *Metronome* editor, with whom he mulled fundamental questions of life and art:

> *"I guess I had the healthiest attitude when I was first coming up," Artie mused. "All I cared about was that the band sounded good to me. You've got*

to have a certain integrity; without it, you're dead. Play what you want to, what satisfies you, not what seems to be commercial. . . .

"I know I may not attain everything I hope for. But in the constant struggle, in the self-criticism, is progress. And progress is what we all want."

Artie thought a while. *"I'm cursed with serious-mindedness,"* he said, *"and I know you can take yourself too seriously. Bix took himself too seriously; his self-concern was pathological. Unless you have the desire to live, to live a good deal apart from yourself, from that overbearing self-concern, you can't play."*

Shaw's rigorous regimen with the analyst was stirring up insights, not all of them pleasant to contemplate. Art admitted, "Very *hard* to say, 'I behaved *stupidly*.' Most people can't—*stand* that. It's terrible to know how stupid you really are, compared to what you gotta *know*."

Some of the hard things Shaw learned were about the marriage he no longer felt part of—if he ever had.

Things came to a head on the night of June 30, when the Kerns gave a dinner celebrating Steven's first birthday. Artie didn't want to go. He liked the boy, but he didn't want to get too close; he sensed he would be breaking up with Betty soon, and if he were still attached to Steven—well that wouldn't be fair, would it, to the boy? Or to Art. He showed up at the dinner but left early, "without warning," his wife said. She and others waited for his return. He didn't come back until three in the morning. "I believe he said he had been driving around," Betty would testify in divorce court.

A few weeks later, in the middle of the night, Art told Betty, "We just don't make sense together anymore." He left and checked into the Garden of Allah. Betty went with Steven to her parents' house.

Shaw's analysis caused him to see the real reason underlying his impulse to marry Jerome Kern's daughter: it was nothing to do with her and everything to do with the yearnings and sorrows of Arthur Arshawsky.

"I wanted to be in that *family*," Art realized. "I wanted to be the son."

CHAPTER TWENTY-NINE

Jumpin' on the Merry-Go-Round

MAYBE BETTY was hoping it was just a trial separation, but Art squelched that when he was seen on the town with a fetching actress. Hedda Hopper was quick to tell the world on August 7: "It isn't a blond Artie Shaw's interested in—it's a beautiful brunette." Three days later, Hopper had her name: "Ramsay Ames."

Miss Ames, a former Powers model, had sung with a rumba band at the Stork Club before coming to Hollywood and being signed by Universal, which pondered presenting her as "a female Tarzan" in *Jungle Girl*. On July 3, the *Los Angeles Times* had printed a photo of Ames in the arms of a uniformed Jackie Coogan, dancing at the Mocambo; Coogan had seen a pin-up photo of Ames while serving in India, the story said, and wrote to ask for a date. Shaw once before had taken a beautiful singing actress away from Jackie Coogan. Did this photo of the beaming Ames and the balding Coogan stir a competitive urge? On August 20, the *Times* ran an article on the leggy Ames, illustrated with a picture of her in a flesh-baring costume, in which she now said, "Surely I like Artie Shaw."

Two days after that, Betty sued Artie for divorce, charging him with "extreme cruelty" causing "great mental anguish." Shaw didn't contest the suit. On September 29, it was decreed that Art would pay Betty two thousand dollars a month support for herself and their child for the next five years; she would have sole custody of Steven until he was six.

WITH RAMSAY AMES seeming to prefer Jackie Coogan's company after all (though soon she'd be dating Xavier Cugat), Artie began seeing Lana Turner in private. Lana, after divorcing and then remarrying the father of her baby Cheryl, had again divorced Stephen Crane in a split that became final that month.

Buddy DeFranco met Shaw with Turner at a movie producer's Beverly Hills bash: "I happened to be hired to play that party," said the clarinetist, then twenty-one. "Dodo Marmarosa was hired with me, to play piano. A lotta well-known stars were there. And Artie, with his ego—he had an unbelievable ego, as everyone knows—he was very polite but kind of standoffish about my *playing*, you know. I don't think he even acknowledged that I played the *clarinet*; he just said hello to this *person*." But Shaw had ears for Buddy's friend Marmarosa, whom DeFranco had worked with in several bands including Gene Krupa's, Charlie Barnet's, and now Tommy Dorsey's. Just eighteen, Marmarosa showed a great harmonic sense and impeccable technique.

Shaw was edging back into the music world, and with everyone from Dorsey to Harry James to Billie Holiday now following his old lead and recording with strings, Artie decided any new band he formed would have just the standard seventeen pieces. He was looking for men to fill those chairs. Dorsey, in town making a movie at MGM, had lots of fine players. After taking note of Tommy's pianist, Shaw had a talk with Dorsey's drummer: his own old employee, back from the Marines, Buddy Rich.

Buddy insisted his contract with Dorsey was firm, but he and Art spent time together in the weeks Rich was working at MGM. Shaw went to Watts several times with Rich and others, including Dorsey, to catch Count Basie's band during its month-long stay at the Plantation.

There, on the night of September 20, an FBI agent served Basie's drummer Jo Jones and tenor-saxophonist Lester Young with draft notices; "Prez" and Jo were to report to an induction center the next morning. Basie had to look no further than his audience for substitutes: "Buddy Rich took Jo's place and Artie Shaw played Prez's part until [saxophonist] Lucky Thompson came in the band," tenor-man Buddy Tate recalled, adding, "Artie Shaw was playing tenor parts on clarinet, but Basie wouldn't let *us* play clarinets."

Basie's band closed at the Plantation on October 4. The Count handed Rich a blank check in return for his help. Rich gave it right back, so Basie sent the drummer a gold watch inscribed "To Buddy from the Count. L.A. Thanks," which Rich wore with pride, in place of the Patek Philippe that Lana Turner had laid on him a couple of years earlier.

Shaw too wanted something from Basie other than money: Art craved the arrangement, or "chart," for a hard-swinging Buck Clayton number the Count featured this season, a number that pulsed with the urgency of a big-city neighborhood, if you took a cue from its title, "Avenue C"—which had special meaning for Artie Shaw, now excavating his past through psychoanalysis. Avenue C, on New York's Lower East Side, was the street where Arthur Arshawsky had lived once upon a time.

MOVING AHEAD with his own plans, Shaw hired Benny Goodman's trumpet-playing brother Freddy—not as a musician, but to road-manage the band Shaw was assembling in the fall of 1944. Auditions began in October, first at RCA Victor's Hollywood studio and then at Shaw's Beverly Hills house.

Through analysis, Artie said, he developed a reason to want to live again. His motive involved going back to work: making a living, making music. Shaw said May Romm approved: "'Work comes first, your life comes first; go ahead. But you couldn't have done this six months ago.' I said, 'No, I couldn't.'"

Another way Romm helped him, Art felt, was in forming a new attitude toward women: "'Cause my *mother* was one of my major problems.

So—[May Romm] became, as a kind of transference thing, my mother, in a way. And, through *her*, I began to realize that—women could be o-*kay*. See my mother gave me this exaggeratedly strange feeling about women—in *general*. She was a—Jewish albatross around my neck."

Art found a spectacular candidate with whom to test his newfound perceptions: a luscious twenty-one-year-old MGM contract actress whose photograph (like Ramsay Ames's) he had also seen in the *Los Angeles Times*. His ex-flame Frances Neal (now Mrs. Van Heflin) knew the young woman—Ava Gardner—and arranged an introduction at the Mocambo supper-club. Ava, who had already been married to and divorced from actor Mickey Rooney, was a big fan of Art's music. The two began dating—every night.

Gardner was taken with Shaw's looks, intelligence, confidence, and charming manner: "I fell in love with him," she would write, "just like *that*." But the two were in no rush to consummate their relationship. For eight months, they went out on the town and just talked: "No funny business. Hands off."

Shaw and Gardner made a terrific-looking couple: she with her dark hair piled high or falling to her shoulders, wearing a smartly tailored, narrow-lapelled tan suit or a black satin dress; he in a wide-lapelled sports jacket, or a dark suit with hand-painted tie. Her phenomenal glamour (English journalist Alistair Cooke would say she was the most beautiful woman he ever met) made the vestiges of Art's wartime trauma look like the traces of world-weary sophistication.

They ate at Lucy's on Melrose, across from the RKO movie studio. They danced at the Mocambo. And, three late-October nights in a row, they checked out clarinetist Woody Herman's hot new band at the Palladium.

"Woody had a good band," Shaw conceded. "I don't know how he did it; he played badly. Played alto pretty *well*; clarinet was sorta— childish-playing. But he did have good bands; they made some good music." The drummer in this Herman herd was the resilient-seeming Dave Tough.

Art's own budding ensemble was accumulating a raft of outstanding men: the trombonist-arrangers Ray Conniff and Harry Rodgers, from Shaw's prewar orchestra; that fine kid pianist from Dorsey's crew, Dodo Marmarosa; Herbie Steward, an eighteen-year-old alto and tenor saxophonist; twenty-one-year-old electric guitarist Barney Kessel; a solid drummer, Lou Fromm; and, as a trumpet player to be showcased as Shaw had presented Lips Page, another "colored" star of long standing, Roy "Little Jazz" Eldridge. The trumpeter was a superlative soloist, full of fire and drive; he would without a doubt up the wattage of Artie's ensemble and spark Shaw to a high level in his own playing. Eldridge would also be in the front line of a new version of Artie Shaw's Gramercy 5.

"Artie knew where the best stuff was, and he admired it," said the African-American writer Albert Murray, who became acquainted with Shaw in the late 1940s. "A guy like Roy would fulfill both the popular part of Artie Shaw—and the hard, musical part, you see? Artie liked the *force* of the music that Roy played so well. The closer that Art got to the lifestyle which was being stylized in that music, the happier he was, because he knew that he could make the horn sound like he wanted it to sound, you know? He had a kind of a technique that was able to play what he could *hear*, you see? He wanted to be *close* to the down-home voicings—so that he sounds natural with 'em, when he's playing with 'em; he could play and still make you *believe* it, at the same time. There's a superior technique involved; and it wasn't just academic; it really was a mastery of the horn. He didn't even think about the restrictions, and so forth, that booking-people had about the Harlem musicians. And of course Charlie Barnet was like that too, you see; and Benny Goodman: 'Don't mess with my musicians!'—that type of thing. But nobody was stronger in that way than Artie. Artie was just as famous, or notorious, for always having outstanding Negroes in his band—not in rebellion against some taboo, but because he liked the way they *sounded*!"

==== CHAPTER THIRTY ====

Little Jazz

SHAW TOOK the new orchestra on a four-month theater tour of the Midwest and East, a jaunt which paid him an average of twelve thousand dollars a week and ended in a five-week stay at New York's Strand Theatre, where a fresh crop of jitterbugs welcomed Shaw and his band like Parisians cheering the liberating Yanks.

"It was a helluva band you're talkin' about!" said trumpeter Paul Cohen, who was with the orchestra during that triumphant Strand booking. Shaw's crew played forty minutes of music each show, Cohen said, to large and appreciative audiences: "During the war, you could hardly get into some of the theaters, they were so crowded; that's why we did *minimum* four shows. Because that *was* the entertainment business at that time."

Each set had stopwatch precision. Every Shaw show began with "Avenue C," Cohen said, the Buck Clayton piece Art dug so much. "We opened with that tune, every show, because it was a swinger." Buster Harding's "Bedford Drive," named for the Beverly Hills street where Artie now lived, was another foot-tapper. Eldridge was showcased with the full band on Johnny Green's "Body and Soul." There were a couple numbers by the Gramercy 5, then a barn-burner with solos from half-a-dozen men. And always there were the Shaw perennials—"Star Dust,"

"Frenesi," "Begin the Beguine"—every show, four times a day, with "Nightmare" as the closing theme.

"And when he played 'Begin the Beguine,'" Cohen said, "there was screaming in the audience. *Screams!* 'He's playing—Be-*gin* the Be-*guine!*' And Artie *hated* it! Because he *had* to play it—every *time*, every *place*, every-*where*! He was bored of playing 'ba-da-da *dee*, ba-day-da-da *dee*'— and he had to play it perfect, every time. That is the hardest thing to do, for a jazz player: play something that became famous. Because now you can't even extrapolate on it anymore; you have to play it note for note, or else people say, 'What happened?' He *had* to play it every show. You know, he was a commercial artist; he wouldn't be somebody who would say, 'I won't *do* that!' No. You either quit, or play it. And he played it. Until he quit!"

When Art did play, Cohen said, it was perfection. "He had a great sense of time; I mean, when he had to come in with his solo, it came in like it was a record date. It was like *right on*; and when he ended it, he didn't interfere with what the band was playing—before, or after. I mean, Artie was a genius, at what *he* did. What a beautiful sound, and he had a—God, a good concept. He always played with a good beat, and with a good sound. You *hadda* like him. There's no way you could not like Artie Shaw."

And Art found ways to keep liking the music he made. "I believe you can always enlarge the musical horizon by giving the public just a little more than what it wants," he told Leonard Feather late one night in a New York bar. ". . . Sure, when you play in theatres you have to do a lot of crummy songs and request-numbers, but on records you can experiment, and sometimes you can establish a new number via records so that it will be accepted in person."

Artie, with the help of a publicist, was making an effort to reconnect with the public and erase the still-lingering memory of that six-year-old anti-jitterbug outburst. But speaking his mind sparked new controversy: when Art, in a canned feature sent out by his PR man, tried to describe forces impeding the making of honest music, he got mocked from *Time* to *Variety* for having "unleashed a scathing denunciation of radio programs in general, publicists, fan magazines, fan club promoters"—and for calling jazz "a dying duck."

Shaw tried to clarify his remarks in the March issue of *Metronome*: What he *meant* to say, the magazine obliged, was that jazz was "not dying, but somewhat emaciated.... And what causes the condition, he said, was the lack of integrity of men in the business, from top to bottom, from bandleader to booker to record executive." More eloquent than anything spoken, maybe, was the photo of a coatless, morose Shaw on *Metronome*'s cover: elbows on knees, a dapper version of Rodin's Thinker, clutching a clarinet in his fists like a weary bargeman poling the river of life. "I never saw him *smile!*" Paul Cohen realized, sixty years later. "At that time, I don't think Artie was happy about *anything.*"

He had hoped and expected to land a movie gig for his band— but Artie turned down half-a-dozen studio offers when none promised a "realistic" treatment of jazz. The radio show he had looked for failed to materialize. In order to meet his band's payroll then—all the men were on salary full-time, for an estimated three hundred thousand dollars a year—he would have to do more live work. "He preferred doing concerts rather than dances," said tenor-man Ralph Rosenlund, who replaced a drafted Herbie Steward, "because of the kids [at dances] jumpin' up and down in front of the bandstand. He wanted people to *listen* to the arrangements and the tonal qualities of everything; that was his idea of music."

YES, ARTIE SHAW was particular. Not even Ava Gardner met with his full approval or had his entire attention—though she certainly drew everyone else's.

Ava was with Art in New York; she sat next to him opposite Leonard Feather in that New York bar as Artie held forth for hours, expounding "on everything from Harry S Truman to the FEPC [Fair Employment Practices Commission] to Count Basie's rhythm section," the critic said. "I found the conversation most stimulating, but [Ava Gardner] scarcely uttered a word all evening."

"I always wanted to be smart," Ava, a farmer's daughter from Grab-town, North Carolina, would tell singer Rosemary Clooney. "People thought I was shy, but I was just afraid to open my mouth, because I thought I'd sound stupid. I always wanted to learn stuff."

Gardner was sidelined with an ear infection during her New York trip. Shaw, at the Strand, was confronted by any number of Manhattan beauties—including Gloria Vanderbilt, the twenty-five-year-old just-divorced heiress and aspiring actress, and a longtime friend of Bill Saroyan's wife, Carol. Art and Gloria spent a good deal of time together in Manhattan. One New York paper quoted him saying he was in love with her. "He certainly was a ladies' man," Paul Cohen would say, "and a good-*lookin'* man. He was that."

But Vanderbilt had other irons in the fire. (In April, she would marry Art's ex–Summit Ridge Drive neighbor, the sixty-three-year-old symphony conductor Leopold Stokowski.) It was Ava, not Gloria, who went back to Los Angeles with Artie in March, moved into his house on Bedford Drive, and at last began a bona fide, unignorable Hollywood affair.

IN L.A. in April, Shaw took his band into the studio for the first of twenty-four formidable recording sessions through the next six months.

"Artie had a contract that he could *not* get *out* of," Paul Cohen said. "So we used to come back from wherever we were performing and go into the studio and do three hours a day, three days a week." The new contract may have been demanding, but it was also rewarding: It guaranteed Shaw a yearly royalty of $100,000 and paid him $1,250 for each 78 made and $1,500 for the occasional 12-inch side. "And he was in control of whatever left the studio," Cohen said, "which was unusual for a bandleader working for a big corporation; at that time, big record companies, they were very much in charge. But Artie said, 'You don't put that mother out until I tell you you can.' And naturally, you know, he made some great records."

One, from April 5, was "Little Jazz," a Buster Harding original fashioned to feature Eldridge. At the same time it was pure Shaw: solid swing with a modern edge.

Art worked hard to get that brilliance. "He's such a perfection-ist," Eldridge reported. "I'll never forget this as long as I live. We were recording one night, and I marked it down: one, two, three, four . . . thirty-eight attempts. And Shaw said, 'Well, we're going to finish this thing if we have to stay here until eight in the morning. If anybody doesn't like it they can go home.' I said, 'Well, I'll go home.' He says, 'I'm not talking to you.'"

Eldridge was the band's sparkplug, well worth the five hundred a week he was said to be getting. Just playing a simple four-bar break, he could jolt the band—and its leader—into higher gear. And when he stood front and center to play the theme of "Summertime," he was an integral part of one of Artie Shaw's most memorable numbers.

The Shaw band's extraordinary arrangement of George Gershwin's 1935 Broadway aria was written by Eddie Sauter, one of the most cre-ative orchestrators in the big-band field. Sauter's inventive settings of others' melodies were often, in essence, original works.

"He was 'the novelist,'" Paul Cohen said. "You want an Eddie Sauter arrangement, you're gonna hear somethin' that you never heard any-body else do before; it's always completely different, musically, at that time. Nobody ever *wrote* like him. 'Summertime'—that in particular, and the way Artie played it, was like a perfect chart."

Shaw's and Sauter's "Summertime" began with Dodo Marmarosa's treble-clef trill, rippling like a heat shimmer on a Harlem street. As the band played an insistent figure sotto voce, Shaw delivered a variation on Gershwin's lullaby lament with intense languor and yearning. "He states the melody in such a *great* fashion," said Buddy DeFranco, "that that's all you need to *hear* from Artie. It was just marvelous." Another lingering trill from Marmarosa—then Roy Eldridge, squeezing middle-register notes through a plunger-mute, played the next sixteen bars like a subconscious reflection of Art.

The band modulated into a passage scored for multiple clarinets: a flight of high-pitched reeds like a flock of birds soaring in the hot July air. A saxophonist wandered below on the boulevard, looked in a café window, saw and heard a lone pianist hunched in reverie. Then the orchestra came back, and Shaw was right with them, spinning a beautiful abstraction of that half-remembered tune, ending in an a cappella cadenza. Other horns uttered single tones in a twist of a sonic kaleidoscope. The whole vision faded into the pianist's final ascending run.

Five minutes was the length of this opus, but it seemed to last only as long as a passing thought. The orchestra honed this "Summertime" in stage performance, and it became a crowd-pleaser. Even Artie thought it came off fine, "one where the band did what it was supposed to do."

But when Art and the men gathered in Victor's Hollywood studio on April 17 to record "Summertime," Eldridge threw a wrench in the works: Though he had used a plunger-mute during the piece for weeks onstage, Roy—winner of this year's *Metronome* poll as "Hot Trumpet" soloist—balked at using the mute on disc, saying it would make him sound like Cootie Williams or some other such growl-*meister*. He flat-out refused.

Without the mute, the piece's whole texture was spoiled, Art felt. All those colors gone from the palette; all that loving work destroyed. Shaw said they might as well all go home right now—because if Roy didn't use the plunger, they were not recording "Summertime." And Roy Eldridge could pay for the day's session.

Eldridge agreed to the mute. "Summertime" was captured in two long takes, each splendid. The record would become a high point of both Shaw's and Eldridge's work.

Friction over the mute, though, underscored the problems Art faced as a leader intent on realizing a particular conception. "I didn't *mind* if we had guys in the band like Billy Butterfield, and they were *stars*," he would say. "Jack Jenney. But I wasn't building a band *around* them. Roy Eldridge had that problem with me. Roy got to be outa *hand*. They get this applause, it drives them crazy; and they read the critics—then they get all these weird notions about themselves. They forget, they are working *in* a *band*. And if it's a good band, it plays within a certain *range* of *styles*. You don't suddenly change your whole band 'cause it's got one guy who wants to do somethin' *else*. You have to be a very strict disciplinarian, when you run a band. It goes against everything I *think*, but—you gotta *do* it."

THE ORCHESTRA was booked for the last week in April at the Golden Gate Theatre in San Francisco.

"We would take a bus up there," tenor-man Ralph Rosenlund said. "Artie traveled separately; he had a Cadillac, and a valet that went along with him. The bus'd go by his house on Bedford Drive and pick up two or three suitcase-trunks of clothing, so that when he got to the theater in San Francisco he'd have a choice of five or six different suits, whatever he wanted to wear; but he went in his own car."

Shaw had more than his valet for company in San Francisco. "Ava Gardner came backstage one time," Cohen remembered, "and she knocked on the door when I just happened to be walkin' out of the first show. She had a tennis racket in her hand, and she said, 'Is Ahtie coming out *soon*?'—in her beautiful, melodious voice. And here I am, a little kid, I'm like nineteen or twenty; I said to myself, 'That's Ava Gardner! Is *she* a beautiful woman, oh my God!' I said to her, 'He'll be out presently, honey . . .' and I walked on. And then I said, '*Wow!*' Artie had a big kick out of it."

Shaw and his band members had to stay in Oakland this trip: the hotels in San Francisco were booked tight with delegates to the United Nations conference. Representatives from scores of countries were gathered to write a charter for an international body that, it was hoped, would bring peace and stability to the world. Artie was all in favor of that—and found a way in which he himself might take part in the worthy endeavor.

According to news reports, Arabia was the only one of the forty-six United Nations countries not to have a national anthem. Shaw vowed to write one for it, "in the interests of international harmony." He began composing it late in the evenings, he said, by candlelight, and came up with a melody in F minor. It was a great anthem, he assured reporters (including one from the Communist paper *People's World*), "as good as the 'Marseillaise' and 'The Star-Spangled Banner.'" It was his own personal contribution to the UN conference, he said; and he invited Saudi Arabian delegates to come to the Golden Gate the night of May 1 for its world premiere. There were no words to the anthem, Art acknowledged, but words could be written; it was a task worthy, he said, of "the greatest poet in Arabia."

The premiere was called off at the last minute though. It seemed there was a good reason why the Arabs had always done without an anthem: "Shaw suddenly learned to his sorrow and surprise," thanks to a helpful Arabian American Oil Company (ARAMCO) executive, the United Press wrote, "that musical instruments, music and musicians are taboo in Saudi Arabia."

CHAPTER THIRTY-ONE

The Grabtown Grapple

L ITERATURE and music were still the twin poles of Shaw's artistic ambitions. Back in L.A. in May, Art—who had spent a memorable prewar New York evening drinking and talking with Ernest Hemingway, and who would maintain a long-term acquaintanceship with Sinclair Lewis—now made a new writer-friend.

"We used to talk about books quite a lot," said Budd Schulberg, whose four-year-old novel *What Makes Sammy Run?* was already considered a classic work of Hollywood fiction. Schulberg and his wife double-dated with Art and Ava several times in 1945. A screenwriter as well as a novelist, Schulberg had grown up the child of a powerful movie-town executive whose antecedents came from Odessa. Schulberg was smart, accomplished, politically engaged, but Shaw treated him with no special deference. "He had a funny way about him," Schulberg said. "He would discover all these books with an attitude of, 'Well you better *read* it'—and they'd always be very famous books, like the autobiography of Lincoln Steffens. But there was something very touching about the way he was so intellectually curious."

Shaw's curiosity, though, did not leave room for his date's participation. Artie shut Ava out of the discussion, Schulberg said: "He wanted to talk with me, but he didn't want to let her into the conversation."

Whenever Schulberg saw Gardner in later years, Ava would remind Budd of his patience answering her questions about books—just the opposite, she said, of Artie's abrupt dismissals. "She said, 'He would say, "Oh you wouldn't understand, you wouldn't know, you're just a dumb broad."' She said, 'Artie was always so mean to me that way, never gave me any credit for having any brains.' She felt that he treated all women that way: sort of like they were just good for one thing, and he would put them down."

Art asked Budd about the mechanics of writing: "How I started, and how much every day, and all of that. We talked a lot about his *own* writing—about the ones he wanted to write. He spoke of wanting to go from somewhat like autobiographical short stories, working toward a memoir, but trying to write them as fiction rather than non-fiction; and we talked about the relationship between the two."

Art also talked politics: "He was very interested, very politically inclined and involved. I thought he was quite naïve in his approach. It was like a little boy learning, like a whole world opening up. I found it appealing in him, even though it could be insufferable, because—if you just mentioned something, he could take off in discourse. I would say he tended to monopolize the conversation; yes, he did. He was sort of nonstop, and I always thought he didn't *listen* all that well. I mean he would mention a book—I don't care *what* it was, Upton Sinclair or something—and if I said, 'Yes, Artie, I know it, I've read it,' it's like he wouldn't hear that; he would tell me all— *all* about it. Like a kid, just discovering something and wanting to share it with you."

Schulberg went to see Shaw and his orchestra perform. "He really was a genius, on that clarinet," Budd said. "He really was a *genius*. But he would stand with his back turned, and he would play these great solos, and he—wouldn't acknowledge the audience." Schulberg chuckled. "He sort of treated them the same way, almost, like he treated Ava. They were just—idolizing him! And he didn't give *them* the time of day either. He was a funny guy, he really was. I liked him. I couldn't help liking him."

. . .

HOLLYWOOD STUDIOS went to great lengths to preserve the whole-some images of their valuable players. Stars signed contracts with morals clauses allowing them to be fired for violating prevailing standards of decency. Syndicated gossip columnists praised or scolded movie-colony residents according to how well they behaved. Ava and Artie provoked this establishment's alarm through their cohabitation. Hedda Hopper and Louella Parsons began calling Shaw and Gardner on a frequent basis: When are you two kids going to get *married*? Can we announce the *date*?

Art devised a scheme to ease the scrutiny. An apartment was rented to serve as Ava's residence; at the same time, Art brought his mother from New York to live in Los Angeles. In theory, Sarah Shaw would reside with her son in his Beverly Hills home. In fact, she would live in the rented apartment, while Ava remained with Artie on Bedford Drive.

IN SUMMER, Shaw's recording schedule moved into high gear. Through June and July, he took the band into the studio twenty times. "We spent six weeks there, in '45," Ralph Rosenlund said. "I was on fifty-two sides with Shaw."

Paul Cohen was even more impressed now with Art's impeccable standards: "When he came into that studio, he was Mister Perfect, you know? Everything he did was precise, and with *taste*." It was the overall effect Shaw cared most about, Rosenlund felt: "That was the difference I think between him and Benny Goodman. I always thought Benny was mechanical, more mathematical; where Shaw was *musical*. Even in his tone, when you listen to Shaw's tone, he had probably the prettiest."

Eldridge noted another difference between Shaw and Goodman: "[H]is best gift was in knowing how to rehearse a band, how to get the best out of musicians, getting them to interpret. He was outstanding at this, whereas Benny Goodman was no good at explaining what he wanted; so a lot of time and effort was wasted at rehearsals, whereas Artie knew exactly what he wanted and could connect with his sidemen."

"He had a lot to do with the selection of everything," Rosenlund said, "tunes and arrangements. Pretty talented man. They weren't the usual three-minutes-and-ten-seconds things. Like 'The Maid with the Flaccid Air,'"—an Eddie Sauter original with a title that punned Debussy's "Maid with the Flaxen Hair"—"that was a *long* arrangement; it went on and on and on."

"Yes, they were incredible sides," Paul Cohen said of the discs Shaw's orchestra cut through the summer of 1945, which included Shaw's own arrangement of Margarita Lecuona's irresistible "Tabu," Ray Conniff's powerhouse original "Lucky Number"; classic midtempo ballads such as "They Can't Take That Away from Me," "Someone to Watch over Me," "Dancing on the Ceiling," and "I Can't Escape from You"; and the Gramercy 5 items "The Gentle Grifter" and "Mysterioso." "At that time, naturally," Cohen said, "we as musicians didn't take note of it too much, because—we thought *everything* we did was great! And if the public accepted it, well that's *enough!*"

Shaw and his men had been working like dogs in His Master's Voice's studio when the world war at last ended with Japan's surrender on August 14. Art gave himself and the band the last two weeks of August off. He and Ava spent the rest of the summer in a rented beach house on Malibu Road, in the midst of an informal artist community.

Next door there was New York playwright and short-story writer Irwin Shaw, in Hollywood to earn screenwriting money; Irwin and his wife gave a weekly Sunday brunch attended by such accomplished types as war-photographer Robert Capa, movie director George Stevens (whose documentary-film unit had just recorded the liberation of Dachau), and screenwriter Ivan Moffat (grandson of Sir Herbert Beerbohm Tree).

Other stimulating salons flourished in nearby neighborhoods, one of them hosted by German refugee composer Hanns Eisler; another was held at the Pacific Palisades home of émigré screenwriter Salka Viertel. Artie, with Ava, frequented several such gatherings, especially at the Viertels', where Shaw encountered many notables. "I met [Aldous] Huxley," he would say. "I met [Charlie] Chaplin. I met [astronomer

Edwin] Hubbell. I was lucky: I got to *meet* those people. Those were heady times."

Most impressive was Arnold Schoenberg, the seventy-one-year-old Austrian-born classical composer whose first works were written in the nineteenth century. "And when I met him," Shaw said, "I was—'Jesus, Arnold *Schoen*-berg?' It was like meeting Beethoven, you know, in a peculiar way. So I said, 'My *God!*' And he was very flattered that I *knew* of him; he was having a tough time. I said, 'How do you live, today?' He said, 'With difficulty.' He didn't have any money; he was broke. And I said, 'Well—you must have some money from royalties.'" Schoenberg had ties with RCA Victor, whose product was distributed around the world. "He said, 'No,' he said, 'it's all impounded.' This is during the war; the war was still on [or just over]. So I said, 'You mean to tell me that RCA won't—advance you some money, on the money that you have? Your German royalties must be very—very large.' 'Well, there's a considerable sum there, but they won't; it's the policy.'"

Artie knew all about policies. Classical or pop, Schoenberg or Shaw, it was the same record business. Art wrote a letter to an executive in New York, asking, Wouldn't it please be possible for RCA to send Arnold Schoenberg some of those monies due him? The label, he said, could insure the transaction with funds drawn from Shaw's own royalties, "if needs be." The label came through.

"I saved Schoenberg's butt," is how Shaw put it, sixty years later. "I got him an advance. And he called me; he was in tears. It was thirty-five thousand dollars—back *then*, 's lotta money. Saved his house."

Another key conversation Art had in Pacific Palisades was with Salka Viertel, who told him her father had been mayor of Sambor, the Austrian burg where Art's mother Sarah was born. It was a revelation for Shaw to learn that the hometown of his parent, a woman he viewed as being of peasant stock, wasn't, as he had assumed, a backwater village with geese flapping in its streets but a cosmopolitan town of some fifty thousand citizens. Still, Art thought, his mother must have come out of a very poor family.

His mother's presence in Los Angeles was an occasion for Art to rediscover his surviving parent's ability to irritate and embarrass him.

She showed up one night at a gig he was playing (maybe the Mexican Independence Day "fiesta dance" at the Shrine Auditorium on September 16), and somehow made her way onto the bandstand. Art shouted at her in the coarsest possible way to get the *hell* off the stage, how *dare* she, what did she think she was *doing*—giving her the same treatment he might give some fan who had riled him to the core.

"She was really goin' a little nuts," Art said. "Because, see—Her husband, she had forgotten about him; and she made me into a sort of surrogate husband. Not *knowing* she was *doing* it; and *I* didn't know she was doing it. Matter of fact she even gave people the impression she was Mrs. Artie Shaw. Very strange kind of thing."

Bolstered by insights gained through analysis, Artie forced a confrontation with Sarah. "We had a little party at my house," Shaw said. "She'd come out to the coast; give her a ticket, she'd come. And I was living with Ava at that time; we hadn't yet got married. And we had a couple of actors and some friends over: 'bout six, seven people, for dinner. My mother was—being so—always trying to, get *into* the *act*, you know." Sarah had just begun smoking cigarettes, at the age of sixty, because it was "the Hollywood thing" to do. "So anyway, around ten-thirty, I said, 'Mom—I think I'll take you home; it's a little late.' 'Cause the—conversation was strained; you had an older person, there. So I got in the car, and I started driving her to Ava's apartment; she was staying at Ava's apartment. And—she didn't say anything. We went into one of those: 'What's the matter?' 'Nothin'.' 'Come *on*, I *know* there's *somethin'*.' 'No, it's nothing.' I *hated* that. So I stopped the car, and I said, 'Look: *somethin's* the matter, you're acting very strangely. What *is* it?'

"'Aw,' she says, 'you're—you're *ashamed* of me.' I said, 'What are you *talking* about? I sent for you; you came *out* here; we had a party, you met all my friends.' 'Well, so why do you make me go home?' I said, 'Because they're *my* friends. And'—because of, in analysis I was thinking that way, I said—'you know I'm not your *husband*, I'm your *son*. As your son, I respect you as my mother. But I'm not—not your husband; if I were your husband, you'd—share my *life*. A husband shares friends with his wife. A son has his own life. You have no business there.' That—scared the shit out of her. She said, 'Who *said*—*husband*?' I was really hitting raw nerve.

"So it *got* to her. But it was a strange period, there, before I could make her understand, that she had to *divorce* from me; from *her* point of view, it was like a divorce. It was a bit *much* for her. Analysis, again, you know: you begin to call things what they *are*. So she changed, utterly, that night. She never did that again."

ROY ELDRIDGE too was having problems with life in California. As a black star in an otherwise white band, "Little Jazz" was still an oddity and racial discrimination still an everyday occurrence in this now-postwar year.

"It was only rough for him when we left the area," thought his section-mate Cohen. "Like, we even went to Mexico. And—it was embarrassing—the customs people in charge, they asked him to disrobe, and—do all those things, to go across the border. Yeah, that bothered me; I was ashamed in fact that we were Americans, and we still—didn't give the man his reputation, as a jazz player. Just *he* was given that kind of going-over, so you *know* it was racial; yeah, at the American side, before he went over to Mexico. Coming back, it was no problem. Maybe those first two guys were racist; maybe the guys coming back were *not* racist. You know, you can't put a stigma on *everybody*, but—I think those two particular people were son-of-a-bitches, what else can I tell you."

Artie had had a Negro trumpet player before, Lips Page, but Lips didn't let the racial stuff get to him. Eldridge had a different temperament. "He was a cute little stocky guy, a feisty guy, in many ways a tragic guy," Shaw told Whitney Balliett. "I told him I could handle racial matters when we were on the stand, but there was very little I could do when we were off. He used to carry a gun, and I'd try and discourage him; and he'd tell me that he'd rather take his chances with the police

Arthur Arshawsky with family: his looming father, Harold; his distraught mother, Sarah; his own wary self at maybe five years old. (Unpublished photograph of Artie Shaw used with the kind permission of the Estate of Artie Shaw)

Art Shaw in Chicago in the summer of 1930: just twenty but already posing for one of the best photographers in town. (David R. Phillips Collection)

Causing a sensation at the Imperial Theatre Swing Concert with his "Interlude in B-flat," May 24, 1936. (Photo by Charles Peterson, courtesy of Don Peterson)

The legendary jam session at Brunswick Records on March 14, 1937: Chick Webb, Artie Shaw, Duke Ellington. (Photo by Charles Peterson, courtesy of Don Peterson)

Artie Shaw and Billie Holiday at the Roseland-State Ballroom in Boston, in the spring of 1938. How young the two of them looked, and were. (Courtesy of Bob Inman)

The King of Swing and the King of the Clarinet: Benny Goodman greets Artie Shaw at the Waldorf-Astoria, 1939. (Wayne Knight Collection)

Shaw's orchestra, with drummer Buddy Rich, on the air for NBC. (Michael Ochs Archives / Getty Images)

Art surrounded by Ann Rutherford, June Preisser, and Lana Turner on the MGM set of *Dancing Co-Ed*, 1939: "All these great chicks—comin' at you." (Courtesy Photofest)

With Betty Grable at the Hollywood Brown Derby in the autumn of 1939, after she sued Jackie Coogan for divorce. (Bettmann/Corbis)

Artie and Lana Turner Shaw arrive in New York City on the 20th Century Limited, spring of 1940. (Bettmann/Corbis)

Shaw with his 1941 trumpet stars, Oran "Hot Lips" Page and Max Kaminsky. (Institute of Jazz Studies, Rutgers University)

Somewhere in the South Pacific, 1943, with Dave Tough on drums. (Frank Driggs Collection)

The star-studded postwar band that included Roy Eldridge, Ray Conniff, Barney Kessel, Dodo Marmarosa (here playing cymbal), and drummer Lou Fromm. (Frank Driggs Collection)

On the town with Ava Gardner in New York City, before the marriage that made the divorce inevitable. (Bettmann/Corbis)

Opening night at Bop City, 1949: critical fiasco, box-office smash.
(Martha Holmes, Time & Life Pictures / Getty Images)

Swearing to tell the truth to the House Committee
on Un-American Activities, 1953: "To the best of
my knowledge, I have never been a member of
the Communist Party." (Bettmann/Corbis)

Artie with Evelyn Keyes, 1967. His longest marriage:
twenty-eight years. (Bettmann/Corbis)

With the Pastor Brothers and their mother on the boys' opening night in New York City, 1971. Artie to Tony Jr. (far left): "I think you should lead my band . . ." (Tony Pastor Collection)

The lion in midwinter: as always, reading a book. (Photograph by William Claxton / Courtesy Demont Photo Management, LLC)

than run up against some crazy guy unarmed. He saw himself as traveling through a hostile land, and he was right."

The trumpet player had a one-year contract with Shaw, and it was understood that he would resume his solo career in November. But events prompted him to leave Shaw's band early.

It started in Del Mar, near San Diego, where the band played in late September. "I got in the hotel all right," Eldridge told Leonard Feather, "but couldn't eat in the dining room. Some of the guys who knew I liked Mexican food suggested that we go to a little Mexican joint. When they refused to serve me, all the other guys walked out with me; but it still started to put me in that mood again."

Things got worse at the San Diego venue: "[M]y name's up on the marquee, big as life. . . . So I walked in that night and the guy says, 'Where you goin'?' and I say, 'I play in the band.' 'You?' he said. 'This is a white band.' I said, 'But look out there, there's my name, Roy "Little Jazz" Eldridge.' But I'm still walking, see, and during those times I always carried a pistol, because you never know—you had to. And this man never knew how close he was to getting it."

Roy said, "When I finally did get in, I played that first set, trying to keep from crying. By the time I got through the set, the tears were rolling down my cheeks; I don't know how I made it. I went up to a dressing room and stood in a corner crying and saying to myself why the hell did I come out here again when I knew what would happen? Artie came in and he was real great. He made the guy apologize that wouldn't let me in, and got him fired.

"Ava Gardner was great, too. She's a very fine person, and she and Artie became real good friends to me. But I finally left the band . . . after another thing where I couldn't get into the auditorium."

Shaw wrote, "The racial pressures were getting to him. I did what I could but there were lots of ugly incidents, and one day when he was mad about everything he pulled a knife on me. I said, 'Roy, if I'm your enemy, who's your friend?' He started to cry and I took the knife away from him. Then I sat him down and told him, 'Look at yourself, it's tearing you up. Go to Europe for a while.' So I had to let him go."

Eldridge went back to New York, taking with him much of what had made this band so special. Roy was no longer standing next to Art in the spotlight, spurring Shaw to his best abilities. And the new Gramercy 5 seemed sort of pointless without Eldridge, whose essence had been such an integral part of its appeal.

OF EQUAL CONCERN to Art was MGM's unrelenting pressure for him and Gardner to marry, which increased as the final date neared for his divorce. Art had qualms about marriage, but he yearned for a settled life; and his sexual relationship with Ava at this point, he said, was "absolutely glorious." Later, when he and she broke up, Artie would claim the wedding took place just to appease her studio: "We got married so we could get divorced." But he would also say every one of his marriages was entered with hopes for success and a feeling that "this is *the* one."

On October 10, Betty Kern received her divorce decree: the last step of proceedings begun one year earlier before Judge Stanley Mosk. On October 17, Ava Gardner and Artie Shaw were married—by the same superior court judge, in his home in Beverly Hills.

Attending the small private ceremony were Frances Neal (Ava's matron of honor) and her husband, Van Heflin; Shaw's new best friend and best man, screenwriter Hy Kraft, and his wife; Ava's sister Beatrice ("Bappie")—and Art's mother.

Ava wore a gray-blue tailored suit, white gloves, and a corsage of white orchids. Artie wore a single-breasted suit of subtle tweed, a hand-painted silk tie, and a white carnation. The twenty-two-year-old Gardner looked breathless and gorgeous. Shaw, thirty-five, seemed proud, rueful—and happy.

THE NEXT THING he did was give his orchestra notice.

"He broke that band up when Ava Gardner and he decided they wanted to make a go of their marriage," Ralph Rosenlund said, "and he couldn't do it on the road with a band, so—that was the excuse he gave us when he called it off. We all went different directions. Bernie Glow, the trumpet player, went back to New York; and [altoist] Rudy Tanza and Barney [Kessel] and I went with [Charlie] Barnet. Everybody sorta scattered, and that was it."

While Art made this new start, the lives of others he had known came to a full stop.

On November 5, Jerome Kern, in New York to write music for a Broadway show about Annie Oakley, collapsed of a cerebral hemorrhage. Six days later he died at the age of sixty.

On November 21, Robert Benchley died in New York, aged fifty-six.

It had been seven years since Art worked with Bob on the Old Gold show. It seemed half a lifetime: one world war and three orchestras ago. In jazz, Artie said, ten years was *two* decades, so fast did the music change. He would have more than a little cause to ponder that phenomenon in the weeks to come.

CHAPTER THIRTY-TWO

The Glider

"REBOP," "BEBOP," or just-plain "bop" were tags given to the new style of jazz that blossomed in the winter of 1945. On first hearing, it seemed a music of jagged rhythms, erratic melodies, and dissonant harmonies, but those willing to keep listening often became converts.

The seeds of bop had been planted four years earlier by (for the most part) black musicians from various big bands: alto-saxophonist Charlie Parker, trumpeter John "Dizzy" Gillespie, pianist Thelonious Monk. In New York clubs including Monroe's Uptown House and Minton's Playhouse, such players met and jammed with like-minded contemporaries—trumpeter Benny Harris, pianist Bud Powell, drummer Kenny Clarke, and Benny Goodman's guitar-star Charlie Christian—as well as with swing-era vets such as Benny Goodman and Artie Shaw. "We listened to Artie Shaw instead of Benny Goodman," said Benny Harris (composer of "Ornithology," one of bebop's seminal pieces). "Goodman swung, but Shaw was more modern."

These musicians were extending the harmonic range of jazz, pushing chords to mathematical limits in efforts to find alternate routes to the sonic realm of Debussy, Bartók, and Stravinsky. The new players were drawn to obscure tunes with interesting "changes" from the repertoires of Duke Ellington and Artie Shaw, including Shaw's 1939 record "Zigeuner" and his 1941 disc "This Time the Dream's on Me."

"There," said clarinetist Buddy DeFranco of the latter record, with its distillation of Shaw's expressive essence, "he played 'Artie Shaw.' Another thing—the way he played 'This Time the Dream's' was similar to the way he played 'Star Dust': in the whole record, the famous one, he never plays the melody, but people generally would think that he did."

DeFranco was one of the first white players to study and absorb the bebop style (as was Dodo Marmarosa). He soon became "the" bop clarinetist, and he knew for a fact that Charlie "Bird" Parker, the phenomenal alto saxophonist whom bop fans and players revered, was an admirer of Artie Shaw's: "Of *course*. Bird and I were talkin' about Artie's playing, yeah, sure, and Bird would talk about certain records that Artie recorded, and certain solos that he liked—and he could play them, on the alto. Yeah, Bird was phenomenal. I know that he liked a lotta stuff that Artie did."

Just as Shaw as a youngster had learned by heart solos by Beiderbecke and Armstrong and Hawkins, so a next wave of jazz players memorized ad-lib flights by Artie and Lester Young and Benny Goodman. "But Benny was more of a swing player," DeFranco said. "So the boppers liked that about Benny: that it was swinging. Benny was more—what?—more obvious, in playing hot. Artie was more subtle, so you had to really *listen*—and think, in terms of the intellect. I have to really intellectually *understand* Artie, although he did swing; I thought his sense of time was *great*."

The boppers were inclined (for reasons of economy, autonomy, and increased soloing opportunity) to perform in small combos. Here too Shaw and other swing-star leaders showed the way, with their "band-within-the-band" small groups such as the Gramercy 5: tight little units that cooked like mad. Indeed, Artie's 1945 version of that group—featuring Eldridge (an influence on Gillespie), Marmarosa, and Kessel—might even have been mistaken, ten or twenty seconds at a time, for a collection of Fifty-second Street beboppers.

Even the 1940 Gramercy 5 sounded fresh this year, when "Summit Ridge Drive" was resurrected for inclusion in the movie *The Story of G.I. Joe.* "Summit Ridge Drive" had done okay in 1940, but when Victor reissued it in the wake of *G.I. Joe*, it became a million-seller: "Took off like a singed cat," Art said.

THE FIRST great bebop combo, co-led by Dizzy Gillespie and Charlie Parker, played New York's Three Deuces club in the spring of 1945. That winter, Gillespie brought his "Six Reboppers" (including Parker, vibist Milt Jackson, and drummer Max Roach) to L.A. for an extended engagement at Billy Berg's club, on Vine Street at De Longpre in Hollywood. All sorts of folk came to hear that group: movie stars, disc jockeys, modern artists, and other scene makers. The most attentive patrons were the musicians, including Marmarosa, Kessel, and Buddy Rich (all of whom would record with Parker in L.A.) and Artie Shaw.

Even as Parker and Gillespie were rending the Hollywood night with their hothouse-bop and congo-blues, Benny Goodman was across town in Culver City at the Meadowbrook Gardens, playing with a new youthful band he wouldn't unleash to play at its vigorous potential, just rehashing his ancient material ("King Porter Stomp," "Somebody Stole My Gal")—and, truth be told, drawing big crowds.

That could never be Art's way. Shaw might not be ready to become a rebopper, but neither would he run with open arms back to 1938. When Shaw made his next records, they'd be modern sounding—not avant-garde, but enough out in front to sound fresh and vital.

And they wouldn't be done for RCA Victor.

ART AND his longtime label were about to part company, after exchanging harsh words. "Artie Shaw isn't hungry anymore," RCA's Eli Oberstein complained. "Artie is no longer willing to put the hard work into his job that it takes to maintain a top-notch band these days. He thinks he can coast along on his reputation." Shaw countered, "Oberstein told me what I should record, and how, despite that my contract clearly stated I was to have full authority. Why should I, or any bandleader who wants to do things that are worthy of respect from musicians and people who know good music, take orders from someone like Oberstein?"

Victor would get back at Shaw by keeping several of his best recent sides (including "Summertime") from release for months or years, then putting them out in limited quantity. Artie, claiming his final session in 1945 had been produced at his own expense, took six discs with him when he went looking for a new label, including three outstanding modern-voiced originals: "Let's Walk," "The Glider," and "The Hornet."

Art brought his talents (and those masters) to Musicraft, a new independent label that signed several other major artists in early 1946 (Duke Ellington, Dizzy Gillespie, singer Sarah Vaughan) in part with the help of Shaw, rumored to own a piece of the company (though he and the label denied it). Artie's Musicraft arrangement was said to give him "unprecedented freedom" in deciding "what, where, when, and how often" to record: "the most generous deal any leader ever had."

It was a freedom Art tempered with business savvy. For his Musicraft debut, he came up with a project that promised both good music and decent sales: *Artie Shaw Plays Cole Porter*, an album (of 78-rpm discs) that matched Shaw's clarinet with a large session orchestra and some of the best singers on Musicraft's roster.

SINGERS HAD COME to the popular-music fore, as a host of males and females followed a gone-solo Frank Sinatra up the hit parade. Now big bands competed with vocalists for the public's attention; jazz and popular taste, brought together a decade ago, drifted apart.

Artie preferred (with exceptions) not to bother with singers, and he didn't care for the words to most songs. But Cole Porter—subject of a movie starring Cary Grant, to be released that year—wrote both music *and* words; a tribute album would have to include *some* lyrics. Shaw had novel ideas on how to present them. One involved a local five-member coed vocal group on Musicraft called the Mel-Tones.

Its Chicago-raised leader, twenty-year-old Mel Tormé, had been a professional performer since age four. He would write,

> I was summoned to a meeting at Artie's home on Bedford Drive, and the door to his neo-English Tudor house was opened by his current wife, the gloriously beautiful Ava Gardner. She smiled warmly and led me into the music room where Artie was seated at a piano, going over prospective tunes for the album with arranger Sonny Burke.
>
> I had been in awe of Shaw for years. Back at Hyde Park High, the controversy had raged daily: who is the better clarinetist, Goodman or Shaw? I was firmly entrenched in the Shavian camp.

For Shaw's versions of Porter's "I Got the Sun in the Morning" and "What Is This Thing Called Love," the Mel-Tones would be integrated into the orchestra's arrangements, with the vocalists' breezy, bebop-tinged phrasings (arranged by Tormé) used like an orchestra section's. "I was interested in recording some jazz-flavored pop music," Shaw told Vladimir Simosko. "That's all I wanted to do and I think it worked well. Using a vocal group as another section was a new idea; with four sections for texture and accompaniment—brass, reeds, strings and voices—there was a wider palette of tonal colors."

Art had another idea: he liked Tormé's voice a lot and wanted him to sing solo on "Get Out of Town." At first Mel thought he was kidding, but he wasn't. It would be the first time Tormé recorded on his own: the perfect start to a fifty-year solo career.

Shaw's initial Musicraft session was on April 30 at Radio Recorders, a new Hollywood facility noted for excellent sound. Among the date's thirty-one session musicians (including fifteen strings) were several old cohorts including Manny Klein, Ray Linn, Les Robinson, Chuck Gentry, Nick Fatool—and Zeke Zarchy, veteran of Artie's first 1936–37 band.

In the studio, old-pro Artie took special care of young Mel, who, in his dark sports coat and checked open-neck shirt, looked like a shy lion cub. "This kid's my favorite singer," Arthur told one and all. "I like the way this kid sings." Shaw made sure Tormé was miked properly: "You could hardly hear him," Art told John Tumpak. "We had to put him behind a lot of baffles, because the band would leak into his microphone." Zarchy said, "When everybody was sitting down and warmed up and everything, and we were ready to go, Artie turned to the control booth—which was run by some *relative* of somebody, was the A&R man—Artie turned to this guy and he said, 'Now when this guy starts to sing'—pointed to Mel—he says, 'Don't touch those dials! That's his natural voice!' We all laughed."

Art's record of "I Got the Sun in the Morning" became a hit. Sessions continued through the summer, yielding gorgeous Shaw instrumentals ("In the Still of the Night," "Night and Day," "I've Got You under My Skin"), Mel's impressive solo "Get Out of Town" (to which Art's clarinet contributed bold splashes of color), a brash and arresting Mel-Tones version of "What Is This Thing Called Love?," and, with twenty-four-year-old singer Kitty Kallen, a reading of "My Heart Belongs to Daddy" that became Shaw's second Musicraft hit.

These records would influence the course of American popular music (though in ways Shaw himself might dismiss or deride): Bob Flanigan, founder of the 1950s vocal group the Four Freshmen, would credit "Mel Tormé's collaborations with Artie Shaw" as a prime influence on his ensemble's sound; Brian Wilson, guiding force of the 1960s pop group the Beach Boys, would cite the Four Freshmen as *his* main inspiration.

Such affinities might (or might not) be gratifying to Art. But in 1946, Zeke Zarchy would be so moved by one of these Musicraft platters that he would express the *true* sincerest form of flattery: "We did that session with the Mel-Tones, and the band was an excellent band. And one of the tunes was 'What Is This Thing Called Love?' And I got so taken with the arrangement on it—you know, as they said postwar, 'the chart'—I *loved* that *chart* so much, and the vocal group and everything, I went out and bought the record!"

CHAPTER THIRTY-THREE

Bedford Drive

Tᴴᴱ ʀᴇᴀʟ trouble began, Ava said, after their Lake Tahoe honeymoon. "He persisted in humiliating me on every turn and disregarded my smallest wish," she would testify of Art, in *her* divorce suit. "When I was silent with friends, he would criticize me for not talking, saying: 'Have you nothing to contribute to the conversation?' But when I tried to say something, he would shout: 'Shut up!'"

Ava's friend Ruth Rosenthal Schecter told biographer Charles Higham, "One night a group of us were at Artie's house, sitting around the living-room floor. Ava was in a chair, with her shoes kicked off, and her bare feet tucked under her. Artie looked at her coldly and said in front of everyone, 'For God's sake, what are you doing? Do you think you're still in a tobacco field?' Well, she went white, she trembled, she cried. It was ghastly."

Artie countered as best he could: "She believed all her own publicity, and that I was the big meany." From his point of view, he was just trying to improve her: help turn her from what she was into what she should be, from a sharecropper's daughter into—well—Mrs. Artie Shaw. But what he was really afraid of, no doubt, was that she made *him* look gauche.

Art gave her a reading list for their honeymoon, Ava said: Sinclair Lewis's *Babbitt*, Dostoevsky's *The Brothers Karamazov*, Darwin's *On the*

216

Origin of Species, Henry Miller's *Tropic of Cancer* ("Holy shit, what a dirty book!" she's supposed to have said). The list lengthened: Marx's *Das Kapital*, Flaubert's *Madame Bovary*, Hemingway's *The Sun Also Rises*, Mann's *The Magic Mountain*. Of the last, she'd write, "I thought I'd never finish that damn book."

"She never got *near The Magic Mountain*," Artie said. "*The Sun Also Rises, maybe*; but—never finished it." As for the oft-told tale that Gardner bought a book on her own (*Forever Amber*, a best-selling "banned-in-Boston" novel of Regency England by Kathleen Winsor), only to have Shaw throw it across the room and forbid her to read "rubbish like that"—Artie would insist to Vladimir Simosko, "Never happened."

But he did find constant fault.

"She knew how to market the merchandise," he would say. "Everything she did was *designed*. I remember we'd go to a party, and she'd show a little too much—tit. 'Geez,' I'd say, 'isn't that a little—' She'd say, 'No no, it's tasteful, it's not gonna—' She knew *exactly* what she was doing. I found that in some way—uh, cheap. It's okay to *be* beautiful, but don't go *selling* it. Whether it's a hooker, or—you know, whatever."

By now it was a pattern: as soon as he married someone, he would start to pick her apart—and see what a bad deal he had made.

"Well he dismissed all of 'em," said Art's later friend Dr. Colter Rule. "First he set 'em up, and then he humiliated 'em. It was part of the repeated battle with his mother. That was a pretty tough scene for Artie as a little kid, to be dependent upon his mother, and particularly as apparently there was a great deal of friction; and I imagine he blamed her for the loss of the father. So . . . I think he was a very lonely guy. A very lonely guy. And he fought against it, and—pretended he didn't care. Pretended he was in charge of everything."

The problem was, he contained two people: Arthur Arshawsky, who craved a home life with a wife who made dinner and joined him in smart conversation, and Artie Shaw, celebrity-artist, who wanted a glamorous wife but didn't like the spotlight on her.

She was two people too—the country-girl nymph Art was charmed by (but deplored), and the headliner she was about to become.

They mixed and mingled their character traits, with disappointing results.

Art paid a Russian grand master to give Ava chess lessons. When she beat her husband in their first match, Artie no longer wanted to play.

Shaw negotiated Gardner's MGM contract up to $1,250 a week—then said he couldn't respect anyone who made her living as a movie actress. ("'Cause they're aiming at a kind of fame that very rarely has anything to do with *abilities*; it's cheekbones.")

Ava (or "Avala," as Art called her, in Yiddish variant) said she wanted a simple, happy marriage; yet as husbands, she picked an irrepressible MGM movie star, then a notorious big-band leader.

She said she wanted a child but never had one.

The sex had been great, they both said—until he lost interest.

"I remember when I was in [post–May Romm] psychoanalysis," Shaw told a radio interviewer, "and I told a joke, and the analyst liked it: There's a guy lying in bed with his wife . . . and he's trying hard—but nothing's happening. And she says, 'What's the matter?' He says, 'I can't think of anybody tonight.' . . . So I said to [the analyst], 'What happens if you're lying in bed with a *goddess* and you can't think of anybody?'"

"I would take a guess," said Shaw's long-time friend Red Buttons, "and say that all his love affairs ended in impotence. Look: it's a tough thing, you know, it's not natural to spend your whole lifetime with just one person. And I guess Artie felt that, eight times! When the physical attraction wore off, I think Artie—could not live with the mundane."

Call it a tragedy. Call it a damned shame. Call it a stupid mistake. Call it quits.

AVA WOULD SAY that she should have known divorce was at the back of Art's mind when he announced he was selling the Bedford Drive house and the two of them would move into a leased San Fernando Valley cottage. By the end of May, Shaw's Beverly Hills residence had new occupants: singer Benay Venuta (wife of Sears Roebuck heir Armand

Deutsch) and her two children. Artie and Ava squeezed into a little Burbank place Gardner found cramped and unappealing. She often stayed instead at her sister's house. Gossip hounds sniffed marriage trouble.

One reporter broached the topic to Artie by phone, on the evening of June 27.

"Do you mean you're living together but not living together as man and wife?"

"I don't see how you could do that. Not in a house this size."

But you could.

LACK OF a happy home life was only one of Art's postwar gripes.

When he had come back from the South Pacific, Shaw would tell a congressional committee in 1953, "I was very angry about a lot of things. There was a lot of black-marketeering and an awful lot of other things going on that I didn't like. I think you can understand a man who has been out in the Pacific and . . . got to the point where he doesn't know whether he's going to be able to make a living again at a profession that he made a lot of money at, can be a little disgruntled. There were a lot of things going on that I was very unhappy about—and I am not the only ex-serviceman to say that, or feel that way. It's an old story."

Hollywood acquaintances steered him toward HICCASP—the Hollywood Independent Citizens Committee of the Arts, Sciences and Professions—an organization dedicated to advancing stronger price controls, full employment, improved housing, health care, and a minimum wage; soon Shaw was on the group's executive council. By then, though, HICCASP was being criticized by both conservatives and Roosevelt liberals for its pro-Soviet positions. A minority of Communist HICCASP members, it was said, was directing the group.

Shaw would tell the congressional committee that in early 1946 he was invited to join the Communist Party. The approach began, he said, with a visit to his small Beverly Hills office from a man who refused to identify himself:

[H]e said if it seemed to me I was interested in the functions of such organizations as HICCASP, it was my clear duty to investigate what the Communist Party offered and how the Communist Party operated within these organizations. . . .

I said, "Well, I'll be very glad to see how they operate." He said, "The only way to do that is to attend some meetings." I said, "Well, I will be glad—very glad—to attend meetings." He said, "You can't attend the meetings unless you are a party member."

I said, "Well, I am not going to be a party member—I want to make that clear—before I know what I am getting into; and I will not sign any cards of an application to become one." . . .

What I did was to sign a piece of paper . . . which was, as far as I could see, not a party card. I read the thing carefully, and he said it was simply something to sign to enable me to go to meetings as a participant or as an observer. . . . I made up some name. . . . And he said, "I am confident if you go to a few of these meetings this will be what you want to do." . . .

At any rate, he gave me the address of a home, at which on . . . some night during the week, there would be a meeting. . . . That meeting concerned itself primarily with . . . how the [HICCASP] executive council . . . could best be moved in regard to establishing an FEPC—fair-employment practices—and an extension of the OPA [Office of Price Administration]. . . . It . . . seemed to me rather harmless at the time. . . .

. . . [A]nd there was [another meeting]. . . . On this one, the Hollywood Independent Citizens Committee of the Arts, Sciences and Professions was redrafting its charter, and one of the purposes . . . was to contain a statement that the [HICCASP] was against communism in any form whatsoever. . . . Certain members of the HICCASP council were against this resolution; others were for it. The thing was pretty well split down the middle. . . . So the thing was a pretty hot issue for a while.

. . . [It] was pretty well determined at that time—all of those present at that meeting who were members of the executive council . . . should vote against the issue of the HICCASP coming out against communism. . . .

At the end of that meeting, I spoke to the person who chaired that meeting; and I said, "Look . . . I am being told what to do, and I haven't yet

decided to join this thing. I am here as an observer; I am not here as a partici-
pant, but as an observer." . . . I said, "Look . . . I don't think I want to come
to any of these things anymore." . . . "Well, you suit yourself," more or less
that was the tone of it; but it was sort of suspicious and sort of incredulous
that I didn't want to belong to this thing. I then heard nothing further from
them. . . .

Be that as it may, Artie acted in concert with "caucus" members
during the HICCASP executive council meeting in Beverly Hills on
the night of July 2. When a faction including the late FDR's son James
Roosevelt, actor Ronald Reagan, and actress Olivia de Havilland tried
to introduce the resolution repudiating communism, "pandemonium"
erupted—with Shaw, along with screenwriters Dalton Trumbo and
John Howard Lawson, among the noisiest protesters.

"A well-known musician sprang to his feet," Reagan wrote in his
1965 memoir. "He offered to recite the USSR constitution from memory, yelling that it was a lot more democratic than that of the United
States." Olivia de Havilland, in a 2006 interview, named the musician as
Shaw: "He said to me, 'Have you read the Russian constitution?' And I
said, 'No I haven't—and how recently have you read ours?'"

Reagan, de Havilland, and others soon resigned from the organization, and in time, HICCASP ("pronounced," Reagan wrote, "like the
cough of a dying man") expired.

IN THE SPRING and summer of 1947, Shaw was attempting to become a
movie producer. He had written, co-written, or acquired various stories,
scripts, plays, and screen treatments. Now, with playwright-screenwriter
Hy Kraft (credited with *Stormy Weather*, the 1943 all-black MGM musical starring Lena Horne), Shaw concocted a script intended as a vehicle
for the "boy singer" he had refused to hire for his band three years earlier. "We worked on a story together," Art said, "which we were going
to try to put together for Frank Sinatra, who was then around Hollywood looking for a screenplay." Shaw and Kraft sold an option on this

script to RKO, but no movie was made. Art said he tried to interest the same studio in a deal involving Les Brown's vocalist Doris Day, but RKO wasn't interested.

So Shaw, using music written during his studies with Hans Byrns, developed an adaptation of "The Pied Piper of Hamelin" for *The Columbia Workshop*, CBS Radio's prestigious Sunday-afternoon program—the same series on which Woody Herman that year performed Igor Stravinsky's *Ebony Concerto*, a work publicized as having been conceived by the L.A.-dwelling émigré composer especially for Woody and his band. In fact, "It was originally written for Benny," revealed baritone-saxophonist Danny Bank, a member of Goodman's band at the time. "Benny didn't wanna do it; it was too *hard*: it required a very fast single tongue. So Woody did it."

Shaw's "Piper," trumpeted as the *Workshop*'s tenth-anniversary broadcast, emanated from CBS Columbia Square in Hollywood. Inspired by the Robert Browning poem, it was an engaging fable set to a contemporary beat. Artie Shaw of course was the man behind the piper's clarinet, and the play's recurring melody was Shaw's self-composed "Pied Piper Theme." One week later, Shaw, the actors, narrator Harry von Zell, and a full orchestra recorded *The Pied Piper of Hamelin* as a children's album for Musicraft. Children's records had become a significant part of the postwar market, and *Piper* would be a popular Christmas item for years to come. "He was a very commercial person, you know," trumpeter Paul Cohen said with admiration. "Artie knew how to make a buck."

=== CHAPTER THIRTY-FOUR ===

A Table in a Corner

OWARD HUGHES, well-known aviator and movie producer, crashed into the news on July 7, 1946, when the prototype plane he was piloting made an explosive landing in a Beverly Hills backyard. Ava Gardner visited him in the hospital the next day; she had dated Hughes before she met Shaw. That same afternoon, Ava moved out of Art's house for good.

Shaw acknowledged the separation to a journalist: "We simply got on each other's nerves." Gardner and her lawyer used different words when they filed for her divorce a month later: "Since the marriage, defendant has treated plaintiff in a cruel manner, causing plaintiff grievous mental suffering."

It might seem odd to some how Shaw and his next partner met, but, as Art well knew, things were different when you were a star.

Kathleen Winsor was famous too in 1946, as author of the then-shocking novel *Forever Amber*: the same book Artie Shaw did or did not forbid Ava Gardner to read ("Never happened"). *Amber*, banned in fourteen states, had sold a hundred thousand copies during its first week after publication. Twentieth Century Fox paid two hundred thousand dollars for dramatic rights and in October would start production on the movie.

Shaw first met Winsor, he would state, on October 7, 1946, "after I telephoned her on the suggestion of my friend, Norman Foley, who had written letters to both of us." The two had lunch at the Beverly Wilshire. "She boasted that she was supporting her husband and that he did not interfere with her personal affairs. About a week later she told me she had forced her husband to leave her house. . . . About two weeks after we met, the question of marriage arose."

It was sudden; but Art was impulsive, and Winsor—a twenty-eight-year-old brunette with a roguish glance—was appealing. "I was working on 'Star Money,' my second book," she would recall, "and Artie was working on a book of his own. He said this had been a lifelong ambition. I think he must have had some vague notion that being married to a writer would have the effect of making him concentrate on writing."

On October 24, Ava Gardner, after a year and a week of marriage to Artie Shaw, had her day in divorce court. The judge granted Gardner's decree. Ava wanted only her possessions from Bedford Drive.

Winsor had secured a property settlement the day before from her husband of ten years, Bob Herwig, a former college football star and ex–Marine Corps captain.

"On October 24, 1946," Shaw later said of himself and Winsor, "we left in my automobile and arrived at El Paso [Texas], where we registered in a hotel as Mr. and Mrs. Arthur Sanders. . . ." Across the border in Juárez, Mexico, they presented their signed property settlements to an attorney and were given Mexican divorces from their mates. On October 28, Shaw and Winsor were pronounced *hombre* and *esposa* by a Juárez judge.

News of Artie Shaw's latest marriage "caused gasps of astonishment" in Hollywood. Bob Herwig said that in his view he and Winsor were still married, since a Mexican divorce wasn't valid in California. The Los Angeles District Attorney's office let it be known that it didn't recognize "quickie" Mexican proceedings, and not only was Winsor still married to Herwig but Shaw was still married to Gardner, since her interlocutory decree wasn't yet final. The DA left open the chance that Shaw and Winsor could be charged with bigamy.

"Artie Shaw and Bride Still Forever Ambling" was the amused headline of a *Los Angeles Times* story in which representatives of the alleged bride and groom claimed no knowledge of either party's whereabouts. The piece concluded, "The band leader was obviously playing bride and seek."

Winsor and Shaw were next sighted in Manhattan. To avoid attention, they dined during off-hours; a *Life* magazine photographer snapped a picture of the maybe-weds seated one late afternoon at a corner table in the Algonquin's otherwise-deserted Chinese Room.

Back in L.A., Winsor's husband had *his* day in divorce court. The name "Artie Shaw" was never uttered as Herwig recited a litany of his wife's marital offenses: On the eve of his World War II departure for overseas duty, he had waited for her at a San Diego hotel from six in the evening to three in the morning, at which hour she showed up with another man. While Herwig was fighting in the South Pacific, she had written him "cool and distant" letters mentioning dates with still other men. When he returned from the war, *Forever Amber* was a hit and his wife "went into a rage" if anyone called her "Mrs. Herwig." "She hinted at having me psychoanalyzed," Herwig said, "so that I would get rid of 'mental blocks' which she said prevented me from making a lot of money."

The jilted husband won his case. The *Los Angeles Examiner's* headline smirked, "Bob Herwig Divorces Shaw's Wife."

ONE LAST vexing matter involving the sale of his Bedford Drive house commanded Shaw's attention in December. The house had been purchased, with contents and furnishings, for ninety-five thousand dollars. The buyer, Armand Deutsch, about to move in, noted the absence of a waffle iron listed on the inventory of contents. It was Gardner's: her sister had given it to her, and she took it as part of her possessions after the divorce. She wasn't about to give it back. But Sears heir Deutsch was adamant: replace or remunerate him for the waffle iron, or the whole expensive deal was off. A furious Artie wrote Deutsch a check for fifteen dollars.

Then, on a quick trip to L.A., he went to J.J. Newberry's and bought a few items.

That inventory, Shaw saw, also mentioned several "glass ashtrays," without specifying they were fine crystal pieces by Steuben and Baccarat. Artie went to Bedford Drive and collected those exquisite objects—and in their place, left dime-store ashtrays from Newberry's for the wealthy Mr. Deutsch.

SHAW AND WINSOR bought an eight-room colonial house on eight and a half acres in Norwalk, Connecticut, for sixty-nine thousand dollars. Here Art and Kathleen—"Kay," he called her—had the isolation and leisure to write as much as they pleased. Winsor made fair progress on a second novel; Shaw claimed to be amassing many pages of an autobiographical work being done with the encouragement of New York book editor Robert Giroux. But Art still found writing a daunting task. He often came up with reasons to visit Manhattan instead.

The latest trend in New York radio was conversation programs hosted by husbands and wives—for instance, Bea Wain and André Baruch. There was talk of Shaw and Winsor doing a breakfast show, but it didn't happen. Despite the good front they presented, "The thing with Kay and me wasn't going that well," Art would admit.

A year later, in court documents, Winsor would allege Shaw often gave vent to a violent temper. One night, around July 5, she sighed in the bedroom while Art was reading: "He leaped out of bed, screaming and yelling obscenely at the top of his lungs, cursing me and threatening to beat and choke me. . . . He said that I had sighed deliberately and maliciously in a 'subtle woman's way' while he was trying to read. His rage continued until dawn. Next day, though his rage had blown itself out, he referred to me as a 'materialistic, money-mad and vindictive bitch.'"

His book writing, too, was giving him trouble.

In mid-July, Shaw sent a letter to William Saroyan in San Francisco, proposing the two of them collaborate on a musical comedy. Saroyan liked the idea, as long as he could work at home. Bill made his own suggestion: Why didn't Winsor and Shaw come for a visit, and Art and Bill could work in person? In September, Art and Kay took the Overland Limited train to San Francisco and found their way to the Saroyans' home on Taraval Street.

"We started to work," Shaw told a pair of Saroyan biographers, "and I began to see that Bill's type of lack of discipline, or whatever you want to call it—He had his own discipline, an inner thing that made him sit down and get those words to spill out; and sometimes I'd envy him that." Art's response was to try to impose *his* method. "I said, 'Look, Bill, if we're going to do this, we have to get a schematic. A musical play requires some kind of approach. You've got to know where act one is, where we are and where we close the curtain. And I can only write music to a specific situation.'"

At last, Shaw said, he told his friend, "'For Christ's sake, Bill, I get the feeling your typewriter is a kind of sexual symbol: you're an autoerotic.' He loved that word, autoerotic: 'Oh, auto-ee-*row*-tic! Auto-ee-*row*-tic!' I said, 'Oh, shit, don't hold me up on a word. I'm making a point. I think what you're doing is jerking off with the typewriter, if you want it in plain language.'"

The friendship survived, in its way; the collaboration didn't. When the Shaws left San Francisco, there had been no progress. Bill sent Art a letter on September 21, saying he had begun work on a long novel and wanted nothing more to do with any musical, except maybe to buy a ticket and see one.

Art was once more on his own.

CHAPTER THIRTY-FIVE

It's the Same Old Dream

BUT THERE was still the psychoanalyst.

When Shaw moved east, it meant the end of his sessions with May Romm. Both he and she thought it useful though for Art to continue analysis. "There are a few islands yet to be explored," was how Romm put it. She recommended a well-known Manhattan man, Abraham (Abram) Kardiner, who agreed to take Art on.

JAZZ MEANWHILE was having an identity crisis: unsure whether to lunge into a bebop future or retreat into a nostalgic past. Shaw stayed out of the fray. Still he managed to place fourth in the clarinet category of *Metronome*'s 1948 readers' poll (behind Goodman, Buddy DeFranco, and Ellington soloist Jimmy Hamilton)—not bad, considering Art hadn't made a single record in 1947.

His old friend Claude Thornhill was getting noticed with his current band, an outfit whose several clarinets, two French horns, and one tuba created beautiful blocks of Impressionist tone-clusters: "The sound hung like a cloud," said Claude's star arranger Gil Evans, who brought bebop expertise and modern soloists into Thornhill's ensemble.

"He had some good men," Art said of Claude's crew. "It was an arranger's band, mostly. Very little jazz, very little jazz. He couldn't *play* jazz, couldn't even beat off the jazz tempo. Claude—had a lotta talent. Marvelous touch, at the piano. Good ears. But—couldn't *improvise*. He *did* it, but it wasn't jazz, it was somethin' else."

Dance band, bop band, ballad band—whatever it was, Thornhill's orchestra caught the ear of the young black trumpet player Miles Davis. "Thornhill had the greatest band . . . during these modern times," Davis told *Down Beat*. The trumpeter modeled his own first ensemble, a 1948 nonet, on Thornhill's sound, and recorded a series of sides with it, which came to be called *Birth of the Cool*.

But in the middle of 1948, Claude broke up his orchestra and went with his current wife to Hawaii. Of Thornhill's disbanded ensemble, Shaw said, "It wasn't bad. If he'd kept it long enough, it might have turned out to *be* somethin'. He had a lotta problems; he had to go to shock therapy. He was a drinker, by the end. Strange cat."

Woody Herman had a progressive band in 1948 with a number of bop-conversant players including a quartet of young saxophonists dubbed "the Four Brothers": Stan Getz, Zoot Sims, Serge Chaloff, and Shaw-alumnus Herbie Steward. (Herman's, and Shaw's, former drummer Dave Tough, not so resilient after all, would die in 1948, at age forty.)

Goodman, who had resisted bop's charms for three years, decided that it might be time in 1948 to explore new ideas—or at least create a context in which others might, while he continued to play in his old familiar manner. For his new sextet, Benny hired a second, more bop-pish clarinet man: Stan Hasselgård, a twenty-five-year-old Swede. "He was pretty good," Shaw allowed of Hasselgård and his modernist skills. "I never heard anything happen that hadn't *happened* before—but he was very good at that, he could do that."

So many things were different in 1948—in jazz and in those who made it.

That was brought home to Art when he went to a sold-out "comeback" concert Billie Holiday gave at Carnegie Hall, marking her release from nine and a half months' confinement, for possession of heroin, in the Federal Reformatory for Women at Alderson, West Virginia.

Long gone was that carefree Harlem beauty. "They got her hooked—she went to jail—all that shit," Art said. "I went to visit her, she was no longer the girl I knew. She was no longer—anybody. She was a—whiner. She had some guy, livin' off of her and—it was no fun. It was not fun being with her. So it goes."

He would remember Billie from happier times: "I used to invite her to parties, and she'd say, 'No, I ain't coming. It's gonna be all ofays; and when the water's too deep, I can't swim.'"

IT WAS at just such a dicty gathering, a birthday party at the Scarsdale home of art-book publisher Harry Abrams, that Art met a young musical-minded woman who would become a lifelong friend.

"Artie was invited by way of a famous pianist, Ray Lev, who was my piano teacher at the time," Sophia Rosoff said. "And my husband and I and my very little boy went. Artie came over to me and he said, 'That is the cutest little kid.' And I said, 'That's *my* little kid.' And we immediately became friends." Sophia's husband, Noah, became Shaw's lawyer. "And Artie lived near where we lived, so that it was easy to visit back and forth."

Shaw kept an apartment in the Beaux Arts Building on East Forty-fourth Street, between Second and First. He spent a lot of time in the city, meeting new people, moving between spheres.

"He was a favorite person of my late husband, Bob Bach, back in the early '40s," said Jean Bach, who became a longtime friend of Shaw's. "Bob and I got married in '48"—Jean had been wed before to trumpeter "Shorty" Sherock—"so that's kinda when I started knowing Artie. Artie was kinda flirting with lefty politics at the time. And that was my interest, but somehow—we had kinda collisions."

Shaw let his name be used in fund-raising ads for third-party presidential candidate Henry Wallace. He was always in respectable company on such lists (Budd Schulberg, Lillian Hellman, Leonard Bernstein, Aaron Copland, Thomas Mann). Artie spurned association with more extreme groups, such as the thirty-two artists who signed a letter of support to Soviet writers urging American intellectuals to "raise their voices against 'the new dangers of fascism, against war, in defense of peace and the brotherhood of peoples.'" Among those who did endorse that particular missive were novelist Howard Fast, screenwriter Alvah Bessie (recently cited for contempt of Congress), Shaw's old Bucks County poet-acquaintance Isidore Schneider—and Ray Lev, the female pianist in whose company Art was often seen in 1948.

Lev, thirty-six, had been born in Russia and raised by a father who had been a New Haven cantor. She had made her Carnegie Hall debut in 1933, and her annual recitals in that venue were well attended through the 1940s. When Ray Lev started seeing Artie Shaw, Sophia Rosoff said, "I thought she was quite keen about *him*, but I think he was interested in her *musically*, that's all."

Stalled in his efforts to write prose, Shaw turned again to music, but with a twist: Art would now become a classical performer.

Benny Goodman had played "serious" music from almost the first year of his big-band success; Goodman had commissioned and debuted clarinet pieces from Béla Bartók, Aaron Copland, and Paul Hindemith (though not without requesting revisions of their more difficult passages). Were Goodman's "highbrow" ventures what inspired Shaw? Whatever prompted him (it may also have been apathy toward bebop), Shaw began a prolonged study.

"He loved classical music," Sophia Rosoff said. "He loved the Ravel *Gaspard de la Nuit*. He loved Bach. Satie. Scriabin was a very favorite of mine, and he did love Scriabin too. There weren't too many performers that he approved of; he was a perfectionist, really; he was *very* critical, about *everybody*. But—there was something about him, he could be *so* charming. And *always* interesting. And even what he said about music which I didn't always agree with—about classic music—I respected it. Because he was very, very intelligent. Brilliant, as a matter of fact. He was very special, even though he was difficult."

Part of that difficult quality came from having to find things out on his own, Sophia said: "Artie had to teach himself; I think he had to find his own way. And he did things with the clarinet because he didn't know that you *couldn't* do it. He would hear something in his inner ear—his ears were marvelous—and he would *find* a way to produce it, in sound. And that's one of the reasons why he has the most beautiful sound on the clarinet that anybody ever had. For instance, in 'Star Dust,' the sound is something just incredible, it's *so* beautiful, and the high notes are so special, but he found a way to get what he heard. Which most of the conservatory people don't *do*, 'cause there are so many rules. He really investigated to the hilt. He was a fascinating person. An extraordinary person."

"The *dream* and *joy* and satisfaction that he derived from his music was very difficult for me to understand," said Dr. Colter Rule, who became friends with Shaw through Lev, "because although I love music, I'm not gifted; it's all a big vast mystery to me. But I knew how beautifully he played, and how natural it was to him." Rule guessed, "I think that his music must have been part of his way out of loneliness. And part of it I think was competition. You know?"

The doctor stayed friends with Shaw for years. "I always *liked* Artie," he said. "And I'm not sure he liked *anybody*—including me. Yeah, I don't think he was attached to anybody. He showed considerable enthusiasm, and whatnot; he had fun with a pretty wide range of people, but I don't know anybody he was close to." So-called trust starts early in life, the doctor said: "And if there isn't an early experience of deep trust, without any sense of danger—if you don't have that early experience, you don't look for it again; you don't think you're gonna find it. So he was pretty much of a lone wolf." But in 1948, Dr. Rule said, Art was at his best as a companion. "Those days with Ray Lev, and Sophia, and that whole gang—he was a little bit human, in those days. Because all they talked about was their crazy love of music." Not since his time in Cleveland with Claude Thornhill, maybe, had Art learned so much and had such a good time.

But that good time would soon end.

HIS PUBLIC NIGHTMARE began with a thirteen-line Associated Press item stating that Kathleen Winsor was asking the New York State Supreme

Court for five hundred dollars in weekly temporary alimony and ten thousand dollars for legal fees to defend herself against an annulment suit to be filed soon by Artie Shaw. Winsor was countersuing for divorce, and she wanted money. Shaw would fight her demands.

Half a century later, Shaw's feelings about Winsor hadn't mellowed. "An unmitigated *c-nt*," he called her. "She was, really."

Had he liked *Forever Amber*?

"Are you *kidding*? It was a piece of shit. She wrote a historical novel—with people having twentieth-century thoughts, and behavior. Not a good thing."

Why had he married her?

"It seemed like a good idea, at the time. I broke with her—a clean break—before we were married. But she said, 'Oh, you're such a wonderful man'—how she admired me, for having such principles, and she could *learn* from me. And I went *along* with that. I guess I wanted to. Boy, I must have been a—bewildered guy. I make big mistakes.

"But now that I look at it, she was scared to death. She was a frightened woman, really—afraid that 'the dream' was going to go away. She never had another [comparably successful] book. . . . So, that was a big *blow* to her—her ego. She thought that she had written a book where she knew what she was *doing*.

"She took me to the cleaners, though. Left one night—without telling me—cleaned out both bank accounts, took everything we had. I never *knew* anyone like that. We had joint accounts, you know? None of the other women I knew, *ever*, would do anything like that. They were cheats, they were whatever they were—but they weren't *this*. She was an out-and-out larceny woman.

"Then she married the lawyer that *got* her that. Everything I owned, she got. I wanted to get out of the newspapers. 'AMBER CALLS ARTIE ——— '—so and so."

"RED" was the word he couldn't bring himself to utter, even half a century later: "ARTIE TRIED TO TURN AMBER RED"—one of the headlines this former New Haven newsboy may have heard shouted on the streets of Manhattan in the autumn of 1948.

"Front-page headlines," Artie Shaw remembered. "I couldn't *stand* that."

THE SHAW-WINSOR chronicles, drawing on the two litigants' dueling affidavits, began running in New York tabloids on the sixth of August; they kept the city's readers hooked for a week.

"She Wanted Him Forever Sterile, Says Artie, Suing to Annul Amber."

Winsor was ready with her own leaked charges. "Last March 5 at the railroad station in Norwalk, Connecticut," she claimed, "he struck me in the face with his hand and knocked me down. . . . On March 20 at my home he threatened to kill me and hurled a heavy lamp at me. . . . He fell on me then and grasped my throat and choked me and beat my head on the floor, also striking me in the face repeatedly." Winsor called Shaw a "gigolo" and said he had married her for her money—over a hundred thousand dollars of which he had seized and refused to return, she stated. She said he bragged of seeing other women and had flaunted lipstick-stained handkerchiefs.

Shaw and his lawyer struck back, saying Winsor's Mexican divorce from her first husband had never been legal. Neither had *his* been, Art claimed: As far as he was concerned, he said, he was still married to Ava Gardner.

Winsor's allegations escalated. On August 10, newspapers carried excerpts from Winsor's statements about Shaw's alleged politics: "He confessed that he had recently become a registered member of the Communist Party . . . and that he considered the Communist way the only way for the United States. . . . He urged me to join the Communist Party if only to demonstrate my loyalty to him."

There it was: "ARTIE TRIED TO TURN AMBER RED."

Shaw denied Winsor's claim that he was a Communist Party member, as he denied her claims of physical violence, but he couldn't afford to let her tabloid "testimonies" continue. In America's postwar political climate, such charges alone could ruin careers. Before even going to trial, Winsor had won. On October 2, newspapers printed this update: Shaw had dropped his annulment action, Winsor had abandoned her counterclaim, and both had reached an out-of-court settlement. The settlement was onerous, Art much later said: "The equivalent of a million bucks."

Winsor went to Reno for an uncontested divorce, a procedure that took all of four minutes. Sounding not unlike Artie Shaw, the novelist joked to reporters: "The first three divorces are the hardest, you know."

CHAPTER THIRTY-SIX

Changing My Tune

S HAW LINED UP concert dates with classical orchestras from Manhattan to Denver; he commissioned works from Morton Gould,
Norman Dello Joio, and Nicolai Berezowsky. His first major appearance was with the Rochester Civic Orchestra, playing pieces by Mozart
and Finzi. Critics gave him good marks for his "flawless technique" and
"sensitive shading."

Art worked out an agreement with Manie Sachs, a record executive
he knew and liked. "I went to Manie and I said, 'Look: I'd like to make
a contract with CBS,'" Shaw said. "'I want total freedom to make anything I want; I don't want a dime from you, except pay the men, pay for
the studio—and I'll get a royalty. Pay me scale, whatever it is—'cause
you can't do it any other way: union.' He said, 'Okay, you got a deal.'"

Time was booked for Shaw and his musicians. "There was a church
they'd bought for a studio," Shaw said. "Marvelous acoustics. I hired
Walter Hendl to conduct the orchestra; it was a Mozart-sized orchestra.
And I came in and *played* these things!"

He recorded eight numbers during the afternoon of March 11, the
shortest of which ran a minute and forty-one seconds; the longest, three
minutes and fifteen seconds. Each selection was performed with precision, delicacy, and feeling. The most striking was a Kabalevsky piece Art

first heard Sophia Rosoff play; orchestrated, it was called "Short Story." Milhaud's "Corcovado" had Latin rhythms handled with aplomb by drummer Irv Kluger, a well-schooled percussionist who had recorded with Dizzy Gillespie. Debussy's "Petite Piece" had been written as an audition test for the Paris conservatory. "Andaluza" was by Granados. There was a Shostakovich prelude and a Poulenc waltz.

A few weeks later, Shaw cut Alan Shulman's "Rendezvous (for Clarinet and Strings)," which combined classical instrumentation with a jazz theme; Art performed it with Shulman's own string quartet, a harpist, and a rhythm section including Irv Kluger. A second Shulman piece, "Mood in Question," sounded like Brahms walking into Café Society. When Barry Ulanov heard these sides, he described them as "a series of variations on the blues." A *New York Times* reviewer said, "Both pieces have refinement and ingenuity. . . . They should attract many musical interests, especially in these imaginative performances."

WHILE SHAW embraced the classics, Goodman toured with a big band featuring pianist-singer Buddy Greco and tenor-saxophonist Wardell Gray. Benny had made a show of at last accepting bebop, but he never called for his new boppish charts until late at night, when he turned the orchestra over to its younger players and left the stage.

In the spring of 1949, Goodman and his band were in L.A. at the Hollywood Palladium, where one afternoon the leader held an open singers' audition. Buddy Greco remembered, "One of the girls who showed up introduced herself as Norma Jean Baker and asked me to back her on 'How Deep Is the Ocean?' She wasn't Marilyn Monroe yet, and she wasn't a blonde, but she was absolutely gorgeous, and all the guys in the band went nuts. Benny looked at her, and when she finally finished, he said, 'I think you're very pretty, but you'll never really get anywhere in show business. I think you ought to go home.'"

Three months later, desperate for cash, Norma Jean Baker called photographer Tom Kelley, who had once offered to pay her fifty dollars to pose nude. She had turned him down but now said she would do it. That night, Kelley covered the floor of his pink-stucco Hollywood cottage with a red-velvet drape; he put on some music, and his wife, Natalie, assisted him in loading and unloading film plates as a naked Norma Jean lay on the velvet, "graceful as an otter, turning sinuously with utter naturalness," striking pose after perfect pose. The experience, Kelley said, was "extraordinary in its intensity."

A year later, the first of Kelley's pictures of a nude Marilyn Monroe was printed on a calendar, "Golden Dreams." More calendars would be published through the decade. Monroe feared that being revealed in time as the "Golden Dreams" girl would hurt her career, but in fact it increased her popularity. In a later interview, Marilyn was asked, Was it true she had really had nothing on when she posed? She said, "Oh, I had something on. The radio."

Monroe biographer Maurice Zolotow, a decade after, asked Kelley if that was true. "It wasn't a radio," Tom Kelley said. "It was a phonograph." And what was it playing? " 'Begin the Beguine,'" Kelley said, "the Artie Shaw version."

RALPH WATKINS, a New York club manager who had made a success of a fried-chicken shack called the Royal Roost by turning it into a bebop showcase, was about to start a much more ambitious new Manhattan venue, and he wanted Artie Shaw as its opening headliner.

Shaw made it clear he would play only concert music, and needed to be paid a lot to reimburse the orchestra. Watkins agreed. And no selling of drinks while the ensemble played, Artie added. The club owner said yes to that too.

Singer Ella Fitzgerald and trombonist Kai Winding's combo were added to the marquee below Shaw. In the thick of an early heat wave, people began lining up at seven in the evening on Thursday, April 14, for admission to the opening night of Bop City at Forty-ninth and Broadway. Police were on hand to control the crowd.

Newsreel and still photographers hustled to record the arrival of celebrities including movie star Kirk Douglas (whose hit picture *Cham-*

pion was playing up the block, and whose next movie would see him portraying a Bix Beiderbecke figure in *Young Man with a Horn*). Broadway comic Frankie Marlowe pulled up in a horse-drawn hansom bannered "Bop City or Bust!" Milton Berle cut the ribbon out front, and the club's doors were flung open.

Bop City was vast; the room held nine hundred people. Three thousand patrons were admitted that night (with fresh ones let in as first arrivals departed); another five thousand were turned away. Tables nearest the canopied stage were filled with the famous: Hazel Scott and husband Representative Adam Clayton Powell, jazz impresario Norman Granz, Charlie Barnet, John Hammond, the handsome young jazz singer Harry Belafonte, and Billie Holiday. In the ninety-cent bleacher seats sat or stood a largely teenage crowd of mostly white bebop fanatics, chewing gum and wearing floppy "bop-ties": spiritual children of the jerky-jitterbugs of ten years ago.

"Mister Artie *Shaw*," an announcer intoned, as a nervous-looking Art in black tie strode onto the bandstand where forty classical players awaited his downbeat.

Things went bad from the start. The air-conditioning was broken, and the room grew humid. Shaw opened with several long selections on which he didn't play clarinet but conducted. The unamplified ensemble could hardly be heard. Flower girls sold corsages table to table. Camera girls asked customers if they would like their pictures taken. When Art picked up his clarinet, the hubbub didn't dim. Shaw glared at the crowd, but the crowd didn't notice: Kirk Douglas had entered the main room.

Art played Nicolai Berezowsky's demanding concerto, a work that baffled the audience; some (to Art's disgust) applauded during pauses, thinking the piece was done. In the bleachers, the bop fans grew restive, shouting, "Let's jump!" "Give us a break, will ya?" "Oop-bop-sh'bam!"

"The plain fact," *Billboard*'s reviewer wrote, "was that Shaw's music was way over this mob's head."

Through the years, Artie Shaw had offended lots of people he had never met ("But critics have to live," he'd once conceded. "Why, I don't know"). Now he had given them the perfect chance to get even.

"Mr. Shaw is a pretentious young man," *Down Beat's* Mike Levin would write, "who evidently feels his abilities are completely unlimited, his horizons unbounded. My impression at this point is that the only things unbounded about him are his ego and his musical ignorance. . . . His phrasing was sterile and stiff, displayed no real firm emotional or intellectual conceptions of the works he was playing. . . . Shaw . . . because of his unbelievable vanity and lack of ability, succeeded in . . . making a laughing stock of himself. . . . [T]his has probably been the worst musical fiasco staged in this country within the last twenty years." *Time, Life, Variety,* and the *New York Mirror* were among other publications that mocked or knocked Shaw's opening-night "bop flop."

During the rest of the one-week engagement, Shaw unbent enough onstage to parry jibes with the cheap-seat hecklers. He shortened his sets and played more clarinet. And once the opening-night scene makers were gone, Art drew a more receptive crowd. Among those present on later nights were Sophia and Noah Rosoff, with Ava Gardner, who, like Lana Turner, was still good friends with her ex. "Ava even had a piano lesson with me," Sophia said, "because she had to play—well, *look* as if she were playing—a piano in a film. But anyway, we went to the Bop City. That was fun."

Despite bad press, Shaw's six nights at the club were a box-office success: ten thousand patrons paid admittance during the week, and *Billboard* guessed the venue grossed forty to fifty thousand dollars on food and drink.

And on the Monday night Bop City was dark, Shaw made his second appearance in Carnegie Hall, this time with the National Youth Symphony conducted by Leon Barzin. The *New York Times* wrote that Artie Shaw "got a chance to play Nicolai Berezowsky's Concerto for Clarinet before a serious audience instead of before the noisy one that hardly listened when he played it last week at the opening of the night club Bop City. . . . His performance had wit, authority, musicality and, in the andante, poignant expressiveness. Despite his jazz background, he was thoroughly serious."

"SERIOUS," THOUGH, was not a much-desired quality in the world of commercial music, as Art learned after delivering his sides to Columbia Records.

"Manie Sachs called me," Shaw said. "'I just got in the Gershwin and the Cole Porter and the two string-quartet things; you want to hear the record?' I said, 'Sure.' He said, 'Come on in.' So I went in—he had this marvelous office, with speakers—and he put them on, and I listened to 'em. He said, 'Wadya think?' I said, 'Geez, I—they're pretty good; sound good to me.' He said, 'Well what am I gonna *do* with 'em, Artie?' I said, 'Wadya *mean*, Manie? Your job is to sell records; my job is to make records.' He said, 'Artie, they're *too beautiful*.' Those words! 'They're too beautiful.' He used *that phrase*.

"And I said, 'Well, what do you want me to *do*, Manie—go back and play 'em a little out of *tune*?' He said, 'Artie, you're missing the point, what are you gonna *do* with these? There's no *dance* music, there.' I said, 'They're not *meant* to be dance music; they're *concert* music.' 'But that's Cole Porter, and Gershwin; it's *dance* music.'"

Shaw had performed Gershwin and Porter tunes in a classical manner, as one might do art songs by Schumann.

"Well, see—I was a *dance-band* leader," Shaw said. "So there was no *category*; it didn't *belong* anywhere. There's a rather narrow road on which you recorded: Over here, Sammy Kaye; over here, Lombardo; over *here*, Benny Goodman; over here, me, and Tommy Dorsey, and other people. That was that. And there was no *room* for this; this went off in some place that—nobody was *ready* for. Except for a few specialized people.

"So, you know, you pay a big *price* for being—off the beat, off the beam. You go off the path that everybody walks on—you need a machete to hack your way through that jungle. I don't blame the record-company people, they got their own business to run; how are they gonna sit around and try to worry about the difference between good and bad, the 'vrai' jazz and the 'ersatz' jazz? I don't know. It's a difficult place to be."

The Gershwin and Porter tunes ended up, along with the more

obvious classical pieces, on *Modern Music for Clarinet,* an album of which Art said, "Nobody knew what to do with that record. Probably sold twelve-and-a-half copies."

SHAW FULFILLED his 1949 concert commitments, which included the world premiere of Norman Dello Joio's "Concertante for Clarinet and Orchestra" done with the Chautauqua Symphony; and a benefit concert for the state of Israel before an Ebbets Field audience of thirty-one thousand, with eighty-five members of the New York Philharmonic conducted by Leonard Bernstein, in which Art played Mozart's "Clarinet Concerto." Artie would do occasional concert dates into 1950, but for commercial purposes, his classical period was over.

Meanwhile, his old Victor material continued to sell. RCA put out an album, *Show Tunes,* of Shaw's 1939 band playing eight Broadway songs, prompting many to observe how much better Artie Shaw's music sounded now than so much other swing-era material. "His band played . . . with style, and his own work with the clarinet had taste and character," the *New York Times'* Howard Taubman wrote. A *Los Angeles Times* reviewer said these vintage Shaw sides were "done with a taste and feeling you seldom hear nowadays."

"I know that that music is still attractive to lots of people," Art told *Metronome's* Barry Ulanov. "I have what you might call documentary proof: my royalty checks." Indeed, *Variety* wrote that "sales of [Shaw's] Victor sides are still hefty enough to have paid him royalties in six figures last year." *Billboard* reported "Begin the Beguine" alone had sold five million copies since 1938.

CHAPTER THIRTY-SEVEN

Innuendo

T HE WHOLE THING had happened in such a rush: Shaw, in frantic rehearsal at Bop City the week before that opening, was waylaid by a petition bearer asking if it would be okay to add Art's name to the many other notables in support of a Soviet-endorsed Cultural and Scientific Conference for World Peace at the Waldorf-Astoria. Art said sure. Now he rued the day.

Columnists like Frank Conniff of the *New York Journal-American* and Lee Mortimer of the *New York Mirror* were all of a sudden calling Artie Shaw "the Communist-loving clarinetist." It was a sign of the postwar times that Shaw was even being knocked in print just for including pieces by Shostakovich on his Bop City bill of fare. "Anybody who plays a program of modern music and doesn't include Russian composers is scratching his left ear with his right hand," Art said. "I'd really be getting political if I ignored them."

But Shaw's every public gesture was being noted now by those who took it upon themselves to keep track of what famous figure promoted or protested this or that action at a time when Stalin had overrun Czechoslovakia, communists had taken control in China, and former State Department official Alger Hiss was under suspicion of holding allegiance to Russia. For a lot of people, Shaw's political activism, such as it was, provided yet another reason to despise this arrogant, much married, artistically pretentious, jitterbug-hating jazzman. "At least one L.A. daily," according to *Down Beat*, "has an ironbound rule that Artie Shaw will have to get arrested to get his name mentioned in it."

IN 1949, Art bought and moved onto the 240-acre "Picardy Farm," in Pine Plains, New York, a three-hour train ride from Manhattan. Here, with the help of staff, he ran a dairy farm: the sort of profitable business he had figured out was the best way to make a living off the country-side, back in his impoverished Bucks County days. Later, he would say the only reason he went back to the music business in late 1949 was to make money for back-taxes the Internal Revenue Service said Shaw owed from 1948.

Whatever the reason, and as weak as the band business was this year, Shaw put together a new orchestra with manager Lenny Lewis, an ensemble that would combine older arrangements with ones "in the modern groove." To *Down Beat*'s John S. Wilson, Shaw said, "I've been away long enough for a whole new crop of musicians to come up. I'll be interested to see what happens."

One of the most avant-garde of this new breed was twenty-six-year-old arranger-composer George Russell. "As a young aspiring musician in Cincinnati," Russell wrote, "I used to listen to radio broadcasts from the Panther Room of the Sherman Hotel in Chicago. I remember hearing Artie Shaw and his orchestra and being astonished and intrigued at the music coming from the console in the living room. Artie set the bar very high for challenging and creative music; he took musical chances, regardless of the popular taste." In the middle 1940s, Russell wrote ground-breaking Afro-Cuban numbers for Dizzy Gillespie and the multirhythmic "A Bird in Igor's Yard," recorded by a Buddy DeFranco ensemble (with Irv Kluger on drums). "As a young composer-arranger in New York," Russell said, "I gathered my courage and asked Artie if he would try my arrangement of 'Similau' with his band. To my relief and gratification, he liked it."

"Similau" (written by Leopold Gonzalez, Arden Clar, and Harry Coleman) was a Latin-sounding pop tune of the season; Russell took apart its components and put them together in a radical manner. His chart—with its shrieking brass, driving beat, and mysterioso mood—was like a post-Hiroshima "Nightmare." With this psyche grabber as its pirate-flagship number, Shaw's new band-book was well and truly launched.

Other arrangers came aboard, including Johnny Mandel, a twenty-three-year-old Juilliard-trained composer. Like Russell, Mandel too had long been a Shaw fan. "I grew up with him, with ear glued to the radio. I paid a lot of *attention* to his records. Benny maybe swung a little more, but he couldn't play a ballad with any great feeling," said Mandel (who would later write such classic modern ballads as "Emily" and "The Shadow of Your Smile"). "And Artie just was the master of that, probably better than any clarinetist *ever* played a melody. And he could swing, too, in his own way; it was a *different* way."

SHAW, SPARING no expense, put together the best modern big band he could, auditioning and rehearsing at Nola's.

"We had paid rehearsals!" marveled trombonist Sonny Russo, then twenty. "Before we went on the road, he rehearsed every day for about a month, which is pretty unusual. Artie was *great*, I tell ya. He had great respect for musicians; he *treated* us good. And he wanted everything to really sound *proper*—which it did."

"In that band," Johnny Mandel said, "he had [on saxophones] Herbie Steward, Frankie Socolow; he had Al Cohn, Zoot Sims, and Danny Bank. The trumpets were great. So he knew with guys like *that*, he didn't have to bring 'em *along*, like he did his earlier bands."

Charlie Parker, co-founding father and sacred monster of bebop, approached Art at Nola's with a startling suggestion. "He came to me one time," Shaw said with a mordant grin, "said, 'Like to play in your band, man.' '*Why?*' 'It's a good sax section—the things you write, for saxes.' I said, 'Bird, you couldn't play in my *band*, you're too much of an individualist! You can't—' 'I know, I know, but I'd sure like to.' That was the extent of the conversation." The notion of this high-flying virtuoso as a mere section man just didn't add up. "But he knew I had great admiration for his *ability*," said Shaw. "He was a remarkable guy. He *learned* to *do* what he *did*. He did it as well as it could be done. Look at the toll it took. Well, a drunk—booze—drugs, everything, you name it." Not the sort of trouble Art cared to court.

Shaw stuck with the men he had, and encouraged soloists to express their modern selves, with occasional nods to the expectations of an Artie Shaw audience.

"With Al Cohn bein' on the band, he's playin' like Tony Pastor's old chair," Sonny Russo said. "He played that solo on 'Begin the Beguine.' So Artie says to Al, 'The only thing I would like you to do, being that it's such a big hit record, when you come in, *start* the solo like [Tony] did—*bup*, ba-dabba-dabba, *doo*-ba-dee-*doo*—and then you can go off into your own thing,' he said. Which Al did."

Artie, though, invoked leader's prerogative *not* to duplicate his own "Star Dust" solo, one of the most-admired choruses in jazz. In part this was to make the point that despite the structured beauty of his sixteen- or thirty-two-bar flights, they *were* improvised. "People used to think I wrote my solos out," Shaw said. "I never wrote a note of my solos."

Russo agreed: "He would have a certain pattern that he'd follow, but he always tried to do different things. On 'Star Dust,' he played it different every time."

Art was able to once more hire Dodo Marmarosa as his pianist. On drums, he lured Irv Kluger from Stan Kenton's orchestra. The electric-guitar chair was filled by Jimmy Raney, fresh from Woody Herman's bebop big band. Raney wrote of Shaw's outfit: "It was a fine band, as good as Woody's; and I got much more to play. I was afraid of [Artie] because I had heard how tough he was to work for, but it wasn't true. If you could play, he didn't bother you. He seemed to care only about the music."

Much of the excitement in this 1949 band came from its forward-sounding arrangements: ear-bendng charts by Mandel, Russell, Al

Cohn, Gene Roland, John Bartee, Tadd Dameron, and others. Shaw's rehearsals at Nola's drew a hip New York crowd of listeners, including Thornhill's arranger Gil Evans and young Gerry Mulligan. The band sounded great, Mandel said. "And they *liked* working for him. And he *loved* that band."

"Well he had so much great stuff in the book," said Sonny Russo. "And you had all those great players, you know. How could you go *wrong?*"

CHAPTER THIRTY-EIGHT

Mucho de Nada

S HAW LEARNED the answer to Russo's question during a tour that stretched from September through December 1949.

Traveling by bus, the guys seemed a happy bunch: sometimes cooled out, sometimes rowdy. Art traveled in his own car, a new Chrysler—the long, heavy, two-door model with the wooden sides—which he picked up in Detroit and drove all the way west.

But the patrons—at the Armar ballroom in Marion, Iowa; the Frog Hop ballroom in St. Joseph, Missouri; and the Tromar ballroom, in Des Moines, Iowa, for instance—couldn't have cared less about Art Shaw's daring new music. "They didn't even know what we were playin'!" Irv Kluger said.

Nevertheless, the drummer insisted, "It was a *wonderful* band!" And Kluger knew one thing for sure: "Artie Shaw loved my playing."

Shaw dug Al Cohn's tenor too, baritone-sax player Danny Bank said; Artie would never solo after Cohn: "*Never.* If the arrangement said 'Al' and then 'Artie Shaw,' he would switch it around. He never wanted to follow Al Cohn. And I don't blame him."

But when it came to maintaining stage decorum, star performers were cut no slack. Shaw called his one and only band meeting of the tour to straighten something out with Cohn and one of his section mates.

"Zoot Sims and Al Cohn were puttin' on," Kluger said, "if somebody asked for 'Begin the Beguine'": rolling their eyes, pulling faces, acting aggrieved in the face of corny customers. "And Artie saw it. He said, 'Al, Zoot, look: I pay good salaries.' Nobody made less than five hundred bucks a week. (I made more than that.) So—Artie's exact words: 'Look—if the people see you puttin' on the tunes that they came to hear, I won't be able to pay you the salaries I pay you. So—lighten up!' And that's all he said! That was it. Very logical man, don't you think?"

"Beguine," "Star Dust," "I Cover the Waterfront"—a lot of the old numbers were done in streamlined arrangements that sounded good if you let them. But most of the book was new, and so far ahead it would still seem fresh half a century later.

There was John Bartee's exotic "Mucho de Nada," which laid down a carpet of cross-rhythms and off-beats for Artie's clarinet to dance on, while the other reeds sighed like sugarcane in the wind.

There was Mandel's "Innuendo," on which Artie's horn swooped above the band like a seagull riding tropical thermals.

There was co-writer Bartee's "Orinoco," another Latin-tinged number full of subtle colors and dynamics. "'Orinoco' was almost a perfect piece of music," Shaw thought.

Art's playing was superb, and on the road, the leader was on his best behavior. "Artie has been making friends by being nice to everyone," *Down Beat* had to admit, "including his fans."

And fans could be a challenge. "We played one place once," Sonny Russo said, "I think it was an Army camp; and one of the guys—a major, or something—comes up to Artie, he says, 'Hey Artie: can you play 'Begin the Beguine,' without the *brass*?' I mean, the brass—that's the whole *arrangement*, you know! Artie says, 'Oh yeah, we'll—we'll try to make you *happy*.' Just—put him aside, you know."

With his own men, Shaw was more direct.

There was the night, for instance, when Artie fired Danny Bank and Al Cohn at the same time. "I think it was in London, Ontario," Bank said. "Someplace between Buffalo and Toronto. We were sitting on the edge of the section, at the end, and he said, 'You two guys are fired.' And

I looked at Al and said, 'Wadya think it's all about?' 'I dunno,' he says, 'but—what the hell—he's gotta [pay to] send us home, and give us two weeks' notice.' So we played another set—and Artie came back, and he says, 'Cancel the firing.' So then I blew *my* top, and I said, 'W-w-w-what the hell's the matter with you?' You know: 'What's your problem?' And he says to me, 'I notice you two guys are pickin' up women in front of the bandstand.'

"People would come up to the bandstand, and instead of dancing they would just *stand* there—and stare at the band. So Artie said, 'You two guys are pickin' up women.' He says, '*You* don't pick up women in front of the bandstand,' he says, '*I* pick up women in front of the bandstand.'" Bank laughed. "Yeah, that's Artie Shaw. Quite a character, I'll tell ya."

DANNY BANK, Al Cohn, Zoot Sims, Jimmy Raney, trumpeter Don Fagerquist . . . it was a bandful of stars, and none shone brighter, as a musician, than Dodo Marmarosa.

At twenty-three, Marmarosa still had a vague, dreamy look as he played those elegant single-note lines and tasteful chords. "The closest thing to Art Tatum I ever heard," Bank said. "But he—he was never in good health, and uh—he only weighed about a hundred pounds. He was—frail, you know what I'm saying? Uh—talented, most talented. Just an ace of a piano, I'll tell you; Bud Powell—that kind of a player. Dodo—Dodo could do anything, in any key. He was great."

But he was "eccentric": frail of mind as well as body. "Well he was nuts!" the blunt Shaw put it, decades later. "Poor little Dodo. Dodo just couldn't handle the real world."

There were those on the band, though, who saw him as colorful, a real goof. This was a man given to speaking to telephone poles; a fellow who painted his bathtub green so he could pretend it was the ocean. There were those wont to use Dodo for their own entertainment— fellows like Zoot and Al.

"Great players," Irv Kluger told writer Bob Rusch, "but they loved their little humor. Things like: Dodo, who was very suggestible—Occasionally there would be a nice strong fellow dancing with a girl, and we were off and maybe a relief band was playing. And one of the boys would say, 'Dodo, cut in,' you know. And he'd tap this guy on the back, and the guy would be ready to punch him. So, to protect him from the beasts, I said, 'Dodo, ride with us,'" meaning Irv and his wife, Phyliss, who had their own Studebaker for the tour. "And Dodo would sit in the back and write music and be happy like he was in his right mind. We just protected him because he needed a keeper."

But no one could protect him from himself.

They were somewhere in the Midwest, at a ballroom in cornfield country. The band played "Frenesi." Shaw's old hits were all these middle-state crowds wanted, not Art's wild new post-bop charts. Within half an hour, someone asked for "Frenesi" again. Once more the band played Artie's second- or third-biggest hit. Then before long came another request for "Frenesi."

"Oh shit, I didn't want to *do* that," Shaw said, "but—people *pay* you, so I thought: Okay, we'll call it. Third time. I gave the number in the book; and Dodo said, 'You play that once again, I'm leavin'.' I said, 'Dodo, I can't—We gotta play it.' So we start. He got up and left. Went back to Pittsburgh. . . .

"Poor little guy. Terribly twisted mind. But he could play the piano."

Shaw's people rushed in another pianist—Gil Barrios—and the band kept rolling.

MANKATO, MINNESOTA; Kaukauna, Wisconsin; Purdue, Indiana . . . the tour, and the crowds' apathy, ground on.

At last, in November, the band reached Chicago for a two-week engagement at the Blue Note Cafe. Chicago—where nineteen summers before, twenty-year-old Art Shaw sat in with Earl Hines at the Grand Terrace Ballroom and heard Jimmie Noone at the Apex Club.

Now Shaw was the headliner, and the hip Blue Note crowd gave him and his cutting-edge orchestra a memorable welcome. "Without question," he told Vladimir Simosko, "that was one of the greatest engagements of my life. That was when that band really came into its own."

And one night during Shaw's two-week stay, a stunning Ava Gardner, dressed to the nines, walked downstairs and into the club. The host ushered her up front, where the band's men couldn't believe their eyes.

"They set up a table right in front of me, a table for two," said Danny Bank, whose baritone chair was at stage left. "And she sat down, and she ordered two martinis: one for her, one for Artie. And he didn't even *look* at her; he didn't even acknowledge her presence. All night we play. And Artie—never mentioned her, never said hello. And, you know, Ava Gardner—beautiful woman. I kept lookin' at her all night, you know. It's a good thing I memorize music very quickly."

One of the standards in the book was George Siravo's arrangement of the Gershwins'"They Can't Take That Away from Me," a song Gardner loved and always associated with Shaw: "The way you wear, your, *hat*," she would sing to herself.

Ava kept ordering martinis, two at a time—drinking one, leaving the other for Artie. At the end of the last set, her little table was full of Shaw's untouched drinks, and Shaw split, without a word.

"She didn't know what to *do* about it," Bank said, "so she invited all the guys in the band—to have a drink. Each one of us got a martini. Yeah, we had a good time in Chicago; yeah."

"It was *very* nice," Sonny Russo agreed.

ART HAD his reasons for giving Ava the cold shoulder. For one thing, he wasn't alone in Chicago, as Bank discovered when the boss invited the baritone player to his hotel room one night for some chess.

"He had a suite," said Bank, an expert chess player. "We played in one room. I won the first game, and we're workin' in the second game—and the door opens, and a young woman walks in wearing a negligee, naked as—You could see right through, you know what I mean? And she was—bringing cakes, and uh—little sandwiches, and coffee; she was serving, you know? I said to Artie, I said, 'Uh, Artie, that's some beautiful woman you got there.' And he looked me right in the eye and he said, 'Yeah, that's my psychiatrist.'" Bank laughed. "I'll never forget that. Yeah, Artie was—quite a character."

As for the chess: "Well, I think I won two out of three. He would never admit it, though, you know."

CHICAGO'S RECEPTION was heartening. The orchestra was also well received in December at Nicky Blair's Click Club in Philadelphia. But it was too little too late, after a long tour that Shaw termed dismal, during which too often "[t]here was a deafening silence when we finished playing." In the shank of 1949, except for a few hip crowds in metropolitan hubs, the paying customers hadn't cared one bit for "The Artistry of Artie Shaw and his Orchestra."

"The people just didn't *hear* that," Johnny Mandel said. "They were as indifferent to that Shaw band as the public was to Woody Herman's 'Second Herd.' It was just a different era from before."

Art would always remember the Blue Note's enthusiasm. But he would never forget the hostile reactions elsewhere. "If you've got a band that you know is the best band in the state of the art at the time," he said in 1990, "and the audience is going like *this* [holding its nose] to you— or making signals like they're pulling a toilet chain—you know you're on the wrong track. And that was arguably the best band of its time, I think. But—the audience *would not have it*. They stayed away in great masses. How can you pay for a band, then? And—it was a helluva band! If the public had had the slightest interest in it, I would have stayed with it, but—there was no *way*."

Jimmy Raney agreed: "Unfortunately, the people didn't care. . . . In fact, they didn't like what we were doing. They wanted to see the man who had married so many movie stars, and hear 'Begin the Beguine' and 'Frenesi.'"

Buddy DeFranco expanded years later on the particular problems

Artie Shaw faced as an artist; for one thing, Buddy said, Art never got his due as a jazz player: "Never. Because he wound up recording songs that became smash hits with the public, and he became what would be called a commercial commodity. He *was* commercial: he appealed to the general public. But he didn't appeal to the general public because he *played* great; his appeal was because of the songs that he recorded that became hits—like 'Begin the Beguine' and 'Star Dust' and 'Frenesi.' You know, you can go on and on with his hits; but they had a commercial appeal. Hidden in that commercial appeal was Artie's real creativity. But he was not recognized by the public for his great playing. And I think later in life, Artie became—soured, because of that.

"Because I think he really believed that the public *knew* what he was doing, musically—in the beginning. I think that's why he got so grumpy over the years, because it finally occurred to him that people didn't *really* know what he was doing; they liked his songs. And the proof was that when he would play a concert and he included so many new things which were, you know, experimental, some experimental, at the time—and the audience got—got nervous, they got—in fact, sometimes they insulted him; which was sad. Late '40s, yes. That's the trouble with becoming well known, in the popular and commercial sense.

"And then suddenly it occurred to Artie, I'm sure, that the people liked the *songs* that he recorded, not so much what he *did* with them. And so that presented a real problem, because—he really could never get to first base with his experimenting and with his developmental—with his real progress. Yeah. Listen, that happens to so many players and so many people in the arts. And then, after they die, somebody'll say, 'My *goodness!* Wasn't that *something!*' And then it *grows* from there, and then he becomes a—a legend, and—finally he gets to be known as—as an artist. But—Artie had a rough time, *while* he was playing. Yeah. That's—that's too bad."

CHAPTER THIRTY-NINE

The Shekomeko Shuffle

SHERMAN BILLINGSLEY'S Stork Club was still one of Shaw's favorite hangouts. On a February night in 1950, Art met the Rosoffs there to celebrate the twenty-eighth birthdays of Sophia and of Art's current girlfriend, Anne, who lived with him in the city and at his farm. "She was a lovely girl," Sophia said, "and *very* bright. We were very good friends, Annie and I were. Artie was very fond of her." At the Stork Club that night, they ran into Charlie Chaplin and Oona O'Neill, who joined them for drinks and talk. On such congenial occasions with compatible people, Sophia said, "Artie could be ex-*traor*-dinarily charming."

Shaw had other reasons to spend time in the city. After gallbladder surgery, he had record dates to fulfill for his new label, Decca. Several sides were cut in January with the remnants of his 1949 band, including the new Gramercy 5 piece "The Shekomeko Shuffle," a paean to his farm (near Shekomeko, New York). After these sessions, Shaw disbanded his latest "million-dollar band."

Again Art contemplated writing a book. In a few months, he could make the time; he had reached a good vantage point from which to contemplate the past. His writing impulse was further provoked by meeting a young man whose debut novel was on its eve of publication.

Jack Kerouac—billed "John Kerouac" for his first work—encountered

Shaw on the night of March 1, after early drinks with Frank Morley, an English editor. Morley's publishing house would later bring out Kerouac's *The Town and the City* in the United Kingdom; March 2 was the publication date of Harcourt Brace's U.S. edition. A lubricated Morley and Kerouac showed up at Shaw's New York apartment, where Artie and Annie entertained them for hours.

Shaw knew Morley through mutual acquaintances. Artie and Jack had people in common too: the twenty-eight-year-old author was friends with David Diamond, and Kerouac's Harcourt editor (and the dedicatee of his book) was Robert Giroux.

Kerouac was a handsome kid of French-Canadian descent, raised in Massachusetts, and passionate about jazz. He hung around the New York clubs to hear and see Bird, Lennie Tristano, Miles Davis, Allen Eager, trying to forge a personal mythology from the secret bebop night.

"I was not impressed by him, see," Art said. "No." But Artie and Annie were gracious, and Kerouac was flying high: waiting for the first important review of his book, to be printed the next day in the *New York Times*. Shaw cautioned him: good, bad, indifferent, don't let what happens throw you off course.

Kerouac was thrilled by the occasion and by this "big conversation" with Artie and Anne. "What a night!" he would write in his journal. At midnight, still at Art's, Jack called his friend Lucien Carr, who worked at United Press International. Carr got hold of the *New York Times* review of *The Town and the City* and read it to Kerouac over the telephone; it was a rave. (Charles Poore hailed the author as "a brilliantly promising young novelist.") Kerouac then had Carr's coworker read the review to Shaw. What a night, for sure.

BUT AGAIN Art put his writing plans aside. In March, he assembled another outfit to play at, of all places, Bop City. This was a much different gig, though, from the one in 1949; now Shaw would front a cut-down, fourteen-piece dance band.

It was a competent bread-and-butter bunch playing standard fare, but a big letdown after Shaw's just-abandoned "million-dollar" ensemble. Art was unhappy (photos show him glowering as he plays), and the music-magazine reviewers, in the wake of Shaw's recent disappointments, were merciless. "Some of the most inept band music that's been heard in years," *Down Beat*'s Michael Levin claimed. *Metronome*'s George T. Simon called this "the worst band of [Shaw's] career . . . a sorry exhibition from a man who apparently has given up."

"It was a good band," insisted Eddie Bert, a member of its trombone section. "I knew all the guys. It was fine, you know. But Artie was like a schoolteacher; he wouldn't let people come near him on the stage. And if we were playin' a dance and people started comin' up, he'd get them away. He was pretty strict. But he was a great clarinet player, you know; he could really play the clarinet."

Ava Gardner was in New York during Art's Bop City stint, in the company of Frank Sinatra, the married singer with whom she had begun an affair. They were staying at the Hampshire House; Sinatra, whose career was at a low ebb, was playing the Copacabana. Without telling Frank, Ava went one night to see and hear her ex-husband at Bop City. According to Earl Wilson's biography of Sinatra, "An employee of the club tipped off the papers, and some Sinatra followers, that Ava was there having a drink with Shaw. 'Get her the hell out of there or there's going to be a murder,' the Sinatra camp warned the Shaw camp." The high-strung singer was jealous of his sultry girlfriend, and no one raised his ire more than her ex: the cocksure clarinetist who'd once turned down Frank's bid to join his band.

One other night that spring, Ava, after a quarrel with Sinatra, telephoned Shaw for advice at his New York apartment: "Artie solved other people's problems in a couple of sentences," she wrote.

> He was at home and his current girlfriend was with him. . . . [H]e said, "Tell you what, Ava. We're going to bed pretty soon, but why don't you come by and have a nightcap before you turn in?"
>
> . . . And off I went leaving my address book open to the page with Artie's phone number.

It was a careless, or mischievous, thing to do. Ava was talking with Art and Anne when Sinatra showed up at Shaw's door, Gardner wrote.

"Why, hello, Frank. Come on in. Good to see you. Yeah, Ava's here. Do you know my girlfriend?" A real smooth customer, Artie, and maybe he had to be at that particular moment.

Frank . . . had his buddy Hank Sanicola with him. . . . Artie knew the score and did his best to act as if this visit was the most natural of social events.

"Frank, sit down and have a drink. You, too, Hank."

Frank shook his head. He turned, his head a bit low, his shoulders hunched. He and Hank walked out. . . . After a few more minutes, I . . . made my way back to the Hampshire House. . . .

[T]he phone rang. It was Frank . . . "I can't stand it any longer. I'm going to kill myself—now!"

Then there was this tremendous bang. . . . I threw the phone down and raced across the living room and into Frank's. . . . And there was a body lying on the bed. . . . I threw myself on it saying, "Frank, Frank. . . ." And the face, with a rather pale little smile, turned toward me, and the voice said, "Oh, hello."

The goddamn revolver was still smoking in his hand. He had fired a single shot through a pillow and into the mattress.

SHAW WENT on the road with his newest orchestra. After touring in the South, the band played the black theater circuit: New York's Apollo, the Howard in Washington, Baltimore's Royal, Newark's Adams Theatre. Art was all business; but there was one occasion, according to Sonny Russo, when Shaw's temperament expressed itself.

It involved another trombonist, Bart Varselona: "He was the first bass-trombone player," Russo said. "You know, in those days nobody used bass trombone except Stan Kenton. Now, Bart was strictly a section player; he didn't play any jazz," didn't improvise. "And you got me and Eddie Bert playing jazz." Varselona's creativity found its expression through gags, Russo said: "He was a *funny man*, Bart; he was like the band clown, you know, the band comedian."

During this tour, the 1940 movie *Second Chorus* was shown on television. Members of the band watched this ten-year-old movie at their hotel. "Before the gig that night," Russo said, "Bart says, 'Hey, Artie—I saw the movie with you, *Second Chorus*, on television today.' So Artie says, 'Oh yeah, really?' And so Bart says, 'Yeah. You had more *hair*, then.'" Russo laughed. "And that's all! He left it at that, right?"

The leader took his revenge that evening, on the bandstand. "Halfway through the night," Russo said, "we come to this one tune where he's featuring guys in the blues, and he's pointin' to everybody: take a *chorus*, play a solo. And he points to me; I play my chorus. He points to Eddie Bert; he plays his chorus. And he points to Bart. Now Bart didn't play *jazz*, so he's—he's shakin' his head, *no*, he says, I don't want to play any solo. So Artie kept pointin', pointin' to him, no, you gotta *play* it. Bart said no no.

"So he forced him to get up, you know. Naturally he—he wasn't a jazz player, right? That's the only time I saw Artie get kinda *mean*, you know," Russo said with a chuckle. "Uh, Bart got up and played a little bit, yeah, you know; he was all right."

TOUR DONE, this band too dispersed. Shaw had lots of sides yet to deliver to Decca though. The label had its own ideas on what those records should be.

In April 1950, Shaw teamed with singer Dick Haymes for "Count Every Star." This platter sold well, and similar collaborations followed. In May, Artie, pianist Gordon Jenkins, and a dismal-sounding choral group did an awkward version of "I'm Forever Blowing Bubbles." Whatever the context, Shaw's musicianship was impeccable. But Art was almost sleepwalking through these dates—doing the Shekomeko shuffle from farm to city and back. The artist who last year had recorded Shostakovich's "Prelude No. 17" was this season noodling "It's a Long, Long Way to Tipperary." Hits made the world go round, as the man who did

"Begin the Beguine" well knew. Shaw also knew, though, that when it's gotten to be one chord for beauty and three to pay the rent, maybe it's time to put down your horn.

BUT NOT yet.

With more performing commitments to fulfill and needing a cash cushion, Shaw had a new manager put together an ensemble for some dates in the hinterlands. Art would now give this year's ballroom public the material it seemed to crave: off-the-shelf stock arrangements of current hit-parade items such as "Bibbidi-Bobbidi-Boo," "A Bushel and a Peck," "Hoop-De-Doo," "If I Knew You Were Comin' I'd've Baked a Cake," "Bonaparte's Retreat," "Gone Fishin'," "Play a Simple Melody," "Sam's Song," "Rag Mop." Into these Shaw would mix his own evergreens, the hits the people yammered for: "Frenesi-Begin-the-Beguine-Star-Dust," as he had taken to saying.

With his union-hall musicians, his obligatory girl singer, and his stock arrangements, Shaw took to the highway. A perverse experiment, he would describe it in later years, a private joke. In his nonplaying moments in front of this band, he disregarded all his stage standards and did what he had never allowed: he clowned around. "I laughed, ogled, waggled my head—in general behaved like a mechanical wind-up doll," he said.

The manager of one of the final venues on this money-making tour thanked Artie: "Mr. Shaw, I'd been told you were a difficult man to get along with but you've convinced me you are a great bandleader. Any time you want to come back with this band, the place is yours. Why, you've played the best music I've heard since Blue Barron." Blue Barron—one of the most cornball, Mickey Mouse band leaders in the business. Artie Shaw knew for sure now that his big-band days were done.

CHAPTER FORTY

Blue Again

EVERYONE WAS giving up their bands this year. Goodman went to England to work with a pick-up ensemble. Barnet, disgusted at being asked to play polkas, cut his orchestra down to a combo. Woody Herman just had a septet now, and not because of finances: he said he couldn't find enough men to play in a big band who weren't "sick" or "unwell"— euphemisms for heroin addiction. "Junk" had hit the New York scene like a powdery plague in the imitative wake of star-addicts, in particular Charlie Parker. Even Count Basie folded his orchestra to front a sextet.

Artie Shaw told the trades that soon *he'd* be out of the business for good.

But still not yet.

If Barnet and Herman and Basie had combos, maybe Shaw could too. But he wouldn't want to just echo his old Gramercy 5; he'd need a modern group. And he'd have to woodshed: hone his playing skills in the current mode.

While Art pursued that goal, his path crossed that of William F. Lee, a young pianist from Texas who had come to Manhattan with the Gene Krupa band—"ninety-one one-nighters, from Fort Worth to New York City"—and stayed on to play with Charlie Parker. Shaw hired Lee in the summer of 1950 for an ad-hoc, low-profile sextet.

"This was a small band," Lee said, "it was six pieces; it was called 'the Artie Shaw All-Stars,'" to differentiate it from any official Gramercy 5. "It only lasted maybe three or four weeks. It started out as a little rehearsal group at Nola's Studios in New York, and then we played one-nighters, mostly in the New York area. We never really had what you'd call a steady gig."

Unbeknownst to Lee and the others, for Shaw this was a rehearsal group. They did new music, Lee said, "Mostly an attempt at the bebop stuff that Bird was playing. Artie really didn't fit into that bag, and—he wanted to *try* it, you know. He'd never really crossed the bridge into bebop, and I think in a way it frustrated him."

Shaw didn't have trouble hearing the boppers' extended harmonies. After all, he had grown up listening to Art Tatum, whose adventurous chords instructed Bird and Diz, and had hired and played with modernists. But the turn-around rhythms of bop improvising hung him up until at last he caught on to how triplets were used as pivot points.

William F. Lee would go back to Texas, marry a girl he fell in love with, have four kids, get a master's degree and then a doctorate, study with Nadia Boulanger, earn prize nominations for his classical compositions, become a significant figure in jazz education, write several books, and see one of his sons (Will) become a well-known New York bassist. But Lee would never forget the summer he worked with Artie Shaw: "He was one of the most unusual guys, because he was so talented, and he was so articulate. His IQ must have been 160, 170. I think music was kind of a drug to him; it's a feeling I always had about him. Because it's one of those strange contradictions: he seemed much happier when he was playing—but he hated to play."

BY THE AUTUMN of 1950, Art felt comfortable enough in a modern combo to hire more established young players for a publicized gig. He had his manager telephone Billy Taylor, a twenty-nine-year-old African-American pianist who'd served as house keyboard player at Birdland, with an offer to hire Taylor's all-black quartet as four-fifths of a temporary Gramercy 5 for a limited engagement at a Broadway venue.

"I was just delighted I got this call," Taylor said. "I had been an Artie Shaw fan for years. Everybody back when I was growing up was choosing sides between Artie Shaw and Benny Goodman, and for me it was no contest: Artie Shaw was head-and-shoulders above what Goodman was doing musically. He was a forward thinker."

So was Taylor. A graduate of Virginia State College, by 1950 he had written several articles and a couple of books on bebop; eventually he would earn a doctorate at the University of Massachusetts. With this already seasoned musician and his colleagues, Shaw held rehearsals at his Upper East Side apartment, where he was quick to establish his modernist credibility.

"He said, 'What about this bebop thing?'" Taylor said. "So I showed him a couple of the things that I had done, and—it takes a musician to understand—I know this is not his style, and he cuts it at sight! 'Oh yeah, that's very nice.' And then we went on back to this stuff that we were gonna play with *him*, you know."

This instant Gramercy 5's book would consist of expected favorites plus newer things: ballads including "Someone to Watch over Me," "Besame Mucho" as a mambo, and Artie's "Pied Piper Theme."

"The style that he had carved out for himself worked in a contemporary jazz field at that period," Taylor said. "He could have played more bebop, but I think that was stylistically more of a corner than he wanted to be pushed into. There were broader things that he heard in terms of his own music, and the things that he liked at the time."

Between practicing, Taylor asked Shaw about William Grant Still, and Art talked about Billy's friend Willie the Lion Smith. "To get to rehearse at his apartment, and hear his thoughts on jazz in particular," Taylor said, "it was like a master class. All in all, it was kind of an oasis for me."

After the oasis, though, the gig.

It was at Iceland, a Scandinavian restaurant-club on Broadway, across the street but a world away from the new jazz mecca of Birdland. The club was in an enormous basement room (*Metronome* called it "the frozen waste") housing a huge smorgasbord table. Iceland had never before presented jazz. The restaurant was "heretofore noted primarily for its Italian tenors," *Down Beat* wrote. "Artie wasn't really thrilled with the club," Taylor said. Shaw was billed as the star of Iceland's "show": a Broadway-style vaudeville with vocal quartet, dancing girls, and a comedian. "He told them, 'Look, the show is fine, but I don't want to be the star of the show,'" Taylor said. "'You do the show—finish it—I'll come on and do my thing.'" Between sets, the leader stayed in what passed for a dressing room. "Artie had to keep the door very tightly closed," Taylor said, "'cause he didn't want to *hear* that!"

Leonard Feather, on duty for England's *Melody Maker*, cornered Artie and found an embarrassed Shaw in a dour mood. "I just came down here to pick up a few fast bucks," Shaw told him. "It's strictly for the loot. You can't make it with music any more—the band business, as we know it, is dead! People don't follow bands and know all the soloists, the way they did."

However out of place he felt, there was no doubt Shaw enjoyed performing with this combo, one of whose members was guitarist John Collins. "John had a harmonic sense that Artie really appreciated," Taylor said. "He played chords a little differently from a lot of other guys. And John played lovely ballads too."

The Gramercy 5 were playing such a ballad one night when the most unforgettable moment of the week occurred.

"We'd been there for a few days," Taylor said. "Coupla nights, things hadn't been the way Artie wanted it, but—one night for some reason or other everything was really hittin' it; I mean, I said, 'Oh man, this is why I took this *gig*! This is really terrific!' It was going so well that Artie had chosen to play a ballad, one of the ballads he liked to play back in those days. The spotlight is on him, and, and—he was *singin'* it, Bill! I mean it was beautiful. And right in the middle of it, a guy comes up onstage out of *nowhere*—and puts his arm around Artie's shoulders! And said, 'You know—I *love* your playing!'

"I thought Artie was gonna deck him, man! He was so furious, man!

He—walked off, and the bouncers had to get the guy, and—I mean—
Then Artie came back onstage, but—but he was *furious*, man. And I
don't blame him, because that was the *one* night—everything was *happening*! That was why he chose a ballad at that point: he knew this was
one of his signature things, and here's some guy who just—spoils it
completely. You know—*why*?

"I thought Artie was gonna quit right then."

CHAPTER FORTY-ONE

He's Gone Away

A RT LOOKED AGAIN at the letter Sinclair Lewis once sent him, with advice on how Shaw should write a book: *One: Be assured you'll never finish. Two: If you do finish, remember it won't get published. Three: If it is somehow published, nobody will read it.*

And at last it worked. "Cleared the decks!" Shaw said. "I was able to write. But it's true! 'What will they think?' 'What will the critics say?' 'What will the readers—?' That's *beside* the point. Get it on paper. When it's bad, fix it. Keep fixing it. Keep doing that—and you may finally end up with a book. That was it! Now—why did I want to *write* a book? Don't ask me. It was important to me. So—so I did."

He never could have conceived of this reflective, philosophical autobiography without years of analysis, Art knew. Now he had enough insights to last him a lifetime; he envisioned a series of at least three books.

Pages accumulated. By the start of 1951, Shaw felt he had made enough progress to warrant a contract. For representation he turned to Ivan von Auw, senior member of the Harold Ober literary agency. Von Auw took the deal to the independent publishing house of Farrar, Straus and Young, whose Stanley Young had married author Nancy Wilson Ross. Artie Shaw had a publishing deal by mid-January. He was paid $1,250 on signing and would get another $1,250 on submission of his manuscript, a work to be titled *The Trouble with Cinderella: An Outline of Identity*.

AS HE WORKED on his book, Shaw kept up his show-business profile. He was a guest on radio and television programs, including a *March of Time* TV report on swing music, and the NBC-radio comedy *Duffy's Tavern*. And Artie made four more Decca sides with singer-golfer Don Cherry.

During a visit to Birdland, Shaw encountered Jack Kerouac again with a bunch of his cronies. The first-time novelist was living through the ambiguous aftermath (querulous reviews, mediocre sales) of the publication of *The Town and the City*. Art, grappling with his own prose and with vexing reactions to his music, was in no mood to sympathize with this youngster whose greatest fame and disappointments lay in the future. "My life at that point—I was feelin' that the audiences were full of shit," Shaw said. "Had the worst band that you could get, and they *liked* it. Well, you know—I didn't have time for his bitterness; I had my own." Still, Art didn't brush the kid off. All Kerouac wanted was for Shaw to remember him. "We talked a little bit," Art said.

Anne, the young woman living with Art, would soon leave him to pursue her work in another country—all the more reason for Shaw to travel into the city, where he had many friends and no doubt a few romances among the Broadway, drama school, fashion, and television crowds. "Artie had a *busy, busy* life," Sophia Rosoff said.

Shaw ran into Doris Dowling, a twenty-eight-year-old actress he had asked for a date once in Hollywood back in 1946. She had turned him down then, but now Doris (who'd advanced her career by going to Italy and costarring in the film *Bitter Rice*) agreed to dinner. She and Artie began seeing each other—"with intermittent fights." Dowling and his book became the twin focuses of Shaw's attention. On a brief trip they took to England, Doris and Art became engaged.

. . .

IT WAS to Stanley Young that Shaw delivered his draft of *The Trouble with Cinderella* in November, but it was John Farrar who had final editorial say. As Farrar read Shaw's manuscript, he dictated his reactions, which became a ten-page memo. To start with, he hated the quotations from classic authors that Shaw had posted at the head of each chapter, and he wasn't crazy at first about the personality Shaw's narrative displayed. Yet as Farrar read further, he saw virtues. Farrar conceded there was a viable work contained within these pages, but he thought the manuscript needed much revision. Shaw wouldn't get his book into print without significant wrangling. But on November 29, Ivan von Auw was sent the remaining $1,250 due the author.

Art stayed in the city a couple of weeks, at the Hotel Langdon. He took in some shows—two of which were star-vehicles for a couple of his oldest friends. At the Winter Garden, Phil Silvers was having the greatest Broadway success of his career in the just-opened *Top Banana*, a musical comedy parodying the new medium of television. Phil's and Art's old friend Judy Garland was having a New York triumph too, in a solo show at the Palace, a tour de force Shaw saw soon after its opening.

"She was my little sister," is how Art in retrospect saw his relationship with the teenaged Judy. "I was totally out of reach, for her; but *she* didn't know that. She had the—hots for me; I didn't have the *faintest idea* of that. Then I married Lana—and that almost *killed* her; she went through a whole *number*. Later, we got to be friends though; we were great friends. And I always respected her; I always thought she had great talent.

"She was the closest thing to a little sister." Far too late, Shaw came to a conclusion about the wrong turn his life had taken. "He always said," his friend Jan Curran would recall, "he should have married Judy Garland."

DORIS DOWLING was no little sister, and in late November it seemed she was having second thoughts about becoming a wife. Hedda Hopper hinted, "You don't have to twist Doris Dowling's arm to learn that her romance and impending marriage to Artie Shaw is pfft. Doris is in New York now, and has been a bit under the weather from it all."

But Artie Shaw could be charming. He and Dowling were far from through.

Now all Art had to do was help John Farrar see the light.

FARRAR HAD paid a freelance editor to rework Shaw's manuscript. "He took my book," Shaw said of the "improved" manuscript his editor-publisher surprised him with, "and turned it inside out. He would 'fix it,' so it would sell. Way he had it, started with me walkin' through the park and saying, 'See all those people there, and those lights?' You know. Well—that's *obvious*; *I* wanted a different kinda book. From there on in, it was like his book *and* my book. He said, 'I didn't change a *word*!' I said, 'I know you didn't, but—you changed the entire accent.'"

It's not as if Art needed the money. If worse came to worst, he could take the pages and leave. That was the great thing about threatening to walk: people knew he wasn't kidding. He had done it before.

Shaw prevailed. "Farrar said yeah; he got it. He let me do it my way."

Artie Shaw's first book was presented to the world on a fortuitous publication date: May 23, 1952, the author's forty-second birthday.

THE WORK was a memoir, a harangue, a sociological exposé, a philosophical argument, a confession, a defense, a work of entertainment, a self-indulgent ramble. It was by turns candid, secretive, earthy, pretentious, open and shut. The author spoke at length on many topics but often seemed to conceal more than he revealed. He wrote to some extent about his mother and father but declared his own marital history off-limits. In some ways, the book seemed painfully honest, with its wealth of excruciatingly personal detail. On closer examination, there were gaps in its revelations, instances of misdirection. How was the aftermath of that car accident resolved? Whatever happened to Betty, the girl from Ohio? How was it possible that Art never heard again from his favorite uncle? Who was the actress Art romanced in 1930 and what became of *her*? The reader cannot ask, for the writer is on to other things: interesting things, expressed with much color and occasional humor.

Cinderella was written in a number of styles, over a period it seemed of several decades. One set piece, about a band rehearsal circa 1938, was as polished and objective as a *New Yorker* sketch from back then. Other sections were done with a modern subjectivity that seemed to originate on a psychoanalyst's couch. And the book's first chapter, a statement of principles hammered out in a labored and ambitious prose, obliquely echoed the opening pages of Joseph Wood Krutch's *The Modern Temper*. In achieving his book-writing goal set long ago on the Bucks County farm, Shaw commemorated the feat by creating his own version of the opening of the work which had humbled him then into postponing that dream until he had learned more and could express it. Emulating Krutch at long last, as he had emulated Goodman in 1936, Shaw in essence said (if only to himself), *See?* I *can do that* too. *I can do that* better.

THE TROUBLE *with Cinderella* was widely reviewed, which was to be expected, given its author's celebrity. More gratifying was that it was taken with the seriousness with which it was written. Most reviewers concluded that the book was like its author: more than a bit exasperating, sometimes seeming disingenuous in ways hard to pin down, often contradictory or illogical; but full of brilliance, energy, and artistry. In short: one of a kind.

The critique Shaw himself was proudest of was the *New York Herald Tribune*'s. "The Trib was a very good paper," he said, "and at the book-review section there was a man named Thomas Sugrue; he was a remarkable reviewer, and he reviewed things like Thomas Merton's *Seven Storey Mountain*. And *he* gave this book one *helluva* review. I was very impressed with that." *Cinderella*, Sugrue wrote, had "an honesty which scrapes as it cleans. Nothing quite like it has come along in quite a while; it is as unpredictable as was its author," a conflicted man who came to realize that "the thing Artie Shaw wanted was tormenting Arshawsky, and the thing Arshawsky wanted was murdering Artie Shaw."

Another equally serious analysis of the book was done for the *Reporter* by the young Frederic Morton, who later said, "I had only one criticism: mainly that Artie rubbed in his intellectual credentials too much by having enormous epigraphs from Sartre to Aristotle, before every chapter." This sole demurral, though, was one too many for *Cinderella*'s author.

"I was living with my parents at that time," Morton said. "I had just gotten out of college. And I got a call from 'Mister Shaw'—and it was Artie. He immediately started to argue with me and said, 'Why don't we have lunch, because I think you've written a very intelligent review, but—' He objected to my objection. We met at the Drake Hotel, and from that rather contentious lunch evolved a lifelong friendship. Despite the fact that I stuck to my guns, or because of it, we became very good friends."

"I wasn't putting all those quotes up there to show what a bright fellow I was, or how well read I was," Art justified years later, the criticism still stinging a bit, even into the twenty-first century. "It was more, 'If you don't want to take *my* word for the conclusions I'm drawing, look at what *these* folks had to say.'"

WITH HIS initial literary work launched, Shaw was ready, after seven months of his first-ever engagement, to plunge into his seventh attempted marriage. On June 14, Art and Doris applied for a license and took required blood tests in North Canaan, Connecticut, for a bare-bones civil ceremony.

Art was a nervous wreck. He rushed the wedding-day drive to North Canaan, almost hitting several cars. Shaw "fidgeted and squirmed and perspired and shook during the ceremony," magazine writer Richard Gehman wrote. "Later a friend asked him why he'd been so nervous. 'Why,' Shaw said, 'with Doris, it's like I've never been married before.'" Arthur Shaw and Doris Dowling were declared man and wife in the eyes of the state of Connecticut—with their secret safe from the wire services for nine days.

LIKE ALL first-time authors, perhaps, Shaw hoped and assumed his book would change his life. One consequence he hadn't foreseen was the conclusion of his psychoanalysis.

Abraham Kardiner always summered in Provincetown. This year when the doctor returned, he was ready with a verbal review of *The Trouble with Cinderella*. "He gave me a few critical points of it," Shaw said. "I didn't agree with 'em. But when the session was over, he said, 'You're discharged; you don't need this anymore.' I said, 'Why not?' He thought about it; he said, 'There's nothing I can tell you about yourself that you don't know. What you're going to do with it, I can't predict.' And I said, 'Geez, that—that's pretty good.'

"So we quit. And I missed it for a few days; I thought, 'Where's my mentor?' Well—that was it. It ended. I've never been back to an analyst, or felt the need to. I can sit now and think my way through most of the problems, and the 'maybe it's me' business comes in pretty handy. A lot of it *is* me. The past, particularly."

ART PROMOTED his book on television, as a featured guest on New York's *Author Meets the Critics* over WABD (Channel 5) and through his second appearance, in August, on the CBS-network series *What's My Line?*

His first time on that show, two years before, he had been the "mystery guest" for the program's third episode. Now he sat on the panel, as substitute for Random House publisher Bennett Cerf—himself the permanent replacement for Louis Untermeyer, a genial poet and man of letters who had been one of the show's original members. Untermeyer had been popular with viewers, but after his name was included on a publicized list of those who'd supported the 1949 Waldorf-Astoria "peace conference"—the same event Shaw had been chastised for endorsing—he had become a focus for protestors who picketed *What's My Line?* broadcasts every week until the sponsor fired Untermeyer. The poet had become part of a growing entertainment-business "blacklist," which looked to get worse before it got better.

It wasn't just a matter of picketers and sponsors, columnists and commentators. People were being called before congressional committees to answer for their alleged sins against the republic—the more famous the people the better, as far as the committees were concerned. Some high school teacher from Brooklyn with ties to the Communist Party might be good for a couple inches of page-eight newsprint; a movie star or a Broadway playwright or a big-band leader meant front-page headlines. A part of Shaw must have braced for the worst. At the same time, why should he worry? He hadn't done anything wrong, just maybe something stupid. If he stayed focused on his work and his home life, why shouldn't everything be all right?

Art gamely looked ahead. He told journalists he had all but finished his next book, a trio of linked novellas. After this, Art thought maybe he would write another memoir—or maybe stick with fiction for a while, *then* go back to autobiography. Was it even maybe possible—contrary to conclusions reached in the semi-dystopic *Trouble with Cinderella*—that some lucky people, in a limited way and under certain special circumstances, just *might* be able to live happily ever after?

CHAPTER FORTY-TWO

It Could Happen to You

Early in 1953 came a proposition for Artie Shaw to do a one-month tour of the Midwest and near-South with a sixteen-man band and a girl singer. The money—$450,000—was too good for Shaw to turn down. The IRS said he still owed them a lot (something to do with penalties for not paying enough tax on the dairy farm's profits) and soon there would be a new Shaw to feed: Doris was pregnant.

Shaw at first told the Texas booker that he wanted to put together a decent new band like his innovative 1949 outfit; he hoped the public's taste had grown enough to accommodate something fresh. But it was no go: if Shaw wanted a successful tour, he was told, he had to stick to his proven hits. So Art dusted off his 1938 book and bought stock arrangements of this season's favorite tunes ("April in Portugal," "Ruby," "Moulin Rouge"). Drummer Tony Papa put together a band for him. Artie and this crew set out in mid-April.

They went to some far-flung places: windblown towns near the Gulf of Mexico—Nagadoches, Palacios—where a couple of thousand people would show up at some makeshift octagon-shaped wooden structure, buy drinks at the wall-long bar, and dance to his music.

Art worked up a story to tell the rest of his life, about a patron in one of these middle-of-nowhere spots, a man Shaw noticed who was nod-

ding and winking at him each time the fellow danced past. Art asked
him what gave.

"I know your secret," the man said, "but don't worry; I won't tell."

"And what's my secret?"

"You're not really Artie Shaw."

"I'm not? And how do you know that?"

"Well—what would Artie Shaw be doing in a place like this?"

SHAW WAS out somewhere in Arkansas when he got word that he would
have to leave his band for a solo command performance in New York
City. He was subpoenaed to appear on Monday, May 4, at the United
States Court House in Foley Square to testify before the House Committee on Un-American Activities, which was investigating Communist infiltration into the educational and entertainment fields.

He had been half expecting such a summons for three years, ever
since this committee first started calling Hollywood figures to account.
As fear provoking as it was, Shaw may have half welcomed this chance to
get things out in the open. Anyway, that's the tack he and lawyer Andrew
Weinberger chose to take. Shaw chartered a plane to Manhattan.

Witness and counsel sat at a U-shaped table, along with seven committee members and staff. It was hot in the court chamber at noon. Big
banks of camera lights lit the scene for Shaw's testimony, which was
televised live in New York and filmed for movie-theater newsreels.

Art was quick to declare himself a cooperative witness. "May I say,
first of all," he told the committee, "that I'm going to answer every
question you ask me as honestly and as fully as I possibly can."

Committee counsel Frank Tavenner asked for a summary of Shaw's
background and professional accomplishments. Art sketched the arc of
his musical apprenticeship up to 1938 and his first great success: "It
came in the form of a hit record, which I made at that time—" Art
paused. ". . . I'm not going to advertise my own recordings here," he said.
But Tavenner insisted: "I think the committee would like to know what
have been your chief productions." Even at this somber moment, there

was no escaping that perennial request. "Well," Shaw said, "in 1938, on the basis of a record called 'Begin the Beguine,' I first came into national prominence as an orchestra leader."

Tavenner read Shaw a part of the sworn statement of Leo Townsend, a screenwriter and admitted one-time Communist (whose credits included the script for *Night and Day*, the movie in which Cary Grant played Cole Porter). Townsend had been asked if he'd seen Artie Shaw at any Party gatherings. "Yes," the screenwriter had said. "He attended five or six Communist Party branch meetings, and he attended four or five Marxist classes." Had there been any friction because of this? "Yes," Townsend had said, "I remember a conversation between my wife . . . and a man named Hy Kraft, who was a friend of Shaw's and who was also a member or had been of the Communist Party. He was greatly annoyed at whoever had recruited Artie Shaw on the ground that Shaw would be a bad Communist."

"Well," Shaw said, hearing this, "I'm afraid he had me right there." Over laughter, he added, "I didn't know that Mr. Kraft was a Communist, I can tell you that now." As for himself, Shaw said, "To the best of my knowledge I have never been a member of the Communist Party."

That needed explaining. Shaw recounted, at length, the sequence of "cloak-and-dagger" events in 1946 through which he was "absolutely misled" and "hoodwinked" into attending some questionable gatherings. He described having been "quite active" in HICCASP and a member of its executive council, and he told of witnessing Communist Party meetings as a bystander. Only later, Shaw said, did he become aware of the possible implications: that others present at those meetings may have incorrectly assumed he was a Communist. Art didn't want to identify the people he had recognized at these "caucuses," he said, for fear of unfairly tainting their reputations. After all, maybe they, like he, had been there as mere observers (although, he said, "Actually, they are names I am sure you know").

The committee took a ten-minute recess, during which they spoke to Shaw in private. Someone much later quizzed Art: Had the congressmen asked him then to name names? "Oh yeah," he said. "I was *given* the *names!* Yeah: 'Here are the people,' who'd been there, who they wanted. I said, 'I can't tell you about those, I don't know them. I can tell you about Dalton *Trumbo.*' Everybody knew about Dalton Trumbo. John Howard Lawson, Jack Lawson; we all knew him, and—Ring Lardner [Jr.].'"

So the committee didn't receive much corroboration or any new leads from Shaw. Counsel Tavenner, though, was at least able to tell the *New York Times* that "Mr. Shaw had divulged these [two or three alluded-to] names during a recess."

When open session resumed, Committee members asked Shaw about political petitions and event endorsements he had signed in the later 1940s. "I feel the use of my name on a lot of these things should have been—should not have been granted," Shaw said, "but at that time I can only say the intent on my part when I granted them was not to do anything disloyal. I have never in my life done anything disloyal to this country." He had changed his ways in the past four years, Shaw assured them. "Not since then will you find my name on anything of any kind outside of the American Federation of Musicians. . . . I wouldn't sign anything today unless I had the advice of seven lawyers and the granting of permission or clearance by this committee."

"You realize, then, Mr. Shaw," Representative Gordon H. Scherer asked, "you were thoroughly duped by the Communist group then, do you not?"

"In this Communist thing," Shaw agreed, "I certainly was. . . .Yes sir. . . . I was a fool; I should not have signed."

He took it further, in an impromptu speech that brought him to the brink of tears. "Well," he told the committee, "I would just like to say one thing. This is no prepared statement or anything. It may sound garbled, but I have, I think, personally, a very large stake in this country, and I want to do everything I can, as I always have, to defend American institutions and American folkways. This country has been very kind to me. I started out as a minority member of a poor family, and I have come a long way for a guy like me; and I have found on the roads I am met with a lot of love and a lot of affection, and when I was serving in the service that same thing happened. . . . I never had any intention of doing anything detrimental or disloyal to the interests of this country." Shaw pressed the palms of his hands to his eyes, apparently to keep tears from flowing. Photographers were quick to take photographs that would be printed on the front pages of that night's and tomorrow's newspapers.

Representative Clyde Doyle had a suggestion: Maybe Artie could end his stage shows with a few uplifting words to young people on the virtues and responsibilities of the American system. "Perhaps you might take a minute for a chosen word or two, as you leave these great audiences in the joy of hearing you and your orchestra play . . . and say something to the audience which has been a great inspiration. Perhaps you might find it convenient."

"I think I have on occasion done that . . . ," Art claimed. "[A]ctually you can upset an audience pretty well that way."

Chairman Harold H. Velde dismissed Shaw with the committee's thanks. Velde and Shaw stood and stretched the width of the table to shake hands, and there it was: the photo *Time* magazine would print with its account of Artie's testimony—to some, a portrait of cooperation and reconciliation; to others, a snapshot of collaboration and capitulation.

Shaw felt he had acquitted himself as best as circumstances allowed, though some would view his performance with dismay and derision— the next day's star witness, for instance, raspy-voiced character actor Lionel Stander, who showed up for *his* Foley Square engagement with a "luscious" blonde female on either arm, and who told the committee, in defiant response to Shaw's having acknowledged being a "dupe," "I'm not a dupe, dope, mope, moe or schmoe." Stander's euphonious declaration would, in the fullness of time and the twisting of fate, be inscribed in stone in a sculpture garden dedicated to the First Amendment at the University of Southern California. There would be no monument anywhere, of course, to Artie Shaw's more cooperative stance.

CHAPTER FORTY-THREE

Sunny Side Up

O N JULY 2, ARTIE SHAW took part in his first Decca session in a year, recording four standards with a thirty-seven-piece orchestra of all-star studio players (including trumpeter Billy Butterfield). The best cut was a three-and-a-quarter-minute version of "These Foolish Things." Shaw's final flourish on this track was an ad-lib cadenza as unexpected and as breathtaking as a Brancusi sculpture. At eighty, Shaw would call that twenty-second flight "the best thing I ever did in my life."

"I did certain things in that cadenza," he said, "that I thought— 'That's good; that's as close to perfection as you're gonna *get.*' So, once in a while, you hit somethin' like that: those few moments, where you have this—peculiar little piece of wood, with the pipes, and the— springs, and—it's a clumsy implement; and you're using all these mus- cles, your lips—tryin' to make somethin' happen that never happened before. Once in a while, you succeed. It's *weird*. But when it happens, it's a bitch; you never forget it. It beats anything. . . . I was a guest lecturer at Oberlin some years ago, at a clarinet conference; somebody asked me, 'Did you ever hit what you really wanted?' And I said, 'Once, in my life.' Well, it's a lot, you know. Once is pretty good."

More good things happened.

On the Fourth of July, in the same year that Shaw's patriotism had been put under a congressional magnifying lens, Doris Dowling Shaw gave birth to a boy, whom they named Jonathan. By all reports, Artie was "wild about his new son," although he was quoted saying one of his first paternal duties would be to teach the kid that all those fireworks every year weren't for his birthday.

Meanwhile, Benny Goodman was coming apart at the seams.

A two-disc 1950 Columbia LP of a rediscovered transcription recording of Goodman's legendary 1938 Carnegie Hall concert had by now sold a phenomenal quarter-million copies. Spurred by this great success, Benny had formed a new big band, studded with Goodman all-stars, for an ambitious spring concert-tour, including a return to Carnegie Hall. But this much-publicized "comeback" turned into a personal fiasco. Goodman had been talked into adding Louis Armstrong as a co-headliner, and the two artists got off on the wrong foot, with Benny hurting Louis's feelings, and Louis retaliating by doubling the length of his scheduled set and pulling out all the show-biz stops, turning Benny's segment into what seemed like an afterthought. Goodman, already nervous about the endeavor, began drinking brandy before shows, played poorly (trumpeter Bobby Hackett said, "He sounded terrible. He just couldn't do anything. It was embarrassing"), argued with spectators, criticized singer Helen Ward onstage, and at last withdrew from the remaining engagements. Biographer Ross Firestone guessed that Benny may have suffered a heart attack as well as a nervous breakdown. The scheduled dates continued, though, with the band playing without Benny. Adding insult to Goodman's injury, the rest of the tour was a great success.

As those events unfolded, New York club owner Ralph Watkins approached Shaw with a much more low-key proposition. Watkins, the man behind the defunct Bop City, now had a more intimate club on Fifty-fourth Street, the Embers. English pianist George Shearing had had a recent success here, leading a quintet with vibes and guitar. (Shearing told Shaw it had been Artie's Gramercy 5 groups that inspired him to form this popular combination.) Watkins suggested that Shaw assemble a similar combo to open the fall season: "You can play the way you feel like playing." Again, the money and the opportunity were too good to spurn.

Art assembled members for a new small group. As in 1950, there was no trumpet player; instead there was vibraphonist Joe Roland, an ex-Shearing man. Guitarist Tal Farlow had also worked with Shearing, as had the black drummer Denzil Best. The black bassist was bop-savvy Tommy Potter, whose most recent job had been with Charlie Parker. As pianist, Shaw hired not Billy Taylor (scheduled to open soon at Watkins's other new club, Basin Street) but Hank Jones, another superb black keyboard artist with a modern technique.

Shaw held paid rehearsals at his four-room flat on East Fifty-seventh Street for an extraordinary six weeks—almost as long as the scheduled eight-week gig. "*Intense* rehearsals," Hank Jones said. "It was a considerable length of time, enough so that we were quite familiar with his music and the way he wanted to play it. Artie was a super-perfectionist: he wanted things *absolutely*, *exactly* the way he intended to have it sound." All the modern players he knew, Jones said, were fans of Artie Shaw's: "Clarinetists, reed players in general, as well as trumpet players, trombone players—*all* musicians admired Artie's style; it was relaxed, and at the same time precise." Especially notable was Shaw's approach to harmony: "Artie was a *master* of interpreting chord progressions. No single chord got by him, you know! He was meticulous as far as interpreting the harmony."

Shaw secured a late-September one-week shakedown gig at Boston's Hi-Hat Club prior to the Embers October opening; he was determined not to duplicate that 1949 "bop flop" fiasco. And, for his first "location" job since 1950, Shaw gave himself a startling haircut.

He'd been complaining that his hair got in his eyes when he swam. "Cut it off," Doris suggested. One night at the farm, Shaw told Dick Gehman, "I took a pair of small animal-clippers from Abercrombie and Fitch and—boom, boom, cut two swaths." He shaved his head bald, saying he hoped to emulate his new little son: "I wanted to look like the baby." The result in any case was that Shaw onstage would now resemble not some middle-aged businessman but a brooding, clarinet-playing Svengali.

ARTIE SHAW'S new Gramercy 5 was a hit from opening night. The Embers was packed with celebrities, jazz devotees, and scene makers. *Variety*'s scribe was knocked out by the mix of hep sounds and boffo box office: "This gig is strictly for listening and [Shaw]'s dishing it out in socko style. . . . [Night-]Spot can count on ropes-up biz for his eight-week run, and if he wants to get back to steady small-room podium work he can just about write his own ticket." Nat Hentoff told *Down Beat*'s readers, "[T]he group swings as few other current jazz groups do. . . . [It's] a gentle gasser." *The New Yorker*'s nightclub columnist wrote, "Artie Shaw . . . one of the truly distinguished jazz soloists of our time . . . played beautifully, and always with the composure of a true artist."

"It was a new kind of music," Hank Jones said, "and I think people were *ready* for something: a new approach, and a new sound." "Chamber jazz" is what Shaw tagged it: a music by turns inventive, lyrical, and witty. "A lot of the things we did, we did in unison," Jones said. "Tal would play unison with Joe Roland on vibes; and sometimes with Artie, and sometimes with the piano. There was plenty of room for soloing." Joe Roland agreed: "Artie let us *play*, a lot."

But Denzil Best wasn't working out as Shaw wished. Irv Kluger was the drummer Shaw turned to for help. "Art calls me," Kluger remembered. "'Irv, I *need* you.' He was playing at a *fancy* nightclub on the West Side which nobody could afford to go there, that loved jazz!" Kluger was in the pit band of the hit Broadway musical *Guys and Dolls*, a job Shaw helped him get back in 1950. "'Irv, I *need* you.' I said, 'Artie! Once you're on Broadway, and the show's a hit—you got run-of-the-show contract: they can't fire you, and you can't quit! *You* can get me out; I can't get out. I been here three years and two months, already, and I *love* it! But—if you need me, I'll *be* there.'"

Art needed him. Art fixed it. Irv joined the new Gramercy 5 in mid-October, twelve days into the Embers gig. Kluger liked the compensation—"Artie *started* me at five hundred a week, that's two thousand a month"—and he loved the musical company: "Sensational. Hank Jones—there's no better piano player. Tommy Potter, bass." And of course, Artie Shaw: "He's a monster musician, and a guy that played with feelings. One of the best clarinet players in the world."

With this squad in place, Shaw worked with pleasure through the heart of this sold-out, "ropes up," standing-room-only success.

THEN, TOWARD the end of the group's eight-week stand, Artie's most famous contemporary stopped by. "Who comes in," Irv Kluger said, "but Benny Goodman. And—and he sits there *all* night. And—Benny's a nutcake!" Kluger cackled. "He's—he's *strange*."

Shaw noted Goodman's presence and came over during a break. "Well he'd heard me *play*," Shaw said, "and his eyebrows went up, into his *head*. 'Cause I did stuff on clarinet he would never *dream* of. Benny had a very limited harmonic sense. Good time, he had that," Art allowed, "time" being that elusive rhythmic nuance essential to jazz.

But instead of remarking on Shaw's formidable harmonic and emotional range, Goodman stared in silence. At last he said, "Swingin' again, uh?"

Yes, Art allowed, he guessed he was.

"So we do the gig," Kluger went on, "and the bass player Tommy Potter says, 'Boy, Benny *loved* the band—but he wasn't too sure with you, Irv.' So I said, '*Fuck* him!' And that's my exact words. What'd I give a shit. I didn't need Benny Goodman."

Benny would later hire Irv though—twice. "And Benny Goodman," Irv Kluger was happy to tell you, "paid *terrible*, man."

CHAPTER FORTY-FOUR

Stop and Go Mambo

SEVERAL RECORD-LABEL reps told Art that this was the best small jazz group they had ever heard—but there was no mass audience for it. To hell with that, Art said. If nobody wanted to record this combo, he would do it himself. He rented a studio, hired a capable engineer, put a microphone on every player, and cut several numbers.

Tapes in hand, Art reached agreements with two independent labels: Bell, whose budget-priced singles were sold like paperback books in drugstores and supermarkets; and Norman Granz's Clef, to which Shaw leased tracks for a series of ten- and twelve-inch LPs.

Shaw's group played clubs in Boston, Toronto, Chicago, Akron, and Cleveland before returning to New York in mid-February 1954, for another ropes-up engagement at the Embers—and more Shaw-financed recording.

At four o'clock every morning after their last Embers set, the men went to Fine Sound at 711 Fifth Avenue, ordered coffee and Danish, and began to play while the tape rolled. Using a Buffet clarinet with a "more intimate, woody sound" than his usual Selmer, Shaw took care not to overblow the other instruments. "In fact," he wrote, "most of the playing I did with that group was so *pianissimo* that I had to hold the instrument very close to the mike and keep the volume way down to where I used just enough breath to keep the reed vibrating. . . . On ballads . . . where I was on the extreme verge of not being heard at all, the result was a warm, highly emotional sound that I don't think can be done much better on a clarinet."

One of the first pieces recorded was "The Sad Sack," a minor-key blues by Shaw and Buster Harding. "Artie was the best *blues* player," Irv Kluger said, "and I played with a lotta good ones, including some of the early blacks; and it was twelve-bar blues—four, four, four—and they were tellin' the story of their *life*. Artie was one of the *best*; he could improvise in any key."

Gershwin's "I've Got a Crush on You" got a tender four-minute reading, with Shaw's melodic flow creating an emotional momentum that Farlow extended; Jones put his own twenty bars' worth in. "When I'm playing with a group like the one I have now," Art told the *Cleveland News*, "it's like a conversation in music."

On the medium-up "Sequence in B Flat," Shaw and Kluger "traded fours" (four-bar solo volleys), during which Shaw paraphrased "Frenesi." Potter took Irv's place for more four-bar exchanges; Roland eased in for a few. "Artie let you live," Kluger told Bob Rusch. "We'd take fours, we'd take eights, we'd take ones, and we'd take twos, I mean it was really fun. . . . He just played and let you play and knew that you would join the Family of Music, just like the Family of Man."

"We would stay in that record studio until maybe eleven o'clock the next day," Hank Jones said, "doing take after take, until Artie felt satisfied with what he was hearing. We were all of the same mind, all the guys in the group; we all wanted to get the very most out of these compositions. It's a case of: 'Did you accomplish what you started out to do on that particular take?' If Artie didn't feel that you did—then you'd do another take." With Art, though, Hank said, "Everything he played had a particular stamp of excellence."

Nothing provoked that excellence more than a ballad. This Gramercy 5 did a number of them: an "Imagination" in which Shaw's flowing ad libs seemed a metaphor of the song's title; a "Don't Take Your Love from Me," during which Shaw poured forth a cascading fountain of gorgeous phrases; a confessional "I've Got a Crush on You," in which Art's fervent clarinet seemed to conjure a state of besotted infatuation; and two breathtaking versions of "Autumn Leaves," each full of startling beauty.

SHAW WAS HEARTENED by the Gramercy 5's nightclub success, and encouraged by *The Trouble with Cinderella*'s good reception. "All he wants," an unnamed editor-friend told *Esquire*'s Merle Miller, "is to be the best and most famous popular musician in the world, which he may be, and to write the great American novel, which isn't impossible."

Art had a long way to go to fulfill that second ambition, but he was still seeking out authors, learning what he might. Shaw made the acquaintance of the African-American writer Ralph Ellison, author of the 1952 novel *The Invisible Man*, which won the 1953 National Book Award. The Tuskegee-educated Ellison, born in Oklahoma, had known guitarist Charlie Christian as a youngster, been a devotee of the early Basie band, and studied trumpet and once hoped to become a composer. Here was a writer with whom Shaw might speak of many mutual interests, from William Grant Still to William Faulkner.

Writer Albert Murray, then a young friend of Ellison's, encountered Shaw at Ellison's apartment. "I met him a couple times, at Ralph Ellison's house, or at Duke Ellington's house," Murray said. "You could always talk to him at a club, or something like that; also at a café that we used to hang out in, in midtown. He liked to stop by and jive with the guys. Artie was very present, very open; and he mixed well. I do remember chatting to him about music, and—he liked the Harlem scene, and so forth; he took the whole thing very seriously. Certainly so far as the relations are concerned, he definitely was as anti-segregationist as you could be. The times I met him, he was in love with jazz, you know? So he liked to be around the *source* of jazz, and had some—*range* in his interests. Yeah, he was okay. I found him likeable—always friendly, always curious, and always had some opinion." Just as Shaw stayed current with music, Murray said, so he sustained an interest in other arts. "Most folks who didn't keep up with what Artie was *doing*—if they'd go somewhere and hear Artie Shaw drop a reference to *Invisible Man*, they would say, 'What the hell does *he* know about it?' You see? I'm sure Ralph read some of it to him, in manuscript."

SHAW ALSO LIKED knowing comedians, including Red Buttons, who in 1954 was doing a popular half-hour live television program from New York; Doris was a guest performer on one episode. After Jonathan was born, Dowling had resumed her acting career; Art helped to get her onto Red's show. "She did a wonderful, wonderful sketch with me," Buttons said, "she did an Italian actress, and I played a bellhop; and they were gonna stage a phony diamond stickup. It was a hilarious sketch, and Artie was there at the rehearsals; and we kind of cemented our friendship, at that time.

"I looked forward to being with him; it was always exciting," Buttons said. "I mean, you knew that you were in the presence of somebody different. Artie was a number-one iconoclast; he just pricked the balloon, all over the place. He was really an original. . . . He didn't schmaltz you; he didn't cater to. . . . Artie, all his days, told it like it was: how *he* saw it, not you. . . . That was his personality."

That personality had blended well for two years with his wife's. Merle Miller described the Shaw-Dowling marriage as "astoundingly successful," and quoted an old friend of Art's: "I think this one is for keeps. Artie is a tough guy to get along with; he shouts a lot, and, when he shouted at Lana and Ava, they burst into tears. Winsor shouted *back*. Doris just laughs, and pretty soon Artie realizes he's been a damn fool. Besides, they love each other and Jonathan."

But Dowling had a mind of her own ("refreshingly outspoken," Miller called her), and the more Shaw made suggestions regarding her newly resumed acting career, the more opportunities there were for conflict.

Then there was Shaw's restless nature. Art was impatient not only with problems but with the status quo—maybe even with happiness. "It may well be that Shaw's neuroses are now completely under control," writer Dick Gehman concluded of Art in 1954. "But . . . no sane man would fade such a bet."

CHAPTER FORTY-FIVE

Yesterdays

ON APRIL 21, 1954, Artie Shaw's *new* new Gramercy 5 opened for four weeks at the just-built Sahara Hotel in Las Vegas.

Art had been given the option of putting together a big band for Vegas, but he preferred to keep his small group. Changes were needed though. Tal Farlow didn't want to travel that far for that long; he was replaced with Joe Puma, who had worked with Joe Roland before. But there would be no room for vibes on the stage Shaw would play on, so Roland was let go.

The group was booked not in the Sahara's main Congo Room but in its Casbar Lounge. "Jazz in those days was not recognized in Vegas as it is today," said Stan Irwin, vice president and executive producer then at the Sahara. "At that time, the headliners—the *major* headliners—were Louis Prima and Keely Smith, Don Rickles, and the Mary Kaye Trio."

The Casbar seated 250. Its semicircular "thrust" stage was behind the bar, with low-stool seats ringed in front and the bartender's trough between. "It was a funny thing," Shaw said, "to be sitting and playing *behind* the bar. You know, 'Artie Shaw' is a big name, so people were sort of astonished—as a drawing point. I didn't give a damn. It was my last year in the business, and I thought: 'When this is over, I'm through.' And I was."

Already he was bored with the grind, discouraged by the public. "One night in Philadelphia," Art wrote in a piece that year for *SEE* magazine, "a drunk in the audience stood up after my new Gramercy Five had played a few numbers and shouted, 'Attaboy, Artie! Go, go, go!' 'Okay, I'll go,' I wanted to say."

The Gramercy 5 worked the Casbar from midnight until six, playing forty-five-minute sets, the last of which began at five. There was no cover charge, no minimum. "Artie would do good business," Irwin said. "Not excellent; good."

Art had no complaints. The money was top dollar. That's what brought him here to this far-western desert town that in 1954 was still as segregated as any place in the Deep South.

"When we were here in the '50s," said Irv Kluger, speaking in 2005 from Las Vegas, where he later moved, "this was an Uncle-Tom *town!* Lena Horne couldn't go into the dining room! Anyone of *color, forget* it. And my wife would stay out with Tommy Potter's wife in my brand-new car, and keep her company until six in the morning when we finished, you know."

"Very tough," said Artie, years later. "The guys in the band—I said before we went, 'Look, we don't have to do this.' One of the guys says, 'Well what's the problem?' I says, 'You can't come into the *room,* where we're playing.'"

The black musicians would reach and leave the stage through a separate enclosed corridor. Between sets, they would stay in a mobile trailer outside, away from all customers. "Came in wherever that corridor led 'em," Art said. "Came in, we played; when they finished playing—back they went. You couldn't go into the room! And when they said you couldn't, you *couldn't,* man.

"They knew: Hank Jones, and—Tommy Potter, bass player? They knew what was goin' on, but they—'Fuck it, let's take the money.' So, that was what we had."

Each man received five hundred a week. "Which was, at that time, respectable money. They elected to go," Art said. The four sidemen were paid by Shaw out of Shaw's fee. So how much did Art make?

Stan Irwin said, "It was good money at that particular time, which I think was $7,500 or $10,000 a week." After paying $2,000 to his men, Artie was left with $5,500 to $8,000, times four weeks in a month, times two or three months . . .

"I made—made a lotta money, while I was there," Artie said. "That's the only reason I went."

It was early days in Vegas—a time, many said, when (at least for whites) the town had a wonderful show-business atmosphere. "All the people from the other hotels would *visit*," Stan Irwin said—make the rounds. "You'd go see Hank Henry at the Silver Slipper, you'd go see Shecky Greene at the Riviera. It was late-night, mobile traffic. Doesn't exist, today. They were very exciting times."

Shaw agreed. "Well when I played there, it was still a little hick town, compared to what it's become. When I played there, the showgirls—It all came together. It was a very, very friendly atmosphere, you know. You stayed in *line*—but you didn't have that *fear*. We played what we wanted to play; they left us alone."

Even in Vegas, some people came to the Casbar just to hear Shaw's group: "the *cognoscenti*," Hank Jones called them. "Those who had a sense of music, and understood the genius of Artie Shaw," Stan Irwin said, "they would appear—usually, at the last show."

"Tommy and Jimmy [Dorsey] were in town," Art said, "and they sat every show. Various people that I knew, came, saw the show—uh, heard us play."

The town was filled with figures from Art's near and distant past. Charlie Barnet was leading a combo at the El Rancho Vegas, across from the Sahara. Don Cherry was at the Sands. Sinatra, whether performing or just visiting, was the city's crown prince.

Shaw seemed relaxed at the Casbar. "I think he was indifferent," Stan Irwin said with a laugh. "It was—a gig! He didn't come in with great expectations. He enjoyed performing, and—He was always well dressed; clothes and he went together beautifully. He was warm to the audience; he signed autographs. Well the Gramercy 5 of course was a *major* group. And comfortable, for him. He was the *star*, you know, and he did all the major takes; it wasn't like Louis Prima, who would blow trumpet and then [saxophonist] Sam Butera would take over. With the Gramercy 5 it was Artie. They all had their—their *moment*; but it *starred* Artie Shaw."

THE GRAMERCY 5 was booked to return to the Casbar in June. In the meantime, they played two weeks at the Down Beat Club in San Francisco, after which the men went to L.A.—not to perform but to record more tracks (from four to eight minutes long) at Shaw's expense.

This newer combo had its own sound and feel. Puma had a nice, rough-hewn approach. "Shaw sounded more deeply involved in some of his solos than ever," Vladimir Simosko wrote, "as if his style was evolving toward yet another level of development." They recorded "Dancing on the Ceiling," "Too Marvelous for Words," "Bewitched, Bothered, and Bewildered," "S'posin'."

It was on the ballads Shaw reached a new intimacy.

Art did a slow, gentle, five-and-a-half-minute version of "My Funny Valentine," full of feeling and nuance. This 1937 Rodgers and Hart tune had just been resurrected by Chet Baker and Gerry Mulligan; next month it would get a heart-stirring vocal treatment from Lee Wiley. Here, in a rendition that matched or surpassed either of those, Puma and Jones played impeccably. But Shaw's was the solo voice one remembered: rueful, thoughtful, filled with emotion recollected in tranquility; from Art's opening arpeggio to his concluding note-flurries (like a hand smoothing the hair on a lover's head). Shaw played so soft and close to the mike you could hear the click of clarinet keys and the tap of leather pads.

Jerome Kern's 1933 "Yesterdays" put a nostalgic capstone on these Hollywood sessions. Hank Jones was superb throughout this six-minute number: from his hushed four-bar intro (setting up Art's lyrical first chorus) to his sensitive chording behind Puma, through his own ad-lib chorus: so perfect one held one's breath. "I'm lost in admiration of Hank," Shaw said later. "Listen carefully to what he does on 'Yesterdays'—it's quite remarkable."

"I don't think Artie was ever completely satisfied with what *he* did himself," Jones guessed. "He may have liked others' performances better than his own."

But there's no second-guessing Shaw's artistry here, as he builds sound castles in the air. "Artie discovered early: the song is a story," Irv Kluger said. "What Artie did was, he played the *song*."

Forty years later, when this and other tracks were re-released or put out for the first time, critics, colleagues, and laymen would grasp for superlatives to describe this extraordinary music. Now, in the quick wake of creation, Artie Shaw—at the summit of three decades' experience—said his own thoughts were, *That's it. That's all I have. That's the best I can do.*

ARTIE SHAW was playing better than he had ever played, with a combo that gave him the greatest freedom he'd ever had. Yet in the press, Shaw was knocked for his politics, mocked for his marriages—and some even wanted to dismiss his music.

Down Beat's Jack Tracy used his pugilistically titled column "In This Corner" to take a swing:

> *Whom is Artie Shaw trying to kid with this new Gramercy Five of his? . . . Artie's clarinet is a mere shadow of the splendid solo instrument it once was, his tone never has transcended mediocrity, and . . . he continues to play the same clichés we've been hearing from him for years. . . . It's tea room music, not jazz.*

Down Beat often seemed to go out of its way these days to knock Artie. Strangest of all, in the magazine's twentieth-anniversary issue published in June, *Down Beat* listed all poll winners since its annual contest's inception—and now claimed the top swing band of 1938 had been Benny Goodman's not Artie Shaw's.

But Art knew what he knew.

"This is near the end of Shaw's musical desires, or engagements,"

Stan Irwin said. "I think already he said, 'I'm gonna give this damn thing up.' And he didn't have that competition with Benny Goodman anymore. You know, he'd made his point, and that was it. In my opinion, as far as *he* was concerned—*he* was the *major* artist on the clarinet; not Goodman. And he had nothing to prove, nothing to disprove. It was settled in his mind; his career was settled in his mind.'"

ART'S MEMORIES roamed through that career, a near-thirty-year span in which he had worked his way from obscurity to the pinnacle of success and then to wherever he now dwelt. It had been a physical struggle as well as an artistic and a business one. Most people didn't realize what labor it was to play an instrument, especially clarinet. Shaw, an active man who enjoyed swimming and horseback riding, was not unaware of symbolic parallels between combative swing-era bandleaders and championship prizefighters; he saw himself in analogy as a boxer, of whom he had met several: Jack Dempsey, Jake LaMotta, and above all Joe Louis, who would soon serve his first of a couple stints here in Vegas—as a casino greeter.

Shaw thought back to the times he had encountered Louis, in both their primes. "I remember being on a reviewing stand in Detroit one time," he said. "It was a parade, and Joe Louis, and I, and the mayor of Detroit, whoever—all the dignitaries—standing there. And I'm standin' next to Louis. Louis was a big *guy*; he didn't *look* like it, in the ring, 'cause he was well proportioned. So I'm—standin' next to him. I said, 'Man, you're—you're somethin'.' He said: 'Heard a *lotta* your records, man. *Killer*.' That's the word: 'Killer.' That's all! He never said another word! He was not a *talker*."

Joe was a doer.

Shaw recalled too that night in Louis's apartment in 1935, the night Joe beat Max Baer in Yankee Stadium. He remembered Joe's trainer saying, "Joe got that. When he lose that, he's through."

And he lost it.

"I don't want to go out like Joe Louis," Art had told Leonard Feather, meaning a champion who lingered past his prime.

"The Mob took care of him," Shaw would say of Louis, referring to the jobs Joe was given in his sunset years. Wrestling-match referee. Casino greeter.

When the end came for *him*, Art knew, there would be no one to look after him but himself.

That's the way it had always been.

And—maybe—that's just how he wanted it.

CHAPTER FORTY-SIX

More Than You Know

Aﬁer disbanding the combo, Art had a chance for one last solo payday: as part of a package tour of Australia with Ella Fitzgerald, Buddy Rich, and Jerry Colonna (who was famous Down Under from wartime visits there with Bob Hope).

Shaw liked seeing Ella Fitzgerald again, whom he had known since the old days in Boston with Chick Webb, and who'd been on the bill with Shaw at Bop City in 1949. "She's beyond compare," he would say in admiration. "She's a minor miracle. Major miracle. . . . Her singing is incredible; she can do anything: any range, high or low . . . from bop to scat to popular songs. She was remarkable. . . . Billie [Holiday] had a unique approach to a song; she made it hers. Ella does that in a different way, entirely different. Of the two, though, I'd say Ella is the more universal musician. . . . But very down-to-earth. I had a lot of respect for her, I liked her a lot. Nice woman. There aren't too many people in the business that you can say that about: totally unaware of how great they are; they just *do* it."

Such was not the case with Buddy Rich, for instance, whom Shaw thought behaved in a despicably egotistical manner during his return to Australia, a continent Rich first played as a child vaudevillian.

The Fitzgerald-Shaw-Rich-Colonna package, booked into boxing stadiums, grossed a record-breaking $103,500. *Time* magazine called the dates "a triumphal visitation," but to Art it was a disaster. The orchestra couldn't play his arrangements properly. He hated what he was doing. "I walked through it for the money," he said. "End of my career."

And, when he got back, end of his marriage to Doris, whose perceived faults and failings trumped the great virtues Art once saw.

Shaw would always have reasons for his marriages failing; near the end of his life, he would say, "I think of Doris Dowling, and I remember her with a rifle, pointed at me. . . . She didn't realize it had a safety. . . . Later I said to her, 'You trying to kill me?' She said, 'Yeah.' I said, 'Why?' 'You made me mad.' I said, 'Well you made *me* mad; I wasn't thinking of *killing* you.'" So it often went—with never a word about anything bad *he* might have done.

Such breakups were inevitable for Shaw, thought his friend Dr. Colter Rule: "Lasting human relationships are almost the hallmark of human maturity, and Artie just did not take that pathway. He may have struggled to take that pathway, and he may have gone through all kinds of agony trying to cling to that pathway, in greater or lesser degree; but I don't think he ever really made it. His capacity for, you know, relaxed trust with another human, was—always limited."

Doris, with Jonathan, moved to L.A.; she would get a Nevada divorce. Art sold Picardy Farm, paid off his eighty-thousand-dollar debt to the IRS, and lived full-time in New York City, once more (in Dorothy Kilgallen's phrase) "the lone wolf of Lindy's." Columnists linked Shaw now with Broadway singer-actress Future Fulton and with Vogue model Theo Graham.

With Shaw off the music scene, a revivified Goodman again came to the fore. He had his own ropes-up Manhattan combo success at Basin Street. Universal Pictures began Hollywood production of *The Benny Goodman Story*, with Benny to be portrayed by Steve Allen, an articulate, jazz-loving New York TV personality who played piano and had published a couple of books.

Art wanted to get back to his own writing. He had done a lot of short stories, three of which were supposed to be gathered in a volume by Farrar, Straus and Young, but the publisher cooled on the project when a paperback reprint house couldn't be found. Shaw then tried to get his stories published in magazines; no interest.

He guessed at first it was because he was a bandleader: people just didn't expect him to be able to write fiction. He proposed an experiment to Dorothy Olding at the Ober literary agency: send out one of his tales under a false name and see if a periodical bit. Sure enough, the first place she tried with his pseudonymous story wanted it—until she revealed its author. Then it came back as if radioactive. Despite (or thanks to) his congressional testimony, Artie Shaw was now, in the damning euphemism of the day, a "controversial figure." Nervous publishers wouldn't touch him. Nor, according to his theatrical agent, could he ever get himself booked on any TV panel shows. It wasn't enough, it seemed, for him to have apologized, at length and in public. The stigma lingered. Others who recanted with greater cause and through naming names—Elia Kazan, for instance—would sooner or later also feel a post-testimony draft.

"All the people I knew were either made invisible or were killed by it," Shaw said of the web of blacklists and counter-blacklists, "killed or as *good* as; anything that was of any value was taken from them."

Shaw wasn't about to hang around and endure that death of a thousand cuts. Now he would flee big time, as Chaplin had—by leaving the continent.

But he still had all those finished short stories, good enough to publish. Why not emulate what a lot of television and movie scriptwriters were starting to do and use a "front," another writer who would pretend to have done the work? In years to come, Art would claim he had published books this way, under another man's name, as his "'private joke' on the rest of the world." How and why a "private joke"? And who was the front? Shaw never said.

SHAW SAILED to Europe aboard the *Queen Mary*. Getting off in Naples, he rented a car and drove up the Italian coast, then into France. He went to Spain—down the southeastern coast, up the Mediterranean's. Driving along the Costa Brava, in Catalonia, through undeveloped agricultural country, he took an old narrow road and came down in a dusty village right out of medieval times: a plaza, a church, a café. Here, in Bagur, on a bare mountainside overlooking a large bay, Shaw chose land on which to build his "castle in Spain."

He lived below the town while construction proceeded. To reach his property, you took a goat path. Art was stunned one day to be confronted in Bagur by an intrepid correspondent on special assignment for *Time* magazine. "How did you *find* me?" Shaw asked. The reporter said *Time* was doing a piece on why the clarinet had fallen into obscurity in modern jazz; they were asking three great clarinetists' opinions. Art wanted to know who the three were. The fellow told him: you, Benny Goodman, Woody Herman. "*Woody* is not in our league!" Shaw blurted.

His house was still being built in November 1956 when the carpenter one day came down the hill on his motorbike to fetch Art up to the plaza's inn, where the old man who ran the place had news for him—half in English, half in Catalan: "Su compadre—has left." Who? "Tomaso—Dor-say." Tommy Dorsey: dead in his sleep (of asphyxia, choking on regurgitated food) at fifty-one.

ARTIE SHAW was forty-six and did not yet wish to be alone. In France, he had an affair with the daughter of a well-known poet. In England, he was seen with starlet Valeria Allen and with his old friend actress Paulette Goddard. Then, in Paris, pals Jules and Joan Buck introduced him to thirty-seven-year-old just-retired movie actress Evelyn Keyes (best known for her roles in *Here Comes Mr. Jordan*, *The Jolson Story*, and *The Seven Year Itch*).

Art had crossed paths with Evelyn in Hollywood, when she'd been married to director John Huston. Now she was unattached (though ex-boyfriend and producer Mike Todd, newly wed to Elizabeth Taylor, still kept in touch). The Bucks arranged a first date for Art and Evelyn at a restaurant near Notre Dame. Evelyn was bright, pretty, politically sympathetic. Art was smitten.

Then a very odd thing happened, right in the middle of Art's first date with Evelyn: all the way from America, in walked Claude Thornhill. "He *found* me," Shaw marveled. "He had *called* Spain; somebody there at the fonda must have told Claude that I was in Paris. So he somehow found where I was, and he showed *up*. Outa nowhere!"

Thornhill, Shaw, and Keyes went to a nearby bar. Keyes wrote, "The two men began reminiscing of those days when [they] went to war . . . under fire on obscure tropical islands, diving for foxholes while bombs and shrapnel fell. . . . 'Survival seemed remote, so I made a run at increasing my odds,' laughed Artie. 'I learned the Japanese national anthem. If they landed I would greet them on the beach playing their song.'"

"We spent the whole night talking," Shaw said of that evening in Paris. "[Claude and I] hadn't seen each other in years, and we were *very close friends*. And we talked about *everything* under the *sun—including* the war." In a way, it was like when Claude and Art first met back in Ohio, when they conversed until daybreak, getting to know one another. "Then," after this Paris reunion, "he went back to America, he married a woman—I think that's the one who had some money, 'cause he didn't have any money at all—and he moved to New Jersey. And I didn't see him or hear from him, ever again."

Evelyn was a different story; Art wasn't about to let her slip away.

"They really connected in a big way, physically," said Fred Morton, who with his wife visited Shaw and Keyes in Spain several times. "They had an affair, and—this was typical of Artie—he fell in love with her. And she was very content to leave it with an affair, but Artie said, 'No you have to at least come and look at my house that I'm building.' And she did. It was about half built; it was spectacular, on a very steep slope; it had three levels. She said, 'Gee, that's *great*.' And he was planting a cactus garden on one of the levels that faced the sea, and she said, 'You know I would put a palm there instead, and this little garden you should put in the *front* because it's a little bare there.' She went back to Paris; a month later, she came back—and discovered that he had done exactly what she had said with that cactus garden. She told me she was so touched by that, that she agreed to abandon Paris, come to Bagur and live with him."

It was delightful to see the effect each had on the other. Morton said, "She was a hard-bitten, tough Hollywood cookie who had been through it all. And Artie really brought a kind of romantic dimension into her life; you know he *had* that, he had that side to him. In addition to that, he opened all kinds of intellectual horizons, which for her was exciting too because she was extremely intelligent and could *really* absorb difficult books. And he also brought out in her a kind of—not exactly family person, but—a *wife*. Now she really became the female part of a *couple*. . . . So they were *extremely* happy." Artie and Evelyn ("Kessi," he called her) flew to Gibraltar and were married there in the autumn of 1957, then returned to Bagur.

Then it all changed. "The tragic thing," Fred Morton said, "is that once Artie had finished a project," such as building his dream house, "he became restless; that was one dimension of it. The other dimension was that—This house was specifically built for him to finally realize himself as a writer. It had a *wing* where he was entirely independent, and there he was going to write his great novel. And he couldn't do it. And he became extremely unhappy." The hardest thing for a fiction writer to do, Art thought, was to keep out of his own way on the page. A novel was different from short stories. He still had not devised a style that would let him say what he wanted in a way that brought this book to life.

He needed a rest from the manuscript, Art said. He and Evelyn took off by car on a salmon-fishing expedition, then drove to Paris, where who should be playing a concert but Benny Goodman. Art visited Goodman at his hotel, and he and Evelyn took in his show: "Thank God I'm out of that racket," Shaw said. They returned to Bagur, but left again with the visiting Noah and Sophia Rosoff, with whom they drove all the way to Switzerland. Back in Spain, they made a trout-fishing trip through Andorra, then left for Vienna to visit the Mortons. Art and Evelyn spent much of 1958 in flight from the Bagur house.

Early in 1959 they took a bigger detour: a month-long trip to New York, where Evelyn dealt with legal matters pertaining to monies she had loaned Mike Todd before his death in a plane crash. It was an exciting time to be in Manhattan.

Among the jazz artists Artie and Kessi saw and heard were Gerry Mulligan, John Coltrane, Ornette Coleman, and Cannonball Adderley. At a Joey Bushkin party, "Artie and Louis Armstrong kissed and hugged." It was great to see old friends, but Art was not so pleased by some of the new sounds and moods in the clubs: "Tremendous amount of hatred and political crap goin' on," he thought. "And black dislike of white. It's all bullshit, I don't *like* that; it's nothin' to do with music. When a guy starts *honking* . . . That's not what music is *about*, for *me*. Why would a guy want to play an instrument and make it sound ugly on purpose? . . . That's got nothing to do with music: *honk*."

What he did like was the Miles Davis group, a contemplative combo playing a modal-based music documented on *Kind of Blue*, which would become the best-selling traditional-jazz LP of all time.

When the Shaws returned to Bagur, Art missed America.

Lester Young had died, at age forty-nine, while the Shaws were in New York. Four months later, Billie Holiday joined him, at forty-four. Giant oaks were toppling. But Shaw still stood.

Evelyn found him in his study one day putting his clarinet together. He gave her a shy look and asked if she would mind leaving the house. She went outside—and scrambled into listening position beneath his window.

It was the only time he attempted to practice after quitting, he would say: "I tried to play the Mozart concerto. I played a couple bars—but then that's all. It was so hard to get *one note* the way I wanted to hear it; if I'd kept that up it would have killed me, I'm sure."

But how had it sounded to Evelyn, someone asked her thirty years later; was it good? "Of *course*," she said. "He was Artie Shaw."

CHAPTER FORTY-SEVEN

Connecticut

W HEN SHAW returned to America to look for a place to live, he had his sites set not on New York but New England. He went house hunting in the company of a youngish writer named Terry Southern, met on his earlier trip to New York through mutual friend John Marquand Jr. Art had read Terry's first novel, *Flash and Filigree*. "He had a great gift of humor, Terry did; I thought he had a lotta talent, of a *kind*."

"They had a good *time* together," said Carol Southern, Terry's wife then. "Terry was very amusing to be around, and Artie *enjoyed* Terry, and vice versa. Terry loved characters, and Artie was *such* a character; he really was."

According to Shaw, he gave Southern the tag scene for his second novel, *The Magic Christian*, the picaresque exploits of a sadistic billionaire, which Art read in manuscript: "He didn't have an ending for it; he said it was like a—a bop piece: it just *stopped*. I said, 'I know, but couldn't you have somethin' there's got a—little *zing*, on it?' He said, 'What would you suggest?' So I gave him an ending: Guy sees these two maiden aunts, and he's—eyeing 'em. They look in the newspaper, and the newspaper says: 'A-Bomb Tests Set to Start in Nevada.' 'Well—off we go,' he says, 'work to do.' So, that's enough of an ending: You know he's gonna—fuck up the *bomb* tests. Terry used it. Unabashedly."

The protagonist of Southern's novel was one Guy Grand, referred to throughout as "Grand Guy Grand." Southern took to calling Shaw "Grand Guy Art."

So it came to pass, in early 1960, that Shaw and the Southerns went house hunting. "Terry and I were looking for something in the Berkshires," Carol said, "and we didn't have much money. Artie was looking for something too, and Artie said, 'I have this great [real estate] agent, Jay, in Sheffield, Mass., and we can stay overnight with him and he will show us around.' So we did this. We looked at lots of wonderful houses for Artie, and he didn't like any of them. Artie was looking at houses for a couple hundred thousand, which at that time was a lot of money. And at the end of the afternoon, Terry said to Jay, 'Do you know of anything for *us*, in the, you know, twenty-thousand range?' And Jay said, 'Yes I do, actually. It's a house that was flooded, and bought by a contractor, and he went broke; so it's sort of midway in terms of renovation.' So we drove up to this wonderful old 1756 house, beautiful old Colonial on a river. And Terry and I immediately said, 'You know, we really are very interested in this.' And Artie said, 'Well actually, I am too.' We were so nonplussed, because Artie could have afforded *anything*."

The farmhouse was in East Canaan, Connecticut. "And Artie immediately took charge," Carol Southern said. "He said, 'Look: You don't have the money right at your fingertips to put down a binder. I'll do *that*.' So Artie put down the money. Then he tried to persuade Terry that he, Artie, really should have the house. Artie was *so* aggressive, and Terry was about to back out. Artie kept saying, 'You know you never would have seen it if it weren't for my agent.' And he was not nice about it. Really, *he* never would have seen it if *we* hadn't been there; Jay wouldn't have thought of *showing* it to him. So his case was very flimsy, besides which not being very friendly. Finally Terry sort of, was able to confront Artie and say, 'Look, this is really for *us*.'"

"He *wanted* to *have* it," is how Art remembered it, "*crying*—kicking the *floor*, like a little kid. He was like a—a rodent—gnawing away at your leg, until he got what he wanted. And he wanted that house, I don't know why. He'd say, '*C'mon*, you can buy whatever house you want; I'll never have another chance like this.' Finally I said, 'All *right*, *take* the house.'"

"Artie said, 'O-*kay*,'" Carol Southern said, "'but I'll keep the acreage across the river.' That was quite considerable; I think it was ninety acres. The acreage around the house was about twenty-nine acres; that was plenty for us, and we got the house. But that's so typical of Artie; I mean, he was a bulldozer." Shaw soon found an equally good property, Carol said: "He bought a wonderful house in Lakeville [Connecticut]. I mean, it really was beautiful; I think it was built in the teens or the twenties, and it was like a *Philadelphia Story* house, so he needn't have fretted."

This was a twenty-two-room mansion, with boathouse-lodge, at the edge of Lake Wononskopomuc. "I bought it for a price I can't believe today," Art said. "The guy told me they were asking $125,000. So I said, 'Make him an offer.' He said, 'What?' I said, 'Give him forty-five.' He said, 'Artie, *I* can't do that.' I said, 'Well if *you* won't, *I* will; you'll lose your commission.' He went in and came out. He said, 'They took it.' It was a *huge* house."

It was the sort of grand mansion that Grand Guy Shaw had been looking for all his life—or at least since the day an eight-year-old Arthur Arshawsky made his poor New Haven parents laugh with the question, "Why can't we live in a *doctor's* house?" Of this fabulous place in Lakeville, Shaw said, "I called it my 'doctor's house.'"

IN CONNECTICUT as in Spain, Art was "the captain" of the marriage ship, with Evelyn a more-and-more begrudging first mate. Shaw found plenty of things to occupy his time: fishing, boating, reading, driving a mowing machine on the huge front lawn. He zipped around the countryside in an Alfa Romeo (accumulating a number of traffic tickets). And he took a creative interest in trying to manage the private lives of certain friends.

Carol Southern said Art showed up at her house on an unsolicited errand of wisdom not long after she gave birth to the Southerns' child. "Terry was in New York," she said. "It was in February; there was a foot or more of snow on the ground. I was in the kitchen, and Artie came up unannounced in his sports car and said, 'I really need to talk to you. You know, you're married to an artist, and—you can't expect him to support you. You've got to—figure it out. And what *I* think you should do—is have a kennel, for dogs.' And I thought, the *presumption*, of this man! It was so *funny*: that he would drive over to Canaan from Lakeville, for this express purpose of telling me that I couldn't expect to be taken care of, and I had to take care of myself! Actually, it was a very good idea; I should have done it."

For his own amusement, Art found a new hobby: bench-press rifle shooting on a target range. "It was just an exercise, to employ his enormous energies," Fred Morton said. "Because the writing that he wanted to do, fiction, was always so difficult, and he was no longer in music. So that was an outlet. He was the only man I think who ever placed in the top five in marksmanship who was over fifty; I mean he got so involved: the same passionate intensity that he devoted to music, or to fly-fishing, he devoted to *that*."

He bought a thirty-six-foot motor home, filled it with shooting supplies, and proposed he and Kessi hit the road to visit rifle clubs, target ranges, and gun shops around the country. Artie could learn all about the shooting-range business. (Shaw, with partners, later opened such a range in Clinton Corners, New York.) According to Keyes's account, the Shaws' motor-home hegira, begun in a Connecticut blizzard, was a nightmare on wheels: a stress-filled, three-month journey marked by Artie's abusive recriminations and Evelyn's developing asthma condition. "Things may have seemed to be the same after that," Keyes wrote, "but they never were."

Evelyn grew cold in body and heart: she bundled herself in layers of clothing, day and night, and withheld herself physically from Shaw. Her asthma grew worse, and she needed to take three trips each week into New York for therapeutic injections. Art too wanted to spend more time in New York; he was trying to get a book of short fiction published—this time under his own name. The Shaws took a Manhattan apartment to live in during the week. Shaw, once more a New York presence, and with the country's political climate changed, was again invited to appear on TV talk programs, including *The Tonight Show* with Johnny Carson. On such shows Artie was wry and curmudgeonly, telling great anecdotes about an era growing more distant each year.

Jean Goldkette died, at sixty-two.

Roger Wolfe Kahn died, at fifty-four.

Benny Goodman, fifty-three, took a big band to Russia on a six-week State Department–sponsored tour.

Other State Department–supported jazz tours had the unexpected result in 1962 of injecting a vital South American musical style into North American modern jazz. Guitarist Charlie Byrd, who had been on such a tour to Brazil, introduced saxophonist Stan Getz (who had not) to the rhythm and tunes of the bossa nova, a new music whose young Brazilian creators were inspired by the "cool" jazz of American instrumentalists, including trumpeter Chet Baker and Getz himself. Byrd and Getz made a bossa nova album in 1962 which became an enormous popular success, touching off a craze that saw dozens of other U.S. artists releasing good- to best-selling bossa nova LPs and singles.

The craze might in fact have started a year sooner, but for some advice given to Dizzy Gillespie by Artie Shaw. Diz had been among the first jazz players to go to Brazil for the State Department, with a combo that included Argentinean pianist (and later composer) Lalo Schifrin. Every night while in Rio de Janeiro and São Paulo, Gillespie went with Schifrin to clubs where the new music was played and learned such tunes as "Desafinado" and "Manha de Carnival." Back in the States in the fall of 1961, Gillespie recorded a sizzling live performance of this Brazilian material—then locked the tapes away. "Dizzy respected Artie Shaw, the bandleader, as a shrewd businessman," Schifrin told Donald L. Maggin, "and Shaw told him that he was not going to have his skills all his life, and that his best insurance was to record all of the things that he was doing and put them away—then when he was older and couldn't play anymore, release the material, which would be very valuable. . . . I said to Dizzy, 'When are you going to release [that concert recording]?' He said, 'I'm not. Artie Shaw said to keep it as insurance, remember?' 'Wait a second. You can keep as insurance . . . all your classics, but this is a novelty. This is going to be a hit. You have to release it right away.' 'Oh no, I'm doing what Artie Shaw said.' A few months later Stan Getz came with his huge bossa nova hit."

CHAPTER FORTY-EIGHT

I've Got Beginner's Luck

THE MOVIE BUSINESS was changing as fast as the music scene. Art knew several people who were finding golden opportunities in a more liberal and less studio-dependent cinematic world. Terry Southern, for instance, hooked up with Art's director-friend Stanley Kubrick (who had just made the film version of Vladimir Nabokov's *Lolita*) and was doing screenplay work on Kubrick's next project, *Dr. Strangelove*, a satire of nuclear politics. Given Art's own excellent (he thought) story sense, extensive show-business and literary contacts, and not-insignificant financial resources, Shaw—who had concluded there was no way he could make a musical place for himself anymore, in a radically altered modern-jazz landscape—thought this the perfect time to revive his own movie-producing aspirations of twenty years earlier.

Artie began scouting books to buy and scripts to promote. He scheduled a flurry of New York meetings and lunches in early 1964 with directors Kubrick, Otto Preminger, Sidney Lumet, Robert Rossen, Martin Ritt, Arthur Penn, and Fred Zinneman; with writers Davis Grubb, Merle Miller, and Robert Lewis Taylor; with actresses Millie Perkins, Elizabeth Taylor, and ex-wife Ava Gardner. He pursued film rights to books by John Gardner, Peter Mathiessen, and Richard Stark (Donald Westlake). He attended screenings of several soon-to-be-released films, including *Fail Safe, Shock Treatment, The Cool World, Good Neighbor Sam, Lilith,* and *The Pawnbroker* (and may have put postproduction money into one or more of these movies).

During the same period, he kept himself in the public eye and picked up extra dollars as a participant on talk and game shows such as *Password.* That fall, Shaw was one of the guests for the debut broadcast over the ABC television network of a new five-nights-a-week conversation program hosted by Les Crane; two evenings later, he was scheduled to take part in Crane's third broadcast, a startling occasion that gathered John F. Kennedy–assassin Lee Harvey Oswald's mother, Oswald-assassin Jack Ruby's lawyer Melvin Belli, and Elizabeth Taylor's new husband, Richard Burton.

IN THE MIDST of all this activity, a figure intruded from Artie's past whom he hadn't had contact with for a while. Sarah Straus Arshawsky—"Mrs. Sarah Shaw," as she was listed in the Manhattan phone book—was now so ill that death seemed imminent. She wanted to see Arthur again. Her doctor—Colter Rule, Art's old friend, whom he also hadn't seen lately—passed the word that Art's presence would be appreciated, and that it was now or never.

Dr. Rule liked Sarah Straus Arshawsky Shaw. He said, "I thought she was fine, and that she did her best, coming from where she had, using what resources were available to her; I thought she was very brave." But he knew Art had trouble relating to or even being in the same room with her: "I think he avoided her; that would be my impression. And I think she felt it. And she may have even hoped that I would *nudge* him *toward* her, and—whatnot." But "Artie couldn't help it; he couldn't snap his fingers and have that resentment evaporate."

"Anyhow," Shaw recalled, close to the time of his own death, "the lawyer got in touch—said, 'She's dying, she'd like you to be there.'" What was he feeling? "Hate, and love. Hate, because of what she did to me, and how she made me, and what she *did* with my life—'cause she steered me." Arthur squirmed and struggled in the grip of opposing impulses toward the mother who had shaped him into a pint-sized performer and shoved him onto the show-biz road.

"I remember when I was forty years old," he said, "and I'd finally *quit*, and I was living on my farm and writing that first book, probably about two-thirds through it—kind of a clearing-of-the-decks, for me: 'Get *rid* of that.' And my mother's sitting there, and she said to me, 'Some day you'll show 'em all again.' And I got so furious at her at that moment—I could have killed her. I suddenly saw my whole past: There I was, in a business I shouldn't have been in—trying to do things I have no natural inclination for. Musically, yes—but I was in the wrong *business*." For years he would wrestle and argue with her galling words: "'Someday you'll show 'em all again.' Who is ''*em*'? And who is '*all*'? And wadya mean, 'show 'em' *what*? 'Show 'em what a big *man* I made'—that's what it came down to: 'I *made* you.'"

Arthur Shaw, like James Joyce's Stephen Dedalus, spurned his mother's deathbed request. He recalled, with tears in his eyes: "I said, 'I'm sorry, I just can't *do* that.'"

"Naw, he couldn't take that kind of intimacy, and—pain, and whatnot," Colter Rule said. "Artie ran away from those things. Yeah, he—he couldn't *enfold* a dying *mother*, in his *arms*!" The good doctor gave a rueful chuckle at the very thought. "Ah—well, I can't blame poor Artie. Artie's character was of a very fragile, self-protective nature. He had an ego problem. When you have an ego problem, you're afraid you're inadequate. And if you're inadequate, you don't feel *safe*. You just don't feel safe."

Sarah Shaw died September 2, 1964, at the age of eighty.

ARTHUR, WITH EVELYN, did attend her funeral at Riverside Memorial Chapel. And it turned out to be a moving experience for Shaw, in a way he had not expected.

"I had always gotten this question," Art said: "'Where did the music come from? Anybody in your background?' Nobody in my background, that I *knew* of. My father had an *ear*, he could play 'My *coun*-

try, *da, da-da*'; one finger [on the piano], he could play. He knew up from down, and he knew the difference in tempo. That's all there was; he must have been *it*. Couldn't have been on my mother's side, I was convinced: My mother had absolutely no ear; she was like a trained *seal*. Note go up, she'd go down; she didn't know the difference between up or down.

"So, my mother was dead—and I was at this funeral, and—there was a young rabbi, who didn't know my mother from a *hole* in the ground; and he made this speech. And oddly enough, it had a certain amount of Irving Howe, in it, you know? And I was touched: about the immigrants who came here to this country, expecting sidewalks of gold, and instead they found sweatshops and so on, and they survived, and they prevailed, and they made children, and so on and so on. So I'm sittin' there, and I'm bein' a little—moved by it. And as he's doing this, a guy gets up from the front row: this typical, New York American, Jewish, Lower East Side guy—double-breasted suit hanging open, ashes on the vest, hat on, a broad fedora—and he walks up to the rabbi and starts tugging at his coat. And it was my Uncle Moishe—Morris; he couldn't speak a word of English. All these years, and he couldn't speak a word of English.

"So a friend of his got up, tried to explain to the rabbi what was going on. And the rabbi turned to the audience—to the, uh, congregation; he said, 'Ladies and gentlemen, this is the deceased's—brother, her older brother, Morris. And he asked permission to sing a lament for the dead.' So he said, 'With your permission, I'll let him.' We were all, 'Okay.' Morris got up and started to sing the Kol Nidre.

"Now that's an interesting piece of music—very interesting and nice piece of music. And he started singing. And—no *voice*, he had no *instrument* left, but—I can hear *music*! He was trying to sing, he had a really musical *sound*. And he—he did it with great feeling, and great emotion; not sentiment—with *emotion*. And you know, isn't this moving; and I—

"Jesus Christ, I suddenly turned to Evelyn and I said, 'You know—this is the first I've ever known in my family, there was *music* there. That

311

came from my *mother's* side. All these years, I—did her an injustice.' Well—whatever that *is*.

"So we left. And I was very moved, and I thought about that, and so on."

A few weeks later, Shaw heard from his lawyer. Except for a few small bequests, Sarah had left her entire estate to Arthur; minus fees, expenses, and commissions, Shaw would receive a bit over twenty thousand dollars. "So he said, 'Meanwhile, when you get a chance, come in, want you to go over some *bills*.' So I did."

There was the bill for the chapel and the funeral arrangements. A fee for the rabbi. And, what's this: "cantor, fifty dollars"?

"'That's Moishe—my uncle Moishe,'" I said. "Fifty dollars, for singing at his sister's funeral! I said, 'That sonofabitch, don't you ever give him a nickel.' I was so *angry* with him." A quarter-century later, Shaw gave a sardonic laugh. "He found a *gig*, you know? That's really a Sholem Aleichem story, isn't it?" As glad as Art had been to learn the source of his musical talent, all the good feeling was wiped out by bitterness. "It was like getting a bill from a nightingale."

NOT LONG after his mother died, Shaw (by Keyes's account) chanced to bump into someone he knew on the street—though, as Art might have put it, you create your own chances—who invited him to a screening of an English film called *Seance on a Wet Afternoon*, written and directed by Bryan Forbes, about a supposed medium and her husband who kidnap a little girl. The movie was acclaimed in Britain, but no American distributor wanted to touch it. Artie bought its U.S. rights that day and went into quick partnership with the fellow who had steered him to the screening: they would be Artixo Productions, "Artixo" ("Artee-show") being the approximate Catalan pronunciation of "Artie Shaw." As fast as that, Shaw was a film distributor. He rented an office on Madison Avenue, alerted the media, and started the bandwagon rolling. He was sure *Seance on a Wet Afternoon* was going to be a major success.

He was right.

On November 5, *Seance* opened at New York's Plaza Theatre. The influential Manhattan movie critics loved it. Kim Stanley's performance was hailed as a masterpiece; she was certain to be nominated for an Oscar, many said. There were lines around the block at the Plaza.

"Artie became overnight a movie guru," Fred Morton said, "because he had picked up what nobody else had picked up. The movie made solid money—not a gold mine, but he got back what he had invested and then a *good* deal more." *Variety* wrote that Artixo had for sixty thousand dollars acquired American rights to a film that might earn a million in rentals.

Art and Evelyn, by her account, had long been at emotional odds and physically estranged. Now—at her suggestion, he would hint; at his persuasion, she would write—he wanted to sleep with another, younger woman. Keyes wrote she gave her "permission" ("Be my guest!") but had second thoughts, which led to fights and to her moving back to Connecticut—where, she would write, she often received Art and his new female companion-assistant as stay-over guests. While still in New York, though, Evelyn was a frequent sight at the Plaza Theatre, where *Seance* played to sold-out houses: "I stop by there every night to see the line waiting to get in," she told the *Hollywood Reporter*. "I never did that for my own movies! Maybe that's because there never *was* any line."

CHAPTER FORTY-NINE

I Was Doing All Right

A VA GARDNER was in a panic. "Whenever she got into a panic, she called Artie," Fred Morton said. "He was still her guru."

In 1965, Gardner was about to start production in a film in which she would portray the nineteenth-century Empress Elizabeth of Austria. "I'm supposed to play an empress," Morton recalled her telling Shaw. "I'm a girl from North Carolina, I don't think I can *do* this."

"And Artie said, 'When do you have to start shooting?' And she said, 'Next week; I'm supposed to fly to Vienna, from L.A.' And he said, 'Well why don't you detour via New York; my friend Frederic Morton is from Vienna, and he's about to do something on that very subject, and—we'll ease you into it.' And that's what she did."

Morton was in the midst of research for his work *A Nervous Splendor*, which would deal with Austrian political and cultural history during the period of Gardner's movie. "My wife and I, and Artie, and Ava Gardner, had dinner at the Regency, where she stayed," he said, "until five o'clock in the morning, just talking. I asked her, 'What did they tell you about the empress?' 'Well simply that she was a Wittelsbach,' a member of the royal family of Bavaria, 'and then she became empress of Austria.' I said, 'Well that's not quite the story; she was part of the collateral line, which is there *only* to provide crown princes and kings if there are no male descendants of the main line. And she grew up on a huge farm; and she was a horsewoman, and she didn't know anything about court life and didn't want to know. Then when suddenly the young emperor fell in love with her—that's one reason for her neurosis, because she suddenly was so restricted and constricted.' And Ava Gardner said, 'You know, my God, that's *my* story: *I* grew up on a farm, and suddenly I became a studio princess and they—controlled everything I did. Hey that's great. Why didn't they tell me that in that little brochure they sent me?' And so—it really *worked*; I thought she was really very good, but the movie itself was one of those hollow, empty, opulent, enormous productions. But you know Ava really kept resorting to Artie, and had that respect for him, that he *knew* so much."

Shaw's reputation as a brilliant polymath and autodidact was at its height in 1965, with *Seance on a Wet Afternoon* a resounding hit and its lead actress Kim Stanley nominated for an Academy Award. His intellectual stock split two-for-one in April when Fleet Publishing brought out Art's second official book, a trio of novellas titled *I Love You, I Hate You, Drop Dead!* (a title Dorothy Kilgallen cheered: "Bravo!").

Art had fashioned a method of writing short fiction that emphasized his strengths (realistic dialogue, for instance) and bypassed his weaknesses (omniscient third-person narration, say). It was like the Hemingway line he liked to quote: "My faults became my style." Shaw drew on the verisimilitude of actual events, then allowed himself freedom to extrapolate—not unlike a jazz player improvising on a melody. He used what he'd gleaned from authors he'd known, especially on how to mix the real with the made-up.

John O'Hara, for instance—though that writer proved less than forthcoming in person. Shaw said, "He was quite a curmudgeon. *Worked* at being a curmudgeon. He had a twisted view of life. I called him up about his [1949] book *A Rage to Live*. I said, 'There's one part of that book that's not fiction, you're writing about yourself: the part about the courting of the woman, where he's planning his campaign to win that woman.' He said, 'Well—I don't know.' I said, 'Come on, in that part you left fiction behind, you were writing autobiography.' He said, 'I can't say yes, I can't say no.' I said, 'You *could* say, but you don't want to.' He was not very pleased, with my saying that. You'd have thought he'd be happy—someone saying, you'd done something so real." Nonetheless Shaw learned from O'Hara's work about how people's speech reveals truths, lies, emotions, and agendas. Some O'Hara-type rhythms and methods found their way into Art's prose, including this trio of novellas: good post-Hemingway vignettes that worked too as suspense tales. The book was covered, and praised, in the *New York Times Book Review* by that journal's detective-fiction critic Anthony Boucher.

But movies had become Art's main interest this season. He went to Europe on a buying trip during which he saw and took notes on dozens of films. Three he picked up for U.S. distribution were announced at a New York press luncheon in late May: *The Power Game*, a German-Swiss psychological drama from a script by Friedrich Dürrenmatt; *Enough Rope*, a French suspense thriller from a novel by Patricia Highsmith; and *How Not to Rob a Department Store*, a Gallic farce.

Artie Shaw was fifty-five years old now: the same age as Claude Thornhill, whom he hadn't seen in ten years. "[I]n the summer of 1965," Art told Whitney Balliett, "I got a phone call at three in the morning from Claude's wife. . . . She said Claude had told her I was his best friend, and then she said that he had just had a heart attack and died. She said he had spent the day in his garden and had told her it had been one of the best days he had ever had. Later, I found out that Claude had been paying frequent visits to my mother.. . . . He had made her promise never to tell me about the visits, and of course he never did either."

"I'll *never know* what that was about," Art said to someone near the end of his own life. "Why was he seeing Sarah, my wife—my, my mother; hear that slip? Why was he seeing her—and telling her not to tell me? And why was she *not* telling me? . . . So then his wife called: 'Used to talk about you all the time.' . . . And that's it. Period! I don't know *anything about* that. One of those mysterious episodes." Tears glistened in his eyes. "I have a feeling that he might have had some slight—tendency toward homosexuality. I think something like that was going on. He was fighting it, I believe. I know I never felt I knew him. It's the only explanation I can—come to. I mean there are no other possible—explanations. Why would you talk to a guy's mother, and tell her not to tell him? You know—that's a strange business."

Art seemed melancholy when he returned to Cleveland in 1965 to promote *Seance*'s engagement there, and lodged at the Pick-Carter Hotel—formerly the Winton, where he and Claude had roomed thirty-five years ago. "Maybe I should have stayed in Cleveland," he told reporter Tony Mastroianni. "I was successful—had a good band job, was making good money, in love with a girl I wanted to marry. I was nineteen and had to make a decision. I decided I had to follow the road. Maybe I'd have been happy here. Or maybe I'd have been miserable wondering what I could have done. I guess I might have been miserable anywhere."

ART HAD AMBITIOUS plans in 1966 to segue from film distribution into movie and television production. He bought screen rights to *The Man Who Fell to Earth* by novelist Walter Tevis, whose book *The Hustler* had become a hit film with Paul Newman, and for a time he interested British performer Bea Lillie in maybe doing a proposed Shaw-produced television situation comedy about an English governess in America. But while Art planned an exciting future, his present success unraveled. It was the success itself that led to his downfall, Fred Morton said: "That was his tragedy, because then he really lost his head: he bought about nine or ten other movies, one of which was wonderful but got terrible reviews—*How Not to Rob a Department Store*." Then there was the animated *Boynng!*, the art documentary *The Impressionists*—not to mention the Italian *Oh, Those Swedish Girls!* "They all lost money. He lost money, so—that didn't work out. It became a very unhappy experience for him."

But not a defeating one.

Shaw told the press he had bought the rights to film F. Scott Fitzgerald's canonical novel *The Great Gatsby*—as a musical, whose book and songs he would commission. And in 1968, Art collaborated in the making of a new Capitol Records LP that rerecorded in stereo his 1938 band's repertoire, performed by an orchestra of New York session players with studio clarinetist Walt Levinsky doing what all agreed was a fine job re-creating Art's original solos.

The "swing era," like the "jazz age," was receding into history, and Shaw's key place in it was coming into sharper focus. Barney Bigard, Duke Ellington's original clarinetist, told Leonard Feather in 1968, "To me, the greatest [clarinet] player that ever lived was Artie Shaw."

BY 1969, Shaw's notion of a movie musical of *The Great Gatsby* had changed into a Broadway show; it was reported he had signed a team of talented collaborators including Hugh Wheeler, and that rehearsals would soon begin.

Fitzgerald's novel had been published in 1925—around the time Artie Shaw met Tony Pastor at the Cinderella Ballroom in New Haven, Connecticut. Tony Pastor died in 1969, of a heart ailment, at age sixty-two. For the past year, he had been coaching his three sons (Guy, John, and Tony Jr.) in a new musical act, the Pastor Brothers. Soon after Tony's death, the Pastor Brothers opened at the Drake Hotel in New York; Artie Shaw was at a ringside table with Tony's widow.

"The show went over very well," Tony Pastor Jr. said. "Artie came up and he said, 'Tony, I have a proposition for you. I think you should be "Tony Pastor Jr." I think you should leave the group, and I think you should *lead my band*, because you have your dad's personality.' My brothers looked at me, like, 'Whaa—Are you gonna—' I said to them, 'Please—relax.' I said, 'Ex-*cuse* me, Artie; we just opened in our first nightclub, you know? And here we are with these bookings, for at least a year and a half.' You know? I thought to myself, Dear God! He was very 'I-am-an-island,' in a way. I mean, his *candor* sometimes was like— knock you off your pins!"

Shaw had other ideas on how to recycle his past. Some of them involved his long-unavailable and mostly never-issued 1954 Gramercy 5 tracks, copies of which he put into friendly hands at Columbia Records.

Gary Giddins, in 1970 a budding young jazz critic, later wrote that the first time he met John Hammond in his office, that legendary producer played him reel-to-reel tapes of these unissued Artie Shaw tracks, "exclaiming that they were possibly the best jazz clarinet records ever made and mourning the fact that Columbia refused Shaw's offer to put them out." The jazz merchants were still not ready to acknowledge the value of Shaw's consummate work.

His oldest records though were still in demand. Shaw was well represented in a *Reader's Digest* six-LP package of swing-band classics. Epic released an album of Artie's Brunswick "strings-swing" material, and many vintage Shaw sides were "re-created" in a Time-Life set of newly recorded versions of swing favorites done (without Shaw's participation) in the mode of Art's Capitol disc with Walt Levinsky.

The more Artie Shaw's musical legacy was appreciated, the more inexplicable it seemed to some that this extraordinary creator was no longer creating. Benny Goodman was still performing with regularity. "Ghost bands" filled ballrooms with the sounds of Tommy Dorsey and Glenn Miller. But an exasperated Shaw told *Down Beat's* John McDonough, "I don't care about 1938, and all that crap about the big-band sound. That isn't it today. Everybody's always talking about the good old days. . . . The good old days led to Hitler and war. I don't believe in that. I don't believe in the 1938 Ford, either. If you're going to buy a Ford, you buy a 1970 Ford." And there would be no new performing or recording gigs for him, either, he said. "Benny keeps doing that. That's not my bag. I haven't got the time."

Much of his time now was taken up with lawsuits.

Shaw sued five investors who he claimed had failed to fulfill obligations to help finance Artixo's film distributing, and won a $563,000 judgment—reduced on appeal to $125,000 and then delayed by further court proceedings.

More ambitious, and less satisfying, was the $5.4 million suit he filed in New York Supreme Court in late 1971 against Broadway producer David Merrick and others, claiming Merrick had "knowingly and maliciously" engaged in a plan to induce Scott Fitzgerald's daughter to breach the licensing agreement she had made with Shaw, in order that Merrick might make a film of the novel for Paramount Pictures.

"I started to do a musical on *The Great Gatsby*," Shaw said years later, "with some very good people. And it just fell apart, because these [other] people just came along and—plucked it out from under me. . . . Merrick stole it from me. That was the subject of a large lawsuit—which I won. We won in the lower courts, but . . . they kept throwing—took me into appellate court, finally, and—I couldn't keep followin' these guys. It's called 'my lawyer's bigger'n your lawyer.' I mean, you can't fight people like that, you know; the law is owned by the rich. . . . The law is a tortuous thing."

"Oh God, that was a disaster," Fred Morton said. "That was a great great blow."

Nonetheless, Shaw took on another behemoth when he sued Time-Life for three million dollars over their use of his name and music in their elaborate *Swing Era* LP package, claiming unfair competition. "It's a flagrant, arrogant violation of every right I have," Shaw told Leonard Feather. "They're putting me in competition with myself by using the phrase 'Artie Shaw Version.' I recognize only one Artie Shaw version, and that's my own. If they want to say 'Time-Life Imitation of the Artie Shaw Version,' that's all right; but not those whole booklets where you have to wade through page after page before finding, way in the back of the book, that it's some modern musicians redoing it in stereo. . . . In words of one syllable, I hate them! . . . I don't give a damn who's playing the clarinet. If they want a re-creation let them get in touch with me! . . . It's my right to imitate me." (In the end, though, Shaw more or less lost this case, when a court ruled one could not copyright a musical style.)

Art (along with many others, from Leonard Feather to Nat Hentoff to Pauline Kael) was also upset by *Lady Sings the Blues*, a 1972 movie in which Diana Ross played Billie Holiday. After Shaw refused to give permission for his name to be used, the film showed Holiday touring with the white "Reg Hanley Band"—and getting hooked on heroin by a fictitious white pianist from that fictitious orchestra.

Shaw had his say on such and many other matters in frequent outspoken or amusing appearances on television talk shows, from Johnny Carson's to Mike Douglas's to Merv Griffin's. Now in the public eye on a regular basis, Artie transformed his sartorial style, shunning business suits for a leather cowboy vest over colorful shirts and turtlenecks, and compensating for his baldness with mutton-chop sideburns and a handlebar moustache. At least he no longer looked like an umpire or a middle-aged farmer (both of which Hedda Hopper had mocked him as resembling).

Trumpeter Paul Cohen saw Shaw around this time, when Art came to hear Count Basie's band at the St. Regis Hotel. Cohen thought Artie was "tryin' to be a hippie," he said with a chuckle. "He wore, like, khaki—like something Randolph Scott Jr. would wear doin' a cowboy movie. And he had a young chick next to him!" But Shaw was still the same unassuming, savvy fellow he had been a quarter-century earlier, Cohen thought: "He was always an honest guy; he never put on airs. He always was—a musician who happened to be a bandleader. And we all respected his opinion, and if you can pick up on something good that this gentleman could tell you—*pick up.*"

CHAPTER FIFTY

(Would You Like to Be the) Love of My Life

SHAW WAS STILL married to Evelyn Keyes, but they hadn't lived together for years. She had moved to London, written a novel, and come back to the States to promote the book. Art spoke of their amicable estrangement in 1973 to Charlotte Curtis of the *New York Times*: "I like her very much and she likes me, but we've found it about impossible to live together." The Curtis piece took a look at the private Shaw, who waxed reflective on his many marriages: "I made an unholy botch of every last one of them," he said. "Of course, I believe I can state, equally accurately and with complete dispassion and objectivity, that I had a good deal of help in making those unholy botches." Yet this "still romantic" Shaw voiced some optimism, Curtis wrote; Art said, "Lately things that have been happening have given me hope. I see the possibility of a *really* good relationship."

"He didn't say with whom," Curtis ended her article, but the young woman in question was Joanne Lupton, a public relations person Art had met a couple years earlier, when he was sixty-one and she twenty-seven. "I was with a firm in charge of arranging art projects for corporations," Lupton said, "and one of my clients was trying to do something

Artie thought was really silly: people were to join hands and span the entire Brooklyn Bridge, and that was supposed to show some kind of unification. I was representing the client at this meeting, sitting on the floor with a lot of other people, and Artie walked in. I had no idea who he was, and he walked directly over to me and said, 'Are you here with anybody?' And I said, 'N-no.' And he said, 'Well is there any reason you shouldn't be with *me*?' I said, 'Well—I guess not!' And that's how I *met* him. Anyway, we were together from about that night on, actually."

Shaw was living at 58 West Fifty-eighth Street, behind Central Park South. He persuaded Lupton to move in with him. Joanne continued her PR work, but soon she was also assisting Art in various ways, including with his many lawsuits. There was also a lot of correspondence to deal with. "Being Artie Shaw," Joanne Lupton found, "was a full-time job."

Shaw had two personae, she said: "He saw himself as *himself*, and then he saw himself as 'Artie Shaw.' And he had to protect 'Artie Shaw,' that was his big job; it was not *him*, it was the *image* of him. When we were out, *that's* what he was protecting, and he *never* let that down. So if it was a public place, you wouldn't see him make a casual remark. If it was at home—if people were there interviewing him, it was still his public space; he would always be thinking, 'How is this gonna look in history? What is it gonna say in a book?' I don't think he would *ever* completely let *that* down."

Shaw and Lupton would be together several years. For a long time, Joanne said, she found Art a joy: "The man was so filled with *life*, he was incredible to be with. So bright, so able to discuss any book—the books were just stacked up next to his chair that he sat in, and all over the house—or anything that I chose to discuss with him, from an intellectual perspective." Their age difference hardly mattered, Lupton said, thanks to Art's forever-young attitude: "He would just leap in to whatever it was that he wanted, just leap in and do it; like a little kid."

She gave an example: "There was a very fancy Chinese restaurant that opened in New York City, that everybody said, 'You have to go, you have to go,' and so one night we went there for dinner. And they were bringing this flaming hors d'oeuvre thing, and he would never even *wait*, you know he would just go *after* something that he wanted—and he goes and he—reaches with his hand—And they're saying, 'No no no no, *no!*' in Chinese, and he gets it—

"And—it was the Sterno. He ate the Sterno."

WHILE A BIG chunk of the country, in the mid-1970s, was rediscovering the joys and merits of an earlier age's movies, popular music, fashions, and happenings, Shaw walked a blurry line between deploring the follies and banalities of olden times and celebrating his own solid accomplishments.

The contrarian Shaw had no patience with the "nostalgia craze" per se and whacked it in a piece he wrote for *Newsday*: "Nostalgia: A blend of several elements, including—but, as the lawyers say, not limited to—dislike of the present, distrust of the future, and a fuzzy memory of the past."

On the other hand—in a year when Johnny Guarnieri and Billy Butterfield played Michael's Pub in New York with an unofficial version of the Gramercy 5, Helen Forrest came out of retirement to sing at Manhattan's Rainbow Room, and Duke Ellington died at the age of seventy-five—Artie Shaw made sure to spell out the true merits of the swing era, a time that represented, he told Leonard Feather, "the confluence of the abilities of a bunch of highly specialized musicians like Tommy Dorsey, myself, Benny, Glenn, et cetera, all of whom knew very well what we were doing. We were playing right up to the peak of our abilities and at the same time meeting the approbation of the mass audiences, which I think is one of the few times in history that anything like that ever happened."

Back in those flush swing-era years, Artie Shaw had no cause whatsoever to pay attention to money. But that time was long past. With much of his funds tied up in lawsuits, Shaw had to be careful now about spending. "New York City was pretty expensive," Joanne Lupton said. "In what I was doing, I sort of had to be at one end of the media axis or the other, so it was either be in California or be in New York. We thought we could live a little more comfortably out in California."

Lupton and Shaw went west in late 1974, in a light-blue Volkswagen van. "I turned thirty in Akron, Ohio, in a Holiday Inn," she said. "He had a lot of possessions that were to come at a later time by moving van; we had everything that was really important to us in that little blue van, so we were guarding it with our *lives*. We drove across the country, into Hollywood. We were in an apartment for a while, while we were looking around; we didn't have a lot of resources. . . . So we were looking around for a place that we could buy in a relatively good neighborhood, and fix up." They found one in the Hollywood Hills, up on Outpost Drive. "It was small," Joanne said, "nothing to write home about, but—we had a lot of fun in that house."

Lupton liked to cook, and Shaw liked to eat, so they did a lot of entertaining. Joanne noticed something about Art, though: "He never really had close friendships; he was pretty much a loner. I don't know whether the people that were very close to him, if he ever truly respected them." People central to his life might be dropped at a moment's notice. "Noah Rosoff, who was his best *friend*, and he was talking to him all the *time*, and his wife was such a good friend of Artie's too, and *had* been, and were so *nice* to him, and then one day, Noah just said something that just hit him wrong—and he never *talked* to him again. I mean he wouldn't send him a *note*, he wouldn't *call* him, and—It was so hard for me to believe that you could just—be a best friend of somebody, and then cut them off like that. But—he did it, to a *lot* of people.

"Frederic Morton: We spent some good times at their apartment, when we were in New York; he was a good friend, Fred was. But then his wife was really sick, and Artie didn't—that didn't interest him. I thought, 'How can you be a really good friend with somebody if you don't care about their family?' But if it wasn't intellectually interesting to him, he really didn't want to know about it. And family was not one of those things.

"And I'm sure Kessi—Evelyn—I'm sure that they must have had some very good times together too, some *very* good times, but—it didn't come *down* to that; it came down to, like, what did you do *yesterday*. Which is really a shame."

But it was consistent with Shaw's "totally truthful" nature, Lupton believed. "They would call him up, when people died," she said, "and they'd say, 'Could you just say a few words about so and so?' And instead of saying 'Oh it's such a sad day, we've lost another musician' or something, he'd say, 'Well he really wasn't all that *good*.' You know! It's like, 'Artie can't you just keep your mouth shut?' But no! That wasn't *him*. It wasn't *him*. I never saw an evil side to him; I just saw a totally brutally honest side."

That brutal honesty sometimes clashed with Art's need to make a living. "One of the things he tried to do to get a little money," Lupton said, "was to go out and give talks and things like that. We went on one cruise on the *QE2*, for people who had become presidents of corporations before they were forty, I think: Young Presidents Association, whatever it was. And there were a lot of interesting other people; Art Buchwald was on it, and Jerzy Kosinski. You would be at a table, and then these young presidents could come sit at that table, and all that. But if they wanted to talk about, 'What was Lana like?' or, 'What was Ava like?'—this is not gonna go anywhere with him! He would not be polite and say, 'Well, that's for another day,' or something; he would just *turn* on 'em: 'That was *not* what I'm here for!' And a lot of it was, again, protecting Artie Shaw. He always felt like he had to *do* that; he had to get a favored-nations clause. It wasn't that it mattered that much to *him*, but it mattered to this protecting the Artie Shaw legacy." Art liked to tell journalists that since putting down his clarinet, he was not in "the Artie Shaw business" anymore. "Yeah but he always was," Lupton said. "He *always* was."

And the Artie Shaw business was looking up a bit in 1976. RCA Victor, having revived its old Bluebird label, used it to launch an ambitious reissue series. Art's Victor product was about to receive the full treatment in *The Complete Artie Shaw*, seven well-packaged and annotated two-LP sets to be released over the next five years.

Nevertheless, in May 1976 Art filed a $1.6 million lawsuit against

RCA, claiming the corporation owed him significant back royalties from as long ago as 1938.

AT SIXTY-SIX and counting, Artie Shaw had outlived many of his contemporaries—but not all. Some of his colleagues and former intimates were now publishing their memoirs, books that often contained vivid and not always flattering portraits of Artie. Songwriter Sammy Cahn, in *I Should Care*, pictured former 1930s crony Shaw as a heartless manipulator and a hollow man. Of greater interest to Art, perhaps, was Evelyn Keyes's autobiography, *Scarlett O'Hara's Younger Sister*, in which Shaw shared anecdote space with several of his current wife's earlier husbands and lovers. Keyes described his obsessive-compulsive behavior minutely, with the sharp eye and keen memory of a smitten-sweetheart-turned-jaded-spouse; she recounted running arguments and ugly scenes in a most convincing way, tempered by an affectionate-seeming above-it-all manner. There wasn't much Art could do but grin (or scowl) and bear it. "She's very good at making herself come off well," was what he would say much later of Keyes's anecdotes. "Very good at that."

For one reason or another, Shaw's own authorial impulse once more itched. He gave a talk at the Santa Barbara Writers Conference, an event run by Barnaby Conrad, an author and one-time secretary to Sinclair Lewis whom Shaw first met in San Francisco in the 1950s. Art began driving up to a twice-monthly writers' luncheon in Santa Barbara attended by Conrad, Ross Macdonald, and a couple-dozen other local lights. His presence there was welcome: "he's a wonderful storyteller," thought novelist Herb Harker. Shaw began committing some of those wonderful stories to paper—but again as fiction: "the last way to tell the truth," he told Nancy Collins of the *Washington Post*, "without hurting feelings and getting sued."

CHAPTER FIFTY-ONE

Imagination

THE COMPLICATED writing project Shaw began was an ambitious autobiographical novel about the education of an American jazz musician with a personal and professional history similar to his own. His model was Romain Rolland's *Jean-Christophe*, a sprawling saga of a German musician-composer that unfolded over several books. Shaw planned his roman-fleuve as at least a trilogy. He would take off from the facts of his own life but not be bound by them.

"Day after day after *day*," Joanne Lupton said, "he would go *up*, and he would write that *book*. And he would go *over* it and over it and *over* it. Oh yeah, I read it. I had a hard time reading his books, actually, because they were so unemotional, to me. So literate in choosing the words carefully, but not painting the pictures of the people the way they really *were*. . . . I was frustrated for him, because I thought, 'You know you're gonna finish this whole thing, and it's gonna be thousands of *pages*—and it's not gonna *go* anywhere!' And he'd have people over, and I'd cook dinner, and we'd sit around talking, and then—they would sit and read it, or he would *read* sections of it aloud, and then he would work to *change* around a paragraph or a sentence here and there, but—I never got that *emotional* aspect out of anything that he had written. So it was difficult for me, because I didn't want to be negative."

Artie had a lot of friends over, some of whom were helpful to him, including a television producer-director named Barry Shear, who gave Shaw small acting parts in TV movies to help him out financially. Other dinner guests were well-known figures Joanne enjoyed having the chance to meet: from Ella Fitzgerald to Marlon Brando.

Art remained fun to be with. Shaw was very affectionate: writing Joanne little love notes all the time, doing sweet cartoon drawings that really looked like her.

At the same time, Lupton found Shaw difficult. "Everything had to be perfect," she said. "Just to give one example—and everything was like this—he liked a glass of freshly squeezed orange juice in the morning, but it had to be a *certain* temperature. So what you had to do was put the orange in the refrigerator to get it cool enough, but then you had to remove it at a certain time before you actually squeezed it, so the timing had to be exactly right. And if you didn't do it exactly right, he would get *very upset*; I mean *really* upset. It would last for a *long* period of time. It could go on for hours.

"And with his coffee—I can visualize that coffee cup right now: it was a black mug with a white inside, and there was a little red *dot* as to where you filled up the coffee *in* that coffee cup; he put the dot *in* there, with red nail-polish! He did. And then you put in a certain amount of this Sweet'N Low. And so if it got above or below that dot, and you put in the wrong amount of Sweet'N Low—I mean he would go ber-*serk*. So, this is not an easy man to live with."

Having to jump through ever-higher hoops was bad enough. But Joanne encountered more fundamental problems. "When we moved out to California," she said, "I wanted to do something else; I wanted to write, or whatever. . . . He said, 'Well, whatever you make, you're never gonna make as much money as me, so why don't you just work for me.' And so, it was the money; that's what he would do. 'Cause I would say, 'I really don't want to *do* this,' and he would say, 'He who pays, commands,' which was his favorite phrase, except he would say it in Spanish. That was the way he saw things. So if you couldn't contribute a lotta money, then you didn't have a voice. And I was never gonna have the voice that he had, 'cause he was always going to be able to make more money. So, why not take my talents and put them into preserving him, and preserving the persona 'Artie Shaw.'"

Lupton, then, took charge of the house: renovated it from the ground up. She learned to give dinner parties for Art's friends, and remembered how much cream and sugar everyone took. She read the books they read and could make informed comments. It worked for a while. But in time she wanted something of her *own*—and then she and Art clashed.

Shaw didn't want her writing women's-magazine articles, he said; that wasn't "real" writing. Doing public relations for big corporations was bogus too, he thought: "spending your life trying to make cannibals look like the Jolly Green Giant." No, he said, the only thing she could do that he would have any respect for was be a teacher or doctor.

Well, Lupton thought she *could* be a teacher, and went back to school. But when it became clear she was doing well and would achieve her goal, Shaw didn't want *that* any longer. "He said, 'Well you're going to get your Ph.D., and then you're gonna wanna go live at some university? I don't know if I wanna go live at that university.' I said, 'Well then that's another door that's blocked off. . . . What can I *do*, and still remain with you?' There just didn't seem to be anything . . . except work for him, which is not what I wanted. He really didn't want me to leave, and I knew that I had to get out."

At last, late in 1979, Lupton took the leap. "When I called up my best friend," she said, "who is *still* my best friend, and I said, 'Patricia, I really have to leave now, I have to move out,' she said, 'Well are you absolutely, one hundred percent *sure* of this? Is this a decision that you've *made*?' I said, 'Yes, it's a decision I've made.' She said, 'I will wire you a thousand dollars tonight!' Yeah. Because that's how strongly she felt, that you shouldn't let yourself stay in that situation for a long period of time. And until this day, she doesn't understand why I did. But I still feel like I'm a better person because of it. Absolutely.

"Well you saw: he was an interesting *person*. Maybe you run into people like that all the time, but I don't; I didn't. It's pretty amazing, and it's exciting just to *know* somebody who managed to pull all of that off.

And he didn't *come* from some *family* that sent him to the right schools, and hired a teacher for him. . . . Nothing was ever handed to him; everything he did, he got for himself."

Their breakup came as Shaw sold the Hollywood canyon home, in late 1979, and bought a house in Newbury Park, halfway between L.A. and Santa Barbara. "I still would drive out there to see him in Newbury Park," Lupton said, "and he came up to see me when I was at U.C. Davis getting my Ph.D. And then he kinda calmed down, and we were friends; but by that time he was onto, you know, another girlfriend. I met *several*, after that." Lupton did indeed relocate out of state: at Texas A&M, where she became a Distinguished Professor of nutrition and food science, a Regent's Professor, a University Faculty Fellow, and holder of an endowed chair in nutrition. As president of the American Society for Nutrition, Dr. Joanne Lupton helped establish the nation's nutritional and exercise guidelines. Shaw would be proud of her many accomplishments—even as he bemoaned her status as "the one that got away."

WRITING—ESPECIALLY WRITING a never-ending bildungsroman, especially living alone—was a solitary business. Shaw ventured out of his home in Newbury Park early in 1982 to conduct a couple of courses at nearby Oxnard College, one of which had as its title and point of departure the poetry line Art had used as a motto for decades: "Three Chords for Beauty's Sake, and One to Pay the Rent." Shaw's second course was on "The Big Band Era," a time period that continued to fascinate a certain segment of the modern generation.

Canadian filmmaker Brigitte Berman was one so intrigued. After interviewing Art for *Bix: Ain't None of Them Play Like Him Yet*, a feature-length documentary that debuted at the L.A. Filmex festival in 1982, she began recording Art for a separate film about Shaw.

By now, Art was keeping company with a twenty-six-year-old flautist from Ventura named Jennifer Carey, with whom he drove to New York City in the fall of 1982. In Manhattan, Shaw looked up Teo

Macero, a musician–composer and record producer he had known since the 1950s. A decade after John Hammond had tried to get Columbia Records to release Artie's 1953–54 Gramercy 5 sessions, Art thought Macero—well known for his work with Columbia star Miles Davis—might assist him in prepping his thirty-year-old material.

"He wanted to mix it down," Macero said. "He had some raw tapes, and I said, 'Let's go do it in the studio.' After we finished, he said, 'I'd like to put it out.' I said, 'Fine, I'll ask these fools here,' at CBS. And [they] turned it down; [they] didn't think it was good enough. And Artie kept saying it's the best thing he had ever recorded. And it's true." Macero, a saxophonist, said he loved both Shaw's and Goodman's playing: "Each of them had their own style. Benny's was a little harder sound; Artie had a softer, mellower tone: the *sound* of that clarinet—Jesus Christ, you wanna *cry*; *uuuh*—brings *tears* to your eyes."

If the powers-that-be still refused to acknowledge Shaw's greatest work, the powers-that-were thought there was still a market for Artie's popular all-time repertoire. Willard Alexander—the legendary agent who had engineered Benny Goodman's 1935 breakthrough and who still, decades later, was booking swing bands—made a trip to Newbury Park to urge formation of an Artie Shaw orchestra to perform those classic charts. Several "ghost bands" had for years purveyed the sounds of deceased swing masters (Art's old trombonist Buddy Morrow led Tommy Dorsey's). Why not a band in memory of a living icon? Shaw at last gave Alexander his consent. To front the band and approximate his playing, Art proposed Dick Johnson, a fifty-six-year-old clarinetist from Brockton, Massachusetts, whose work he had heard on compact disc. Alexander was enthusiastic; Johnson was amenable. By the spring of 1983, the band (which Shaw would own) was ready to play its first West and East Coast dates, with its namesake accompanying it as guest conductor and emcee. At seventy-three, Artie Shaw would once more take an orchestra on the road.

CHAPTER FIFTY-TWO

Dancing in the Dark

PETER LEVINSON, a veteran jazz publicist, was hired by Alexander to promote the new Shaw ensemble, a seventeen-piece band of young players including several graduates from Boston's Berklee School of Music. Levinson went to Boston in early December to watch Artie rehearse in the ballroom of the Hilton Hotel. "Artie had a wool cap on, with a brim, and sweat clothes," Levinson said, "and when I walked in, he was saying, 'No no, the saxophones gotta do so-and-so, while the trumpets—' I said, you know, here he is, he really *knows* how it works, *still*; he knows the structure, and the way the sections should go. I watched him about forty-five minutes, and I was just fascinated; this completely new band. I certainly saw the awe that these guys had for him."

Shaw held all-day rehearsals preparing for the orchestra's official debut at the about-to-reopen Glen Island Casino at New Rochelle, where filmmaker Berman would be on hand. "It was just two or three weeks later, at the most, we were having to do that reopening," said Daryl Sherman, who sang with the band for its first six months, "and he knew what he had in front of him: not only to get them to play the right notes—they were fine musicians—but to get them to play like a band, to jell together, and stylistically to get those nuances. He spent time on that for sure, because he was a stickler for detail."

The three-day Glen Island Casino gig was a hit, packed with gray-haired swing enthusiasts from throughout the tri-state area. "The place was beautiful," Daryl Sherman said, "and it was just filled [that first night] with great fans and all kinds of people who were very very excited. The first thing he counts off of course is his theme song, 'Nightmare.' And this is the first time I'd experienced it; you know it's not exactly a sweet sprightly thing, it's very *dark*—and I'm on the stage, and I'm feeling the excitement and the tension of this dark song, and then witnessing, with my eyes, everyone in that room standing up, you know, *cheering*, and practically running to that bandstand. I thought, my God! How do you follow *this*? But he hit it, and just went through: 'Back Bay Shuffle,' and all the things that we were doing. It was a great night. Lots of 'industry people' there, as we say. And as they went into the song 'Dancing in the Dark,' who should get up with his wife Ellie to dance—and even he would laugh at this, 'cause he has a sense of humor—but George Shearing."

"This is a kick-ass band!" Shaw crowed to the *Los Angeles Herald-Examiner*'s Tony Gieske, the day of its concert at L.A.'s Dorothy Chandler Pavilion in the spring of 1984. And Dick Johnson's performance as Shaw's doppelganger won over critics, as Johnson hewed close to Art's solos on earlier numbers and showed his own creative chops on the modern charts.

Yet there was something peculiar about the whole endeavor. "The presence of Shaw, looking trim, dapper and eminently fit to re-create his distinctive, piercing sound but not playing, even on 'Begin the Beguine,' is initially a little eerie," *Newsweek*'s David Gates wrote. "Shaw talks, conducts and talks some more," the *Toronto Globe and Mail*'s Mark Miller wrote, "in effect curating his own exhibit." Viewed in a certain light, Artie Shaw seemed a figure trapped between worlds: the onlooking leader of his own live ghost band, protagonist in the second act of an American life written not by F. Scott Fitzgerald but by Pirandello.

The disorientation intensified on a Thursday afternoon in November when Shaw, his bandsmen, Brigitte Berman, and a few press people attended a screening at Toronto's Film House of Berman's just-completed, nearly two-hour documentary, *Artie Shaw: Time Is All You've Got.* "Fasten your safety belt!" Artie shouted as the lights dimmed. Berman's film was an adroit mix of archival footage and photographs with contemporary interviews. There were bits of reminiscence from John Best, Helen Forrest, Mel Tormé, and Frederic Morton, and there was a long, effective, affectionate segment with Evelyn Keyes. Most of all, there was Artie Shaw: telling droll tales on himself and others, viewing the past through his own custom lenses, being viewed in turn by the filmmaker. "It's very strange seeing yourself through someone else's eyes," Art told the *Toronto Star's* Sid Adilman. "It's like looking through a triple mirror. . . . It's a distillation of a lifetime. Only I know what was left out."

Artie Shaw: Time Is All You've Got played at the L.A. Filmex festival in early 1985. The documentary's title (from a statement by Shaw) underscored life's fleeting nature and urgent priorities—as did a clutch of sudden deaths among Art's contemporaries and colleagues: Count Basie in 1984, at eighty; the seventy-six-year-old Willard Alexander, in the autumn of 1984, leaving Shaw to continue his orchestra venture on his own; Johnny Guarnieri in January of 1985, at a mere sixty-seven.

People were coming to see the band, but not in huge numbers. "We're still fighting the battle of getting an audience out there," Art told Chip Deffaa, "aside from that for Cyndi Lauper, Prince and Madonna." But Shaw loved this new orchestra. "The band is swinging its head off," he told Deffaa. "It's a hell of a bunch of players!" He made plans to go out with Dick Johnson and crew again for the 1985 season.

As his personal assistant for that tour, Art hired Jan Curran, a journalist and publicist and a single mother of four whom he had met in Santa Barbara and been friends with for seven years. Curran was with Shaw on a Wednesday in July when he and the orchestra played the Hollywood Bowl on a bill with singer Mel Tormé, forty years after Art gave Mel his first solo record date. Here Curran got her first taste of Shaw's show-business temperament: "We shared a dressing room with Mel Tormé," she said. "Artie didn't like that I allowed that."

Tormé told Chip Deffaa, "I got to the Bowl for afternoon rehearsal. And a producer runs up to me, frantic: 'Oh Mel, I don't know how to tell you this. Oh God! Artie Shaw took your name off the main dressing room, and put your nameplate on the back dressing room, and he took your dressing room! I don't know what to do.' I said: 'Don't do anything. He's Artie Shaw. He's my hero. And he was my mentor. And if he wants that dressing room, of course.' I never said a word about it to him. And he never said, you know, like, 'Gee, I didn't think you'd mind.' He just automatically—*I'm Artie Shaw*. I happen to love the man. I adore him."

The Bowl concert went well, and afterward the headliners repaired to their backstage quarters. "Artie's instructions," Jan Curran said, "were, 'Do not let *anybody* into the dressing room; no crowds in here.' I was supposed to answer the door. Mel Tormé just rolled his eyes, because— who was gonna *come* back there, you know?" But a knock came. "I am never intimidated by anybody," said Curran, whom many at the time said resembled Ava Gardner in her prime. "But it was Evelyn Keyes—with Tab Hunter," the tall and handsome 1950s movie star. "I was stunned; I just *stared* at Tab Hunter. He had the blue sweater tied around his shoulders, the blue eyes; I thought, 'My God! He's an eight- by-ten glossy!' Artie couldn't figure out why I wasn't saying anything, so he walked over—looked at Tab—looked at me, and he said, 'Jan, you remember Dorian Gray, don't you?'"

AFTER A WEEK'S work at Disneyland, the orchestra headed east. Shaw and Curran took a flight from L.A. International, giving Jan another close-up view of "Artie Shaw" in volatile action.

"When we went to board the plane," she said, "he quickly gave me his garment bag—because, he says, 'Headliner doesn't carry a garment bag.' I said, 'Nobody calls themselves a headliner.' So we get inside the plane, in the little first-class area; there's no closet. I'm sort of befuddled. The stewardess is standing there, young girl—very young—and she asks if there's a problem. I said, 'I was looking for the closet.' She said, 'Well we don't have a closet.' And then Artie just screamed at her; my God, it was terrible: 'I'm a *headliner*, and I've gotta go onstage, and my clothes have gotta look good; don't you *understand* that? This has to be hung up!' Nowadays, they would have kicked him off the plane, you know; called the cops. He was yelling at her: 'Don't you know who I am?' That really was a surprise, because he never wanted anybody to know who he was. 'I'm Artie *Shaw*. Now—get a closet.' I just turned to him and said, 'Artie—she doesn't know big bands, she doesn't know a "headliner," she probably never hearda *you*, and you're making a scene. Siddown, because I don't want to see this in the *New York Times* tomorrow.' And so he sat down. But he was worried: where was I putting the garment bag? He kept watching me; I had to lay it out like a body, you know, up above us. When I sat back down, I said, 'Stop worrying. I will never let you go onstage looking like a schlump. You'll always be perfect, so— that's my problem, not yours.' It was a bad scene, very bad scene. But I think it was just him being nervous. He could be impossible that way."

The centerpiece of the orchestra's East Coast trip was a one-week August gig at the Blue Note in New York City. Peter Levinson found a two-bedroom apartment for Shaw and Curran to stay in, within Man-hattan walking distance of the club. On the several days before and during the Blue Note gig, Jan saw a more relaxed side of Art. "He was wonderful," she said. "We went sightseeing, and I took picnics in the park, and nobody recognized him. We did goofy things. He acted younger than I did. There were lotsa times when we could say Yiddish expressions to each other around a situation, and people wouldn't know what we had just said; for instance he could tell me about somebody, 'This guy's a little *shmegege*,' a little jerk. We would walk holding hands; we just had this wonderful time, and he was so sweet and terrific to me. He never made any *moves* on me, you know, but he would *look* at me romantic, in his eyes. You can look at somebody and you're telling them, 'I care about you.' Maybe all his insecurities held him back, not to express himself, not to tell anybody his feelings, 'cause what if they mocked him? A lot of it was because he was so shy."

Speaking with Jan in the apartment one afternoon, Art told her of the woman he had been married to long ago. "The first wife was a nurse. They'd married when he didn't have two dimes, just a lot of dreams. She was the sole support or the major breadwinner for a while; he wanted to write. Yes, he had loved her. Loved her very much. I'm not sure how long they were married, but long enough for him to start to become famous. . . . 'She didn't want to be married to a famous person; she just wanted to be married to *me*,' he told me. . . . Yes, she loved him; but she didn't want a life in the spotlight. He didn't mention her getting remarried. Maybe she never did.

"He told me all this about the first wife . . . and I swear to you, it was so emotional; he had tears. . . . He got out the phone book. I didn't move to join him; I stayed seated. He held the book and looked at it and ran his hand over a page, the left-hand side. He said to me, 'She's here, she's still here.' Mostly he was saying it to himself. He toyed with calling her: yes, no, maybe. Not now, he's too upset; the memories and all. . . . I said I would leave the room so he could call her. No, he said, it would be too hard; he couldn't handle making that call. He just wanted to see if she was still there. It was a relief—a relief to find her there, listed.

"He looked so God-damn sad."

CHAPTER FIFTY-THREE

Autumn Leaves

S HAW AND CURRAN walked each afternoon to the Blue Note gig,
talking all the way. Artie enjoyed this daily stroll, which took them
past a park filled with nannies and babies. Shaw carried a garment bag
that held his tuxedo jacket. Half a block from the club, he would give
it to Curran: "Stars don't carry their own garment bag." And always he
warned her about the line of patrons waiting ("this big *mob* that was
supposedly gonna be outside; there'd be maybe three or four people"):
"Keep 'em away from me; keep 'em all away from me."

One afternoon, one of the people waiting in front of the Blue Note
was a fellow about thirty years old, intent on speaking with Shaw. Art
shoved him and said, "*Get* away from me." After seeing Art safely inside
and into his dressing room, Curran went back to check on the young
man still standing in front. He told her he was Artie's son Jonathan,
Shaw's child by Doris Dowling.

Curran brought Jonathan into the club and upstairs, and hid him in a
small office until the show began, when she brought him backstage. The
two of them sat in the dark, watching and listening. When the set was
over, she put Jonathan in Shaw's dressing room, then went to the wings
to wait for Art's stage exit.

"He would take one arm," she said, "and then we'd go up these stairs into his dressing room. So he opened the door to the dressing room, and Jonathan's standing there. First of all, Artie screamed at *me*: 'How can you *do* this to me? *How* can you do this to me?' Screaming horrible things. Jonathan kept saying, 'I just came to tell you—' And Artie wasn't listening; he just kept screaming at *him*: 'I don't want to *look* at you. You look like *her*. You remind me of her, that's why I don't ever want to *see* you, I don't want anything to *do* with you.' It was so sad. I finally just walked in front of Artie and told him to shut up: 'This boy's trying to tell you something important.' So he shut up. And Jonathan told Artie he was gonna be a grandfather, and then Artie cried. And—they hugged each other. And talked for a long time. I think we all went out to get something to eat. And then the kid either came back and stayed with us, or came back the next day to the apartment; I think we saw him two, three days running. So Artie was trying to establish a relationship with him. It was a sad thing, for the kid, I think. But then Artie did such a quick turnaround, from yelling at him to then loving him. You know? He could do that: that quick turnaround."

BUT THERE was no such turnaround for Benny Goodman.

Shaw's jealousy of Goodman persisted into the 1980s—and the jealousy was reciprocated, according to Loren Schoenberg, the saxophonist and bandleader who was Goodman's assistant during this period. "Artie and Benny," Schoenberg said, "actually had kind of an almost childish rivalry, even in the later years. It sounds like something cartoon-like, but—they *really did*! Kind of funny, in that they were so different; and their music was so different."

Goodman invited Peter Levinson to lunch around this time, the publicist said, for the express purpose of talking to him about Shaw: "He wanted to know, why didn't Artie Shaw play the clarinet anymore? 'He could have gotten it back in six or seven months, and he was very good.' He couldn't understand that. I said, 'Well Benny, he felt he went as far as he could go on the clarinet, and it doesn't mean that much to him, but he wanted to come back, to work with a band and play his hits, and he could—lead the band and talk to the audience.' 'Yeah, but he should *play*, and—' Because Benny Goodman's whole world was the clarinet; there was nothing else that was important to him."

Goodman called Shaw's apartment during Art's Blue Note stay, to welcome him to New York. Curran answered the phone (Shaw liked to give the impression he was surrounded by staff). Artie wouldn't talk to his old colleague, Curran said. "I'm sure it hurt Goodman's feelings. . . . Also he said he wanted to come to the Blue Note. Artie said to tell him not to come."

Benny Goodman, seventy-six years old, in and out of the hospital these days and only sporadically active as a guest performer, mulled and pondered the actions of the man he often referred to as "the competition." Loren Schoenberg said, "Actually, the resurgence of the Artie Shaw Orchestra with Dick Johnson I think is what spurred Benny on to want to have [another] band in the last year of his life."

Goodman agreed to perform with a band for a PBS-TV fundraising special in the autumn of 1985. For the necessary crew, he hired Schoenberg's full swing ensemble, which included a few Goodman alumni. After the special was taped, offers came in for Benny and this band to do more shows and concerts. "Encouraged and energized," Goodman's biographer Ross Firestone wrote, "he . . . made several major changes. Before playing his next engagement . . . he eased out Loren Schoenberg, in effect firing him from his own orchestra."

BENNY GOODMAN'S appearances with Loren Schoenberg's former band gave him a brief but satisfying last hurrah, despite his failing health. Then, on Friday the thirteenth of June 1986, Goodman had a heart attack at home, playing Mozart on the clarinet. Benny Goodman: dead at seventy-seven.

Many people's thoughts turned to Artie Shaw. Some folks were cruel. San Francisco columnist Herb Caen was moved to a gesture Artie found hard to forgive.

"Herb loved Benny," Barnaby Conrad said, "since he was a kid. And he was with a bunch of friends, and they were all drinking a lot and playing Goodman records. It was a Saturday night. And Herb really wasn't that mean, but for some reason he felt mean, and he called up Artie Shaw, and he said, '*Hey Artie*—we're sittin' here, and we want you to listen to a *real* clarinetist'—and they put the phone up to the gramophone. Artie called me the next morning, said, 'Hey that *friend* of yours up there, Mr. Caen, listen to what he *did*,' and he told me, and at great length. He said, 'Doesn't he realize that *stars* have feelings too? No matter how big the star is, he's got feelings; I've got feelings, you know. That hurt my *feelings*.' And Herb wrote him a note and apologized, said, 'I was drunk, I shouldn't have done it.' And Artie called me up again and read it to me, and he said, 'That doesn't do any good. He meant it at the time.'. . . He could dish it *out*, he just couldn't take it."

Shaw's contributions to the big-band era were nonetheless being recognized by a new generation of jazz critics and chroniclers. In 1986, the *New York Times*' John S. Wilson wrote two essays noting Artie's key part, through his purposeful choice of material, in the creation of the concept of a "great American songbook" of enduring work by the best Broadway show composers. A PBS documentary on Billie Holiday included an interview of Shaw vividly describing that vocalist's pioneering stint with Art's orchestra.

The compact-disc revolution was taking hold in earnest. With CDs replacing LPs in the marketplace, major labels were busy repackaging catalog items, including some of Shaw's most vital work.

On the night of March 30, Brigitte Berman's film *Artie Shaw: Time Is All You've Got*, in a tie with another nominee, was co-winner of the Academy Award as best feature documentary. Shaw was typically unable to express unalloyed pleasure. "I feel like George Bernard Shaw did after he received the Nobel Prize," he told the *Toronto Globe and Mail*. "'It's like sending out a life-boat after I've already swum to shore and safety.' What do people think I've been doing all these years, spinning my wheels?"

Three days later, Buddy Rich died in Los Angeles, aged sixty-nine. He kept his wise-guy wit to the end. Asked at the hospital, where he went for treatment of a brain tumor, if he was allergic to anything, Rich said, "Yeah, country-and-western." Artie Shaw—along with Frank Sinatra, Johnny Carson, Jerry Lewis, Robert Blake, and Mel Tormé—spoke at Rich's funeral. "Artie had a way of saying things that sounded like he was putting everybody else in the world down," Terry Gibbs wrote. "Buddy's lying there in the casket, and Artie Shaw said, 'I went to see Buddy's band some years ago and I told him, "You know, you played loud bass-drum when you played for me, and you play louder bass-drum now."'"

"I didn't *like* him, as a guy, at all," Shaw said later of Rich. "I said he had one quality, though, which was exuberance; he was full of that. It bubbled! That's what came out in his playing. Later I'm talking to Mel Brooks, outside the funeral home. And Georgie Auld—he turned out to be a fucking *gangster*, horrible guy—he comes up: 'You're fulla shit. You're fulla shit.' 'Wadya *mean*, George? Wadya talkin' about?' 'You're fulla shit.' I said, 'Is that your considered opinion? Is there anything you want to *add*, to that?' He was disappointed he wasn't called on to speak, and he was very *angry*. 'You're fulla shit.' That's all he could *say*! Chagrin! What—I dunno, he identified himself with me, and he never could quite *make* it, as a *star*; you know, whatever it *was*. Angered him. Infuriated him. When I quit the music, man, [in 1939] I *gave* him the *band*; I gave him my *book*. He could not make it *work*. He *didn't* have the *quality* that it *took*. Certain people don't."

CHAPTER FIFTY-FOUR

That Old Feeling

I N 1989, A LITTLE while after Evelyn Keyes at last served Artie with divorce papers, Shaw had his third book published: *The Best of Intentions and Other Stories,* a short-story collection from Santa Barbara publisher John Daniel which included a stand-alone chapter, "Snow White in Harlem," from Art's novel-in-progress. (In 1996, another fragment from his book manuscript, "Music Lesson," would be printed in an issue of the Chicago journal *The Baffler.*) From the evidence of these pages it seemed Shaw had indeed succeeded in finding a satisfying way to write engaging fiction about his own extraordinary life. If Art managed to finish his massive novel, it might well turn out to be some sort of a masterpiece; at the least, it would be a unique and engrossing chronicle.

The Best of Intentions received mixed but respectful reviews, and after five or six years, its edition of two thousand copies sold out.

GEORGIE AULD died of lung cancer in January 1990, at age seventy.

Ava Gardner died a few weeks later, of pneumonia, at sixty-seven.

Later in the year, Ava's memoir was published, a work that indicated Shaw's failings as a husband but was generous in its final judgment of him. Artie's exes, whether or not through his influence, turned out to be a bookish lot. Lana too had published a memoir, and soon Evelyn Keyes would produce her second autobiographical work in which (as in her first memoir) the colorful Shaw loomed large.

Meanwhile Artie kept working and working on his novel, known at different times as "Sideman" and "The Education of Albie Snow." He always seemed to be about seven chapters from the end.

Art turned eighty in May 1990, occasioning lengthy profiles in *Los Angeles*, the *Los Angeles Times*, and the *Philadelphia Inquirer Magazine*. Also in 1990, the independent label MusicMasters released a CD of the transcription discs made by Shaw's 1949 band, which drew brief but appreciative reviews by knowing critics such as Francis Davis, who (writing in *Connoisseur's World*) said George Russell's arrangement of "Similau" "boldly fuses mambo and Russian-period Stravinsky" and marveled that Shaw's 1949 "Star Dust" solo had been even "more free-floating and melodically indivisible, less anchored to the bar line and the beat" than his classic 1940 turn.

More important in many ways was the release in 1992 by MusicMasters of a two-CD box of *The Last Recordings*: Artie Shaw's self-produced 1954 sessions with his final Gramercy 5s, his lasting legacy and ultimate statement as an improvising musician. These were the tapes Art himself had paid to make in 1953 and 1954—the ones both John Hammond and Teo Macero later failed to get Columbia Records to market. MusicMasters's discs came out in time for Shaw's eighty-second birthday, and their beauty, virtuosity, and very existence stunned jazz critics young and old.

Time's Christopher Porterfield wrote that these sessions, held mere months before Shaw retired as a player, showed Artie still at the height of his powers: "Shaw contributes one revelatory solo after another. His tone is crystalline, his lines distinctively long and sinuous, full of witty, sometimes startling interjections and exuberant flurries into his laser-like top register, but always settling back into a sleekly lyrical groove. He probes the recesses of ballads . . . with a risky intimacy. On middle-tempo numbers . . . he twists and flashes through the beat with a finger-snapping insouciance." Most enthusiastic and articulate was the *Village*

Voice's Gary Giddins, who judged these tracks "among the finest performances by one of the great clarinetists of the century, and among the most enchanting small band recordings in jazz history, virtually unique for occupying a thoroughly persuasive crossroads in the nexus between swing and bop. . . . The music is romantic, daring, and exquisitely played . . . a personal triumph for Shaw as clarinetist, arguably the pinnacle of his work on the instrument. . . . [Y]ou may wonder how jazz ever got along without these recordings."

WITH THE STIR caused by *The Last Recordings* came a renewal of that old lingering question: Why did Shaw quit? How could he have abandoned that magnificent gift?

What better time for Artie Shaw to once more make a splashy return (in a nonplaying capacity of course) to the music stage?

It was clarinetist Bob Wilber's idea: The sixty-four-year-old instrumentalist (a one-time student of Sidney Bechet's) wanted to perform a classical-and-jazz concert in London, to feature himself in both Mozart's clarinet concerto and Shaw's "Concerto for Clarinet." He asked Artie to conduct, and Art said yes. Shaw would make his British concert debut in the Royal Festival Hall at the age of eighty-two.

He was accompanied to England by his much younger friend Kay Pick of Beverly Hills. "It was a hundred percent pure friendship," she said of her relationship with Shaw. "But I went to London with him— and it was like being with Elvis Presley. I mean, when I got off the plane they looked at me and said, 'Who are you?' I said, 'I'm his grandmother.'" In England, Shaw was treated like a major celebrity. "It was fabulous to go different places with him; he was well regarded by many people." Pick said Art's energy was amazing. "When we got off the plane, I was knocked out; I went to my room and went to bed and slept, and woke up about six hours later and called his room. There was no answer! He'd gone on to do interviews. After my nap, he strides off the elevator; he says, 'Give me half an hour'—and then we went out to dinner!"

Major stories about Shaw's visit were printed in several newspapers, with their writers also startled and charmed by the vitality of this famous visitor, who could be both curmudgeonly and beguiling: "A remarkably handsome and upright old man with a head like a Rodin sculpture," wrote the *Daily Mail*'s Corinna Honan. "His eyes positively kindle with intelligence. The sex appeal is still palpably there, twinkling away, barely dimmed."

"It was jammed at the Royal Festival Hall," said *Los Angeles*'s editor in chief Geoff Miller, Shaw's friend who with his wife, Kathryn, was at the London concert, which also included jazz medleys by an ensemble of well-known players. "All these Britishers had spent their entire lives listening to this guy and admiring him. And he pulled his usual thing of asking people not to applaud solos; applaud at the end of the piece! He's not just conducting the orchestra, he's giving the audience orders. A number of star British performers—Kenny Baker, for instance, a rather famous trumpet player—onstage playing, although Artie was rather casual about introducing them." Barney Kessel was on guitar. "It was a memorable evening." Later the Millers went backstage. "God, he was just *mobbed* afterwards," Geoff said. "And he takes that in stride, because—he'd experienced it all, you know." But even Artie Shaw was touched by the "huge standing ovation" he received, and that the musicians joined in the applause. "At the end of the show," wrote the *Glasgow Herald*, "he was in tears as he left the stage."

But when the English fans who crowded into his dressing room begged him to sign their precious Shaw records and photos, he said no to every single one of them.

BY NOW Artie Shaw was adept at conducting occasional courses and seminars at local colleges, giving talks at writers' conferences and jazz conventions, and doing interviews (on the road or in his Newbury Park house) that often lasted several hours.

On such occasions, Shaw railed against the banality and ugliness of popular culture and contemporary life, and he celebrated his own survival and achievements. "Every story was burnished beautifully," said

Aram Saroyan, the author son of William and Carol, who heard many of Artie's tales in the course of researching a book he and Shaw hoped to do but never did, "and he told them wonderfully. It was almost like what replaced music, for him. He was *always* the central figure; he *never* would cede the center of the stage to *anyone*. And the *attitude* in the stories was the *same*, from beginning to end: 'I'm a gifted—supremely gifted—human being; and from the beginning, the world has endeavored to drive me crazy. And—here's the proof.' The stories are great; they're fascinating. And then every so often—in theatrical terms—he's a little appalling."

Artie used interviews to settle scores, air grievances, show himself in the best possible light, and put others to blame. But some of the things he said seemed so mean-spirited, they put *him* in a bad light. Of his two children: "I hardly see my sons; there's no point worrying about things that are over." Of his most recently deceased ex-wife: "Ava died of confusion; her beauty ruled her." Of his departed contemporaries: "All I can say is that Glenn [Miller] should have lived, and 'Chattanooga Choo Choo' should have died," and "I'm too straight-talking for most people. Today, you gotta say, 'I love you madly,' and then you become Saint Ellington, who they're all now busy canonizing."

LANA TURNER died in the summer of 1995, at seventy-five.

Later that year, Shaw, whose first major screen exposure came in a movie with Turner, went to the Library of Congress to attend a showing of Brigitte Berman's documentary and give a talk. With every year that passed, the collective perception was growing of Shaw as a living master, a national treasure, a still-vital legend of American cultural history. Biographers sought him out for incisive comments on famous figures he had known and survived: Bing Crosby, Judy Garland, Tommy Dorsey, William Saroyan, W. C. Fields. In 1996, *Down Beat* magazine voted Shaw into its Hall of Fame, an honor long overdue, such as it was; as Art himself said, "It's about time."

It was past time too for Brigitte Berman's documentary to have wider exposure, but the film had been tied up in litigation for years. Shaw had sued Berman in 1990 for breach of contract, seeking half a million dollars in damages or thirty-five percent of the film's profits, and possession of the movie. The case at last came to trial in Ontario, Canada, in December 1996. Shaw, using a cane, a hearing aid, and reading glasses, took the stand and claimed the film was a "collaborative product." Berman, in her testimony, told her lawyer, "I maintain as God is my witness that that is my work of art." Of Shaw, she said, "He likes to talk, but I don't think he likes to do much real work." Shaw grew irritable as the trial wore on.

In March 1997, Shaw's action against Berman was dismissed by Mr. Justice Romain Pitt of the Ontario Court, General Division, who found no basis for Art's claim. "I'm absolutely thrilled and relieved that it's finally over after ten years," Berman told the *Toronto Star*. "It has been nightmare." But it wasn't over. Shaw filed an appeal which claimed, "The learned trial judge erred in misapplying the law to facts presented at trial." Later, Art would pursue his case in American courts. Those wishing to see *Time Is All You've Got* would have many more years to wait.

CHAPTER FIFTY-FIVE

Hop Skip and Jump

VARIOUS WOMEN companions entered and exited Shaw's life as he made his way toward ninety. He also had several female secretaries, but each proved unsatisfactory; one, he said, lasted but a single day: "She said, 'I'm not gonna be able to work for you if you're gonna quibble about every little bit of punctuation in a letter.' I said, 'Well there's a solution to that.' She said, 'What's that?' I said, 'You came *in* through a door—'"

In the mid-1990s, Art hired as personal assistant a young man named Larry Rose to work in an office at the Newbury Park house seven hours a day, five days a week. He would be with Shaw for eleven years. "I didn't really know what I was getting into," Rose later said with a smile. "He was not an easy man to work for. But he was never mean. He would get angry, and he could be insulting, but he was never malicious, not once. But sometimes the anger would not be because of something that I did; it was because of a conversation with the attorney, or with the accountant, or something he was upset about that he didn't have any control over right at that moment and he needed to vent. And there I was. That happened. And he could really rattle your cage. There were many times when I had to really tie the knot and hang on, and keep repeating to myself: 'Mortgage. Mortgage. Mortgage.'

"He had very high expectations, and he expected you to think like he did, which was difficult. Sometimes we clashed on the particulars of how a letter should be structured, or how a filing should be done. And one particular moment, I almost walked out. I was trying to explain to him how the satellite cable-box remote control worked. Trying to explain electronics to this man, or anything related to a computer, was a Herculean task. I can't begin to find the words to describe how difficult it was, and I've been told by many people, long before I met Artie, that I have the patience of a saint. I used to be a schoolteacher. So I'm trying with all the patience I can muster, to help Artie understand how this device works. And he's just not getting it. We're on probably the tenth attempt, of me going back to square one, and he having to try it himself—well he screws up step two, and then it doesn't work. Then you're trying to explain why he screwed up step two, and he's not understanding that, and it just snowballs, and we're both getting frustrated, and he says to me, 'Well you must not have been a very good *teacher*.' You know. And I came *that* close to just opening the door, walking out, getting in my car, and leaving. But I didn't. And finally I said, 'You know, I'm too frustrated with this right now, and I don't think we're going to make any progress with this, so can we just switch to something else.' And he agreed: 'Yeah, I think that's a good idea.' And that's how we survived."

After about a year and a half, though, Rose said, he was considering that if the right opportunity presented itself, he might leave the challenging service of Artie Shaw. But then something happened that made the whole idea moot: "It would have been a rather cheesy thing to do, if I were to have bailed at that point. He fell and broke his leg. It just turned his whole world upside-down."

KAY PICK remembered how it came about: starting in the Viper Room, a Sunset Strip club that had been the site of actor River Phoenix's death by drug overdose. "Kurt Elling was singing there," Kay said, "and he was a friend of Johnny Depp," who was considering portraying Artie Shaw in a movie, "so Artie wanted to hear him. So me, Artie, and Elliott Kastner," Art's movie producer friend, "a rather strange grouping for that place, all went to the Viper Room. And Artie's telling us he's going to get a German shepherd. I said, 'Get a *small* dog, Artie.' Elliott said, 'Don't get *any* kind of an effing dog.' Artie paid no attention to either of us."

Art had had dogs in the past and loved them as loyal companions. He recalled one such mastiff acquired by chance in his band-leading days, around 1950. "I went out in the alley, back of a theater in the black ghetto, for a smoke between shows," he said. "There were all kinds of people around, and kids playing—and there was this dog there. Wonderful dog, he looked at you; he just had a *manner* about him. One of the kids says, 'Oh, that's Dickie Davis.' Of the *dog*! I said, 'Dickie *Davis*?' 'Yeh, his name is Dickie, and he belongs with the Davis family.' 'Think I could buy him?' 'Well,' the kid says, 'it'll *cost* you.'" Art held up an open hand to show all fingers. "*Five dollars* I paid. Which was a *lot*, then. Took the dog home to my farm, where he lived happily. Until—" Art gave an embarrassed chuckle. "He was shot for a woodchuck."

Another canine Art had adored was an English sheepdog named Chester, whom he nicknamed Chaucer. Artie got Chester/Chaucer as a birthday present from friends, Joanne Lupton said: "He was just the most lovable dog in the whole world. That dog was like a *person*. Actually it was a lot *nicer* than a lotta people; it was a great dog. I was crazy about that dog. And when we were breaking up, he said, 'I own that dog; that dog is *my* dog. If you go, the dog stays with me.' Well, that was probably the hardest thing about leaving—was leaving the dog!"

In time, Chester/Chaucer died. Shaw never thought of getting another canine—until years later, when he heard on the radio of a kennel where German shepherds were practically being given away. "A hundred bucks," he said. "All you had to do was come pick one up. I thought it would be nice to have a German shepherd around the place. So I drove all the way to heck out there, past Glendale—and one dog there sort of stood out from the pack. I wanted *that* one. Took it home. First night, I put it on a leash to take it for a walk. It's a big dog, I hadn't realized. When the dog pulled ahead, I had to jump. Anyhow, we're walking, and this other dog jumps out of nowhere, barking; my dog takes off after it. I got tangled in the leash, fell—broke my femur. Then the dog came and—bonded with me! Crouched by me, wouldn't let anyone else come near. Finally someone from animal services comes with a noose harness, slips it over the dog's neck, pulls it away. I was rescued. I didn't ask what became of the dog."

For a while, using a cane, Art continued to travel and give talks at various gatherings. More and more, though, people came to him in Newbury Park, to hear what he had to say about the twentieth-century sights and sounds he had been a part of. "He was a master storyteller," Larry Rose said. Shaw had a fine opportunity to exercise that skill when director Ken Burns and his film crew visited Newbury Park early in 1998 to interview him for the PBS-TV documentary-series *Jazz*. Several commentators would single out Art's onscreen segment as one of the documentary's highlights.

A more extensive set of interviews was conducted with Shaw later in the year by Ted Hallock, a Peabody Award–winning Oregon broadcaster, ex-state senator, former *Down Beat* associate editor, and longtime Artie Shaw fan.

Hallock first crossed paths with Shaw in Detroit in early 1942, when he snapped a backstage picture of Lee Castaldo shaking hands to commemorate resuming possession of his own orchestra from Shaw—"this hostile, handsome man," in Hallock's recollection. Fifty-five years later, Berman's documentary (which he may have seen during its brief run on cable TV) rekindled Hallock's Shaw fascination. "That film really pissed me off," he said, "'cause the man she dealt with—one almost wouldn't have known he was even a *musician*, let alone that he was a great clarinet player. I said to my wife, 'Who the hell *is* he? What *is* he?' And she said, 'Why don't you find out?'" The seventy-seven-year-old Hallock secured some Oregon foundation money (to combine with his own funds), and Shaw agreed to be interviewed. Hallock and a technician came to Newbury Park in May.

"It started with, 'Be careful of where you put your things on the coffee table,' literally," Hallock said. "And, 'Don't ask me a question when your eyes are on a book.' Dictating terms, and getting *me*, intellectually, in his *sites*. His ego edge is always there: he is making God damn sure you know who is in charge, and I think with one intellectual hand behind him is brushing his trail to make sure that there are no footprints."

Hallock persisted through twenty-two hours of raw tape, later edited into a thirteen-hour series, *The Mystery of Artie Shaw*, which ran on several public radio stations and three times on the CBC. "It's a sort of a music worshiper's guide to Artie Shaw, that does not have the depth about the man that I hoped to have," Hallock said, "nor has anything else that I've ever read about him, by the way. It was a positive experience, yes, but from my standpoint I guess disheartening. I dunno what I wanted: my hero to ride in on his charger, and go off into the sunset, and I would have uncovered—I don't know what I was after. Uncovering the secret of his clarinet playing was impossible; that was uniquely his. But I thought I could get something intellectually more out of his mind than I did.

"His favorite clichés are, 'Watch what you dream for, you may *get* it'—which he *had*, and then it turns to dross in his hands. Then the other thing is, 'No matter what it is, you're never going to play it adequately,' and so forth. But the final thing about him is that absolutely he's got to have been the most selfish man that ever lived. So you've got this enormously narcissistic man in a cocoon, who is quite happy. There's no *tragedy*, I *guess*—other than for some of the women, and the two sons."

As Hallock completed editing each episode, he sent it to Shaw for Art's verification and approval. Shaw's only objections had to do with the few other interviews Hallock conducted with people who had worked with Art. One of these, singer Imogen Lynn, recounted the time Art's mother came onstage in 1945, Hallock said: "The thrust of her anecdote was that he'd been just *brutal* in his language toward his mother, telling her to get the *fuck* off the stage, and *what* are you doing and how *dare* you, blah blah blah. Well, he came apart when he heard this portion; and for the first and only time since we talked—he was on the telephone, but he was almost literally on his knees begging me, imploring me, to take this out: 'What *good* will it do?' he said—not at all saying, I never spoke this way to my mother. So—like a fool, or like a human being, I took it out."

After a year and a half, the project was completed. "One day he says, 'I admire your persistence.' I thought, Oh my God—the Congressional Medal of Honor! And at the end, he said, 'Well that was pretty good— wasn't it?' I said, 'Well—' And he said, 'Yeah; I know what you mean.' Near as we got to accolades."

CHAPTER FIFTY-SIX

Don't Take Your Love from Me

T HE YEAR 2000 SAW publication of Vladimir Simosko's *Artie Shaw: A Musical Biography and Discography*, an intensely researched work that marked the culmination of its author's lifelong interest in his subject. "I had fallen in love with his music as a kid," said Simosko, a scholar born in Pittsburgh who became curator of the Institute of Jazz Studies at Rutgers and then music librarian at the University of Manitoba. "I had *The Pied Piper* records when I was a preschooler; I used to play them as a child, in the late '40s. Much later, when I became interested in taking up the clarinet, it was immediately obvious to me that Artie was just in another dimension, musically: the tonal color of his horn, the fluidity of his style. So at that point I began collecting and really studying, and that evolved into my entire interest in music; I wound up teaching jazz history, and so forth. At the time I was working for the Institute of Jazz Studies at Rutgers in the late '60s and beginning of the '70s, my first published jazz article was on Artie's Gramercy 5 for the Institute of Jazz Studies' journal. And in the process of working on it, I felt that I had a good excuse to actually bug Artie! I called him up; at that time he had Artixo Productions in New York City. We talked on the phone; he gave me a lot of information. I mentioned I would like to do a full-scale musical biography documenting his entire musical career;

he said, well, get something together and we'll talk about it. Well, what with marriages and divorces and kids and moving up to Canada, it took me a while, but I finally did get it together, and I contacted him. By then he was in California, and nearly twenty years had passed; it broke the ice when I said, 'At least you have to admit I haven't been bugging you in the interim!' He enjoyed that. So he invited me down. Twice I visited him for over a week, going over the book to make sure there were no terrible mistakes. We really hit it off, frankly; we talked about everything under the sun. I was very flattered: he actually called me at work a couple of times, to ask me kind of tricky questions about the era of his own career! So, we had a lot of fun. Yeah, I really really enjoyed knowing Artie."

Also that year, there were significant Shaw appreciations just before his ninetieth birthday, on the arts pages of the *New York Times* and the *Wall Street Journal*, and, right after, in the *Los Angeles Times Magazine* and the *Boston Globe*.

The press attention generated further contacts. Pianist Marian McPartland, English-born host of National Public Radio's long-running *Piano Jazz* program, said, "I was looking through the *Wall Street Journal*, which I don't usually do; there was a picture of Artie Shaw at ninety, and I read the piece, and I thought, 'Boy, he would make a great guest for *Piano Jazz*.'" McPartland had been a Shaw fan since her adolescence in England, she said: "'Frenesi,' I *loved* that tune; I'd sit down and play it on the piano." In 1953, in Manhattan, she had caught a glimpse of Art onstage at the Embers with his Gramercy 5: "Jimmy, my husband—McPartland—and I went over there, and the place was so crowded, we stood at the entrance to the club; we couldn't really get in. And that was actually my only time of seeing him live: you know, handsome guy with the band all around him. Of course I knew all those guys."

Now, in mid-2000, McPartland called Shaw, who was pleasant if maybe not much aware of the pianist's award-winning radio series. The two agreed to meet for lunch when McPartland visited California. He came to pick her up at her hotel in the San Fernando Valley, driving his Prius and wearing a jaunty cap. McPartland found him easy to be friends with. "We talked about all kinds of things. He kind of demurred a little bit about [doing] *Piano Jazz*. I said, well maybe you'd like it to be something like, uhm, 'The Artie Shaw Special,' something like that? And that seemed to go down well with him. And we—said goodbye. It's funny, he leaned over and gave me a big kiss, which I—sort of really wasn't expecting. He just was very *sweet*." The events of September 11, 2001, and Shaw's later illnesses forced cancellations of dates they made to tape a show. Eventually, McPartland, with the assistance of Richard Sudhalter, assembled a Shaw *Piano Jazz* episode using Art's prerecorded comments.

RCA Victor missed its chance to put out a significant Artie Shaw release in time for his ninetieth, but the label made up for it soon after, proposing a CD boxed-set to be supervised by Orrin Keepnews, the highly regarded producer and reissue master who had already worked with Shaw a couple of years earlier to assemble a single disc of what Art thought were some of his *Personal Best* RCA Victor tracks. This new package, *Self Portrait*, would extend that concept to cover five discs of a multilabel career retrospective: ninety-five tracks, with a booklet of notes largely written by Art himself.

"I *told* him," Keepnews said, "that when I was growing up, if you were at all interested in popular music, it became necessary to make that choice, you couldn't equivocate. You had to be *for* Artie Shaw or *for* Benny Goodman, and I felt very pleased that I had made that original decision to be an Artie Shaw person."

Artie and Orrin did a lot of long-distance telephoning, and Keepnews came to California to work with Shaw in person. "I did some *prodding* with him, here and there," Keepnews said, "but fundamentally, the idea was, *he* was making the repertoire choices. You know, I got a kick out of *that*. There is *no* comparable circumstance, working on sessions involving pre-tape material, of having the *artist* to work with; that was the one and *only* occasion. I mean, he is definitely one of the few artists who lived into his own reissue period! I had a wonderful time with him."

The two assembled a superb treasure box of Shaw material, including some fine Brunswick sides, the cream of RCA's material, and several roof-raising airchecks. There were Musicraft gems, eleven numbers by the 1949 band, the MCA "These Foolish Things" with Shaw's extraordinary cadenza, and more than an entire disc's worth of music from the 1953–54 Gramercy 5 (issued in 1992 on the independent MusicMasters label but since fallen out of circulation). At last, fifty-eight years after Art paid to record what he thought was the best music he'd ever made, a major record label vindicated his belief in its ultimate worth. It seemed especially apt that RCA's Bluebird, home of Shaw's first "Begin the Beguine" triumph, would be giving its imprimatur to his final masterwork.

Keepnews and Shaw went to lunch one day, near Newbury Park. "I remember my tremendous trepidation over the fact that *he* was driving," Keepnews said, "but actually, I hope I'm as good a driver at ninety as he was. And our waitress must have been about eighteen or something, and at the end of the meal, she came back over and said to him, 'Are you Artie *Shaw*?' And he said, 'Well I *was* when I came *in*.' And so she proceeded to tell him that when she was growing up, her *grandmother* had all of his records! He wasn't too happy with *that* aspect of it, but he was very gracious and friendly, and he asked her her name. She said her name was Amber. And he said, 'Oh, one of my *wives* wrote that!' She didn't know what the hell he was talkin' about. *Forever Amber* was not in her knowledge."

ART'S LEFT LEG had never quite healed—he had a herniated disc, which pinched a nerve in his spinal column—making it necessary to use a cane. Then, in early 2001, he got sick and was hospitalized for two months. "He had a very bad case of pneumonia," Larry Rose said. "Almost died." Once home, Shaw needed much more care and attention. "He always had this habit of offering me a carrot, you know," Rose said. "'Well you'll be well taken care of when this is all over.' 'Well, Artie, don't worry about that; I'm not going to abandon you. You're payin' me a salary, and I'll do whatever you need me to do.' But—I think he was afraid that it'd be too much for somebody, and they'd just walk."

Kay Pick, alarmed by Art's state, called Shaw's son Jonathan, now forty-seven, and told him of his father's condition. "Jonathan showed up," Larry Rose said, "and he made an effort to develop a relationship with his dad. And I really have to give Artie credit: he made a very genuine effort to do that."

By the fall of 2001, when *Self Portrait* came out (and made "best-of-the-year" lists from the *New York Times* to the *Economist*), Art was once more giving at-home interviews. By January 2002, he was again attending public events such as the International Association for Jazz Education's annual conference in Long Beach, where Shaw sat onstage and spoke to a capacity crowd for ninety minutes, then autographed every *Self Portrait* box purchased. "Louis [Armstrong] started it," he told the jazz educators. "He was the first guy who played what you could call present-day kind of jazz. He took a tune and did things with it. And the first time I ever heard him . . . it made such an impression on me that I thought, 'This is God.' This wasn't a man. Louis became God for me."

"I loved hearing those stories," said movie producer Elliott Kastner, who saw Shaw often at Newbury Park. "Fabulous stuff, that I enjoyed so much—'cause he was *there*. Going backstage to see Louis in Chicago, in the '30s, you know? Poked his head in, and he saw Louis sitting there with that stocking, you know how they used to wear, over their head? And, braid it. And he said, 'Oh Louis loved to write, he was always at the typewriter, you know?' So he gave me this visual of Louis sitting there with the stocking cap, you know, pecking away at some Underwood, and he said, 'Hey Pops, what's up?' And Louis swings his head around, looks, and he says, 'White folks, are still in the lead.' I mean, lotsa stuff like that, that I enjoyed, that he told me. I mean he was there in 1938, in Musso Frank's, having lunch with Bing Crosby. . . . I mean, Artie was a treat! It was stimulating; it was like listening to good music. I loved him, I just loved him; the guy, to me, was so interesting. He was *gigantic*."

Not that Kastner wasn't aware of Shaw's faults and failings. "He was very arrogant. And offensive. But I loved him. Even though I was resentful, or didn't like him because of his selfish posture, and his unwillingness to admit that he was an asshole at times—I still was so attracted to him. What can I tell you."

Art would have liked for Elliott to produce a feature film on his life, Kastner said: "He was too proud to really ask me directly, so it was always planting seeds: encouraging me to meet with *this* screenwriter and *that* director, and I met with these people. And I just never said, 'Okay Artie, let's make a deal.'"

The main reason for Kastner's hesitation was his involvement with another project he was already trying to develop about the early days of white jazz: "I had this wonderful, delicious screenplay called 'Hot Men,' of two guys in their late twenties: one couldn't read music, and smoked dope and drank and cursed; and the other guy didn't smoke or drink, and of course he read music—and that was Benny Goodman; and the other guy was Gene Krupa. Which I was gonna *make*, about twenty years ago, with Nick Cage and Matthew Modine, and I had a train wreck with their agent, I attacked him physically. . . . Anyway . . . You know I could never *mention* it to Artie, because, you know, I just thought—I had better—I just never *did*. That's why I felt so un-*comfortable*; because I had this screenplay, that I had *commissioned*, actually, and *loved* it. And I probably never went *back* to it, out of deference to Artie. You know: how could I *do* this, to my friend? It's true!"

IN LOS ANGELES, at eighty-five, Ray Conniff died.

In Pittsburgh, at seventy-six, Dodo Marmarosa died.

In Newbury Park, at ninety-two, Shaw talked to his son Jonathan about his own father, Harold, and about wounds that never went away and scars that never healed. "I think to myself in bed," he said, "'I'm ninety-fucking-two years old.' My father died at fifty—that prick. He had no use for me. . . . He gave me the contempt I had, that eventually made me quit the music business. It wasn't a manly thing to do, to go up there and—blow a horn in front of a lotta people. In the deepest sense, he gave me that; that's what his heritage was, with me. I'd-a stayed in the business if I'd any respect for it; 'cause he gave me that *contempt*. I think,

'If you were around now, you *prick*—and see the letters and the honors that I get, and the amount of people that have been influenced by what I do'—you know, I would say, '*Up* your *ass*.'

"But—I was a kid. He left when I was . . . thirteen or fourteen. . . . He and my mother, fighting to the point where I used to *cringe*, under the—Thought he was gonna come and kill her, and *me*! . . . What a way to live. It's a wonder I didn't get to be an alcoholic. I found the horn; that saved my life. That really saved my life."

But to what end? Art admitted that after a lifetime of living, reading, and thinking, he still hadn't a clue. "What is life about, what is it all about? It's a big joke. Like the man said: 'There's only three things: God, human folly, and laughter. And since the first two pass our comprehension, let's do the best we can with the third.' . . . I don't know a damn thing. I don't know what it's about. The longer I live, the more mysterious it all is."

CHAPTER FIFTY-SEVEN

Long Ago and Far Away

S*ELF PORTRAIT* WAS nominated for two Grammy Awards in 2003, one for Art's liner notes. Shaw's boxed-set didn't win either prize, but Shaw had the satisfaction of being the only nominee in the "Best Historical Album" category to still be alive.

The iconic rhythm-and-blues soul singer and pianist Ray Charles included Shaw's "Star Dust" in his *Artist's Choice* CD compiled in the spring of 2003 for Hear Music, a line sold at Starbucks stores; "I mean, it makes you want to cry, man, so much feeling in that thing," Charles said of Art's 1940 recording. He told music executive and historian Joe Smith, "Ever since I was a kid Artie Shaw was someone I loved. Everybody used to be excited about Benny Goodman. I'm not saying he wasn't great, but Artie Shaw had so much feeling in his notes. Every note you could feel in his heart. Artie Shaw was one of the greatest musicians that ever lived."

"Ray Charles came out to meet me one time," Shaw said in Newbury Park. "Yeah he was all *over* me. What a guy! 'Why aren't you *playin'*, man?' He was sittin' there, practically in my *lap*. I played him some Glenn Gould, he wasn't impressed; I mean, he didn't seem to be *listening* very hard. I said, 'Listen to this guy.'. . . Certain pieces Glenn Gould plays, swing like a bat outa hell. . . . Charles himself can swing like hell, sometimes."

A few days after Art's ninety-third birthday, Kathleen Winsor died, in

Manhattan, aged eighty-three. Carol Marcus Saroyan Matthau died in July, at seventy-eight. Benny Carter died at ninety-five.

And, despite his formidable energy, Art's own health was in decline. "He had adult-onset diabetes for many years," Rose said. "He was on a lot of medication to keep his blood sugar under control, but he just ate whatever the hell he felt like. He'd test his blood sugar, but it didn't mean anything to him; it was just a number. 'If it's over that number, okay that's not good but—wadya gonna do about it.' 'Well, Artie, you don't drink the orange juice, and you don't eat the pasta.' He just waved his hand at me, like, aah, you're fulla shit. You know. So, that got very frustrating. Finally, the doctor said, 'Let him eat what he wants; it's not gonna change anything, at this point.'"

Other headstrong behavior worsened matters. "He didn't listen to the physical therapists," Rose said. "They told him specifically, 'Don't sit on a recliner. You need to stretch out on a bed, to make sure that your muscles and your hip don't lock into a bent position and you're not able to stand up straight and walk properly.' Well of course—Artie knows better than anybody else, about anything, and so he slept in his recliner, 'cause he felt *safe* there. So then when he *would* try and walk, he couldn't straighten up. And he blamed everything on the doctor. . . . He just wasn't willing to do the physical work it would have taken to have corrected everything, or at least made it better. And that got him, in the end; his muscles atrophied, and he just got weaker and weaker and weaker."

But Art rallied one morning in August 2003 for a car trip to nearby Westlake Village. There a wheelchair-bound Shaw received the James Smithson Bicentennial Medal for his "lifetime achievement and contribution to American culture and music," and Shaw donated to the Smithsonian Institution two clarinets with which it was said he had recorded his final Gramercy 5 sessions (a Buffet) and his 1938 hit "Begin the Beguine" (a Selmer).

"This is lagniappe," Art said in thanks for his medal, which he termed "a sort of significant honor." When a questioner asked what was so special about the Selmer clarinet with which he had recorded "Beguine," Shaw answered, "Nothing is special about it. It was *me*."

. . .

"ARTIE WAS probably the most egocentric person I've ever known," his son Jonathan said. "Artie was so full of rationalization that he felt it necessary to tell the same stories over and over and over and over again, to whoever would listen: radio talk shows, interviewers, biographers, friends, acquaintances, gas station attendants. It was 'The Artie Shaw Show,' here it *comes*—and you could never get *beyond* that with him, *never*. There was never any *dialogue*, with Artie; always a monologue. I don't think he was really very interested in what you were thinking or feeling, and if you offered a different point of perspective to the stories—'Well you know Artie, there's two ways of lookin' at that'—he'd just be like, 'Aw, you're fulla shit!' He just—cut you right off, 'cause he felt threatened. You know.

"Artie was *defeated* by his intelligence—in the sense of somebody who seeks to find some peace of mind in a world that's full of apparent injustice and hardship and trouble. He couldn't see that there's a higher point of perspective to all these slings and arrows of life; he didn't have the ability to sort of shift gears and get out of himself, so that he could see that maybe there's more things on heaven and earth than he dreamed of in his philosophy. And that made him a deeply unhappy man, and unable to find the sort of comfort that, you know, religious people find, because—he'd seen the ugly side of that *too*, you know, and he figured, well, religion is for chumps; religion is for—weaklings.

"Artie didn't love anything or anybody, because he didn't have that in his character; he was un-*able*. It's not his *fault*. He was a prisoner of his intellect, and you can't find love through the mind. 'Cause *all* he *wanted* was love. And the closest he could come to that was in the music. 'Cause he felt himself to be so alone, and so apart from humanity. He was abandoned and cast aside as a little child, and he had to make his *way*. He was—

"Just like me.

"Artie was unable to see that he had any accountability in fathering children and just—walkin' away. To him, that was a perfectly natural state of affairs. Because that's what *his* father did. That's what his father *taught* him. So that's what he taught *me*. And when I said I don't think that was a very good lesson, I think I'm gonna go the other way—to find this son of mine, and make myself accountable, and say 'I'm sorry I abandoned you, I'm here now, how can I be of service to you?'—he became furious. That's . . . when we had our big falling-out.

"'Cause we were gettin' along pretty good there. There was a point at which we were really bonding. And God forgive me—maybe one of the reasons that he got so pissed off at me for goin' back to Brazil to find this son of mine was because I think there was a part of him sayin', 'What, you're just gonna *leave* me here, now that we've gotten close? Now you're just gonna—go off and leave me, like a stranger?' When actually what I was doing was going to redeem myself, *him*, his father . . .

"Yeah, after all those years of therapy, all those books he read, and all those conversations he had with other intelligent people—I think his ultimate failure was his inability to forgive his father. Therefore he was unable to receive the forgiveness of his son that was handed to him on a silver platter. . . . So he justified himself as having been the victim of all these—harms and hurts, that he couldn't possibly forgive or excuse. Well, that's the tragedy of his life: that he was unable to give or receive love—because he'd never been given any love, as a kid.

"Music is what intervened. That was the saving grace, for Artie. He made beautiful music. He made beautiful art. He was redeemed by his talent and his drive, and his obsession; I mean, it's noble. He was born to lose, and he lived to *win*. And you know, that's—to his credit."

"THE LAST YEAR," Larry Rose said, "he pretty much didn't do anything but just sit in that chair. And sleep. You know, he'd get up to have a meal, but then towards the end, he wouldn't even get out of the chair to do that.

"It was the diabetes that caused the macular degeneration, which caused the eyesight to go. That's what really did him in, is when he lost his eyesight and couldn't read; that was kind of the last straw."

"Good thing my mind is stocked," Art told a visitor in the spring of 2004, "otherwise I'd go nuts. I can't read. Not even big print. I barely can see your face; it's a blur. Well—what are you gonna do? That's what it is. You take the horse you're given, and ride it. I'll be ninety-four next month. I feel—great. But the outward symptoms are not good.

"What I do now is mostly just—I look up at the ceiling and I think, 'Why is there something instead of nothing?' It'd be very easy for there to be nothing. Why are there so many things? And who did it? How did it come about? You can't say 'evolution,' for the universe—although it might be. Makes one wonder.

"What do I think about? Oh, all sorts of things. Old songs, and how they came to be. 'Why did he write it that way?' There are no answers, you know. People tell you there's an answer; there isn't.

"Asked Jerry Kern one time, why a tune he wrote called 'Long Ago and Far Away'—nice song—" He hummed it. "That low note: in the key of C, that would be an F. I said, 'Why not a G? With everything that followed—why not?' He looked up. He said, 'It sounded better.'

"Words, when you write a book. 'Why did you say it this way, and not that way?' It's just—one big hodge-podge."

He had abandoned his long novel-manuscript at last, he said—sent it off to an editor-friend in New York, to do with what she could. "I didn't finish it; I took him up to a certain place—and left him there. It's as good a pausing place as any, but it wasn't the end. It was the beginning of his emancipation from the problems of livelihood; he had a band, he was just starting—and the world was open to him. He knew it wasn't right, it wasn't right—but the people—Ah, it's a complicated story.

"You write a *long* book, it takes a commitment of time and purpose; you gotta clear the decks, at least I do. I can't work part-time. If I'm gonna do a book, I have to sit down and say, 'I've got a year and a half, and that's what I'm gonna do.' That hasn't happened. I couldn't get the time clear, to sit down and do the whole thing. I recognized how long it would take, and I couldn't do it. The old line of, 'Life is too much with him.' Life got in the way. Couldn't beat that."

But he had sketched out the book's ending, long ago: "Guy's in Spain, many years later. He's been writing books, and he's writing a book about the arachnidan, and among them, he comes across a thing called the rectangular spider. It's a spider that makes a rectangle, roughly;

then it takes the corners, and joins them—radii—and more radii—more radii—and when it's through, it's constructed a web, which is the way it makes its living: like a fisherman. And anything that flies into that, sticks to it. Makes it cunning.

"When you think about it—for an unrational creature to *do*, that's a pretty amazing feat. So—my guy, writing about this, says, 'We could be sitting even an inch from that spider, watching it work—and it has no conception you're *there*.' And as my guy writes this, he thinks to himself, 'What is sitting watching *me*, while I'm doing the equivalent of making my *own* web?' It's an eerie thought; he never gets over it.

"So maybe that's what we mean, when we say 'God.'"

Unnerved by cosmic-sized thoughts, Shaw retreated to his lifelong contemplation of the self.

"You take what's given, and you make what you can out of it. I was given a sense of music. But that was a gift. Had nothin' to do with where I went with it. I didn't know I was gonna become one of the so-called immortals, in that field. Had no *intention*. I knew I had to be better. Had to be better, better, better. It always could be better.

"When I quit, it was because I knew I couldn't do any better. I did some things with that small group—I mean, Jesus, I ain't gonna do any better; that's *it*. So when you get to that, and you put in all this *effort* to *do* that, and you say, 'This is fucking hard *work*, man—and I've already *done* it; why do *more*?' 'Cause you were only gonna *repeat* yourself. There was a limit, the audience would not accept any more than that, and you don't have an audience, you can't pay your band. You can't pay your band: forget it. So you can have all the ideas in the world, but the last band I had, in '49—I couldn't keep that.

"So, where did it come from? I dunno. Where does anything we do come from? We manufacture it. Where does the spider's silk come from? That's the spider's destiny, to do that.

"But it was *honest work*, you know.

"Writing is the same. Writing, I've never given it a fair shake. That takes, you know, sitting down on your butt—and working at it. But I had too many other things, by that time, interfering with my life:

personal problems. Women I married, thinking that could make some sense. I sure picked 'em. I decided the best thing to do is walk away; you can't talk to them."

"AT HEART, he was really a nice guy," Larry Rose said. "I think he was just—lonely. I think he kept hoping there'd be that—someone, that he never seemed to be able to find."

"HOW LONG have you been together, you and your wife?" he asked a visitor one day.

"About twenty years," came the answer.

"And, do you—care for one another?"

"Well—sure."

"Oh—" Arthur made a sound between a sigh and a sob. "That is so—beautiful," he said. He almost reached out and touched the man.

"I WENT OUT to see him, with Kay Pick," Geoff Miller said. "He had just heard about Joey Bushkin dying," on November 3, 2004, in Santa Barbara, at the age of almost eighty-eight. "You know he never acknowledged anyone's passing, whether it was Ava, or—But he said, 'I can't imagine a world without Joey Bushkin on piano.' And for him to have even acknowledged someone passing from the scene was so unlike him, you just knew it was a different Artie."

"Around Thanksgiving," Rose said, "he really became despondent, and—just the indignities of all of it. . . . Finally I knew he'd reached a point where he was going to give up. . . . He just sat and looked out into space and said, 'I don't know what to do.'

"We ordered in-home hospice care the next day. He was having a lot of pain in his right leg—his right hip and right thigh—and he had some swelling in his right knee. We know he had arthritis in his right leg. But he refused to go to the hospital to allow anybody to examine his leg further; in no uncertain terms, he didn't *ever* want to go back into a hospital. So I ordered the hospice care. And that helped a lot, to make him more comfortable.

"He had a sense of humor, right up to the end. At one point, Pattie [Porter, Artie's caregiver] and I were changing his bedclothes, which is difficult, and painful for him, but—we'd try and get him through it as best we could, and after one episode, Pattie leaned down to him and said, 'Are you comfortable?' And without skippin' a beat, he looked up at her with a grin and he said"—the old Myron Cohen line—"'I make a living.'

"I thought he was gonna hold on for a while longer, if not rebound completely. We had on the calendar to get things in place, as far as finances and whatnot. And he went suddenly. Thursday morning [December 30, 2004,], Pattie called me and says, 'I can't get a pulse.'"

Artie Shaw, king of the clarinet, dead at ninety-four.

YEARS AGO, he had written his own epitaph: "He did the best he could with the materials at hand." Later he rewrote it: "Go away." Still later, he said this was his final life statement: "Leave things a little better than you found them."

As death approached, Shaw claimed to know what his final words would be, when the end came at last and he gazed on whatever lay beyond:

"Oh."

FOUND AMONG Art Shaw's papers after his death was a letter from Herb Caen, written six years after Caen cut Shaw's feelings to the quick with his taunt about Benny Goodman. In 1992, Shaw sent Caen the new CDs of his 1953–54 Gramercy 5 tracks, and in return received the written response he had sought, a simple admission: Herb Caen did indeed agree that Artie Shaw's last recordings represented the ultimate and unsurpassable end-point of jazz clarinet-playing.

Acknowledgments

INTERVIEWS

I am grateful to the many people who agreed to be interviewed in person or by telephone or (in a few cases) email.

Artie Shaw was good enough to speak with me for many hours, in the course of several interviews and visits with him between 1990 and 2004.

Al Gallodoro shared his memories of seeing Art Shaw with Roger Wolfe Kahn's band in New Orleans, in 1932, and of later encounters.

Buddy Morrow and Zeke Zarchy told of playing with Art Shaw and His Orchestra of 1936 and 1937. George Avakian remembered what it was like to see and hear that band in person.

Bea Wain recalled her 1937 recording session with Art Shaw and His New Music.

Tony Pastor Jr. talked at length and with warmth of his father's close association with Artie Shaw, which reached its professional apogee in Shaw's orchestra of 1938 and 1939. Joseph Tauro told wonderful stories of seeing that band's members in informal circumstances. Jack Klugman described Artie Shaw and Billie Holiday performing in Wildwood, New Jersey, in 1938 as if it were yesterday. Jerry Wexler, Noni Bernardi, Bill Finegan, Van Alexander, Dr. Paul Tanner, James T. Maher, and Lee Young added further perspective on the swing era.

Diana Cary recalled Artie Shaw's sojourns in Hollywood in 1939 and 1940. Paula Fox remembered a glittering Hollywood party where Artie Shaw and his new bride were the talk of the town. Jane Yolen was surprised to learn her father, Will, had been friends with Artie Shaw.

Benny Carter remembered a record session he did with Shaw in the summer of 1941.

Paul Cohen and Ralph Rosenlund revisited their happy tenures with Shaw's 1944–45 band.

Buddy DeFranco afforded insight into Artie Shaw's achievements and frustrations as a great American popular artist.

Albert Murray verified the high regard in which Shaw was held by African-American musicians and listeners.

Lewis Erenberg, Victor Navasky, Norman Corwin, Bella Stander, and Norman Lloyd helped describe Art's social and political spheres in the mid-twentieth century.

Michael Goldfarb expanded on themes developed in his excellent NPR program, *Jews and Blues*.

Sophia Rosoff brought a pianist's sensitivity to her descriptions of Art's classical studies and doings circa 1948 and 1949. Dr. Colter Rule shed much light on Shaw's behavior in those and later years.

Danny Bank and Sonny Russo reminisced about life on the road with "The Artistry of Artie Shaw and his Orchestra" in late 1949, and Jon Raney added things said by his father, Jimmy. George Russell and Johnny Mandel told what it was like to write for that band.

Eddie Bert and Sonny Russo helped document Art's brief 1950 big band.

William F. Lee told the unknown story of "Artie Shaw's All-Stars" from later that year.

The singer Don Cherry had only good things to say about making Decca records with Art in the early 1950s. Bill Holcombe also shared memories of Decca sessions he did for Shaw. Bones Howe, Billy James, and Don Asher shed light on the 1950s jazz scene.

Dr. Billy Taylor with erudition and wit spun the saga of Artie Shaw's problematic 1950 gig at a club called Iceland.

Sue Carson remembered her theater date with Artie in London in 1951.

Dr. Nicholas Johnson explained how his father, Wendell, helped Artie edit the manuscript of *The Trouble with Cinderella*.

Hank Jones, Irv Kluger, and Joe Roland gave vivid pictures of being three-sixths of the 1953–1954 version of Artie Shaw and his Gramercy 5.

Jonathan Shaw was courageous in exploring his relationship with his father, and generous in sharing recordings he made of conversations with Art.

Stan Irwin brought Artie Shaw's Las Vegas engagements to life.

Nat Hentoff, Ira Gitler, Joe Goldberg, Mike Zwerin, Dan Morgenstern, Richard Sudhalter, Charles Champlin, David Kamp, Mark Cantor, Doug McIntyre, Al Martinez, and Whitney Balliett described how it was for journalists, broadcasters, critics, and archivists to deal with Shaw. William Claxton spoke of taking Art's photograph.

Lee Konitz, Phil Woods, Bud Shank, Buddy Colette, and Dave Pell attested to Art's influence on a later generation of reed players.

Jeff Walker passed along stories of his parents' and others'.interactions with Artie in the 1950s.

Red Buttons and Jerry Lewis each had sharp observations to make about Art.

Frederic Morton, Carol Southern, Elliott Kastner, Kay Pick, Jean Bach, Dr. Dan Geeting, Geoff Miller, Kathryn Miller, Barnaby Conrad, and Marian McPartland described the pleasures and challenges of being friends with Artie Shaw. Annie Dillard remembered her brief correspondence with Art.

Dr. Joanne Lupton was good enough to speak at length of the fun and pain of living with Art Shaw. Evelyn Keyes shared a few stories about Shaw in 1990, on the occasion of his eightieth birthday.

Daryl Sherman, Peter Levinson, Jan Curran, and Bill Curtis were there when Art once more took a band on the road in the 1980s.

Vladimir Simosko, the kindest of scholars, went out of his way to assist a fellow biographer, in addition to telling what it was like to write a book about Artie Shaw.

Aram Saroyan spoke of trying to write a book with Artie Shaw. John Daniel talked about publishing a book by Artie Shaw. Ted Hallock recounted his adventures making an Artie Shaw radio documentary.

Orrin Keepnews, Teo Macero, and Michael Bloom each had pertinent things to say about various Shaw reissue projects.

Ruth Price recalled Art's frequent visits to the Jazz Bakery.

Loren Schoenberg had the unique experience of being friendly with Artie Shaw while also serving as Benny Goodman's assistant.

Larry Rose, Artie's personal assistant, spoke about Shaw with candor and affection.

Not every person named above is quoted, but I treasure each one's contribution.

INSTITUTIONS AND INDIVIDUALS

Copies of articles, correspondence, documents, and sound recordings were provided for research purposes by Millersville University, California Lutheran University, the New York Historical Society, the Thomas Jefferson Library at the University of Missouri, the Hamilton Jazz Archive at Hamilton College, the Department of Special Collections in the Stanford University Libraries, Archives & Special Collections of the Ganser Library at Millersville University, the Harry Ransom Center at the University of Texas, the Manuscripts and Archives Division of the New York Public Library, the Boston Globe Library, and the Margaret Herrick Library at the Academy of Motion Pictures Arts and Sciences.

Ryan Maloney, at the Institute of Jazz Studies at Rutgers University, located much interesting Shaw-related material. Tad Hershorn there was a godsend and a lifesaver.

Rhonda Green, at the Cleveland Research Center of the Cleveland Public Library, found several fine items regarding Shaw's days in Ohio.

Isabel Cymerman discovered vital documentation on the lives of Arthur, Sarah, and Harold Arshawsky.

Keith Pawlak, music curator of the Artie Shaw Collection at the University of Arizona, explained some intricacies of Art's orchestra arrangements.

The Artie Shaw Collection, created by Shaw in his lifetime, contains the bulk of his several bands' books: the scores used by his orchestras from 1936 through the early 1950s. Administered by the School of Music at the University of Arizona, the archive also includes a considerable assortment of Shaw business documents, professional and personal photographs, and career memorabilia. It is an essential resource for all Shaw scholars. Its finding guide is online at www.library.arizona.edu/speccoll/search/az_manuscript/s-t.html.

My greatest thanks, as before, goes to Mary Rousson, whose inspired and diligent research uncovered great things no one knew existed.

The music libraries at USC, UCLA, UC Santa Barbara, the Brand Library, and the Los Angeles Public Library, and the libraries at UC Irvine and Hebrew Union College were invaluable resources.

Special gratitude to Mary Alice Wollam and the staff at the Casa Verdugo branch of the Glendale Public Library.

Loretta Weingel-Fidel continues to be the best and nicest agent anyone's ever met.

Amy Cherry at Norton was this author's excellent and ideal editor.

Her assistants, Erica Stern and Laura Romain, made the production process a pleasure.

Mary Babcock expertly copyedited the manuscript.

Ed Ezor, Artie Shaw's friend and executor, was generous in assisting this work into print.

Barbara Watkins and Bobb Lynes went beyond the call of friendship in transferring and preserving key material. Dave Amaral sent radio interviews I'd never heard.

Brad Riesau and Diana Nazareth at DL Media put me in touch with two of the legendary players who worked or were friends with Art.

The actor and author Hank Jones, Ida Giragossian, Marty Meyers, Annette Meyers, Nancy Coble Damon, Joan Long Sweeney, Kathryn and Geoff Miller, Jerre Lloyd, Todd Everett, Richard Layman, Jim Fusilli, Dick Lochte, and Larry Dietz all encouraged me at crucial times.

My wife, Mary, makes writing possible and life worth living.

The late Peter Levinson urged me to start chronicling Artie in 1990. I wish he could read this.

Joe Goldberg said: "It's a necessary book."

Nick Meyer said: "You were born for this one."

Peggy Mims said: "Artie Shaw—how cool!"

Artie Shaw, after reading my biography of Ross Macdonald, said: "You'd do for *me* what you did for *him*?"

Yes.

═══ Notes ═══

Page   **PREFACE**

xiv   a lifetime supply of semi-aliases: "Arthur Arshawsky" was his given name, "Art Shaw" his first professional identification; a friend nicknamed him "Sid Shawfellow"; when he hit it big overnight in 1938, *Variety* dubbed him "Mr. Cinderella"; in the New York phonebook, he used the name "Arthur J. Shaw"; he sometimes signed hotel registers as "Arthur Sanders"; in France, where his name sounded like the word for artichoke, he was known as "Artichaut"; in Spain, where he lived in the 1950s, they pronounced "Artie Shaw" as "Artixo"; "James Braddock" was a *nom de plume* he wanted to use on a book (prizefighter Jim Braddock, who came up quick in the 1930s at the same time Shaw did, was dubbed "the Cinderella Man"); "Albie Snow" was the Shaw-like character in the novel Art worked on for years; "A Shaw" was a later-years telephone listing.

xiv   "with ice water in his veins": Peter Levinson to Tom Nolan, 2006.

xiv   "He was like a prism": Tony Pastor Jr. to TN, 2006.

xiv   from P. G. Wodehouse to Thomas Pynchon, Jack Kerouac to Philip Roth: P. G. Wodehouse, *The Mating Season* (1949); Thomas Pynchon, *Vineland* (1990); Jack Kerouac notebook entry, 1950 (re "summer of 1941"), *Windblown World: The Journals of Jack Kerouac* (2004); Philip Roth, *The Human Stain* (2000).

xv "Every time you write a letter": Artie Shaw to Tom Nolan, from interviews and conversations between 1990 and 2004.

CHAPTER 1: AVENUE C

1 "I don't know how old": Artie Shaw to Jonathan Shaw, from conversations recorded in 2002.

3 "There's somethin' to be said": AS to JS.

3 "Sick unto death": AS to TN, from interviews and conversations between 1990 and 2004.

3 "My mother was a plodder": Ibid.

4 "There was a little girl": AS to JS.

4 "Go on home and say": Artie Shaw, *The Trouble with Cinderella: An Outline of Identity* (Farrar, Straus and Young, 1952), p. 33.

4 "Nobody'd ever seen one before": AS to TN.

5 "I didn't think he knew": AS to JS.

5 "As a boy": Colby Driessens, "Elm City Newsboy Now King of Swing," *New Haven Register*, January 29, 1939.

6 "Mom": AS to TN.

6 "I had dreams": AS to JS.

CHAPTER 2: DREAMY MELODY

8 "Open hand": AS to JS.

8 "average": New Haven High School records, Arthur Arshawsky, 1923–26.

9 "You gotta walk": Larry Rose to TN, 2006.

9 "Five dollars": AS to TN.

9 "I remember him": AS to JS.

10 "I used to *cringe*": Ibid.

10 "He had to be": Ibid.

11 "Every night": Tony Pastor, "Artie Shaw Used to Carry My Saxophone Case: He's One of the Most Misunderstood Guys in the World," *Music and Rhythm*, March 1941.

11 "As 'Arthur Arshawsky'": AS to TN.

11 "I was nobody": Kristine McKenna, "Altered Chords: Artie Shaw on Music, God, Sex & Fame," *LA Weekly*, November 12–18, 1999.

11 "The nuances of playing": AS to JS.

12 "'In Prohibition'": Ibid.

13 "Thought the thumb": AS to TN.

14 "We drove out": Karl Fleming and Anne Taylor Fleming, *The First Time* (Simon and Schuster, 1975), pp. 267–268.

15 "When you heard him": AS to John McNally, *Castaway's Choice*, KCRW-FM (Santa Monica, CA), 1984.

15 "When he blew into that band": "The Semantics of Jazz: A Symposium," California Lutheran University, September 12, 1987.

CHAPTER 3: I'M SITTING ON TOP OF THE WORLD

17   "He was a bug": Bill Dvorak, "Artie Now Is 'Jitter' King," Cleveland newspaper clipping, March 30, 1939.

17   "It wasn't long": Ibid.

18   "Fletcher had *no* band": AS to TN.

18   "Coleman Hawkins was so taken": Rex Stewart, *Jazz Masters of the Thirties* (Macmillan, 1972), p. 82.

19   "BIX COMING TO CLEVELAND": *Cleveland Press*, December 2, 1927.

20   "The first time": Fleming and Fleming, *First Time*, p. 268.

20   "a funny-looking gent": Whitney Balliett, "Bright Unison Clarinets," in *Barney, Bradley, and Max: 16 Portraits in Jazz* (Oxford University Press, 1989), p. 85.

21   "Although I had only": Shaw, *Trouble with Cinderella*, p. 148.

21   "She was like a *leech*": AS to TN.

21   "Oh yeah!": AS to JS.

22   "I never thought": AS to TN.

CHAPTER 4: WHY WAS I BORN?

23   "We'd play records": AS to TN.

24   "He practiced things": Balliett, "Bright Unison Clarinets," p. 85.

24   "He called me Shawfellow": AS to TN.

25   "I couldn't believe my ears": AS to Doug McIntyre, *Red-Eye Radio*, KABC-AM (Los Angeles, CA), February 15, 2003.

25   "They were the best there was": AS to McKenna, "Altered Chords."

25   "I couldn't make": AS to TN.

26   "Just for the hell of it": Shaw, *Trouble with Cinderella*, p. 128.

26   "Jesus": AS to Ted Hallock, *The Mystery of Artie Shaw* (radio documentary made possible in part through funding by the Meyer Memorial Trust), 1998.

27   "He couldn't believe": AS to JS.

CHAPTER 5: THE GIRL FRIEND

29   "He would go": Theodore Dreiser, *The "Genius"* (Boni and Liveright, 1923), p. 96.

30   "He was a good player": AS to TN.

30   "I heard some music": Hallock, *Mystery of Artie Shaw*.

31   "I couldn't make myself *feel*": Shaw, *Trouble with Cinderella*, pp. 210–12.

32   "Shaw's car struck and killed": "Car Kills Man, Pair Held," *New York Times*, October 16, 1930.

33   "I came around a corner": AS to JS.

34   "I was the only white guy in the place": AS interview in 2000, in *Willie the Lion* (television documentary produced and directed by Marc Fields), 2002, available at www.njn.net/arts/williethelion/transcripts.html.

34   "He had a peculiar way": AS to JS.

Notes

34 "First time I heard him play": AS interview, in *Willie the Lion*.

35 "We got to know each other pretty well": AS to JS.

35 "Willie was my open-sesame": AS interview, in *Willie the Lion*.

36 "He is a good blues-man": Willie the Lion Smith, with George Hoefer, *Music on My Mind: The Memoirs of an American Pianist* (Doubleday, 1964), p. 169.

36 "He didn't know that I was Jewish": AS interview, in *Willie the Lion*.

CHAPTER 6: JUST ONE MORE CHANCE

38 "He was sweating out": Geoff Miller to TN, 2006.

38 "He'd come up for sessions": AS to TN.

39 "Tommy and Jimmy took turns": Peter J. Levinson, *Tommy Dorsey: Livin' in a Great Big Way* (Da Capo, 2005), pp. 41–42.

39 "He was telling me": LR to TN.

39 "I remember being": AS to TN.

41 "Bing was an enormous influence": Gary Giddins, *Bing Crosby: A Pocketful of Dreams, The Early Years 1903–1940* (Little, Brown, 2001), p. 265.

41 "See all those windows": Shaw, *Trouble with Cinderella*, pp. 250–51.

41 "They used the best": Vladimir Simosko, *Artie Shaw: A Musical Biography and Discography* (Scarecrow, 243), p. 31.

43 "breadlines stretching": Pee Wee Erwin, as told to Warren W. Vaché, Sr., *Pee Wee Erwin: This Horn for Hire* (Scarecrow/Institute of Jazz Studies, 1987), p. 76.

43 "And I met him!": AS to JS.

43 "One": AS to TN.

CHAPTER 7: A DESERTED FARM

44 "John Coffee": AS to JS.

45 "*Theory of the Leisure Class*": AS to TN. See also Ross Wetzsteon, *Republic of Dreams: Greenwich Village: The American Bohemia, 1910–1960* (Simon and Schuster, 2002), p. 383.

46 Polish-Russian: Late in life, Shaw (with no proof but his own intuition) came to think his father's people were of Polish origin, from Warsaw, and that "Arshawsky" was a corruption of "Warshawsky"—"of Warsaw." AS to TN.

47 "I used to play lead alto": AS to TN.

51 "Shaw and Teddy Wilson": John Hammond, with Irving Townsend, *John Hammond on Record: An Autobiography* (Ridge Press/Summit, 1977), p. 127.

CHAPTER 8: BROADWAY RHYTHM

52 "Dick was okay": AS to TN.

53 "Artie . . .": Arnold Shaw, *The Street That Never Slept: New York's Fabled 52d St.* (Coward, McCann and Geoghegan, 1971); reprinted as *52nd Street: The Street of Jazz* (Da Capo, 1977).

53 "And I was not *known*": AS to TN.

53 "Hey Mac": See Levinson, *Tommy Dorsey*, p. 62.

54 "She hadda choose": AS to JS.
54 "That was a real marriage": AS to TN.

CHAPTER 9: THERE'S SOMETHING IN THE AIR

58 "He brought it down": *Piano Jazz*, National Public Radio, 1991.
59 "We went up sometimes": Chip Deffaa, *In the Mainstream: 18 Portraits in Jazz* (Scarecrow/Institute of Jazz Studies, 1992), pp. 71–72.
59 "Just for some relaxation": Artie Shaw, "I Don't Like Saxophones!" *Melody Maker*, January 23, 1937.
60 "A stillion bucks": Wingy Manone and Paul Vandervoort II, *Trumpet on the Wing* (Doubleday, 1948), p. 124.
60 "I was terrified": Richard M. Sudhalter, *Lost Chords: White Musicians and Their Contribution to Jazz 1915–1945* (Oxford University Press, 1999), p. 577.
60 "an essay in contrasts": Ibid., p. 577.
61 "Artie Shaw and his string swing ensemble": "'Jitter-Bugs' Thrill at N.Y. Jam-Session," *Down Beat*, June 1936.

CHAPTER 10: NO REGRETS

63 "She had a voice": AS to JS.
64 "Most people": AS to TN.
65 "I just wrote": Rod Soar, "Artie Shaw Update," *Jazz Journal International*, November 1987.
65 "It sounded kind of nightmarish": AS to McIntyre, *Red-Eye Radio*, KABC.
65 "It *reached* me": Nat Hentoff to TN, 2006.
65 "The *hazan*": Nat Hentoff, "My Debt to Artie Shaw," *Jazz Times*, April 2005, available at http://jazztimes.com/articles/15595-my-debt-to-artie-shaw.
65 "I rushed": NH to TN.
66 "Artie and his boys": Mel Adams, "Artie Shaw: Top Band of the Future," *Swing*, November 1938.

CHAPTER 11: IT AIN'T RIGHT

67 "I'm a singer": Gerold Frank, *Judy* (Harper and Row, 1975) p. 92.
67 "When we went through": Zeke Zarchy to TN, 2006.
68 "I gave up": Buddy Morrow to TN, 2006.
69 "I remember standing": AS to TN.
69 "I was never so nervous": Shaw, "I Don't Like Saxophones!"
70 "I wanted to play": Sudhalter, booklet notes, *Best of Big Bands: Artie Shaw*, Columbia Legacy, 1993.
70 "Goodman came along": AS to TN.
70 "That was a wonderful band": George Avakian to TN, 2006.
70 "We played a noon session": ZZ to TN.
71 "To be a *good guy*": AS to JS.
71 "I told Artie": ZZ to TN.

72   "Monkey see": AS to JS.

72   "I'm gonna get": Buddy Morrow to TN, 2006.

CHAPTER 12: I GOT RHYTHM

74   "I was a wild man": Shaw, *Trouble with Cinderella*, p. 333.

75   "He could *allude* to notes": AS to TN.

76   "Artie would wear two hats": TP to TN.

78   "[T]he people that hired": Sheila Tracy, *Bands, Booze and Broads* (Mainstream, 1995), pp. 230–31.

CHAPTER 13: IF IT'S THE LAST THING I DO

79   "He talked": Max Kaminsky, with V. E. Hughes, *My Life in Jazz* (Harper and Row, 1963), pp. 95–96.

80   "Wasn't a big romance": Bea Wain to TN, 2006.

80   "I didn't like singers": "Star Dust" (episode two), *Soundtrack of the Century*, American Public Television / BBC Worldwide Americas, 2004.

81   "What he did": BW to TN.

82   "When he hit Boston": Max Jones, "Youngsters of the '30s," *Melody Maker*, January 30, 1954.

82   "He gave us one thousand dollars": Simosko, *Artie Shaw*, p. 58.

82   "It meant two broadcasts a week": Jones, "Youngsters of the '30s."

82   "He listened to a rehearsal of my band": Hallock, *Mystery of Artie Shaw*.

83   "I got in the car": Simosko, *Artie Shaw*, p. 58.

84   "I gave her a record": AS to TN.

84   "[T]hose college students": Count Basie, as told to Albert Murray, *Good Morning Blues: The Autobiography of Count Basie* (Random House, 1985), p. 204.

84   "the new Shaw-Holiday combo": J. F. Considine, "Boston's Back Bay Rockin' Solid," *Metronome*, May 1938.

84   "One night [Art] asked": *The Swing Era* (Time-Life Records, 1971).

86   a stinging piece in *Down Beat*: George Frazier, "Should Shaw Tell Pluggers to Go to Hell?," *Down Beat*, May 1938.

86   "Art Shaw will keep": "On the Upbeat," *Variety*, May 4, 1938.

86   "I went to a record store": John Best interview by Monk Rowe, February 15, 1998, Hamilton College Jazz Archive, Clinton, NY.

87   "The band was on the stand": Warren W. Vaché, "Best on the Bandstand," in *Jazz Gentry: Aristocrats of the Music World* (Scarecrow, 1999), p. 17.

CHAPTER 14: GREEN KEY JUMP

88   "Billie Holiday was singing": Cliff Leeman interview by Milt Hinton, Jazz Oral History Project, 1979, Institute of Jazz Studies, Rutgers, State University of New Jersey, Newark, NJ.

88 "the greatest attraction of the month": J. F. Considine, "Swing Shakes Bay State," *Metronome,* June 1938.

89 "The mob howled": Bernie Woods, "Outdoor Swing Carnival Developed Oddities; Addicts Finally Got Tired," *Variety,* June 1, 1938.

90 "Dad and he": TP to TN.

90 "I was a seven- or eight-year-old kid": Joseph Tauro to TN, 2006.

90 "If you've got": Holiday, with Dufty, *Lady Sings the Blues,* pp. 73–74.

90 "She was very nice": JT to TN.

91 "She was sen-*sational!*": Jack Klugman to TN, 2003.

91 "It wasn't like": Hallock, *Mystery of Artie Shaw.*

CHAPTER 15: BEGIN THE BEGUINE

93 "a complete waste of time": Shaw, *Trouble with Cinderella,* pp. 333–34.

93 "Why throw in": Cole Porter, quoted in David Grafton, *Red, Hot & Rich!: An Oral History of Cole Porter* (Stein and Day, 1987), p. 98. "The only critic who mentioned it was Robert Benchley, who said, 'Why throw in just another rumba?'"

93 jotted in a notebook: William McBrien, *Cole Porter: A Biography* (Alfred A. Knopf, 1998), p. 188.

93 "the longest popular song": Alec Wilder, edited by James T. Maher, *American Popular Song: The Great Innovations, 1900–1950* (Oxford University Press, 1972), p. 240.

93 "By 1938": *The Swing Era* (Time-Life Records).

93 "It all started": Burt Korall, liner notes, *The Complete Artie Shaw, Vol. I, 1938–1939* (Bluebird, 1976).

94 "One day at a rehearsal": Kaminsky, with Hughes, *My Life in Jazz,* p. 101.

94 "Jerry Gray scored": Leeman interview.

94 "Everyone wants": Simosko, *Artie Shaw,* p. 63.

94 "We rehearsed it": *The Swing Era* (Time-Life Records).

95 "He's . . . amazing": Holiday, with Dufty, *Lady Sings the Blues,* pp. 71–73.

96 "Especially in the South": Donald Clarke, *Wishing on the Moon: The Life and Times of Billie Holiday* (Viking, 1994), p. 145.

96 "Holding back nothing": "Artie Shaw Collapses in Swing Battle," *Metronome,* October 1938.

97 "That was the beginning of the end": AS to TN.

CHAPTER 16: NON-STOP FLIGHT

99 "And [when] we left town": Leeman interview.

100 "It was very funny": Clarke, *Wishing on the Moon,* p. 143.

100 "[I]n the middle": Leeman interview.

100 "What is 'Begin the Beguine'?": AS to TN.

101 "I don't know why": Ibid.

101 "Porter was pleased": William McBrien, *Cole Porter: A Biography* (Alfred A. Knopf, 1998), p. 188.

CHAPTER 17: INDIAN LOVE CALL

102 "We followed him": BW to TN.

102 "Benny took me": Ross Firestone, *Swing, Swing, Swing: The Life & Times of Benny Goodman* (W. W Norton, 1993), p. 233.

103 "Jazz was the big thing": Albert Murray to TN, 2006.

103 "That's when they came": Leeman interview.

103 "He hadn't been there": Jones, "Youngsters of the '30s."

103 "A lot of people": Helen Forrest, with Bill Libby, *I Had the Craziest Dream* (Coward, McCann & Geoghegan, 1982), p. 59.

104 "She quit because": AS to JS.

104 "The woman who ran": Ibid.

104 "There aren't many": Holiday, with Dufty, *Lady Sings the Blues*, p. 81.

105 "Buddy provided a spark": Burt Korall, liner notes, *The Complete Artie Shaw, Vol. III, 1939–1940* (Bluebird, 1978).

105 "a classic stand": John Dunning, *On the Air: The Encyclopedia of Old-Time Radio* (Oxford University Press, 1998), p. 448.

106 "His blends": Abel Green, "Paul Whiteman's 8th Jazzique Rally Gala; Six 'First Performances,'" *Variety*, December 28, 1938.

106 "He's not here!": Paul Whiteman, 2-CD *Carnegie Hall Concert: December 25, 1938* (Nostalgia Arts, 2005).

106 "Did you ever": AS to TN.

CHAPTER 18: KING FOR A DAY

107 "I felt as if": John McDonough, "Artie Shaw: Nonstop Flight from 1938," *Down Beat*, January 22, 1970.

108 "I went there": AS to TN.

109 "It followed": Forrest with Libby, *I Had the Craziest Dream*, p. 61.

110 "that snake eyes": Sudhalter, *Lost Chords*, p. 503.

110 "The one I wish": AS to TN.

110 "You'd ask him": Ibid.

111 *"Abee gesunt"*: Carleton Smith, "On the Record," *Esquire*, October 1939.

111 "Every time we went into the ['Nightmare'] theme": Mel Tormé, *Traps, the Drum Wonder: The Life of Buddy Rich* (Oxford University Press, 1991), p. 44.

111 "At the Shubert": "Jitterbugs in Jersey," *Time*, March 6, 1939.

111 "If Goodman": Bernie Woods, "Battle of the Killer-Dillers in New'k All This Week; Goodman vs. Shaw," *Variety*, February 22, 1939.

112 "Rivalry": "Goodman, Shaw Battle to Swing Draw!" *Metronome*, March 1939.

112 "When Benny played": AS to TN.

112 "a number guaranteed": *Melody and Madness* broadcast, issued in part on Jazz Guild 1007 (date unknown).

CHAPTER 19: ONE FOOT IN THE GROOVE

115 "something about one chance": Shaw, "Music Is a Business."

115 "I can't even keep": Babette Rosmond, *Robert Benchley: His Life and Good Times* (Doubleday, 1970), p. 197.

115 "The one-night stands": Artie Shaw, with Bob Maxwell, "Music Is a Business," *Saturday Evening Post*, December 2, 1939.

117 "I respected her": AS to JS.

117 "violent": Lupton A. Wilkinson, "Fame Is Fun for Judy," *Los Angeles Times*, October 8, 1939.

117 "You could live out where there were trees": AS to TN.

118 "I never had mike-fright": "Artie Shaw, Young Man with a Woodwind," *Boston Globe*, August 19, 1939.

118 "Artie was despised": Lana Turner, *Lana: The Lady, the Legend, the Truth* (Dutton, 1982), p. 48.

118 "I'm pretty awful": "Hedda Hopper's Hollywood," *Los Angeles Times*, July 27, 1939.

118 "All these great chicks": AS to JS.

118 "She had the most": AS to TN.

119 "ready cash": Diana Serra Cary, *Jackie Coogan: The World's Boy King* (Scarecrow Press, 2003), pp. 183–184.

119 "She called": AS to TN.

120 "I'll tell you": Joe Smith, *Off the Record: An Oral History of Popular Music* (Warner, 1990), p. 22.

120 "cocky": Bob Bach in *Metronome*, quoted by George T. Simon, *The Big Bands* (Macmillan, 1967), p. 404.

120 "Oh, he was": AS to TN.

120 "I've gone as far": Clarissa Start, "New King of Swing," *St. Louis Post-Dispatch*, August 8, 1939.

CHAPTER 20: NIGHTMARE

121 "But the crowd": Robert Lewis Taylor, "Middle-Aged Man Without a Horn," *The New Yorker*, May 19, 1962.

122 "they went wild!": Erno Rossi, *Crystal Beach: The Good Old Days* (Seventy Seven Publishing, 2005), pp. 44–45.

123 "shorter and heavier": "Weary Artie Shaw's First Thought Is for Betty Grable," *Cleveland Press*, September 8, 1939.

123 "We met one time": AS to TN.

123 "estranged wife": "Weary Artie Shaw's First Thought."

123 "No, we're not": Ibid.

123 "I don't like the damned music business": Michel Mok, "A Band Leader THINKS," *New York Post*, September 26, 1939.

124 "I meant the ones": "'I Still Don't Like Jitterbugs,'" *Metronome*, November 1939.

124 "The show was built": Ibid

124 "He asked us": "'Glad to Release Shaw'—Agency," *Metronome*, November 1939.

124 "Why don't you?": "Betty Grable Returns to Push Divorce from Jackie Coogan," *Los Angeles Times*, October 9, 1939.

125 "We are just friends": Ibid.

125 "He comes in": AS to TN.

125 "I can't marry": Sidney Skolsky, "David Niven of Movies Is Offered a Column," *New York Post*, October 12, 1939.

125 "That time": Dave Dexter Jr., "Artie Shaw Fed Up with Music Racket," *Down Beat*, October 15, 1939.

126 "It's funny": Henry Duckham, "A Masterclass with Artie Shaw," *Clarinet*, Spring 1985.

126 "Big star": AS to JS.

126 "Stop!": AS to TN.

127 "made under duress": "Oberstein Sues Artie Shaw Who Claims 'Duress,'" *Variety*, November 1, 1939.

127 "The band's morale": "'I Still Don't Like Jitterbugs.'"

127 "With me": AS to TN.

127 "I thought": Ibid.

128 "I realized": Gary Giddins, "Shaw 'Nuff," *Village Voice*, February 4, 1992.

128 "So that's why": AS to TN.

129 "At the stage": Shaw, *Trouble with Cinderella*, p. 351.

129 "When we finished": Forrest with Libby, *I Had the Craziest Dream*, p. 89.

129 "If I stay": Ibid., p. 90–91.

129 "When Shaw broke up": JT to TN.

130 "I took it": Forrest with Libby, *I Had the Craziest Dream*, p. 95.

130 "It was like": *The Swing Era* (Time–Life Records).

130 "go away": "Artie Shaw, Heedless of Fame, Coin, Walks Out on His Own Orchestra," *Variety*, November 22, 1939.

130 "It was a bitch": Forrest with Libby, *I Had the Craziest Dream*, p. 64.

130 "The crew is billed": Strand opening-night review, *Billboard*, September 30, 1939. Cited by Simosko, *Artie Shaw*, p. 78.

130 "There we were": Korall, *Complete Artie Shaw, Vol. III* (Bluebird LP), 1978.

CHAPTER 21: OVER THE RAINBOW

131 "Artie Shaw, Jivist": "Artie Shaw, Jivist, Will Do Comeback as String Dance Band," *Variety*, November 29, 1939.

132 "Mr. Shaw, it was said": "Band Leader Quits Because of Illness," *New York Times*, November 22, 1939.

132 "It was a big surprise": JT to TN.

132 "Artie Shaw Saves Girl from Death": *Down Beat*, February 1, 1940, p. 1.

132 "I could have bought": AS to TN.

132 "Any commentary": B. R. Crisler, "News and Comment in a Quiet Week," *New York Times*, November 26, 1939.

133 "He didn't have": AS to TN.

134   "If only he'd ask": Gerold Frank, *Judy* (Harper and Row, 1975), p. 143.

134   "[Artie] complained": Phil Silvers, with Robert Saffron, *This Laugh Is on Me: The Phil Silvers Story* (Prentice-Hall, 1973), p 104.

135   "because she might": Silvers with Saffron, *This Laugh Is on Me*, p. 104.

135   "He was always afraid": Jan Curran to TN, 2006.

135   "Artie built": Turner, *Lana*, p. 42.

136   "It was a dare": AS to TN.

136   "I married": Ibid.

136   "It was destined": Turner, *Lana*, p. 50.

137   "There I was": Corinna Honan, "Fame? No Way, I'm Going to Live a Bit Longer," *London Daily Telegraph*, January 1, 2005.

137   "I had never heard": Turner, *Lana*, pp. 51–52.

137   "I never *touched*": AS to TN.

137   "She wasn't": AS to TN.

CHAPTER 22: SUMMIT RIDGE DRIVE

139   "Oh I believe": AS to McIntyre, *Red-Eye Radio*, KABC.

140   "We thought": AS to TN.

141   "Look, baby": Inez Robb, "Mrs. Artie Shaw Sees the Ghetto," International News Service, *Cleveland Plain Dealer*, March 30, 1940.

141   "I think he was": Colter Rule to TN.

142   "Her mother": AS to JS.

143   "He doesn't want Lana": "Hedda Hopper's Hollywood," *Los Angeles Times*, April 10, 1940.

143   "It was one of the first": JT to TN.

143   "[Benny] says": Jerry Jerome interview by Monk Rowe, April 12, 1996, Hamilton College Jazz Archive, Clinton, NY.

144   "By the third day": Turner, *Lana*, p. 55.

144   "Lana used to": AS to TN.

145   "Clean up": Turner, *Lana*, p. 59.

145   "He told me": JC to TN.

145   "We lived": Turner, *Lana*, p. 55–56.

145   "I saw marriage": Honan, "Fame?"

146   "Won't you please": Frederick C. Othman, "Swing Man Artie Left by Lana, or Is He?," *Cleveland Press*, July 2, 1940.

146   "one of the wildest-eyed interviews": Frederick C. Othman, "Lana Turner, Artie Shaw Swing Apart," United Press, July 1, 1940.

146   "I'll *never* forgive him": Turner, *Lana*, p. 63.

146   stole Artie Shaw's best clarinet: Cheryl Crane, "Lana Turner & Artie Shaw: A Brief Interlude Atop Coldwater Canyon for the Actress and the Bandleader," *Architectural Digest*, March 2006. Lana's daughter Cheryl Crane wrote that Turner "got away with his prized clarinet, which sits proudly on my bar today."

CHAPTER 23: IN THE MOOD

147 "Artie managed": Ted Toll, "Chicago Jumps Again after Too Many Weeks of Quiet," *Down Beat*, August 1, 1940.

147 "Glenn doesn't even count": AS to TN.

148 "But finally": Ibid.

149 "How could it not be": Jerome interview.

149 "I said, 'Artie'": *Piano Jazz*, National Public Radio.

149 "with Butterfield's muted trumpet": Simosko, *Artie Shaw*, p. 89.

150 "Everything was made": Alan Littlejohn, "Billy Butterfield," *Jazz Journal International*, February 1985.

150 "The group was": Korall, *Complete Artie Shaw, Volume III* (Bluebird).

150 " [T]he way he used": Littlejohn, "Butterfield."

151 "It's the Saturday tea": Herb Caen, "What Is San Francisco?," *San Francisco Chronicle*, October 22, 1940.

151 "one of those remarkable": Herb Caen, "Days of Our Years," *San Francisco Chronicle*, May 16, 1995.

151 "the two men often": Lawrence Lee and Barry Gifford, *Saroyan: A Biography* (Harper and Row, 1984), p. 71.

152 "I think I paid": AS to TN.

152 "People ask me": AS to JS.

152 "I loved painting": Hallock, *Mystery of Artie Shaw*.

153 "But I don't use": AS to TN. See also Levinson, *Tommy Dorsey*, p. 136.

154 "His chorus on 'Star Dust'": Terry Gibbs, with Cary Ginell, *Good Vibes: A Life in Jazz* (Scarecrow, 2003), p. 37.

154 "It's the greatest": Whitney Balliett, "A Difficult Instrument," in *Barney, Bradley, and Max: 16 Portraits in Jazz* (Oxford University Press, 1989), p. 196.

155 "Certain things": AS to TN.

155 "I'm not gettin'": Ibid.

CHAPTER 24: CONCERTO FOR CLARINET

157 "A well-known clarinet player": Artie Shaw, booklet notes, "Good Enough Ain't Good Enough," *Self Portrait* (Bluebird/BMG, 2001).

157 "The Frances Neal–Artie Shaw twosome": Jack Egan, "Duck Draft, Wind Up in Panama!" *Down Beat*, November 1, 1940.

158 "I recall at Christmas": Burt Korall, liner notes, *The Complete Artie Shaw, Vol. IV, 1940–1941* (Bluebird, 1980).

158 "Christmas, I was playing": AS to TN.

158 "There was a masculine intensity": Yvonne De Carlo, with Doug Warren, *Yvonne: An Autobiography* (St. Martin's, 1987), p. 59.

159 "My music is still solid": William Brennan, "Artie Shaw Is Now a Symphonic Sender," *New York World-Telegram*, February [14], 1941.

160 "a combination": Inez Robb, "F. D. Jr.—'He's Dynamite, a Junior Farley'—Is One

of 10 Dream Prince–Glamour Boys," International News Service, *Washington Post*, April 8, 1941.

160 "it's a great big disappointment": George Frazier, "Benny's New Band Is Too Much Like Benny's Old Band," *Down Beat*, March 15, 1941.

160 "Goodman no longer": Dave Dexter Jr., "K.C. Jazz Album Rated as Best of Current Wax Releases," *Down Beat*, May 1, 1941.

160 "Benny used to edit": Firestone, *Swing, Swing, Swing*, p. 263.

161 "pastor-ized swing": Bill Gottlieb, "Swing Sessions," *Washington Post*, May 18, 1941.

161 "Benny Goodman once confided": Ibid.

CHAPTER 25: THIS TIME THE DREAM'S ON ME

162 "Lena was the type": AS to TN.

163 "Shaw's current inspiration": Jimmie Fidler, "Jimmie Fidler in Hollywood," *Los Angeles Times*, August 27, 1941. See also Fidler's column, same paper, September 5, 1941.

163 "a really sensational biscuit": Dave Dexter Jr., "20 Inches of Shaw Blues Pace New Record Output," *Down Beat*, June 15, 1941.

164 "Artie's a little more": Peter Vacher, "Nick Fatool: The Good Life," in *Soloists and Sidemen: American Jazz Stories* (Northway [London], 2004), p. 166.

164 "Watching him": Dave Dexter Jr., "'$1,164,166 Talent' in Shaw Band," *Down Beat*, September 1, 1941.

164 "[Shaw] has assembled": George Frazier, "Frazier's Thumbs Go Up for New Shaw Band," *Down Beat*, September 15, 1941.

166 "I think it was in Kansas": Ray Coniff interview with Chris Popa in 1983, quoted in Michael P. Zirpolo, "Artie Shaw and his Symphonic Swing—1941 (Part Two)," *IAJRC Journal*, Summer 1998.

167 "Hot Lips Page was playing": AS to TN.

167 "I liked Lana": Simosko, *Artie Shaw*, pp. 91–92.

168 "I had a friend": AS to TN.

168 "I never married": Honan, "Fame?"

168 "I introduced": AS to TN.

168 "I've been looking": Earl Wilson, "Artie Shaw Back, Same as Ever," *New York Post*, August 4, 1941.

CHAPTER 26: SOMEONE'S ROCKING MY DREAMBOAT

170 "I went back": Terry Gross, *Fresh Air*, National Public Radio, 1985.

171 "It's not a question of making": Paul Eduard Miller, "'String Music Helps . . . Keep Our Sanity!' says Artie Shaw," *Music and Rhythm*, December 1941.

171 "[W]e were doing": Kaminsky with Hughes, *My Life in Jazz*, p. 127.

172 "One night Mother and Lee": Carol Matthau, *Among the Porcupines* (Random House, 1992), pp. 17–18.

173   "We quickly became": Lena Horne and Richard Schickel, *Lena* (Doubleday, 1965), pp. 125–26.

173   "They have our blessings": "Jerome Kern's Daughter Is Married to Artie Shaw," *New York Times*, March 4, 1942.

174   "She called me": "Hedda Hopper's Hollywood," *Los Angeles Times*, May 5, 1942.

174   "This isn't a fancy-pants job": Mike Levin, "'This Is No Fancy Pants Job!,' Says Artie Shaw," *Down Beat*, May 1, 1942.

174   "Shaw had cleared": "Shaw, O. Tucker Will Join Navy, Others Called," *Down Beat*, May 15, 1942.

174   "I went in": Gross, *Fresh Air*, National Public Radio.

175   "I had a breakdown": Ibid.

CHAPTER 27: I ASK THE STARS

176   "They'll get you": Taylor, "Middle-Aged Man."

176   "He *begged* me": AS to TN.

177   "I was the leader": Ibid.

178   "Since it was night": Kaminsky, with Hughes, *My Life in Jazz*, p. 143.

178   "We hitch-hiked": Mike Daniels, "Musician of the Year," *Metronome*, January 1944.

179   "I was the lowest": Taylor, "Middle-Aged Man."

179   "Sometimes we'd be set up": Simosko, *Artie Shaw*, p. 102.

179   "The idea was": Daniels, "Musician of the Year."

180   "We were on this battleship": Art Hodes and Chadwick Hansen, eds., *Selections from the Gutter: Jazz Portraits from "The Jazz Record"* (University of California Press, 1977), p. 190.

180   signed a pact: See Charles Davis Jr., "Benefit to Aid Widow of Famous Trumpeter," *Los Angeles Times*, November 15, 1964.

180   "I just took off walking": AS to TN.

180   "A few days later": Taylor, "Middle-Aged Man."

181   "After we got down": United States House of Representatives, Hearings before the Committee on Un-American Activities, Eighty-third Congress, First Session, Investigation of Communist Activities in the New York Area—Part 1, "Testimony of Artie Shaw, Accompanied by His Counsel Andrew D. Weinberger," May 4, 1953.

181   "While Kiwi dads": "Diary," *Wellington* (New Zealand) *Dominion*, January 5, 1999.

182   "[H]e was a natural target": Kaminsky, with Hughes, *My Life in Jazz*, p. 139.

182   "Only one": AS to TN.

CHAPTER 28: DEARLY BELOVED

183   "[There] a guy": Lee and Gifford, *Saroyan*, p. 108.

184   "For him": Daniels, "Musician of the Year."

184   "I couldn't do anything": AS to TN.

184   "a virtuoso": Gerold Bordman, *Jerome Kern: His Life and Music* (Oxford University Press, 1980), p. 378.

184   "wide-ranging and probing": Ibid., pp. 390–91.

184   "Artie told me": Steve Jordan, *Rhythm Man: Fifty Years in Jazz* (University of Michigan Press, 1991), p. 37.

185   "It was all too much": McKenna, "Altered Chords."

185   "I rented a car": Hearings before the Committee on Un-American Activities, "Testimony of Artie Shaw."

185   "I guess I had": Barry Ulanov, "Shaw in '44," *Metronome*, September 1944.

186   "Very *hard* to say": AS to JS.

186   "without warning": "Composer's Daughter Divorces Artie Shaw," *Los Angeles Times*, September 29, 1944.

186   "I wanted to be": AS to JS.

CHAPTER 29: JUMPIN' ON THE MERRY-GO-ROUND

187   "It isn't a blond": "Hedda Hopper Looking at Hollywood," *Los Angeles Times*, August 7, 1944.

187   "Ramsay Ames": *Los Angeles Times*, August 10, 1944.

187   "Surely I like": Edwin Schallert, "Atmosphere Tingles as Volatile Ramsay Ames Reaches for Ice Bag," *Los Angeles Times*, August 20, 1944.

187   "extreme cruelty": "Artie Shaw Sued for Divorce by Elizabeth Kern," *Los Angeles Times*, August 23, 1944.

188   "I happened to be hired": Buddy DeFranco to TN, 2005.

189   "Buddy Rich took Jo's place": Stanley Dance, *The World of Count Basie* (Scribners, 1980), p. 124.

189   "Work comes first": AS to TN.

189   "'Cause my *mother*": AS to JS.

190   "I fell in love": Ava Gardner, *Ava: My Story* (Bantam, 1999), pp. 88–89.

190   the most beautiful woman: Richard Corliss, "Alistair Cooke: PBS's Rock Star," *Time*, November 23, 2008.

190   "Woody had a good band": AS to TN.

191   "Artie knew where": AM to TN.

CHAPTER 30: LITTLE JAZZ

192   "It was a helluva band": Paul Cohen to TN, 2005.

193   "I believe you can": Leonard Feather and Paul Eduard Miller, "The Rhythm Section," *Esquire*, July 1945.

193   "unleashed a scathing": "Shaw Speaks His Mind," *Metronome*, March 1945.

194   "not dying": Ibid.

194   "I never saw him *smile!*": PC to TN.

194   "He preferred doing concerts": Ralph Rosenlund to TN, 2006.

194   "on everything from Harry S Truman": Leonard Feather, "Artie Shaw: Mr. Swing in Spite of Himself," *Los Angeles Times*, February 6, 1972.

195   "I always wanted to be smart": Rosemary Clooney, with Joan Barthel, *Girl Singer: An Autobiography* (Doubleday, 1999), p. 257.

195   "He certainly was": PC to TN.

195   "Artie had a contract": Ibid.

196   "He's such a perfectionist": Roy Eldridge interview by Arthur Smith, quoted in John Chilton, *Roy Eldridge: Little Jazz Giant* (Continuum, 2002), p. 145.

196   "He was 'the novelist'": PC to TN.

196   "He states the melody": BD to TN.

197   "one where the band": Orrin Keepnews and Artie Shaw, booklet notes, *Personal Best* (Bluebird, 1992).

197   "I didn't *mind*": AS to TN.

198   "We would take a bus": RR to TN.

198   "Ava Gardner came": PC to TN.

198   "in the interests of international harmony": "Shaw Is Writing for Saudi Arabia," United Press, April 28, 1945.

199   "Shaw suddenly learned": "Artie Shaw Finds His Anthem Is Taboo," United Press, May 1, 1945.

CHAPTER 31: THE GRABTOWN GRAPPLE

200   "We used to talk": Budd Schulberg to TN, 2006.

202   "We spent six weeks": RR to TN.

202   "When he came": PC to TN.

202   "That was the difference": RR to TN.

202   "[H]is best gift": Chilton, *Roy Eldridge*, p. 143.

203   "He had a lot to do": RR to TN.

203   "Yes, they were incredible": PC to TN.

203   "I met [Aldous] Huxley": AS to TN.

205   "She was really goin' a little nuts": Ibid.

205   "We had a little party": Ibid.

206   "It was only rough": PC to TN.

206   "He was a cute little stocky guy": Whitney Balliett, *American Musicians II: Seventy-one Portraits in Jazz* (Oxford University Press, 1996), p. 196.

207   "I got in the hotel": Leonard Feather, "No More White Bands for Me, Says Little Jazz," *Down Beat*, May 18, 1951.

207   "[M]y name's up": Eldridge interview by Smith, quoted in Chilton, *Roy Eldridge*, p. 148.

207   "When I finally did": Feather, "No More White Bands for Me."

207   "The racial pressures": Shaw, "Good Enough Ain't Good Enough," *Self Portrait* (Bluebird/BMG).

208   "absolutely glorious": Kristine McKenna, "Altered Chords," *LA Weekly*, November 18, 1999.

208   "We got married": JC to TN.

208   "this is *the* one": AS to TN.

208   "He broke that band up": RR to TN.

CHAPTER 32: THE GLIDER

210 "We listened to Artie Shaw": Dick Hadlock, "Benny Harris & the Coming of Modern Jazz," *Metronome*, October 1961.

211 "There . . . he played 'Artie Shaw'": BD to TN.

212 "Artie Shaw isn't hungry": "Shaw-Victor Split Confirmed," *Down Beat,* December 1, 1945.

212 "Oberstein told me": "Shaw Will Sign with New Firm," *Down Beat*, December 15, 1945.

213 "unprecedented freedom": "Trade Buzz on Ellington Switch to Musicraft," *Down Beat*, May 6, 1946.

214 "I was summoned": Mel Tormé, *It Wasn't All Velvet: An Autobiography* (Viking, 1998), p. 88.

214 "I was interested in recording": Simosko, *Artie Shaw*, p. 111.

215 "You could hardly hear him": John Tumpak, "Artie Shaw's Post-War Musical Odyssey," *L.A. Jazz Scene*, September 2003.

215 "When everybody was sitting down": ZZ to TN.

215 "Mel Tormé's Collaborations": Gary C. W. Chun, "Let's Swing," *Honolulu Star-Bulletin,* August 4, 2006.

215 "We did that session": ZZ to TN.

CHAPTER 33: BEDFORD DRIVE

216 "He persisted": "Wife Divorces Artie Shaw as 'Utterly Selfish,'" *Los Angeles Examiner*, October 25, 1946.

216 "One night": Charles Higham, *Ava, A Life Story* (Delacorte, 1974), p. 60.

216 "She believed": AS to TN.

217 "Holy shit": Lee Server, *Ava Gardner: "Love Is Nothing"* (St. Martin's, 2006), p. 392.

217 "I thought I'd never finish": Gardner, *Ava*, p. 91.

217 "She never got *near*": AS to TN.

217 "Never happened": Simosko, *Artie Shaw*, p. 110.

217 "She knew how": AS to TN.

217 "Well he dismissed all of 'em": CR to TN.

218 "'Cause they're aiming": AS to TN.

218 "I remember when": AS to McIntyre, *Red-Eye Radio*, KABC.

218 "I would take a guess": Red Buttons to TN, 2006.

219 "Do you mean": Artie Shaw, Ava Gardner Still Together, He Says," *Los Angeles Times*, June 28, 1946.

219 "I was very angry": Hearings before the Committee on Un-American Activities, "Testimony of Artie Shaw."

220 "[H]e said": Ibid.

221 "A well-known musician": Ronald Reagan, with Richard G. Hubler, *Where's the Rest of Me?* (Duell, Sloan and Pearce, 1965), p. 166.

221 "He said to me": John Meroney, "Olivia de Havilland Recalls Her Role—in the Cold War," *Wall Street Journal*. September 7, 2006.

221 "pronounced": Reagan, with Hubler, *Where's the Rest of Me?*, p. 166.

221 "We worked on a story together": Hearings before the Committee on Un-American Activities, "Testimony of Artie Shaw."

222 "It was originally written for Benny": Danny Bank to TN, 2006.

222 "He was a very commercial person": PC to TN.

CHAPTER 34: A TABLE IN A CORNER

223 "We simply got": Michael Levin, "Notes between Notes," *Down Beat*, July 29, 1946.

223 "Since the marriage": "Artie Shaw's Ava Gardner Asks Divorce," *Los Angeles Times*, August 16, 1946.

224 "after I telephoned her": Alfred Albelli and Neal Patterson, "Divorces Illegal, Still Wed to Ava, Artie Tells Amber," *New York Daily News*, August 7, 1948.

224 "I was working on 'Star Money'": "People," *Time*, March 30, 1953.

224 "On October 24th": Albelli and Patterson, "Divorces Illegal."

224 "caused gasps of astonishment": "'Forever Amber' Author Married to Artie Shaw," *Los Angeles Times*, October 29, 1946.

225 "The band leader": "Artie Shaw and Bride Still Forever Ambling," *Los Angeles Times*, November 1, 1946.

225 "cool and distant": "'Forever Amber' Author Divorced by Herwig," *Los Angeles Times*, December 10, 1946.

225 "Bob Herwig Divorces Shaw's Wife": *Los Angeles Examiner*, December 9, 1946.

226 left dime-store ashtrays: Kay Pick to TN, 2006.

226 "The thing with Kay and me": Lee and Gifford, *Saroyan*, p. 139.

226 "He leaped out of bed": Alfred Albelli and Neal Patterson, "She Wanted Him Forever Sterile, Says Artie, Suing to Annul Amber," *New York Daily News*, August 6, 1948.

227 "We started to work": Lee and Gifford, *Saroyan*, p. 140.

CHAPTER 35: IT'S THE SAME OLD DREAM

228 "There are a few islands": AS to TN.

228 "The sound hung": Dan Morgenstern, "Miles Davis," in *Living with Jazz: A Reader*, edited by Sheldon Meyer (Pantheon Books, 2004), p. 212.

228 "He had some good men": AS to TN.

229 "Thornhill had the greatest band": Pat Harris, "Nothing but Bop? 'Stupid,' Says Miles," *Down Beat*, January 27, 1950.

229 "It wasn't bad": AS to TN.

229 "He was pretty good": Ibid.

230 "They got her hooked": AS to JS.

230 "I used to invite her": McKenna, "Altered Chords."

230 "Artie was invited": Sophia Rosoff to TN, 2006.

230 "He was a favorite person": Jean Bach to TN, 2005.

231 "raise their voices": "Authors Defend Open Letter," *New York Times*, May 24, 1948.

232 "I thought she was quite keen": Sophia Rosoff to TN.

232 "The *dream* and *joy*": CR to TN.

233 "An unmitigated": AS to TN.

233 "ARTIE TRIED": Alfred Albelli and Neal Patterson, "Artie Tried to Turn Amber Red, Ruled Her 8 to Bar, She Cries," *New York Daily News*, August 10, 1948.

234 "Front-page headlines": AS to TN.

234 "She Wanted Him": Headline on Albelli and Patterson story, *New York Daily News*, August 6, 1948.

234 "Last March 5": Neal Patterson, "Artie Shaw Asks to End Marriage," *Boston Post*, August 6, 1948.

234 "He confessed": Albelli and Patterson, "Artie Tried to Turn Amber Red."

235 "The equivalent": AS to TN.

235 "The first three divorces": "Artie Shaw Divorced by Kathleen Winsor," *Los Angeles Times*, December 4, 1948.

CHAPTER 36: CHANGING MY TUNE

236 "flawless technique": Ross Parmenter, "The World of Music," *New York Times*, March 13, 1949.

236 "I went to Manie": AS to TN.

237 "a series of variations": Barry Ulanov, "Elder Statesman Returns," *Metronome*, September 1949.

237 "Both pieces have refinement": "In the Popular Field," *New York Times*, June 4, 1950.

237 "One of the girls who showed up": Firestone, *Swing, Swing, Swing*, p. 352.

238 "graceful as an otter": Maurice Zolotow, "Marilyn's Dreams of Romance Fade in Glare of Starlet Standards," *Washington Post, Times Herald*, December 7, 1960, excerpt from *Marilyn Monroe: A Biography* (Harcourt, Brace; 1960).

239 "Let's jump!": *wil*, "Much Confusion as Ella, Shaw Open Up Bop City," *Down Beat*, May 20, 1949.

239 "The plain fact": "Night Club Reviews," *Billboard*, April 23, 1949.

239 "But critics have to live": "No Hollywood for Me!" *Click*, July 1940.

240 "Mr. Shaw": Michael Levin, "This Is Arty? P'Shaw, Says Mix," *Down Beat*, May 20, 1949.

240 "Ava even had a piano lesson": Sophia Rosoff to TN.

240 "got a chance": "Barzin Conducts Season's Finale," *New York Times*, April 19, 1949.

241 "Manie Sachs called me": AS to TN.

242 "His band played . . . with style": Howard Taubman, "Records: New Opera for Children," *New York Times*, April 3, 1949.

242 "done with a taste and feeling": J. M., "Records of the Month," *Los Angeles Times*, February 13, 1949.

242 "I know that that music": Ulanov, "Elder Statesman Returns."

242 "sales of [Shaw's] Victor sides": "Shaw to Make 1st Pop Disks for Col.," *Variety*, May 25, 1949.

242   "*Billboard* reported": "Artie Shaw Goes to GAC; ABC Loses Out," *Billboard*, July
2, 1949.

CHAPTER 37: INNUENDO

243   Columnists: "[T]he blasts loosed . . . by Frank Conniff . . . who attacked [Shaw]
for appearing on the list of sponsors of the recent Cultural and Scientific Conference for World Peace" cited in "Shaw Hits Back at Critics," *Down Beat*, June 3,
1949. Mortimer's piece calling Shaw "the Communist-loving clarinetist" quoted
by Levin, "This Is Arty?"

243   "Anybody who plays a program": "Shaw Hits Back at Critics."

244   "At least one L.A. daily": Hal Holly, "The Hollywood Beat," *Down Beat*, July 29,
1949.

244   "I've been away long enough": John S. Wilson, "This Time Shaw Will Play as
Dancers Ask, He Says," *Down Beat*, September 23, 1949.

244   "As a young aspiring musician in Cincinnati": George Russell to TN, 2006.

245   "I grew up with him": Johnny Mandel to TN, 2006.

245   "We had paid rehearsals!": Sonny Russo to TN, 2006.

245   "In that band": JM to TN.

245   "He came to me one time": AS to TN.

246   "With Al Cohn": Sonny Russo to TN.

246   "People used to think": AS to TN.

246   "He would have a certain pattern": Sonny Russo to TN.

246   "It was a fine band": Jimmy Raney, "Things *Down Beat* Never Taught Me," August
3, 2006, at http://jonraneyblog.blogspot.com.

247   "And they *liked* working": JM to TN.

247   "Well he had so much great stuff": Sonny Russo to TN.

CHAPTER 38: MUCHO DE NADA

248   "They didn't even know": Irv Kluger to TN, 2005.

248   "*Never*": DB to TN.

249   "Zoot Sims and Al Cohn": IK to TN.

249   "'Orinoco was almost": Hallock, *Mystery of Artie Shaw*.

249   "Artie has been making friends": "Pat and Artie on the Cover," *Down Beat*,
December 2, 1949.

249   "We played one place": Sonny Russo to TN.

249   "I think it was in London": DB to TN.

250   "Well he was nuts!": AS to TN.

250   "Great players": Bob Rusch, "Irv Kluger," *Cadence*, August 1990.

251   "Oh shit": AS to TN.

252   "Without question": Simosko, *Artie Shaw*, p. 120.

252   "They set up a table": DB to TN.

252   "It was *very* nice": Sonny Russo to TN.

252   "He had a suite": DB to TN.

253 "[t]here was a deafening silence": Hallock, *Mystery of Artie Shaw*.
253 "The people just didn't *hear*": JM to TN.
253 "If you've got a band": AS to TN.
253 "Unfortunately": Raney, "Things *Down Beat* Never Taught Me."
254 "Never": BD to TN.

CHAPTER 39: THE SHEKOMEKO SHUFFLE

255 "She was a lovely girl": Sophia Rosoff to TN.
256 "I was not impressed": AS to JS.
256 "big conversation": Jack Kerouac, edited by Douglas Brinkley, *Windblown World: The Journals of Jack Kerouac* (Viking, 2004), p. 275.
256 "a brilliantly promising young novelist": Charles Poore, "Books of the Times," *New York Times*, March 2, 1950.
257 "Some of the most inept band music": Michael Levin, "Shaw's New Ork Proves 'Can't Turn Clock Back,'" *Down Beat*, April 21, 1950.
257 "the worst band": George T. Simon, "In Person," *Metronome*, May 1950.
257 "It was a good band": Eddie Bert to TN, 2006.
257 "An employee of the club": Earl Wilson, *Sinatra: An Unauthorized Biography* (Macmillan, 1976), p. 106.
257 "Artie solved other people's problems": Gardner, *Ava*, pp. 129–30.
258 "He was the first bass-trombone player": Sonny Russo to TN.
260 "I laughed, ogled": Sudhalter, *Lost Chords*, p. 612.

CHAPTER 40: BLUE AGAIN

261 "ninety-one one-nighters": William F. Lee to TN, 2006.
263 "I was just delighted": Dr. Billy Taylor to TN, 2006.
264 "the frozen waste": Barbara Hughes, "In Person," *Metronome*, December 1950.
264 "heretofore noted": "Shaw Debuts Gramercy 5," *Down Beat*, October 20, 1950.
264 "Artie wasn't really thrilled": BT to TN.
264 "I just came down here": Leonard Feather, "'Strictly for the Loot!'—Says Artie Shaw," *Melody Maker*, November 18, 1950.
264 "John had a harmonic sense": BT to TN.

CHAPTER 41: HE'S GONE AWAY

266 "Cleared the decks!": AS to TN.
267 "My life at that point": AS to JS.
267 "Artie had a *busy, busy* life": Sophia Rosoff to TN.
267 "with intermittent fights": Richard Gehman, "Artie Shaw," unpublished article manuscript (marked "Cosmo"), February 3, 1954, Gehman Collection, Archives and Special Collections, Ganser Library, Millersville University, Millersville, PA.
268 Farrar conceded: John Farrar to Stanley Young, November 19, 1951, Manuscripts and Archives, New York Public Library, New York City, NY.

268 "She was my little sister": AS to JS.

268 "He always said": JC to TN.

269 "You don't have to twist": Hedda Hopper, "'My True Love Won't Spoil Dow Honeymoon,'" *Los Angeles Times*, November 24, 1951.

269 "He took my book": AS to JS.

269 "Farrar said yeah": AS to TN.

270 "The Trib was a very good paper": Ibid.

271 "an honesty which scrapes": Thomas Sugrue, "Artie Shaw vs. Abraham I. Arshawsky," *New York Herald Tribune Book Review*, June 15, 1952.

271 "I had only one criticism": Frederic Morton to TN, 2006.

271 "I wasn't putting all those quotes up there": AS to TN.

271 "fidgeted and squirmed": Gehman, "Artie Shaw" manuscript.

272 "He gave me a few critical points": AS to TN.

CHAPTER 42: IT COULD HAPPEN TO YOU

275 "I know your secret": AS to TN, JC to TN.

275 "May I say, first of all": Hearings before the Committee on Un-American Activities, "Testimony of Artie Shaw."

276 "Oh yeah": AS to TN.

277 "Mr. Shaw had divulged": Peter Kihss, "Artie Shaw Says He Was Red 'Dupe,'" *New York Times*, May 5, 1953.

277 "I feel": Hearings, "Testimony of Artie Shaw."

278 the photo *Time* magazine would print: "The Name Is Familiar," *Time*, May 18, 1953.

CHAPTER 43: SUNNY SIDE UP

279 "the best thing I ever did": AS to TN.

279 "I did certain things": Ibid.

280 "wild about": Gehman, "Artie Shaw" manuscript.

280 one of his first paternal duties: Richardson Howard, "Artie Shaw Back in Town But Parking Is Off Key," *Cleveland News*, February 10, 1954.

280 "He sounded terrible": Firestone, *Sing, Sing, Sing*, p. 379.

281 "You can play": Gehman, "Artie Shaw" manuscript.

281 "*Intense* rehearsals": Hank Jones to TN, 2006.

281 "Cut it off": Gehman, "Artie Shaw" manuscript.

281 "I wanted to look like the baby": Alan Frazer, "My Boston," *Boston Globe*, September 25, 1953.

282 "This gig is strictly for listening": Gros., "Band Reviews," *Variety*, October 14, 1953.

282 "[T]he group swings": Nat Hentoff, "Shaw's New Gramercy 5 'Not Just a Copy of Old'," *Down Beat*, November 18, 1953.

282 "Artie Shaw . . . one of the truly distinguished jazz soloists": D.W., "Tables for Two: The Pied Piper," *The New Yorker*, October 17, 1953.

282   "It was a new kind of music": HJ to TN.
282   "Chamber jazz": AS to TN.
282   "Artie let us *play*": Joe Roland to TN, 2008.
282   "Art calls me": IK to TN.
283   "Well he'd heard me *play*": AS to TN.
283   "So we do the gig": IK to TN.

CHAPTER 44: STOP AND GO MAMBO

284   "more intimate": Shaw, "Good Enough Ain't Good Enough," *Self Portrait* (Bluebird/BMG).
285   "Artie was the best *blues* player": IK to TN.
285   "When I'm playing with a group like the one I have": Howard, "Artie Shaw Back in Town But Parking Is Off Key."
285   "Artie let you live": Rusch, "Irv Kluger."
285   "We would stay in that record studio": HJ to TN.
286   "All he wants": Merle Miller, "Jazz and Jabberwocky," *Esquire*, September 1954.
286   "I met him a couple times": AM to TN.
287   "She did a wonderful, wonderful sketch": RB to TN.
287   "astoundingly successful": Miller, "Jazz and Jabberwocky."
287   "It may well be": Gehman, "Artie Shaw" manuscript.

CHAPTER 45: YESTERDAYS

288   "Jazz in those days": Stan Irwin to TN, 2006.
288   "It was a funny thing": AS to TN.
289   "One night in Philadelphia": Artie Shaw, "Dixie, Swing, Bop or What?" *SEE*, September 1954.
289   "Artie would do good business": SI to TN.
289   "When we were here": IK to TN.
289   "Very tough": AS to TN.
290   "It was good money": SI to TN.
290   "I made—made a lotta money": AS to TN.
290   "All the people from the other hotels": SI to TN.
290   "Well when I played there": AS to TN.
290   "the *cognoscenti*": HJ to TN.
290   "Those who had a sense of music": SI to TN.
290   "Tommy and Jimmy": AS to TN.
290   "I think he was indifferent": SI to TN.
291   "Shaw sounded more deeply involved": Simosko, *Artie Shaw*, pp. 136–37.
291   "I'm lost in admiration": Dan Morgenstern and Loren Schoenberg, liner notes, *Artie Shaw: The Last Recordings* (MusicMasters, 1992).
292   "I don't think Artie was ever completely satisfied": HJ to TN.
292   "Artie discovered early": IK to TN.

292   "Whom is Artie Shaw trying to kid": Jack Tracy, "In This Corner," *Down Beat*, March 10, 1954.

292   "This is near the end": SI to TN.

293   "I remember being": AS to TN.

294   "I don't want to go out like Joe Louis": Feather, "'Strictly for the Loot!'"

294   "The Mob took care": AS to TN.

CHAPTER 46: MORE THAN YOU KNOW

295   "She's beyond compare": AS to TN.

296   "a triumphal visitation": "U.S. Stars Down Under," *Time*, February 7, 1955.

296   "I walked through it": Hallock, *Mystery of Artie Shaw*.

296   "I think of Doris Dowling": AS to TN.

296   "Lasting human relationships": CR to TN.

296   "the lone wolf of Lindy's": Dorothy Kilgallen, "Maggie May Bow in Night Club," *Washington Post, Times Herald*, February 3, 1955.

297   "All the people I knew": AS to TN.

297   "'private joke' on the rest of the world": Simosko, *Artie Shaw*, p. 139.

298   Shaw never said: It's intriguing to note that Steve Allen—the jazz-loving, multi-talented, Manhattan-dwelling polymath chosen to play Benny Goodman in the movies—published two books of short stories in the middle 1950s, to excellent reviews. What better "private joke on the rest of the world," from Shaw's point of view, could there be? Shaw and Allen were friends the rest of their lives.

298   "How did you *find* me?": AS to TN.

298   "Su compadre": Ibid.

299   "He *found* me": Ibid.

299   "The two men": Evelyn Keyes, *Scarlett O'Hara's Younger Sister: My Lively Life in and out of Hollywood* (Lyle Stuart, 1977), p. 242.

299   "We spent the whole night talking": AS to TN.

299   "They really connected": FM to TN.

300   "Thank God": Keyes, *Scarlett O'Hara's Younger Sister*, p. 265.

301   "Artie and Louis Armstrong": Keyes, *Scarlett O'Hara's Younger Sister*, p. 274.

301   "Tremendous amount": AS to TN.

301   "I tried to play": Ibid.

301   "Of *course*": Evelyn Keyes to TN, 1990.

CHAPTER 47: CONNECTICUT

302   "He had a great gift": AS to TN.

302   "They had a good *time*": Carol Southern to TN, 2006.

302   "He didn't have an ending": AS to TN.

303   "Terry and I were looking": CS to TN.

303   "He *wanted*": AS to TN.

304   "Artie said": CS to TN.

304 "I bought it": AS to TN.
304 "I called it": Ibid.
305 "Terry was in New York": CS to TN.
305 "It was just": FM to TN.
305 "Things may have seemed": Keyes, *Scarlett O'Hara's Younger Sister*, p. 300.
306 "Dizzy respected Artie": Donald L. Maggin, *Dizzy: The Life and Times of John Birks Gillespie* (HarperCollins, 2005), pp. 308–9.

CHAPTER 48: I'VE GOT BEGINNER'S LUCK

309 "I thought she was fine": CR to TN.
309 "Anyhow": AS to TN.
309 "Hate, and love": AS to JS.
310 "I remember when I was forty years old": AS to TN.
310 "'Someday you'll show 'em'": AS to JS.
310 "I said, 'I'm sorry'": AS to TN.
310 "Naw": CR to TN.
310 "I had always gotten": AS to TN.
313 "Artie became overnight": FM to TN.
313 *Variety* wrote: Vincent Canby, "His First Film for Distribution a Prospective $1,000,000 Grosser, Artie Shaw Yens to Produce 'Em," *Variety*, April 4, 1965.
313 "permission": Keyes, *Scarlett O'Hara's Younger Sister*, p. 303.
313 "I stop by there": Radie Harris, "Broadway Ballyhoo," *Hollywood Reporter*, December 1, 1964.

CHAPTER 49: I WAS DOING ALL RIGHT

314 "Whenever she got": FM to TN.
315 "Bravo!": Dorothy Kilgallen, "Romy Sporting New Beau in Paris," *Washington Post, Times Herald*, November 10, 1964.
315 "He was quite a curmudgeon": AS to TN.
316 "[I]n the summer of 1965": Balliett, "Bright Unison Clarinets."
316 "I'll *never know*": AS to TN.
317 "Maybe I should have stayed": Tony Mastroianni, "Artie Still Swings on Another Beat," *Cleveland Press*, February 16, 1965.
317 "That was his tragedy": FM to TN.
318 "To me, the greatest": Leonard Feather, "Barney Bigard: Jazzman in the Classic Mold," *Los Angeles Times*, July 21, 1968.
318 "The show went over": TP to TN.
319 "exclaiming that they were possibly the best": Giddins, "Shaw 'Nuff."
319 "I don't care": McDonough, "Artie Shaw: Nonstop Flight from 1938."
319 "knowingly and maliciously": "Miscellany," *Variety*, December 22, 1971.
320 "I started to do a musical": AS to TN.
320 "Oh God": FM to TN.

320 "It's a flagrant, arrogant violation": Leonard Feather, "Artie Shaw: Mr. Swing in Spite of Himself," *Los Angeles Times*, February 6, 1972.

321 "tryin' to be a hippie": PC to TN.

CHAPTER 50: (WOULD YOU LIKE TO BE THE) LOVE OF MY LIFE

322 "I like her very much": Charlotte Curtis, "Artie Shaw at 62: Still the Romantic," *New York Times,* February 18, 1973.

322 "I was with a firm": Joanne Lupton to TN, 2006.

324 "Nostalgia": Artie Shaw, "A Memorable Slap at Nostalgia Craze," *Los Angeles Times,* January 20, 1974.

324 "the confluence of the abilities": Leonard Feather, "Artie Shaw Gets Back in the Swing," *Los Angeles Times*, May 19, 1974.

324 "New York City": JL to TN.

327 "She's very good": AS to TN.

327 "he's a wonderful storyteller": Tom Nolan, *Ross Macdonald: A Biography* (Scribner, 1999), p. 345.

327 "the last way to tell the truth": Nancy Collins, "It's Back to Writing after Time Out for Music, Fame, Women and Alimony—the Elvis of Swing," *Washington Post,* March 26, 1978.

CHAPTER 51: IMAGINATION

328 "Day after day": JL to TN.

332 "He wanted to mix it down": Teo Macero to TN, 2006.

CHAPTER 52: DANCING IN THE DARK

333 "Artie had a wool cap": PL to TN.

333 "It was just two or three weeks later": Daryl Sherman to TN, 2006.

334 "This is a kick-ass band!": Tony Gieske, "Shaw's 'Stardust' Memories," *Los Angeles Herald-Examiner,* April 21, 1984.

334 "The presence of Shaw": David Gates, "Artie Shaw Swinging without His Clarinet," *Newsweek,* January 2, 1984.

334 "Shaw talks": Mark Miller, "Shaw's Return to Music Goes beyond Nostalgia," *Toronto Globe and Mail,* November 6, 1984.

335 "Fasten your safety belt!": Sid Adilman, "Local Producer's Film a Kick for Artie Shaw," *Toronto Star*, November 9, 1984.

335 "It's very strange seeing yourself": Ibid.

335 "We're still fighting": Chip Deffaa, *Swing Legacy* (Scarecrow, 1989), p. 17.

335 "We shared a dressing-room with Mel Tormé": JC to TN.

336 "I got to the Bowl": Deffaa, *Swing Legacy*.

336 "Artie's instructions": JC to TN.

CHAPTER 53: AUTUMN LEAVES

339 "Stars don't carry": JC to TN.

340 "Artie and Benny": Loren Schoenberg to TN, 2006.

340 "He wanted to know": PL to TN.

341 "I'm sure it hurt Goodman's feelings": JC to TN.

341 "Actually": Loren Schoenberg to TN.

341 "Encouraged and energized": Firestone, *Swing, Swing, Swing*, p. 449.

341 "Herb loved Benny": Barnaby Conrad to TN.

342 "great American songbook": John S. Wilson, "Rarities Illuminate the Days When Pop Music Meant Jazz," *New York Times*, March 9, 1986; John S. Wilson, "Lee Wiley Sings Show Tunes in a Jazz Setting," *New York Times*, November 30, 1986. Wilson wrote Shaw's obituary for the *Times* in advance; by the time it ran, in late 2004, Wilson himself was deceased.

342 "I feel like George Bernard Shaw": "Courting Oscar Pays Off for Canadian Winner," *Toronto Globe and Mail*, April 21, 1987.

343 "Yeah, country-and-western": Levinson, *Tommy Dorsey*, p. 315.

343 "Artie had a way": Gibbs, with Ginell, *Good Vibes*, p. 78.

343 "I didn't *like* him": AS to TN.

CHAPTER 54: THAT OLD FEELING

345 "boldly fuses mambo": Francis Davis, "Artie at Eighty," *Connoisseur's World*, June 1990.

345 "Shaw contributes": Christopher Porterfield, "The Man Who Walked Away," *Time*, May 18, 1992.

346 "among the finest performances": Giddins, "Shaw 'Nuff."

346 "It was a hundred percent pure friendship": Kay Pick to TN, 2006.

347 "A remarkably handsome and upright old man": Corinna Honan, "The Man Who Couldn't Help Marrying Beautiful Women," *London Daily Mail*, June 11, 1992.

347 "It was jammed": GM to TN.

347 "At the end of the show": "Artie Shaw swings in to the UK, at 82," *Glasgow Herald*, June 12, 1992.

347 "Every story was burnished": Aram Saroyan to TN, 2006.

348 "I hardly see my sons": Honan, *London Daily Mail*.

348 "Ava died of confusion": James Brady, "In Step With: Artie Shaw," *Parade*, July 19, 1992.

348 "All I can say is that Glenn [Miller] should have lived": *Entertainment Weekly*, 1993, quoted in Gary Susman, "Goodbye," *Entertainment Weekly*, January 3, 2005.

348 "I'm too straight-talking": Tom Nolan, "Still Cranky after All These Years," *Los Angeles*, May 1990.

348 "It's about time": John McDonough, "Hall of Fame: Artie Shaw," *Down Beat*, August 1996.

349 "collaborative product": Thomas Claridge, "Film Not Profitable, Producer Tells Court," *Toronto Globe and Mail*, December 13, 1996.

349 "I'm absolutely thrilled": "Artie Shaw Loses Lawsuit over Film," *Toronto Star*, March 5, 1997.

349 "The learned trial judge": "Artie Shaw Seeks Second Film Trial," *Toronto Globe and Mail*, April 3, 1997.

349 many more years to wait: As of 2009, *Time Is All You've Got* had yet to be available on commercial DVD.

CHAPTER 55: HOP SKIP AND JUMP

350 "She said, 'I'm not gonna be able to'": AS to TN.

350 "I didn't really know": LR to TN.

351 "Kurt Elling was singing": KP to TN.

352 "I went out in the alley": AS to TN.

352 "He was just the most lovable dog": JL to TN.

352 "A hundred bucks": AS to TN.

353 "He was a master storyteller": LR to TN.

353 "this hostile, handsome man": Ted Hallock to TN, 2005.

CHAPTER 56: DON'T TAKE YOUR LOVE FROM ME

356 "I had fallen in love with his music": Vladimir Simosko to TN, 2006.

357 "I was looking through the *Wall Street Journal*": Marian McPartland to TN, 2005.

358 "I *told* him": Orrin Keepnews to TN, 2006.

359 "He had a very bad case": LR to TN.

360 "Louis [Armstrong] started it": "Artie Shaw on Artie Shaw," *Jazz Times*, May 2002.

360 "I loved hearing those stories": Elliott Kastner to TN, 2006.

361 "I think to myself in bed": AS to JS.

362 "'Like the man said'": Paraphrasing a line by author Aubrey Menen ("There are three things which are real: God, human folly, and laughter. Since the first two pass our comprehension, we must do what we can with the third"), from *The Ramayana: As Told by Aubrey Menen* (Scribner's, 1954).

CHAPTER 57: LONG AGO AND FAR AWAY

363 "I mean, it makes you want to cry": Ray Charles, *Ray Charles Artist's Choice* (Hear Music, 2003).

363 "Ever since I was a kid": Smith, *Off the Record*, p. 75.

363 "Ray Charles came out to meet me": AS to TN.

364 "He had adult-onset diabetes": LR to TN.

364 "lifetime achievement": Smithsonian press release, August 28, 2003.

364 "This is lagniappe": TN notes.

365 "Artie was probably the most egocentric person": Jonathan Shaw to TN, 2006.

366 "The last year": LR to TN.

366 "Good thing my mind is stocked": AS to TN.

369 "At *heart*": LR to TN.

369 "How long have you been together": AS to TN.

369 "I went out to see him": GM to TN.

369 "Around Thanksgiving": LR to TN.

370 "He did the best": AS to TN.

370 "Oh": Ibid.

370 a letter from Herb Caen: seen by TN in lot 1026, auction held by John Moran, Incorporated, Pasadena Convention Center, September 16, 2008.

═══ Select Bibliography ═══

BOOKS BY ARTIE SHAW

Artie Shaw Clarinet Method: A School of Modern Clarinet Technic, with Arnold Brilhart (Robbins Music, 1941).

The Trouble with Cinderella: An Outline of Identity (Farrar, Straus and Young, 1952; with new introduction, Da Capo, 1979; Fithian Press in association with Artixo Books, 1992).

I Love You, I Hate You, Drop Dead! (Fleet, 1965; with new preface, Barricade Books, 1997).

The Best of Intentions and Other Stories (John Daniel: Santa Barbara, 1989).

UNCOLLECTED PIECES BY ARTIE SHAW

"I Don't Like Saxophones!," *Melody Maker*, January 23, 1937.

"Artie Shaw Expresses His Opinions on Swing and Its Various Forms,", *Bandstand*, February 1939.

"I'm Not a Monster," *Upbeat*, March 1939.

"Music Is a Business," with Bob Maxwell, *Saturday Evening Post*, December 2, 1939.

"No Hollywood for Me! (One Experience Was Enough)," as told to *Click*, July 1940.

"Bandsman Artie Shaw Dropping His Baton States His Glowing Credo for Our American Jazz," *Washington Post*, January 26, 1941.

"I Want to Lead a Symphony!," *Music and Rhythm*, April 1941.

"Jazz, Swing and the Popular Song," speech prepared for the Institute of Music in Contemporary Life (Los Angeles), September 17, 1944.

"No Categories, Please!," *Woodwind Magazine*, March 1949.

"Facts, Figures and No Flamboyance" (book review of *The Musicians and Petrillo* by Robert D. Leiter), *Theatre Arts*, September 1953.

"Dixie, Swing, Bop or What?," *SEE*, September 1954.

"A Memorable Slap at Nostalgia Craze," *Los Angeles Times*, January 20, 1974.

"Music Lesson," *The Baffler*, no. 8, 1996. Excerpt from Shaw's novel in progress.

"Address to the IAJRC Convention," August 15, 1998, *IAJRC*, Winter 1999.

"Good Enough Ain't Good Enough," booklet notes for *Self Portrait* (Bluebird, 2001).

"Artie Shaw on Artie Shaw," remarks at the 2002 International Association of Jazz Education conference, *Jazz Times*, May 2002.

BOOKS ABOUT ARTIE SHAW

Vladimir Simosko, *Artie Shaw: A Musical Biography and Discography* (Scarecrow, 2000).

John White, *Artie Shaw: His Life and Music* (University of Hull Press, 1998; revised edition, Continuum, 2004).

MEMOIRS BY EVELYN KEYES

Scarlett O'Hara's Younger Sister: My Lively Life In and Out of Hollywood (Lyle Stuart, 1977).

I'll Think About That Tomorrow (Dutton, 1991).

SHORT STORY COLLECTIONS BY STEVE ALLEN

Fourteen for Tonight (Holt, 1955; Dell, 1955).

The Girls on the 10th Floor (Holt, 1958; Popular Library, 1959).

= Permissions =

All quotations from unpublished interviews and conversations with Artie Shaw are used with the kind permission of the Estate of Artie Shaw.

Excerpts from an unpublished magazine article by Richard Gehman are used with the kind permission of the Gehman Collection, Archives & Special Collections, Ganser Library, Millersville University, Millersville, Pennsylvania.

Quotations from an interview with Cliff Leeman are used by kind permission of the Institute of Jazz Studies, Rutgers, State University of New Jersey, Newark, New Jersey.

Quotations from interviews with John Best and with Jerry Jerome are used by kind permission of the Hamilton College Jazz Archive, Hamilton College, Clinton, New York.

Certain Artie Shaw quotations in this book first appeared in these articles by Tom Nolan:

"Still Cranky After All These Years," *Los Angeles*, May 1990.

"The Secret Love of Artie Shaw," *Philadelphia Inquirer Magazine*, August 1990.

"Star Dust Still Falls on Artie Shaw," *Wall Street Journal*, February 20, 2003.

"Ends the Beguine: Remembering Artie Shaw," *Wall Street Journal*, January 4, 2005.

Index

411

Index

Index

Index

Index

Index

Index

Index

Index

Index

Index

Index